The Death of WCW

The
DEATH OF
WCW

R.D. REYNOLDS & BRYAN ALVAREZ

10th ANNIVERSARY EDITION
OF THE BESTSELLING
CLASSIC

REVISED AND EXPANDED

Published by ECW Press
665 Gerrard Street East,
Toronto, Ontario, Canada M4M 1Y2
416-694-3348 / info@ecwpress.com

Library and Archives Canada Cataloguing in Publication

Reynolds, R. D., 1969-, author
The death of WCW / R.D. Reynolds & Bryan Alvarez.
— 10th anniversary edition of the bestselling classic, revised and
expanded.

Includes bibliographical references.
ISBN 978-1-77041-175-3 (paperback); 978-1-77041-176-0
(hardcover)
also issued as: 978-1-77090-641-9 (PDF); 978-1-77090-642-6 (ePub)

1. World Championship Wrestling, Inc.—History. 2. Wrestling
promoters—United States. I. Alvarez, Bryan, author II. Title.

Editor for the press: Michael Holmes
Cover design: David A. Gee
Cover images (front and back): © George Napolitano

Printing: Friesens: 10   9   8   7   6   5
Printed and bound in Canada

★ ★ ★ CONTENTS ★ ★ ★

Foreword ix

1st Edition Foreword xviii

Preface xxii

Introduction xxv

PART I THE BIRTH

ONE 1988–1996: Mr. Turner's Baby Boy 3

TWO 1996: The War Begins 69

PART II THE RISE

THREE 1997: The Waiting Game 101

FOUR 1998: Momentum Is Money 127

PART III THE FALL

FIVE 1999: Gambling on a Savior 191

SIX 2000: Everything Falls Apart 267

PART IV THE DEATH

SEVEN 2001: The Ultimate Swerve 359

1st Edition Epilogue 375

Epilogue 2014 399

Endnotes 415

Acknowledgments 419

To Dixie and Bob

★ ★ ★ FOREWORD ★ ★ ★

Ten years ago, when the original edition of this book was released, World Championship Wrestling had just closed up its doors three years earlier. That company's demise ended a legacy that stretched back to the days of territorial pro wrestling, with promoters like Paul Jones in Atlanta and Jim Crockett Sr. in Charlotte, dating back to the depression.

The pro-wrestling industry was territorial in nature prior to 1984, when things started to change with the advent of cable television. What's notable is that many of the same opportunities arose in the late 1940s and early 1950s, when the birth of network television garnered the major promotions national prime time exposure. The mentality in that era was that the dozens of wrestling companies would work together; the promoters who had national television had a key to the gold mine and would utilize that exposure to broker their top stars to the local promoters for a nice booking fee, usually based on a cut of the gate. This led to thriving promotions all over North America and in many other parts of the world.

The National Wrestling Alliance is a name that dates to about 1940, originally used by a promotion based in Kansas City. But the famous NWA, the one that led to the creation of the titular WCW, was a conglomerate of regional promotions that dated back to meetings in 1948. By the '50s, they had set up an arguably illegal monopoly of the business; one so overarching that it even led to a Justice Department investigation.

The various promoters would respect territorial boundaries. If an outside promoter came along, the alliance could help in many ways, such as send top talent to the promoter in a jam. They could also go with a more heavy-handed approach, such as threaten to blacklist talent that appeared for a non-NWA member. A key rule was that an NWA promoter could only recognize the NWA World champion, voted by the board of directors at the annual conventions.

For most of the 1950s, the NWA was the dominant force in pro wrestling. But there was always opposition, leading promoters who couldn't get along or simply didn't want to get along. In 1957, when the alliance champion, Lou Thesz, quit to wrestle overseas, he handpicked his replacement in Dick Hutton, one of the greatest U.S. amateur heavyweights in history. But while Hutton was top of the line as a real wrestler, he wasn't particularly colorful and couldn't draw like Thesz. A number of promoters decided he wasn't worth the 13 percent of the gate-booking fee (10 percent to the champion and 3 percent to the alliance itself) charged. Over the next several years, the alliance nearly crumbled.

New major champions were created. The World Wrestling Alliance was based in Los Angeles and its champion was recognized in Japan, where wrestling was on highly rated prime time network television, although it rejoined the NWA in 1968. The American Wrestling Association was based in Minneapolis, as another former amateur star, Verne Gagne, who for political reasons never had a shot at the NWA title, bought controlling interest in the promotion and made himself AWA champion. But Gagne always worked harmoniously with the NWA, except for a brief period in the late '60s when he arrived in Los Angeles.

But bigger problems were coming. In 1962, the NWA champion was "Nature Boy" Buddy Rogers, who was being booked by Northeast promoter Vincent James McMahon, the father of today's Vincent Kennedy McMahon. McMahon kept the champion working in the Northeast the majority of every month. While the NWA's strongest cities, like St. Louis and Toronto, got steady championship matches, smaller territories weren't getting dates on Rogers. This led to more promoters creating their own champion.

A showdown was about to take place.

In late 1962, Sam Muchnick, who headed the NWA, scheduled Thesz to beat Rogers for the title. Things got hairy, as strange things began to happen, such as convenient injuries by Rogers. This led to the match continually being delayed. D-Day came on January 24, 1963, in Toronto. In the ring, Thesz, one of the great legitimate submission wrestlers of the era, told Rogers, "We can do this the hard way or the easy way," a line that had already become part of pro-wrestling's lexicon from Thesz's mentor, Ed "Strangler" Lewis. It remains used to this day in the business, kept alive in modern interviews by Stephanie McMahon.

The fallout was McMahon's champion lost, but McMahon wanted no part of Thesz as champion. Thesz never drew well in his cities, and Rogers, in 1962, was the hottest thing going. Originally, McMahon tried to pretend the Thesz-Rogers match never happened, still billing Rogers as champion. When that became impossible, he announced that Rogers had won a tournament in Rio de Janeiro, Brazil, to become the World Wide Wrestling Federation champion. In 1979, the WWWF was shortened to WWF, as in World Wrestling Federation. Today, the promotion is known as World Wrestling Entertainment, or WWE for short.

McMahon and Muchnick still worked together, and in 1965, decided to unify the titles. McMahon's new champion, Bruno Sammartino, was to beat Thesz, and they'd work out the dates. But for a number of reasons, the deal the promoters worked out fell through, as Sammartino refused a schedule that would have him on the road every single day. Ironically, Thesz wasn't happy with the arrangement either.

In 1971, McMahon rejoined the NWA, and the WWWF World Heavyweight title, as it was called during the first Sammartino reign that lasted from 1963 to 1971, was simply called the WWWF title. It was never really known to fans that the WWWF had rejoined the NWA, nor that McMahon had influence on picking the NWA champion.

By the late 1970s, cable television emerged and would change the game.

Jim Barnett, who ran the Georgia office, was the first beneficiary. It was almost a fluke. The local Channel 17 in Atlanta broadcasted highly rated Georgia Championship Wrestling every Saturday and Sunday. As cable companies around the country started picking up the station, first called WTBS and then just TBS, wrestling was its most popular program. The stars on the station started to develop a national following.

Barnett had been around pro wrestling since the 1950s, and even though for years he was not allowed to be an NWA member because he was gay, he was eventually brought into the fold. He refused to expand against his fellow promoters, even though he had the capability due to the exposure.

In 1982, Vincent James McMahon sold his Northeastern promotion to his 36-year-old son in a complicated deal, where Vincent Kennedy McMahon used the old company's money to make his payments to the old owner.

By this point, the territorial foundation began a full collapse. Gagne had expanded the AWA into San Francisco, causing promoter Roy Shire to retire rather than fight. Barnett was forced out of Georgia, accused of embezzlement, where longtime booker and star heel Ole Anderson (Alan Rogowski) took charge and started moving into new regions. But the most ambitious of all was McMahon, who started running first in

Los Angeles.

Wrestling changed in 1984, when McMahon signed Gagne's biggest star, Hulk Hogan, and started buying television time all over North America. He bought some companies and took the biggest names away from the other territories. He also hired Barnett as his director of operations.

The whirlwind really began to spin during this period. In a secret meeting, unbeknownst to Anderson, McMahon was able to purchase more than 50 percent of the stock of Georgia Championship Wrestling. This gave him the television contract on TBS and the traditional time slots of the most widely viewed pro-wrestling shows in the country. While the relationship only lasted one year, it was key to what happened next.

TBS was owned by Ted Turner. When Turner put Channel 17 on satellite, he was a laughing stock in television; seriously, who could possibly want to see an Atlanta UHF station in Los Angeles or Dallas or New York? But he had three very unique ingredients that made it a success, the first being Atlanta Braves baseball and the second being *The Andy Griffith Show*, a television staple a generation earlier. But the third was the most popular of all: pro wrestling every Saturday and Sunday. In 1981, his two-hour Saturday at 6:05 p.m. wrestling show did a 6.4 average rating for the year. His Sunday show, starting at the same time, did a 6.6. Nothing else in cable came close. Wrestling was the first star of cable television, not unlike it was during the early days of television itself.

In 1984, when McMahon purchased the company that had the TBS contract, he first came across Turner. It wasn't pleasant. McMahon had spent $750,000 to get the time slot, which at the time was significant money to him. But Turner got so many complaints from wrestling fans about not getting their Georgia wrestling with popular announcer Gordon Solie, that he gave Anderson an earlier hour on his station. Later, he gave Mid South Wrestling an hour and wanted to get into the wrestling business with Bill Watts. In an embarrassment to McMahon, the small group that taped TV at a Boy's Club in Shreveport, Louisiana, drew more than a full point higher in the ratings in a non-traditional time slot.

Turner attempted to kick McMahon off, noting that ratings were falling and McMahon wasn't producing a show at his studio. In 1985, McMahon sold the rights to the station to Jim Crockett Jr., whose Charlotte-based promotion had become the second strongest in the country, behind stars like Dusty Rhodes, Ric Flair, The Road Warriors, Wahoo McDaniel, and others.

Eventually, Crockett, whose father became wealthy promoting wrestling and everything else imaginable in the Carolinas, became McMahon's key opposition. He took over in Georgia, Florida, and the NWA changed from a group of promotions working together to almost synonymous, in the fans' eyes, with Crockett Promotions. Most companies faded away. In 1987, Crockett Jr. bought Mid South Wrestling from Watts, who was losing too much money trying to be a third national group.

The game changed in 1984 when McMahon started buying television time slots. As an example, he offered the television station in San Francisco that had been airing Gagne's show approximately $2,500 per week and a percentage of every house show in the market. Soon, instead of stations airing wrestling as low-cost programming that drew ratings, it was viewed like the Sunday morning religious programming and was the predecessor to infomercial time. Television realized they were in the driver's seat.

Without them, there was no local wrestling, so they started charging local promotions. This sped up the inevitable decline of those companies, who couldn't generate enough money to pay for their TV time. This was a major reason why ECW folded as well, as they simply couldn't generate the amount of money needed to pay their television bills.

Both Watts, who paid to establish national syndication, and Crockett, who bought out Watts largely to get his network, ended up deep in debt with the new changed business. McMahon, through opening up merchandise, pay-per-view, and doing strong arena business behind Hulk Hogan, had remained profitable through all this.

In late 1988, Crockett was out of cash and sold his promotion to Turner Broadcasting. Ted Turner was in the wrestling business and was McMahon's only real adversary.

Though Turner's company struggled in its early years, the cable ratings for the WWF and WCW, as Turner's company became known, were not that different. Wrestling fans would watch wrestling on television and weren't loyal to a particular promotion as far as TV viewing went, as would be the case in another generation. McMahon's company always had an edge with kids and was stronger at the arenas and on pay-per-view.

In 1993, things again began to shift, as Hulk Hogan quit the WWF after feeling insulted that he was asked to lose the championship to Bret Hart. Business was in a tailspin, so he left to pursue acting, including a television series called "Thunder in Paradise." The show was being taped out of Orlando, Florida, where WCW was also taping. By this time, after going through one failed manager after another, WCW was in the hands of Eric Bischoff. Bischoff and one of WCW's top stars, Flair, talked Hogan into returning to wrestling in 1994, but with them, based on what was an incredible contract for the time. Hogan was such a star that pay-per-view business grew significantly.

However, Turner was not satisfied and wanted to know why WCW wasn't beating WWF. Bischoff said it was because WWF had a Monday night prime time show on USA. So Turner gave Bischoff a Monday night show, and the war was on.

That led to the most exciting period in television wrestling history. *Nitro* expanded to two hours. Then *Raw* expanded. Monday night wrestling viewership grew from about four million in 1995 to consistently topping ten million a few years later, peaking at twelve million in 1998 when both companies were strong. The money-losing WCW was suddenly very profitable and blew past WWF in popularity for a short period of time. It was an amazing time to be a wrestling fan.

But as quick as it rose, everything collapsed, as WCW never planned for the future. WCW started struggling as Steve Austin caught fire for McMahon. Infighting was rampant in the company as fingers were pointed in every direction, leading to creative in 1999 and 2000 possibly being the worst in the history of pro wrestling. They had completely lost touch with their audience, which eroded away at a rate never seen before or since.

Since WCW folded, many of those who were in charge have created a number of narratives for why it failed. WCW, as its zenith, was the hottest pro-wrestling company the world had ever seen. It had more talent than any company in history. A pro-wrestling company as part of the Turner family was a panacea. At one point, they had Vince McMahon on the ropes.

But they never planned for the future, and in desperation, the television and arena product got worse and worse.

This book explains, sometimes on a week-to-week basis, what built WCW into the most successful pro-wrestling company in history, only to be squandered all away. It's a story of how that bright future was basically destroyed in one horrible calendar year, and why, just over one year after that, it was gone.

Ten years ago, we wrote in the original book that pro wrestling may never be the same because of it. With the benefit of a decade of hindsight, that is no longer speculative. Today's WWE is a stable business, which through technological changes has remained profitable for the most part. The big change from a business standpoint is that, unlike in the '80s when McMahon led the way in television stations wanting money to put wrestling on the air, the plethora of cable stations hungry for anything that will deliver ratings has made wrestling, or as McMahon now calls it, sports entertainment, into a product that gets paid nine figures annually by NBC Universal through rights fees each year.

As screwed up as WCW was, had it survived five more years, it would have benefited from the changing economy. In the creative state of 1999 and 2000, that wouldn't have been enough. But in the right hands, the company may never have died. And if it didn't, it may have even thrived economically.

But now, the costs of getting in, starting up, and competing with WWE are too high. A generation only knows one major-league version of wrestling, and that is WWE. The vast majority of fans aren't open to an alternative. And it certainly doesn't help that the largest alternative, TNA Impact, has been run nearly as ineptly for most of its existence as WCW was during its dying days.

WCW always had a traditional fan base dating from the territory days. For the most part, when *Nitro* was canceled that one fateful night in March 2001, they quickly drifted away and never came back.

There are so many lessons to be learned from WCW's downfall that you would need a book to detail them all. This is that book. It's a book that everyone in wrestling, even those who lived through the famed Monday Night Wars, should read to learn from those mistakes.

—Dave Meltzer, October 2014

1st EDITION
★ ★ ★ FOREWORD ★ ★ ★

When the ultimate history of American pro wrestling is written, there is probably no story more important, with the exception of the history of Vince McMahon Jr. and the World Wrestling Federation, than that of World Championship Wrestling.

It's a story about what should have been. WCW was, at its zenith, the single hottest company the wrestling world had ever seen, a title it should have held for years. The idea of a pro-wrestling company being part of the Turner family was a panacea. Wrestling had, in most parts of the country, been a hand-to-mouth business. In many parts of the country, it was a huge TV ratings success, and many cities had traditions of drawing good crowds on a regular basis. But every place had its ups and downs. Many formerly flourishing cities over the years, from Detroit to San Francisco to Los Angeles to Atlanta to Toronto to Montreal to St. Louis, had great long-standing traditions. In all cases, however, they went down the tubes in very quick order. That was the nature of the beast.

But being under the Turner umbrella could have, and arguably should have, changed everything. The backing of a billion-dollar company should not only have opened the doors to better marketing, but also (in theory) have created a promotional synergy that would put the company on the entertainment map that its rival, McMahon's WWF, had been on since 1984. But to those in charge of the wrestling end of things, it was questionable whether anyone in the Turner regime had a single clue what promoting professional wrestling was all about. Indeed, by the time Ted Turner suggested putting *Nitro* head-to-head with the WWF's flagship program *Raw* on Monday nights, pro wrestling in North America was in a terrible depression. The thought of splintering the audience between the two promotions was seen by many in the wrestling business as suicide.

Instead, something amazing happened. *Raw* and *Nitro* didn't split a finite group of wrestling fans, but instead spent the next several years creating millions and millions of new viewers. The Monday-night wrestling audience grew from about 4 million in 1995 to more than 12 million at its peak in 1998, when both companies were on a roll.

And make no mistake about it—WCW was on one hell of a roll. It went from being a company that no one had much interest in to being the most powerful company in the history of wrestling, one capable of drawing 30,000 people to major stadiums without even having to advertise one match.

The man behind WCW's rise to fame was Eric Bischoff, who raised the stakes by paying top dollar and getting the most marketable talent in the world. He brought fans big-name stars and filled the undercards with the best wrestling anywhere. He brought in big-name celebrities, many of whom actually drew money for the company. But Bischoff's biggest contribution was probably the fact that, under him, WCW modernized the in-ring style of American pro wrestling, a style that had languished behind those of both Mexico and Japan for years. Other promotions, such as Paul Heyman's Extreme Championship Wrestling, tried to do the same, but they never had the money to keep the talent they were developing, and they were doomed when WCW started copying their style.

Even the mighty WWF didn't have the star power, or the talent depth, and its "big man" style suddenly looked slow and outdated compared to the far more athletic product WCW featured at the time.

The irony of Bischoff being the man who did all this is nothing short of amazing. Prior to his rise up the ranks, Bischoff was little more than a backup announcer, hired largely because he wasn't very good and thus would never be a threat to lead announcer Jim Ross. He grew frustrated at how badly the company was run, and he somehow leapfrogged over everyone to gain control over a business of which he had limited knowledge. His battle plan was really not all that different from McMahon's years earlier: that is, he would spend huge money for the top talent and raid the opposition. McMahon did this in 1984, and his rival promoters laughed at him for overspending. But it was McMahon who had the last laugh, as those promoters quickly went bankrupt while he became the most successful wrestling promoter who ever lived.

In the mid-1990s, Bischoff gave McMahon a taste of the medicine he'd given the rest of the wrestling world. The end result should have been the same, except, in the end, Bischoff didn't understand his fan base. Perhaps even more crippling was the fact he was so close with pro wrestling's ultimate charmer, Hulk Hogan, that he thought he'd never have to worry. Bischoff really believed that Hogan *was* pro wrestling, because for so many years, he had been. In addition to Hogan, Bischoff also had every other huge star under contract: Roddy Piper, Randy Savage, Ric Flair, and countless others. Hogan's initial matches with all these men were huge hits, and cast the die for years to come.

The problem was that, after years of seeing the same men in the main events, fans yearned for something new. What Bischoff and WCW were presenting became very stale. This wasn't the same as the Rolling Stones doing a tour every few years; this was the wrestling legends of the '80s attempting to dominate television shows in 1999.

It wasn't only Bischoff's lack of foresight that led to the company's downfall. The wrestlers themselves took advantage of and ruined the greatest system they could have possibly ever worked under. Bischoff would often allow these men to have total control of their careers, although he'd learn (only not soon enough) that putting old wrestlers in charge of a business that had changed rapidly, but that they still thought was the same as it had been in 1991, was a recipe for disaster. WCW had squandered its future because the hungry younger wrestlers were not allowed into the main events. The guys in those spots jealously guarded them, ran them down to management, and soon all the fresh young stars began to hate their jobs and sought employment elsewhere. Before long, every advantage WCW had was gone, and its future was mortgaged at the feet of the older wrestlers. It would never get that bright future back.

In the end, WCW was a victim of its own success. Bischoff had created a successful formula, one that he held on to for far too long, and one that ultimately started the downfall of the company. Once the snowball started to roll, those in charge had no idea how to stop it.

This book explains, sometimes on a week-to-week basis, how the company was built into the most successful pro-wrestling promotion in history, only to be squandered all away. It's a story of how a bright future was basically destroyed in one horrible calendar year, and why, just over one year after that, it was gone. Sadly, pro wrestling may never be the same for it.

There are so many lessons to be learned from WCW's downfall that you would need a book to detail them all. Thankfully, the book has finally been written. It's a book that everyone in wrestling—even though most lived through it—really needs to read in order to remember the mistakes and avoid repeating them.

Because, sadly, since the death of WCW, we've seen far more examples of copying what killed it than of copying what made it successful.

—Dave Meltzer, August 2004

★ ★ ★ PREFACE ★ ★ ★

Since the original version of *The Death of WCW* was released, we've received countless emails—and death threats.

Thankfully, the former greatly outnumber the latter, and for that we say "Thank you."

What may have shocked us most during the last decade is the utter lack of correspondence regarding our original dedication. It simply read: "To Hunter and Steph." We thought that was a fairly clever if somewhat subtle way to begin the proceedings back in 2004.

Perhaps it was just a bit *too* subtle.

In short, yes, we were referencing Paul and Stephanie Levesque. That would be Triple H (Hunter) and Stephanie McMahon, the heirs apparent to Vince McMahon's cash cow known as World Wrestling Entertainment. In fact, the original layout of *The Death of WCW* was that of a handbook, a guide stating everything that a wrestling company could possibly do wrong, using WCW illustrations to prove the points. We thought if we penned a guideline of the exact items that killed WCW it would guide future wrestling promoters and help them out. Of course, the layout of the book changed because, honestly, the original concept was kind of a mess and not very fun to read. Still, the basic issues that destroyed the company all made it in there.

Make no mistake—we knew neither Hunter nor Steph would ever actually read the book. Still, we had hopes that someone within that company might, and perhaps, somehow, in some way, derive some wisdom from it that would help their company as Vince McMahon morphed into Rich Uncle Pennybags, having vanquished all realistic opposition in the pro-wrestling industry.

The past ten years have shown us that didn't happen.

While we are certain there are people within WWE who have read the book, they have taught those in charge very little about the demise of their largest competitor. Since 2004, WWE has made many, many of the same mistakes that led to WCW's downfall. Granted, there has been nowhere near the level of stupidity that we saw in Ted Turner's "rasslin" company (honest-to-God, after reviewing and expanding the WCW 2000 chapter, that would be impossible), but still, lessons were there to be learned and were simply ignored. Due to ignoring the past, money has been lost—money that will never be recovered.

In short, they should have read the book. And not just because we dedicated it to them.

But it's not just WWE. Amazingly, and most bafflingly, consider the fact that those who were at the helm of WCW during its colossal collapse have found new jobs. In the wrestling business, no less! Why wrestling companies would want to hitch their wagons to the horses that pulled WCW off a cliff is, quite frankly, baffling; a question that can never be answered. But that hasn't changed the fact that those in charge of TNA Impact Wrestling have decided to do just that. Whenever ECW Press calls us to ask what book we are going to write next, the answer is always the same: "*The Death of TNA*; you can just change the letters 'WCW' on the cover to 'TNA,' and reprint the rest.

Oh, and don't forget to send us our royalty checks."

Seriously, look at the front cover of the original *The Death of WCW*. Who do you see? Vince Russo, Eric Bischoff, Hulk Hogan, Scott Hall, and Kevin Nash. Who has been the head writer for TNA during the bulk of its existence? Russo. Who, when they saw that wasn't working out, did they throw money at to come in and right the ship? Hogan and Bischoff. And what has the company garnered from Russo, Bischoff, and Hogan's years of said guidance? The same issues WCW had and the same result: losses of millions of dollars. All that plus a never-ending string of 1.1 television ratings, and a whole heapin' helpin' of stupidity that was so plentiful we decided to add in a listing of it at the end of this book.

However, as we're sure they won't bother to learn from history either, we're going to try to go one step further and note the same mistakes both WWE and TNA have made that WCW did years prior. To be sure that no one can miss this, we've not so subtly tagged these sections with bold **"LESSON NOT LEARNED."**

We've also added a ton of quotes from those who saw WCW implode, just to shut up all the people who mistakenly thought we wrote about what happened without knowing folks behind the scenes. Additionally, you'll find other items and notes that weren't in the original version of the book.

Finally, and most importantly, we're changing our decication. Instead of "To Hunter and Steph," this book will be dedicated "To Dixie and Bob."

Why we bother, we don't know. It's apparent that those in the wrestling business will never learn from the past.

We do, however, hold out hope that one day we, the authors of this book, will learn a lesson. Perhaps when the *20th* anniversary edition of this book is digitally uploaded directly into your brain, we'll get smart and dedicate it to our wives and kids instead.

★ ★ ★ INTRODUCTION ★ ★ ★

Here Lies World Championship Wrestling 1988–2001

World Championship Wrestling was not supposed to die.

Anyone with even a basic understanding of its inner workings knew this to be true. As the company began to hit its peak around 1997, all signs indicated that WCW was destined to thrive and prosper. The promotion had so many unfair advantages, it seemed that not only would it continue to expand its profits, but it would also eventually turn every other wrestling promotion in the country into dust.

And why wouldn't it?

More importantly, *how* couldn't it?

The promotion had the single greatest array of talent the wrestling world had ever known. The two men who defined professional wrestling in the 1980s, Hulk Hogan and Ric Flair, both made their home in WCW. The most popular wrestlers of the 1990s, including Sting and Bret Hart, competed in WCW rings, as did Scott Hall and Kevin Nash, who revolutionized the business as the Outsiders, and shortly thereafter formed the nucleus of the infamous New World Order. The company had the most talented in-ring workers: men like Chris Benoit, Eddie Guerrero, and Dean Malenko, as well as the greatest high-flyers from around the world—Rey Mysterio Jr., Juventud Guerrera, and countless others. And, perhaps above all, WCW also employed the man who would lead the industry into the next millennium, the man fans flocked to arenas to see: Bill Goldberg. Such a roster of talent had never been seen in a single pro-wrestling promotion before.

When their flagship show *WCW Monday Nitro* was created, many older fans returned to watch the stars they'd grown up on, creating the largest wrestling audience the cable industry had ever seen. WCW was in a place no company had been since Vince McMahon took the World Wrestling Federation national in the mid-1980s: that is, poised to kill the WWF once and for all. Many wrestlers were eager to jump ship to WCW, some looking to increase their paydays, others out of fear that the WWF wasn't long for this world. Essentially, they were looking to survive.

WCW was looking beyond that. *Nitro* had surpassed not only *Raw* in the ratings, but every other program on cable television. They weren't just the number-one wrestling show; they were the number-one cable show, period. Every week, *Nitro* presented three hours of live action, featuring cutting-edge storylines, amazing matches, and production values the likes of which the wrestling world had never seen before. In addition to the skyrocketing ratings, WCW was one of the biggest and most profitable touring groups in the country, as fans swarmed to arenas for live *Nitro*s and for the monthly megashows. Fans who couldn't attend the matches live ordered in record numbers via the miracle of pay-per-view, spending upwards of $30 a month just to watch the special events. And let's not forget the insane amounts of merchandise sold, from T-shirts to posters to magazines to bandanas to wrestling teddy bears to key chains to beanie babies to sipper cups to every stupid tchotchke piece of crap imaginable—all with the WCW logo slapped right on it.

Everything was making the company money, to the tune of more than a $55 million profit in a single year.

So let's restate once more, for the record, that WCW was not supposed to die.

In fact, not only was WCW never supposed to vanish from the face of the Earth, but the mere thought that the company could ever perish was laughable.

How could this company go the way of the dodo? WCW zealots would tell you—inaccurately, but that's beside the point—that it had been around for over 100 years. *One hundred years!* Not only had it been around longer than any other wrestling company, they'd insist, but also longer than almost any other viable form of entertainment. It had been around longer than movies or television. It had been around longer than the National Football League. By God, WCW wasn't just a wrestling company, it was an American institution!

As impressive as it was that the company could trace its roots back "nearly to the days of Abraham Lincoln," more impressive was the fact that it was owned by the biggest media mogul in the entire universe, Ted Turner—the real reason why the company could not, would not, die. There was simply too damn much money behind it. Turner had purchased the company in the late 1980s almost as a toy, a hobby, and, if truth be told, he wasn't greatly concerned if the thing ever made a dime. Anything it lost was just pocket change, and anything it made likely was as well. But since wrestling had been a cornerstone of the Turner networks since the launch of the Superstation, he pledged to keep it around, no matter what.

So he had their shows airing on his networks, TBS and TNT, and in prime viewing hours: Monday nights, Wednesday nights, Saturday nights, and Sunday nights. Think about that: in any given week, more often than not, WCW was being featured on the Turner networks during prime time. If another time slot was needed for a new show, or perhaps a bimonthly special, Uncle Ted was just a phone call away. Backed with the power of the Turner networks, promotion of the pay-per-view events was nothing short of grandiose.

How on Earth could anyone imagine that World Championship Wrestling might die?

After all, if the company was going to die, it would have done so years before it ever hit it big. WCW would have died in 1993, when it lost $6 million filming expensive promotional movies featuring exploding boats and one-eyed midgets. It would have died when it lost its number-one draw, Ric Flair, to the competition.

It would have, and perhaps it should have, but it didn't.

World Championship Wrestling didn't die; in fact, it laughed in the face of death and came out smiling, making more money in 1998—over $50 million—than it had lost in all its previous years put together. WCW wasn't dying; it was growing and expanding, becoming the wrestling company against which all other wrestling companies would ever be measured. WCW was the benchmark of success in the wrestling industry. The fans knew it, the wrestlers knew it—even the WWF and Vince McMahon knew it. WCW was so successful, in fact, that it didn't matter what stupid mistakes were made because the revenue would always keep coming in. The ratings that came in on Tuesday mornings would justify whatever they did, as would the incredible buy rates and live attendance figures.

Yes, WCW was on top, and it knew just how to stay there: by never changing anything. After all, why shuffle the card around in order to give new talent a chance on top? The stars it had been using for years—the Hogans and Nashes and the rest—well, they'd been stars for years, and they'd certainly be on top for many more to come. Sure, there were younger and arguably more talented guys on the roster, but they weren't proven commodities. The fans couldn't buy these guys as main-eventers; after all, these wrestlers had never been put in such an important position before, and who knew if they could handle the pressure? Besides,

Hogan and Nash were the big stars in the eyes of the fans. If anyone tried to convince the WCW brass otherwise, these two wrestlers would be more than happy to explain their role in bringing WCW out of the dark ages and into its rightful position as the number one wrestling company on the planet.

Question: Why fix what wasn't broken?

Answer: Because if it wasn't broken, it was certainly worn out.

Almost as quickly as they had grown, the ratings tanked. As the WCW fan base began to depart in record numbers, the ratings spoke volumes. Audiences were tired of seeing the same old, same old, and they voted with their remote controls. Not only did the ratings collapse, but the all-important pay-per-view buy rates also tumbled, eventually falling right off the cliff. The wrestlers who'd supposedly brought the company to its zenith began to quarrel backstage, some choosing to vanish like thieves in the night rather than shoulder any blame that this was somehow partially their own doing.

Countless millions were spent on quick fixes that did nothing but drive fans away. Regimes changed backstage. New script writers were brought in. New sets were built. New pay-per-view events were created. Rock and roll bands were brought in to do mini concerts.

None of it made a damn bit of difference. All these short-term fixes amounted to little more than putting a bandage on a cancerous tumor.

World Championship Wrestling wasn't supposed to die?

Right.

★ ★ ★ ★ ★ PART I
THE BIRTH

*"Ted called me up and said 'Hey Vince,
guess what? I'm in the rasslin' business now!'"*
—Vince McMahon, Owner, World Wrestling Entertainment

CHAPTER
★ ★ ★ ONE ★ ★ ★
1988–1996:
MR. TURNER'S BABY BOY

While many believed World Championship Wrestling could never die and were stunned in 2001 when it actually did, an even larger group believed the company probably should have died countless times before then, since it had consistently lost so much money. And perhaps it should have. But the misconception that WCW was a huge money-loser in its formative years should be dispelled right off the bat. In truth, WCW lost around $6 million per year in the first five years of its existence—not a horrible figure at all, considering what they were giving Turner: four hours of excellent ratings every single week of the year. Some within the Turner organization squawked at the losses, but Ted Turner himself didn't. In fact, Turner was such a cheerleader for the company that when his board of directors suggested shutting WCW down in 1992 (their argument was that they'd save tons of money putting movies they already owned in the WCW time slots), he told them that wrestling built the Superstation, and as long as he was in charge it would always have a home there. He also told them never to bring the idea up again.

They didn't.

Since Turner was so strongly behind WCW, it seemed that regardless of what happened or how much money the company lost, it would always be around. No matter what, no matter how bad things could get, many within the company were unafraid, and unfortunately this sense of security often led those in charge to make bad decisions. They could throw away money, alienate their employees and even their fans—none of it mattered, as Ted Turner would always be there to bail them out of a jam.

For all the reasons why the company could have and arguably should have died, it did have history on its side. After all, this was a company that had been around almost 100 years . . . or at least that's one of the myths rabid WCW supporters would have you believe.

The truth is a bit different. When promoter "Big" Jim Crockett died in 1973, his assets—including Jim Crockett Promotions, which ran pro-wrestling shows—were eventually passed on to his son, Jim Jr. For decades, the Crocketts, like other National Wrestling Alliance (NWA) promoters nationwide, tried to bring prestige to their organization by claiming that their main title, the World Heavyweight championship, dated back to 1905. Their champ, they claimed, wore a belt with a lineage that could be traced to such turn-of-the-century legends as George Hackenschmidt and Frank A. Gotch.

Truth be told, the NWA that helped form WCW has roots in 1905 about as much as the rap group NWA does. The confusion stems from the fact that there were two different NWAs: the turn-of-the-century National Wrestling *Association*, and the modern-day National Wrestling *Alliance*. Today's NWA was formed in 1948 by six promoters at a meeting in Waterloo, Iowa. They named Des Moines promoter Pinky George the first president and Kansas City promoter Orville Brown the first champion. Lou Thesz won the title in 1949, then won the National Wrestling Association title in 1950. Because the group controlled all the major titles, the NWA championship became the most prominent belt in the world for almost forty years. In April of 1984, it was one of three "big" titles in the U.S., along with the World titles of the AWA, promoted by Verne Gagne, and the WWF, promoted by another junior, Vincent Kennedy McMahon.

The original Vince McMahon—Vincent James McMahon, to be precise—was the son of boxing and wrestling promoter Jess McMahon. Vince Sr. had promoted the World Wide Wrestling Federation (they dropped a "W" in 1979) since 1963, running throughout the Northeast. The highly successful promotion, based in Madison Square Garden, was built around such legendary stars as Bruno Sammartino, Superstar Billy Graham, and Bob Backlund. But Vince Sr. was getting old, and his son—the handsome, fast-talking announcer on his wrestling shows— was eager to make a serious impact.

Vince Sr. wasn't so sure about his son. He never wanted him to be a wrestler, and probably didn't want him to be involved much with the business at all. Plus, the young McMahon seemed to have some pretty grandiose ideas. Wrestling had always been a territorial business, with different groups promoting cards exclusively in "their" areas of the country. There was Roy Welch in Alabama; Nick Gulas in Nashville; Leroy McGuirk in Oklahoma; and Sam Muchnick in St. Louis; among over two dozen others. While promoters would sometimes venture into opposing territories, no one had ever attempted to do what Vince Jr. was planning on such a massive scale. Vince Jr. wanted to promote wrestling wherever he pleased.

Amazingly, had Vince Sr.'s wish that his son never become a wrestler come to pass, the history of wrestling might forever be different. A key turning point in the war between WCW and the WWF was Steve Austin's blood feud with his most famous in-ring rival: none other than Vince McMahon himself. Vince was a great heel; his chemistry with Austin was a large part of what turned the tide. While his early stint as a babyface cheerleading announcer was little to pay attention to, and his later stint as a song and dance man (really!) crooning a ditty called "Stand Back" was more something for folks to laugh at, the evil Mr. McMahon's pumped-up faux-pro-wrestler persona was one to whom nearly every fan could relate; after all, who hasn't had a boss they wanted to pummel? No doubt Austin would have been a huge star regardless, but no one can argue the impact that the vile Mr. McMahon foil had on Austin's rise to fame. And that rise to fame was what gave wrestling fans options, options that led in part to WCW's fall.

Contrary to what many believe, Vince Jr. wasn't the first wrestling promoter to go national. His father's Madison Square Garden cards aired regionally on the MSG Network and nationally on HBO in the early-to-mid-'70s. Other promotions had been syndicated nationally as early as the dawn of television in the late 1940s, while others, such as Jim Barnett, tried national expansion in the '60s and '70s. And when Ted Turner's Atlanta WTCG UHF station went up on satellite as the Superstation in 1976, it took Jim Barnett's Georgia-based promotion nationwide, airing two shows on the weekends: *Georgia Championship Wrestling* on Saturday nights (6.4 average rating) and *Best of Georgia Championship Wrestling* (6.6 average rating) the following evening. The station quickly grew to serve 15 million people, and the wrestling show was the first program to draw over one million viewers on the station and the first TV show in history to ever reach one million homes on cable television.

The NWA promoters were leery of this newly configured nation-wide coverage, but Vince Sr. argued that it would be ridiculous for him to stop promoting in the Garden (as long as he promoted there, MSG Network was going to broadcast the shows regionally and nationally through HBO), and Barnett simply said that no matter what, his show still featured mainly Georgia wrestlers. Several years later, however, Turner requested that the name be modified to something less regional in scope, and therefore the show was changed from *Georgia Championship*

Wrestling to *World Championship Wrestling*, which just so happened to be the name of a promotion Barnett had successfully promoted in Australia a decade earlier.

Cable, Barnett would later say, could not be stopped. And he was right.

In 1982, Vince Sr. finally caved and sold the World Wrestling Federation to his son. The deal, though, was that if Vince Jr. missed even one of his quarterly payments he'd lose the promotion back to Vince Sr.'s three original partners: Bob "Gorilla Monsoon" Marella (who eventually got a lifetime announcing gig out of it), Phil Zacko, and Arnold Skaaland. While some believe that Vince Sr. was never aware of his son's lofty plans, most with knowledge of the situation feel otherwise. The sense was that even if Vince Sr. did know, he didn't believe that his son could pull it off. Shortly after selling the company, Vince Sr. was diagnosed with cancer, and he died a few months later.

Those who doubted Vince Jr. couldn't have been more wrong. Not only did he take the WWF national, he created a near monopoly for himself within five years of doing so. One of his first major offensive moves was to offer lucrative contracts to stars (and sometimes guys nobody in their right mind would consider star material) from other territories, most notably from Verne Gagne's AWA. Vince had already offered to buy Gagne's promotion outright, but he'd been shot down. His next step, therefore, was to buy Gagne's talent, including his hottest star of all: a young, bleached-blonde muscleman named Hulk Hogan. Hogan ended up being the chosen one, and McMahon quickly moved his WWF title from his father's long-term champion Bob Backlund to the dastardly Iron Sheik. On January 23, 1984, just twenty-eight days later, Hogan beat Sheik in Madison Square Garden with his dreaded Legdrop of Doom, and Hulkamania took off.

Widespread TV was the next major step. In those days, many wrestling promoters got along swimmingly with their local TV affiliates. In many territories, the television people would air the programming for free and make money off the advertising. The wrestling people, meanwhile, would write shows to compel fans to go to the local arena and pay for tickets. In some territories—Jerry Jarrett's Memphis is a good example—the TV stations would actually pay the promoters for the programming. Vince Jr. went from territory to territory and not only offered the station managers his slick TV tapes in place of their current, often poorly filmed local wrestling shows, but also offered to *pay* to get them on the air.

Further into his expansion, McMahon purchased Georgia Championship Wrestling for $750,000 in a deal actually made behind Ole Anderson's back. The company had gone from a money-loser under former promoter Jim Barnett (a notoriously lavish spender who, during a money-losing period in 1982, was forced out by his own booker, Anderson, and other shareholders over allegations of embezzlement) to a moneymaker under Anderson. However, the shareholders were disgruntled that they weren't making any money—all of the profits appeared to be going into the pockets of the highly paid Anderson. Two of the shareholders, former legendary grapplers Jack and Gerald Brisco, talked the other shareholders into banding together to sell a majority of the stock to McMahon.

The entire point of the purchase was for McMahon to gain control of the coveted Saturday and Sunday 6:05 p.m. time slots on TBS. Adding those time slots to his traditional Monday night time slot on USA Network (which eventually became the home of *Monday Night Raw*) gave Vince a virtual monopoly on the best television real estate for pro wrestling in the entire country. His plan, obviously, was to replace tapes of the Georgia wrestlers with tapes of his WWF superstars. The problem was that there was a vast in-ring difference between the two products: the Georgia show featured an emphasis on in-ring action with talented workers, and the WWF show featured a bunch of one-sided "squash" matches that had already aired on the USA Network.

Problem: viewers didn't want WWF wrestling. When the switchover took place on "Black Saturday," July 14, 1985, over 1,000 fans angrily complained to the Superstation. Many asked specifically for "Gordon Solie Wrestling" to return, a reference to the legendary GCW announcer. Turner's response was to give Ole Anderson a Saturday 7:00 a.m. time slot so that he could start a new company, Championship Wrestling from Georgia, Inc. (which didn't last long). Then, the following year, Turner gave Bill Watts' *Mid-South Wrestling* a one-hour time slot on Sunday, and agreed to finance him so that he could compete nationally against McMahon. Vince, who thought his purchase of *GCW* would give him an exclusive on TBS, was outraged, particularly since he paid nearly $1 million for the time slots and Turner gave Watts the new time slot for free. Turner, of course, disagreed, feeling that Vince had reneged on a stipulation in the contract that required him to produce a separate weekly program from an Atlanta studio. If Vince wasn't going to do it, well, someone else would. Thus began the two-decade war between McMahon and Turner.

What made things worse for Vince was that *Mid-South*, a tremendously well-booked and entertaining show, immediately started to destroy all of his programming in the ratings despite the weird time slot and having no promotion whatsoever. At its peak, the show was averaging a 5.2 rating, not only beating McMahon's shows, but also becoming the highest-rated show on all of cable television. Turner, who had promised to bankroll Watts, wanted to kick Vince off the station, but couldn't until the contract the two had signed expired. When that day drew near, who should return to the fold but former GCW promoter Jim Barnett, who had jumped to WWF after being ousted by Ole, and who just happened to be a close personal friend of Turner's. Barnett negotiated a deal between Vince and Jim Crockett Jr., the then promoter of Mid-Atlantic Championship Wrestling, which enabled Crockett to purchase the TBS slots with exclusivity for $1 million. Turner was ecstatic: not only was he rid of Vince, but he had also regained popular wrestling stars like Dusty Rhodes and Ric Flair, plus Crockett agreed to do what Vince wouldn't, promote a local Atlanta studio wrestling show. Watts felt betrayed. He claimed Turner had promised to give him McMahon's time slots when McMahon's contract expired, only to turn around and give them to Crockett instead. Despite the affront, on the final episode of *Mid-South Wrestling*, Watts went on television and put over Crockett's performers, saying fans would get to see great NWA action from now on.

Vince, however, gave Crockett a very stern warning, noting, "You'll choke on that $1 million."

Heading up the top two promotions in the country, McMahon and Crockett continued to feud over the next few years. The smaller territories couldn't compete with the level of TV exposure these companies had, and subsequently, most died off. Among the promoters who didn't make it was Watts, who tried to go national after losing the TBS slots but couldn't afford it in the end. He was paying for national syndication but was losing $50,000 each week due to a combination of falling business and economic turmoil in the region. He finally sold to Crockett for $4 million, although he only ended up receiving $1.2 million when all was said and done because Crockett, despite having had a great two-year period under booker Dusty Rhodes after the McMahon TBS buyout, ultimately couldn't afford to go national either.

After buying Watts' company, which was known as the Universal Wrestling Federation at that time (you know, because the universe is bigger than the world—seriously, that's why it got the name), Crockett Promotions booked an ingenious invasion angle that consisted of having all their guys destroy all the UWF guys, making them look like total losers. "Crockett didn't know how to book," noted Bill Watts. "He never booked, he couldn't book, so he was at the mercy of his booker. And Dusty was a brilliant person, but if you look at Florida, it went broke under Dusty. Every place he booked went broke.

Because as good as he was at drawing gross gates, he had no consciousness of a bottom line . . . nothing was bottom-line oriented. [And] Crockett couldn't make the tough management decisions needed to rein it in."[1] In terms of bad booking, Crockett was years ahead of his time, because like the WWF/WCW invasion in the summer of 2001, the plan was so ingenious that instead of leading to a period of business boom built around a "promotion versus promotion war," they killed the invaders immediately and it died a painfully quick death.

Crockett had many brilliant ideas, few of which would ever be learned from. He signed guys to huge guaranteed deals he couldn't afford. He snubbed loyal fans by moving *Starrcade* (the NWA equivalent of *WrestleMania*) out of the South for the first time ever, and running it in Chicago instead. He flew himself and the top stars around in an expensive private jet and partied it up on the flights. Scratch that, he didn't have *a*, as in one, private jet, he actually had *two* of them . . . and thus had to keep two pilots on payroll at all times.

And he allowed Dusty Rhodes to ultimately book the company into oblivion with cheap finishes that outraged fans. In fact, Dusty's penchant for having a babyface (or good guy) win a belt or match and then later reversing it became commonly known within the industry as a "Dusty Finish." (Dusty himself actually got the finish from booker Eddie Graham when he was learning pro wrestling in Florida in the 1970s.) Another Crockett moment of genius saw mid-carder Ron Garvin beat perennial champ Ric Flair for the World title . . . then saw Garvin, who we remind you was a babyface, announce he would not be defending the title again until *Starrcade*. Umm, what? Although Garvin was supposedly the hero prior to his title win, fans didn't see him as a man who should be beating the Nature Boy, and ratings plummeted from the 4.0 range to a 2.8—the fastest drop in history.

In late 1987, Crockett announced that the annual Thanksgiving-night *Starrcade* show would be broadcast for the first time on PPV on

November 26. Like McMahon did with the first *WrestleMania*, Crockett was betting his company's existence on this show's success, having run up some huge debts with all his crazy spending. McMahon, knowing the stakes were high for Jim Crockett Promotions, announced that he was going to be running a Thanksgiving-night pay-per-view as well: the first annual *Survivor Series*. Crockett didn't want to run head-to-head with McMahon, who was doing great pay-per-view numbers at the time, so he offered to move the *Starrcade* show to Thanksgiving afternoon. The cable companies were thrilled to hear this, since they expected wrestling fans to buy both shows and basically sit in front of their TVs watching wrestling all day. But Vince had other ideas. He announced that any company that aired Crockett's PPV would not be allowed to air *Survivor Series* or the next *WrestleMania*. Since he was the established king of wrestling PPV at the time, and since *WrestleMania III* had been such a huge financial success that it basically made the genre, all but five companies across the country chose to air the *Survivor Series* over *Starrcade*. Crockett was dead in the water before his show even aired.

Struggling to keep his company alive, Crockett planned his revenge. He booked his next PPV, the *Bunkhouse Stampede*, at the Nassau Coliseum, a building right in the middle of McMahon's home territory. Nobody is quite sure why he thought this was such a great idea, because his product had absolutely no history in the area, and it inevitably bombed at the gate, drawing just 6,000 fans and $80,000. But it got worse. McMahon had a plan of his own: to air the first-ever *Royal Rumble* (a modified battle royal in which new men enter the match at two-minute intervals) live from Hamilton, Ontario, on the USA Network, head-to-head with Crockett's PPV. The *Rumble* ended up doing an 8.2 rating, the highest number for any wrestling show in history on that network—and that includes the Monday Night Wars. And, if all of that wasn't bad enough for Crockett, the *Rumble* was widely regarded as the superior show since Crockett's PPV, headlined by Flair versus Road Warrior Hawk, had yet another hackneyed Dusty Finish.

But Crockett was not yet done. His next idea was to run a free *Clash of the Champions* on TBS on March 27, 1988, head-to-head with *WrestleMania IV*. This time, his plan was somewhat a success, as the *Clash* did a 5.8, and the Flair versus Sting main event ended up being at the time the most-watched match in the history of cable television, peaking at a 7.8. *WrestleMania IV*, on the other hand, was a miserable show headlined by Randy Savage, who beat Ted DiBiase to win the vacant WWF title.

Despite Vince having done exactly the same thing with the *Royal Rumble*, the cable industry was irate with Crockett and Turner for having the audacity to air a free show opposite *Wrestlemania*, despite the fact that *Mania* did 585,000 buys—the most in history. The problem was that the universe for PPV had doubled that year, and even though they set a purchase record, the feeling was that the show would have done substantially better without the competition. Wrestling companies were starting to make the bulk of their money through PPVs, and cable companies were getting a nice slice of the pie (to the tune of approximately 60 percent of the gross!). Turner was told never to allow something like that to happen again. To make matters worse, CNN ran a news story on the major pro-wrestling show of the day . . . and it was *WrestleMania*. Turner's own wrestling company was completely ignored in the story.

Despite the *Clash*'s huge success, Crockett was informed shortly thereafter that his company was going broke. The disastrous year, the huge-money contracts he was paying off, and all his jet flying and limousine riding and kiss stealing and wheeling and dealing were finally coming to roost. Crockett himself would later admit that he loved the lifestyle too much. "I probably had too many beers with the boys," he noted. "That was back in the day; they were great people to be around."[2]

Crockett figured he would make huge money on PPV and through national advertising. Unfortunately, Vince had stomped all over his PPVs, and advertisers believed only inbreds watched pro wrestling and weren't willing to pay much for commercial time. And to be fair, that is a feeling that exists to this day. At the time of this writing, WWE *Raw* is one of the highest rated programs on all of cable television. Despite having a massive audience, their ad rates are far, FAR lower than programs drawing half their ratings.

"The reason it [Crockett Promotions' collapse] happened was because maybe I had too much ego," Crockett himself noted. "Maybe I should have brought in people with expertise in areas other than wrestling. People that don't like Dusty will say it was Dusty's fault. I don't know why people would ever blame Dave Johnson [Crockett's accountant], he almost went nuts trying to save the company, trying to tell me what was really happening because he understood all the ramifications of cash flow. If anyone is to be blamed, it's me."

Turner got wind that things were bad and took an interest in buying. He had a soft spot in his heart for wrestling, as the success of Barnett's program years earlier had helped to convince him that he hadn't made a mistake and that his Superstation could indeed be a success. So, late in the summer of 1988, shortly after Crockett took out $600,000 in loans to make payroll, Turner purchased Jim Crockett Promotions for $9 million. While Turner didn't end up owning the entire NWA, he did own its biggest member promotion and its biggest stars. The Crockett family was given a minority interest (they were bought out a few years later), and everyone in the family was given a job. This included Jim himself, who, after all his years in the business, became a consultant whose ideas were never used.

In the following years, audiences sat through the highs and lows of what would become World Championship Wrestling, thinking to themselves that as horrible as some of it was, with a billionaire like Turner bankrolling everything it would never go out of business.

"I'm sure you have most of the stupid stories," said Jim Cornette of his memories of the promotion. "But one of my favorites was when they booked Centre Stage for TV and we all showed up only to find it in the middle of renovations with no seats in the building, just concrete ledges with dust all over them, and so we had to do TV the next day in Huntsville. Or the time we did a big angle for the Saturday night show at Centre Stage and somehow they didn't record it. Or letting Iron Sheik's $100,000 contract roll over for another year after they only used him about ten times the first year. I never mind being on the record about how stupid WCW was."

For the early years of WCW's life under the Turner empire, the booking duties ping-ponged between two men: Dusty Rhodes and Ole Anderson. Amazingly, despite both having had successful booking runs in regional promotions in the past, neither man seemed to have any clue as to how to run a wrestling company on a national basis. Both had their own agendas, namely pushing themselves and their friends to the high-paying main event slots. And when things didn't go their way, they tended to act like little babies, doing things that did neither the company nor, ironically, themselves any good. A perfect example of this came in 1988, after Dusty and WCW vice president Jim Herd had a blowup. Dusty was upset at Ric Flair and as a result wanted to book him to lose the NWA title in five minutes to Rick Steiner at *Starrcade*. The idea was that Steiner was a legitimate tough guy, and if Flair was in the ring with him Flair would have no choice but to drop the title, even if he didn't want to. Flair was so upset that he threatened to quit the company. Herd didn't want him gone, so he went over Dusty's head as booker and instead put Flair versus Lex Luger at *Starrcade*, which Flair won. Dusty, outraged that he'd been usurped and upset with a decree that there be no more blood or weapons on TV, retaliated by having the Road Warriors come out to the ring, grab a huge metal spike, hold him, and jam it into his eye. Suffice to say, Rhodes' orbital socket soon resembled a crimson version of Old Faithful. To the shock of no one—save perhaps Dusty himself—Herd immediately fired him as booker, and within a few weeks fired him as talent as well.

With WCW no longer his home, Dusty looked north for employment, turning to Vince McMahon and the WWF. McMahon was more than happy to welcome him to the WWF. He even bought him some new outfits. And what outfits they were, with Dusty's flabby frame somehow squeezed into the tightest latex imaginable. Oh—and gigantic bright yellow polka dots! He was introduced to WWF fans through a series of asinine vignettes in which he delivered pizzas, cleaned toilets, and shoveled horse crap. See, that's the way a lot of folks in wrestling operate. You, the promoter, don't like someone in a rival organization. Circumstances arise in which that person is unemployed and in need of a job. Instead of simply denying him employment, you bring him into the company and completely humiliate him. Do the fans in the stands want to see this? No. Does it matter? No, because it's all about showing the guy you don't like who has the power.

The polka-dot outfits weren't the first time McMahon took a shot at Rhodes either. In 1987, the WWF created a manservant character named "Virgil," so named because Rhodes' real first name was Virgil. If that wasn't childish enough, years later, when the WWF's Virgil jumped to WCW, he was renamed "Vincent" as a shot against Vince McMahon. Vincent/Virgil ended up making a career of spoofing folks, as later in his WCW tenure he was renamed again, becoming "Shane," an inside rib on Vince McMahon's son. Which persona was most memorable? Well, to this day Mr. Mike Jones can be seen on the wrestling convention circuit (and elsewhere, randomly), usually alone at an empty booth with a black and white sign that reads "Wrestling Superstar Virgil." The image of him sitting alone with no fans within 1000 yards has been immortalized countless times on the internet, including on a website titled LonelyVirgil.net.

The stellar booking of Ole Anderson in 1990 cannot be ignored. During the period, he scripted many incredible angles, including a match between Sting and Sid Vicious wherein the WCW title changed hands. For approximately forty-five seconds. During the encounter, Sid and Sting fought toward the backstage area, then returned to battle in the ring. However, when Sting came back out, he had apparently grown six inches in height and about fifty pounds in weight. He lifted Sid up for a bodyslam, collapsed (likely from gaining fifty pounds in the span of thirty seconds), and was immediately pinned. New champion!

But wait, no! It turns out that "Sting" was actually Barry Windham in disguise, and the real Sting emerged from the back and then *he* pinned Sid to keep the title. How, exactly, the referee who had just counted the other Sting down for a three count suddenly deciphered that the real Sting had been taken to the back, beaten up, and replaced by Windham in less than a minute was never explained.

For the record, though, to this day, Sid Vicious states that not only did he not know what was going to happen ahead of time, he also was unaware that the man he pinned was not actually Steve Borden: "I didn't even know that," Sid notes. "I didn't know anything. I didn't know Barry Windham was even in the building, I don't think anyone did. If they did, maybe I was the only one that didn't. I ran Sting through the back door, I was told he was supposed to come back out holding his head like somebody whacked him. And when he got back in the ring, I just rolled him up, one-two-three. When he got in there, of course it wasn't him, it was Barry, and I didn't notice it until I got him down. I still had not been told anything. I had to use some quick thinking there."[3]

QUICK THINKING.

Suddenly, some of the interviews the big guy did in the dying days of WCW make more sense.

With Sting having dispatched Sid, and the company not wanting to push Flair as his challenger for whatever reason (likely because he was "too old"—yes, in 1990), a new foe was needed, and thus Ole unveiled his greatest creation: a mystery man known as the Black Scorpion. The Scorpion was a masked being (we weren't sure he was a wrestler, at least in the beginning) who would be shown in what appeared to be a black

This is the man Sid Vicious believed was Sting at *Halloween Havoc 1990*. Really. For the record, it was Barry Windham. [WADE KELLER/PWTORCH.COM]

lit closet, giving Sting cryptic clues to his identity and their shared past. "Oh yes, you know me," Scorpion explained via a garbled voice box recording to Sting. "Or at least you *did*. But don't try to track me down, it won't help. Even if you saw my face in light, you wouldn't recognize me. My face doesn't look the same!" He then promised that he would make Sting "terrified."

And "terrified" would describe anyone who bore witness to Scorpion's live appearances, wherein he generally chose not to wrestle, but rather perform his evil black magic.

EVIL.

BLACK.

MAGIC.

Such sorcery included, but was not limited to, sticking a dude's head in a box and spinning it around like a top and then throwing him into another box and turning him into a tiger.

Really. We're not making this up. This was to entice folks to spend their hard-earned cash on a wrestling match.

Behind the scenes, things were just as laughable. Despite all this build, there was no real plan as to who, precisely, the Scorpion would be unveiled to be. You'd think that would have been a prerequisite going into such an angle, but as you'll soon learn, logic and WCW often chose not to co-exist.

All of this tomfoolery led to the biggest pay-per-view of the year, in which Sting would finally battle the Scorpion mano a mano inside a steel cage. As Gary Michael Capetta announced the stipulations, the Black Scorpion made his way to the ring. Followed by another Black Scorpion. Then another. And another. Eventually, a giant spaceship lowered from the ceiling, from which the real Scorpion emerged.

Yes—the Scorpion was able to not only perform magic, but travel intergalactically as well.

Ready to drop some coin yet?

So Sting came down to the ring (without the aid of a flying saucer), and the two had a match. And for those in attendance, it was a somehow familiar match. This would make sense, as following the defeat of the Scorpion, Sting ripped the mask off to reveal . . . oh yes . . . Ric Flair.

Somehow this led to Ole being fired. Shocking, we know.

His replacement?

Dusty Rhodes, of course!

Dusty, after being made to look like a complete jackass in the WWF, returned once more to the Turner empire, this time to clean up the mess Ole had made in 1990. Who knows why anybody would have thought that rehiring him was a good idea, given his track record of pissing off upper management and booking himself as the star of the territory. The man behind the decision was Jack Petrik, who was in charge of the

Turner wrestling division at the time. He felt that Dusty's problem was that he always booked everything around himself, so his solution was to bring him back with the stipulation being that Dusty could book, but not wrestle.

Dusty came out flying, too, with one of his greatest creations: War Games. It was a ten-man tag match that placed two rings side by side and surrounded both with a steel cage. The participants entered the cage in two-minute intervals. A coin was tossed beforehand, and the winner of the toss would have the upper hand throughout the opening stage of the match, with a two-on-one, then a three-on-two, a four-on-three, and finally a five-on-four advantage. The match could not be decided until all ten men had entered, at which time the "Match Beyond" would begin. It was an ingenious concept, and it created some memorable bouts. *Wrestle War* was no exception, as top heel Sid Vicious nearly sent Brian Pillman through the roof of the cage before depositing him neck first on the mat. If Dusty was looking to impress his bosses, old or new, he did just that in booking this showdown.

It wasn't just madness in the ring, though, For instance, the company was looking to diversify its portfolio by dipping its toe into electronics. Really. Look, we don't blame you for not believing us. So we'll let the *New York Times* tell you the story:

> The group [WCW] is working on electronic contraptions to heighten interest among children. When completed, the gadgets will be shown to focus groups of young fans to get a reading on them.
>
> In development, for instance, is a "rage-meter" that will somehow measure the amount of rage a wrestler is feeling at any given time. Fans will be able to learn, say, whether a wrestler who has just had his teeth kicked out feels blood-curdling rage or perhaps just mild displeasure. Another device being studied is a

"slam-meter." It will reveal the force of a slam to the mat. Was it a back-breaker of a slam? Was it a career-ender?[4]

How much money was spent on what was certain to be a miraculous piece of electronics is unknown, as it was never mentioned again.

There were no American PPVs until May, but the company did put on a co-promotional show with New Japan Pro Wrestling in Tokyo called *Rumble in the Rising Sun*, featuring stars from both promotions (but sadly no rage- or slam-meters). The event featured World champ Ric Flair dropping his title to Tatsumi Fujinami . . . kind of, sort of. The storyline was that Fujinami pinned the champ, but this happened after Flair was thrown over the top rope—grounds for a disqualification in WCW. It was not, however, grounds for a DQ according to New Japan, so Fujinami was recognized by that group as the new NWA World champion.

This led perfectly into WCW's next domestic PPV, *SuperBrawl*. The show saw Flair regain the title in a decent match, as well as a rare baby-face versus babyface showdown between the most popular tag teams in the company: Sting and Lex Luger took on the Steiner Brothers in a match that absolutely tore the house down. Sadly, just as Scott Steiner appeared to be catching fire, he suffered a torn biceps that put him out of action for about a year. The only other notable match on the show featured El Gigante beating Sid Vicious in a match known to cause nightmares for anyone fool enough to watch it. Vicious was leaving for the WWF. His WCW contract didn't expire until the fall, but WCW agreed that if he lost to Gigante in a stretcher match (loser had to be taken out of the building on a stretcher), they'd let him out of his deal early. However, they told him that if he no-showed *SuperBrawl*, they wouldn't give him a release and he wouldn't be able to go to WWF until September. WWF, obviously, urged him to show up. WCW was so certain he wouldn't show that the format backstage listed the match as Gigante versus One Man Gang. But alas, Sid did show up to participate in an all-time terrible battle (described by Dave Meltzer as a match that appeared to feature two blind men wrestling). He lost as scheduled, but instead of being carted out on a stretcher, he just stood up immediately after being pinned and walked out. WCW still let him out of his deal.

As bad as this was, nothing could compare to the fiasco that occurred in June, when one of the biggest wrestling cataclysms ever took place. To explain how it all began, let's back up a bit and look at what had been going on behind the scenes between Ric Flair and WCW vice president Jim Herd. Herd felt that Flair, at forty-two years old, was over the hill and ought to be replaced. He even went so far as to claim that Flair should cut his trademark bleached-blonde hair, wear an earring, and change his name to Spartacus. Perhaps most of all, however, he didn't care for Flair's contract. (Flair was the highest-paid wrestler in the company at a time when they were losing millions every year.) The animosity wasn't one-sided, however, as Flair didn't see Herd as anything more than a corporate suit. And indeed, looking at his employment history, that's exactly what he was: Herd had been a higher-up at Pizza Hut prior to his arrival at Turner. Obviously, the two businesses were radically different. To be fair, Herd did have a minor background in wrestling, in a former life working as a television director for *Wrestling at the Chase* under Sam Muchnick in St. Louis. But despite his friendship with Muchnick, one of the great promoters in wrestling history, Herd had a tough time grasping some of the basic concepts of pro wrestling, including the notion that WCW fans would pay to see Ric Flair perform. Flair was willing—unhappy, but willing—to take a massive pay cut to sign a new two-year deal, less than half of the $750,000 per year he had been making. Herd refused. The two bickered back and forth for months, with Herd calling for Flair to drop the WCW title repeatedly and Flair refusing to do so unless his contract demands were met. In the end, Herd finally just gave up and fired Flair before Flair had a chance to drop the title. The plan was that WCW would declare the title vacant.

All fine in theory, but unfortunately for WCW, Herd failed to realize that Ric Flair, despite now being billed as the WCW champion, was still technically the NWA World Heavyweight champion and thus believed he owned the physical belt. While the NWA largely only existed on paper at that point, WCW was not only promoting Flair as their company champion, but also as the champion of the National Wrestling Alliance, an organization to which they still belonged and whose rules they still had to follow. The NWA board (which didn't really exist in 1991 since most of the promoters had been put out of business by then) was supposed to vote on and approve all title changes. In those days, the NWA champion leased the belt—meaning he had to put down a $25,000 deposit which was held in case he refused to drop the title when asked. Since Flair never lost the belt in the ring and never got his $25,000 back from either the NWA or WCW, he just figured the belt was his to do with as he pleased. He even went so far as to send the belt to Vince McMahon, who began showing it on his television shows. Manager Bobby Heenan claimed that the "Real World champion" was on his way to the WWF. Fans watching WWF TV at home were stunned to see this turn of events, and eager to finally see the long-awaited dream match: WWF champion Hulk Hogan versus WCW/NWA champion Ric Flair.

The Hogan versus Flair series in the WWF ironically turned out to be something of a disappointment. Despite years of wrestling magazines hyping it as the biggest potential match in wrestling history, the WWF gave it a run on house shows. This was puzzling, as most thought it could easily be a **WrestleMania** main event. There were apparently those within the company who viewed Flair as solely a regional act, and thus relatively little promotion was given to what was his first match with the WWF's biggest star. That first match took place in Dayton, Ohio, on October 21, 1991, in what was originally scheduled to be a bout between Flair and Roddy Piper. Hogan and Flair wrestled again three days later in Oakland, California, which according to WWE canon was their first match. While the early bouts in the feud drew very well, it quickly fell off; it appeared that the longer Flair was on WWF television, the less drawing power he had. The appeal was truly when Ric was "WCW champion," and when it became obvious Flair was just another WWF performer, people tired of it. Following the 1992 Royal Rumble where Flair won the title, **WrestleMania VIII** was originally promoted as Hogan versus Flair. That was soon scrapped, however, with Flair instead battling Randy Savage. The feeling was that Hogan versus Sid Vicious/Justice was a bigger main event to the masses than Hogan versus Flair, plus with Hogan leaving to shoot a movie after **WrestleMania** it made no sense for him to beat Flair (he wasn't losing) and then disappear with the belt. At the end of the day, despite both having appeared in the company at the same time in both the '90s and '00s, the greatest dream match of the 1980s, Hulk Hogan versus Ric Flair, never took place at **WrestleMania**.

Herd may have breathed a sigh of relief when Flair left WCW, but once that belt showed up on WWF TV, chaos erupted within the entire company. Herd caught hell from everyone—from Turner officials to the wrestlers themselves. It certainly didn't help that Ted Turner's personal favorite wrestler was Ric Flair. Herd immediately went into a full-blown panic and tried to lure Flair back into the company with an offer twice what Flair had offered to stay for originally (in other words, back to $750,000 per year or so). Flair, irate with how everything went down and having already made a verbal agreement with McMahon, told him no.

Unable to get Flair back, Herd knew he damn well had to recover that title. WCW went as far as to have Jim Barnett (yes, he's back) convince one of the seven members of the NWA Board to switch his allegiance to the side of the WCW members of the board (Gary Juster, Jim Crockett Jr., and, yes, Jim Herd), which then allowed Herd to be named the new NWA president and give WCW controlling interest over the NWA title. This allowed them to proclaim Luger the current NWA champion, after which a lawsuit was filed that eventually forced Flair to return the belt. It also set a legal precedent that would have a major impact on wrestling years later: the court ruled that a pro-wrestling belt was a valuable symbol for the promotion it represented, and if Flair continued to wear it on WWF TV, WCW could sue for damages. So the WWF tried to make a fake WCW belt for Flair to wear. The court wasn't happy. So WWF gave him a tag belt and digitized it on television. The court still wasn't thrilled. Finally, the WWF just had Flair win their version of the World title and scrapped the other version entirely.

Years later, Herd would admit that his decision to drive Flair from the company was the defining moment of his tenure in WCW . . . and it was indeed a poor one. "Regret it?" he laughed. "It was a stupid act on my part. [He was] the best performer in the company . . . by far."[5]

To Herd, the Flair nightmare finally appeared to be in the past. In reality, it was only just beginning.

Herd's first order of business was to crown a new champion. A plan was set in motion to do just this at the upcoming *Great American Bash* pay-per-view from Baltimore. WCW really needed this show to be a success. Fans had not been happy with Flair's sudden disappearance from the promotion, and they made their feelings known with chants of "We Want Flair!" and "Dusty sucks!" at every venue. With an already irritable crowd, it was crucial that the *Bash* entertain fans to prove that WCW could succeed without Flair.

The show rushed right out of the gate with a scaffold match. For those of you who have never seen such an encounter, a scaffold match is pretty much just what it sounds like: a scaffold is erected above the ring, and the combatants attempt to knock each other down to the floor. This type of match is not only incredibly dangerous, with the workers dropping somewhere between fifteen and twenty feet from the scaffold, it's also pretty boring—after all, no one wants to get shoved off before they're ready to make the drop. The scaffold match was a feud-ender. First, build up a huge rivalry between two men and have them duke it out in conventional matches to no satisfactory conclusion. Then, with no other way to resolve the matter, have them square off in a match so dangerous that it would not only settle the rivalry, but could also end careers at its conclusion.

It made little sense to open the show with the match, and even less sense to open it with a bunch of mid-carders like "Rapmaster" P.N. News, a 400-pounder who would likely have collapsed not only the ring, but also the concrete floor underneath had he made the drop. Still, the four men did their best, tiptoeing around the platform and doing everything they could to not lose their balance. After about ten minutes of "action," the bell rang. Since no one had fallen from the scaffold yet, this appeared to be a major screw-up on someone's part. But it wasn't. The match ended because one of the contestants had captured the other team's flag. This was a new rule, one that had never been instituted in a scaffold match before. Despite the fact that this had been advertised for weeks as a standard scaffold match, the rules were changed on the night of the show so that no one would have to take the fall. It was basically a bait and switch, an increasingly common theme in WCW shows. A few boos began to scatter through the arena.

Following the scaffold match fiasco, WCW carted out cartoonish characters—a wizard (Oz), a lumberjack (Big Josh), and a hooded executioner (Black Blood)—all of whom put on horrible matches. A showdown between longtime partners Ricky Morton and Robert Gibson disappointed, as did a goofy chain match featuring Sting and Nikita Koloff. The crowd, which had been presented a horrendous card thus far, was on the verge of turning not only against the show itself, but against the promotion as well. And they did just that during the main event of the evening: Barry Windham pitted against Lex Luger for the WCW World title.

Lex Luger had been a major player for the company since his debut in 1987. With his chiseled physique, many pegged him as Flair's inevitable successor. He had, after all, been chasing the WCW title for the better part of the past four years. When the card for the *Bash* was first announced, it was to be Flair defending the belt against Luger, and every fan in the country believed that Luger would finally step up to the big time and win the belt (which was the plan had Herd and Flair come to terms on the contract extension). When Flair left the company, it seemed obvious that Luger would be the next champion, although the fact that he never beat Flair himself would haunt Luger throughout his title run.

While it certainly made sense that Luger would be in the main event, the other half of the match was puzzling. There was no doubt Barry Windham had been a solid performer in both WCW and the WWF for years, but he was never a true-blue, main-event player. He had worked a few main events (generally against Flair) throughout his tenure, but for most of 1991 he was nowhere to be found. He had been buried in a silly feud with Brian Pillman, who was running around as the masked Yellow Dog—yet another goofy Dusty creation. He was nowhere near the title scene when Flair was champion, and the sudden decree that he was the top contender to the belt seemed preposterous. Fans simply didn't buy Windham as a contender because he hadn't been presented as one in years.

The match took place within the confines of a steel cage—probably a good thing, since fans had taken to throwing garbage toward the ring. Windham and Luger proceeded to "entertain" the fans with one of the most boring title matches in years. At this point, it seemed the crowd was just looking to release its frustration with the promotion. Random cries of "We Want Flair" began to build throughout the arena, finally culminating in a deafening chant that was clearly audible not only live, but also to everyone watching the PPV broadcast.

It wasn't over yet. In a moment of infinite wisdom, WCW did decide to book Luger to win the match, but not before heel manager Harley Race came out to help him. Yes, WCW turned Luger heel, the mind-set being that Flair was always a draw as a heel, so Luger should try to duplicate that act. It wasn't a bad idea in theory (although comparing

Luger to Flair in any way was comically absurd), but turning him on a night when so much else was going wrong probably wasn't the best idea, since it sent the crowd right over the edge. Despite everything else they were forced to endure, the one thing fans knew they could always count on was a celebration at the end of the night with a babyface champion. Instead, Luger and Race hugged to the crowd's catcalls.

Presenting Luger with the belt was a problem in and of itself, since WCW was not in possession of the title at the time (Flair had taken the belt to WWF). To "solve" the problem, WCW took an old regional title (the Western States Heritage title, to be precise) and glued a plate that read "World Champion" on top of the embossed representations of Texas, Arizona, and New Mexico.

The situation was starting to resemble a riot. And that was the last thing WCW needed: not only was the promotion in no position to mend the bridge with Flair, but he was headed straight for their competition. The company had needed to turn things around when Luger was on top, and now they had to do it with Luger as a heel. So they did the only thing they could possibly do: they put Luger into a feud with Ron Simmons, a guy who had never been over and had competed primarily in tag teams throughout his entire WCW run.

Simmons was granted the next title shot on PPV at *Halloween Havoc*, live from Chattanooga, Tennessee. The most shocking thing about the entire show was that there was not one run-in or screwjob finish on the entire show, and yes, Dusty booked it. That's not to say the show was perfect, or anything close to that. The kickoff bout was an extra special bonus attraction: an abomination known as the Chamber of Horrors. The object of this ten-man cage match was to strap your opponent into an electric chair ("THE CHAIR OF TORTURE"!!!) and pull the switch. Read the sentence again. You'd think grown men hitting each other with shrunken heads would be entertaining—at least in a morbid sense—but you'd be wrong. It didn't help that the switch (excuse us, "THE FATAL LEVER"!!!) kept falling down prior to the end of the match. On the plus side, the company had strapped a mobile camera to the top of the referee's head to give fans a jerky look at what was happening inside the cage. The so-called "Refer-eye" (again, not making this up) was such a sensation it was never used again. The match ended with Abdullah the Butcher being "electrocuted" (read: "shaking in the chair uncontrollably like he had ants in his pants").

The remainder of the card was just a series of squash matches, followed by the Simmons-Luger match, which did little to excite the crowd, and while it wasn't bad in the ring, it was a stark reminder that Lex Luger was not, in fact, Ric Flair. There was, however, one noteworthy match: the debut of the WCW Phantom, who completely annihilated his opponent for the evening, Tom Zenk (brilliant booking given Zenk was scheduled to headline house shows for the title against Luger in the coming weeks). Later in the show, the Phantom was unmasked, and was revealed to be Ravishing Rick Rude, one of the WWF's top heels for the past several years. It didn't make much sense not to at least promote Rude's appearance on the show—advertising his involvement might have generated a few last-minute buys. Still, the company had a new top heel on their hands, and this would come in handy as the calendar turned to 1992.

The year ended for the company with what had traditionally been their biggest show of the year, *Starrcade*. In the past, the show had featured the settling of feuds, and it was generally the showcase for the year's most important World title defense. This year, however, in an effort to change things, Dusty came up with the Lethal Lottery, in which randomly paired tag teams would square off against each other, and the winning pairs would take part in a big battle royal at the end of the night, the Battle Bowl.

The catch in this case was that the lottery picks were so bizarre it appeared for all the world that the draw was, in fact, random. It wasn't, but it might as well have been. The card became a weird mishmash of matches between guys who had no business being in the ring with each other. Fortunately, WCW did plot a proper ending to the night: the final pair ended up being Luger, still the World champ, and Sting, the man many fans saw as the top contender to the belt. Sting triumphed over Lex in the non-title bout to set up the one match that WCW fans were actually interested to see, a championship match between the two.

The only problem was that now Luger wanted to get out of WCW, just like Flair had six months earlier. His dream of becoming WCW World champion had become a nightmare, and he had no desire to stick around for more "We Want Flair!" chants. As had been rumored for over a year, his plan was to leave WCW for Vince McMahon's new World Bodybuilding Federation. (Yes, Vince McMahon was starting a PROFESSIONAL BODYBUILDING PROMOTION during a time when a steroid scandal was rocking the pro-wrestling industry and making national headlines.) The idea was that he'd spend a year doing the bodybuilding and then likely shoot an angle that would result in him becoming a WWF wrestler. Why spend a year bodybuilding? You see, his WCW contract didn't expire until March 1993, so to get around that, instead of going to WWF as a wrestler he left to become a body-builder for the WBF. The loophole allowed Luger to make big money with Vince McMahon as a character on WWF TV by making appearances on *Superstars of Wrestling* in a role plugging *WrestleMania* and the new WBF All Stars show. None of this was a mystery to inside fans, so it was more than a bit anticlimactic when he dropped the title to Sting at *SuperBrawl* on February 29.

Luger wasn't the only guy to depart. When rumors in wrestling got out that Dusty Rhodes was returning, Herd was outraged. Both Petrik and Dusty told everyone that the rumors weren't true, but when Jim Herd found out that Petrik, who had been his friend for a long time, was lying to him, he told Petrik, "Either he goes or I go." To his shock, Dusty was kept on and Herd was fired—sadly before his desire to create a pair of hunchback wrestlers could come to fruition. (This is true. Why hunchbacks? What concept could be more fascinating than two wrestlers who could not physically have both shoulders pinned to the mat?)

Petrik, after replacing Herd, was replaced himself by Bill Shaw. Got all that? If so, you're further ahead of the game than many were in 1992.

Herd, who after being fired by Petrik was offered a role in the TBS syndication department but refused, was replaced by Kip Frey, who had a novel approach to the task of turning the company around. It involved, believe it or not, the wrestlers themselves. His concept was simple: reward the men who did their jobs the best. In fact, he created a new bonus system in the company in which a $5,000 award was distributed to those who performed the best match on each pay-per-view event. Raises were also introduced. This led, amazingly enough, to workers suddenly being motivated in the ring, which in turn gave fans events worth watching.

It was something new, something wholly unexpected by the boys in the back. For years, they had listened to grizzled veterans and grumpy bookers like Ole Anderson tell them to shut their mouths and just do as they were told. Anderson, in particular, would basically try to get higher-priced young talent to quit so he could bring in his old pals at a reduced rate. Of course, this wasn't what the fans wanted to see, but that mattered little to Ole. He'd grown out of touch with the business, seemingly stuck in a time warp in which he and other geezers were still the belles of the ball. After years of being held down, it looked as though the younger guys in the company, such as Brian Pillman, Steve Austin, and Tom Zenk, were about to catch a break. Unfortunately, the downside of Kip Frey's approach was that his bonuses and increased payouts to re-signing talent started to sink the company back into the hole again.

One of the big issues with WCW in the early '90s was that they had a revolving door of people in charge and nobody knew what the goal was.

Were they supposed to cut costs and get the budget under control? Were they supposed to spend money, bring in talent, and try to compete for the number-one spot in the country against Vince McMahon? Nobody could ever quite figure it out. Frey didn't last long in this environment and eventually quit the company.

"Kip Frey was a good guy who was challenged to rebuild WCW but had virtually no product knowledge," said a former big name WCW talent from that era. "He got the chance to move from being an IP attorney to running a department within Turner's empire. He was and is an entrepreneurial spirit. I'm not sure why he left. Kip wasn't a vocal, strong leader and was easily duped. He got little support from Turner upper management, none of whom liked pro wrestling except Ted. My belief is that Frey was ready to move on and may have made that clear to his bosses." Today, Frey is a professor at Duke University and president and CEO of EvoApp, Inc.

Frey's successor was, of all people, Bill Watts, last seen selling his UWF to Crockett in the late 1980s after losing $50,000 per week trying to go national. The good news was, after a string of non-wrestling people attempting to steer the ship, a wrestling person was now in the office. That's about where the good news ended. In his first few weeks in office, it became very apparent that Watts hadn't watched a single match since his company had folded. He was old-school, damn it, and that's the way he liked it. Therefore, effective immediately, he was going to make WCW matches seem much more "legitimate." He did this via a bizarre series of rule changes that made little sense to anyone other than old-timers like himself.

He immediately instituted a ban on all moves off the top rope. His idea was that he wanted wrestling to be more realistic (yes, jumping off the ropes is unrealistic, but BOUNCING off the ropes is completely believable), and guys coming off the top rope illegally behind the ref's back would get lots of heat. This was true—in the 1970s. In the 1990s this effectively killed any Cruiserweight matches, which had begun to help differentiate WCW from other organizations. In fact, the 1992 showdown between Brian Pillman and Japanese sensation Jushin Liger at *SuperBrawl* had been heralded by many fans as the best wrestling match on the entire planet. He also removed the protective mats that surrounded the ringside area. This was done in an effort to make the workers look tougher when they took bumps outside the ring, certainly tougher than those WWF guys who fell down on the pretty blue mats. Watts had an affinity for legitimate tough guys—one of his favorite performers ever was Steve Williams, who once got busted open during an afternoon card and returned to work later that night with 108 stitches in his head. Why Watts would want to encourage such dangerous working conditions by removing the mats is anyone's guess, and it did little to drum up support for the Cowboy backstage.

The de-emphasis of the Cruiserweight division led to a lot of bad blood between Pillman and Watts, which escalated when Watts told Pillman (among numerous others) he was looking to cut his pay. Pillman had signed a big-money contract with Kip Frey, worth nearly a half million dollars over two years. Watts, who hadn't watched any wrestling since the late '80s and obviously hadn't seen the revolutionary Pillman versus Liger matches that had lit WCW on fire, was baffled at these numbers. He told Pillman that he wanted to cut out the incentive portion of Pillman's contract, which was ironic because Watts had spoken out against guaranteed contracts, claiming that wrestlers with guarantees had no incentive to perform. Pillman did not like this idea. Watts said the performance bonuses were based on Pillman's push, so Pillman had a choice—he could agree to have his bonus cut as Watts had requested, or, to avoid paying out the bonus, Watts was going to have Pillman lose every night. "Fine," Pillman replied. "I'll be the world's highest-paid jobber."

Not that it mattered to Watts; it was apparent from the beginning that he cared little about what the boys thought of him. He was brought in to steer the ship away from the iceberg and stop the bleeding. He cut payroll. He eliminated catering at events. He outlawed wives and families from visiting the wrestlers backstage. And in an apparent effort to piss everyone off, he set forth a rule that forbade any wrestler to leave the arena until the entire show was over. Even the opening-match guys had to sit around for three hours until the final bell rang. In short, Watts was not popular among his employees.

It got worse when Watts brought in a new wrestler who was immediately pushed to the moon, despite having approximately zero talent and somehow even less charisma. Why would he do this, you ask? Because, silly, it was his son, Erik. Yes, just like Dusty Rhodes, who had pushed his son Dustin up the card despite his being totally unprepared, Watts fell into the trap of bringing up his untalented son and giving him more than his fair share of the spotlight. It didn't help that Erik was hired at the same time that massive pay cuts were being made. Wrestlers who had worked for years hoping to get a push were aghast at this turn of events. Not only were the workers unimpressed, but so were the fans—and they damn near booed poor Erik out of the building on a nightly basis.

One guy who did connect with fans, however, was Leon White, who worked as Big Van Vader, an import from Japan. A 400-pound powerhouse monster, Vader was booked as the top heel for the promotion, and he immediately began to lay waste to everyone in his path. No one could stop him, and within weeks, fans knew that only one guy had a prayer of doing him in: Sting. This was classic pro-wrestling booking, as the unstoppable heel faces the plucky, popular babyface champion. Even more shockingly, WCW didn't drop the ball with Vader, as he defeated Sting in a stellar match at the *Great American Bash* and established himself as a viable World champion both to the fans and to the boys behind the curtain.

After defeating Sting, Vader was inexplicably booked to drop the title to Ron Simmons, the guy whose feud with Lex Luger had failed to generate much interest the year prior. Actually, it wasn't completely inexplicable, as Watts thought that by putting the belt on Simmons and making him the "first black World Heavyweight wrestling champion" (and keep in mind, this term was being used by WCW here in 1992, not 1972), he would be able to duplicate the success he had attained in his old Mid-South promotion with the Junkyard Dog. But while Dog was charismatic and adored by the fans, Simmons was merely passable on the mic, and garnered little reaction. It didn't help matters that he was booked in World title bouts with lifelong mid-carders like the Barbarian. A champion, after all, is only as good as the folks he beats, and the fans knew that beating a stiff like Barbarian meant nothing. Worse, despite being champion, he worked the 1992 *Halloween Havoc* (one of the worst shows of all time, incidentally) in the semi-main position under a Sting versus Jake Roberts coal miner's glove match main event (where Jake's snake accidentally bit him in the face during the match, two weeks before Jake checked himself into rehab at the Betty Ford Clinic). Simmons needed all the help he could get to be perceived as a main event champion, and positioning him below Sting and Roberts made him come off even less as the top guy. On the bright side, he was positioned better here than he was the following month, when he was one half of a mid-card tag team match at the *Clash of the Champions*, or at *Starrcade*, WCW's biggest show of the year, when he was sixth from the top on a nine-match card. The experiment a failure, Simmons dropped the belt back to Vader on December 30 in Baltimore.

Watts' style of running a promotion may have worked in the mid-'80s, but he seemed to have no clue about how to change with the times, nor any inclination to do so. (You may be noticing a trend with WCW bookers here.) But it wasn't just his wrestling philosophies that were outdated; Watts' people skills were lacking as well. He was used to being his own boss, not answering to a bunch of suits. Watts' temper was definitely not his ally, and it led to shouting matches with those who disagreed with his tactics. Everything came to a head as a result of an interview he had done prior to his hiring in the *Pro Wrestling Torch* newsletter. In the 1991 interview, he stated that he believed restaurant owners shouldn't have to serve blacks or gays (using, it should be noted, much more offensive terminology) if they didn't want to. The interview flew under the radar of Turner management for over eighteen months. Then, in late 1992, a former employee of the Cincinnati Reds claimed that team owner Marge Schott had made a number of very disparaging racial slurs that ended up getting her suspended from the day-to-day operations of the team for the 1993 season. Home run leader Hank Aaron, at the time the vice president of the Atlanta Braves, had supported the suspension in an interview with the *New York Times*. A month later he just happened to show up at *Starrcade*. Noting that Aaron had appeared at a show booked by Watts, Mark Madden of the *Torch* faxed Aaron the interview Watts had done eighteen months earlier, asking for comment. Aaron immediately took the interview to TBS president Terry McGuirk, and the next day Watts announced his resignation.

Watts was able to pull off one final, huge coup before his departure. By the end of 1992, Watts was in dire straits and knew there was only one man who could bail him out: Ric Flair. Yes, *that* Ric Flair. The same guy who had departed the company under the Jim Herd regime, the same guy fans had been chanting for since his departure. In an effort to boost WCW's sagging ratings, Watts decided to air classic Flair bouts, such as those with Ricky Steamboat and Terry Funk. It worked—Flair was simultaneously a star in WWE and pulling good ratings for WCW on *Main Event*.

Despite achieving success in the WWF in the form of a pair of World titles, Flair's run on top was coming to an end. After dropping the WWF title to Bret Hart in Saskatchewan, Flair knew he could make an immediate impact in WCW if he returned. With WCW waving huge money his way, Flair went to McMahon and asked to be released. McMahon had always told him that if he was ever unhappy with his position in the company or wanted out, all he had to do was ask. And McMahon was true to his word, giving Flair his release and asking only that he put over one of his top stars, "Mr. Perfect" Curt Hennig, in a loser leaves town match on an early episode of the company's new flagship program, *Monday Night Raw*. It was a clever move by McMahon. Instead of leaving fans with the perception that Flair had voluntarily left WWF to go to greener pastures in WCW, it appeared that Flair had been forced out of WWF and had no choice but to return to the second-rate WCW.

After that, it was time to go back home, back to his most loyal fans. And it was time to do everything he could to make the company competitive with McMahon's. Although Flair couldn't wrestle for several months due to a non-compete agreement with McMahon, he kept himself busy both on-screen, in a non-wrestling segment entitled "Flair for the Gold" (alongside Wendy Barlow, aka Fifi the Maid, who twenty years later would become Flair's live-in girlfriend after his fourth divorce), and behind the scenes, eventually becoming the lead booker of the promotion.

Regaining Flair convinced Ted Turner to open his wallet in an attempt to lure in more big names. It took nearly a half-million dollars to bring Sid Vicious back into the fold, a move many in the industry justified by the fact that he had main-evented *WrestleMania* less than a year earlier against Hulk Hogan. They also signed "British Bulldog" Davey Boy Smith to an inflated deal—a bit puzzling, seeing as he had been a mid-carder (as half of the British Bulldogs tag team) for most of his WWF career. He had main-evented exactly one PPV—admittedly a huge success, as it drew over 80,000 fans to *SummerSlam* in 1992 at Wembley Stadium in London. But that was the catch: he was a star overseas, namely in his "homeland," England. He'd never drawn in the U.S., where WCW was promoting all of its shows.

Not only did WCW begin to sign names, but at the advice of their PPV head, Sharon Sidello, they also began to film expensive skits in an effort to sell their upcoming shows. These weren't cheap-looking productions filmed with standard television equipment; they were professionally filmed, and they looked like honest-to-God movies. And why not? They had the Turner family behind them, and if anyone could make such a production look high-end, it would be them.

The only problem was that these skits were so horribly written and acted that the results were laughable, at best. Take, for instance, the showdown between Vader and his new nemesis, Cactus Jack (Mick Foley). The storyline for this one had already been set up by Vader and Jack's knock-down, drag-out affair on *WCW Saturday Night*, the promotion's flagship show at the time. Vader pulled back the blue mats around the ring, exposing the concrete, and set up Jack for his powerbomb. Announcer Tony Schiavone, mortified, said if Vader executed this move Jack would be killed. Well, he executed the move. Jack was not killed. That's the good news. The bad news is that even though Vader tried to let him down as gently as you can let a 300-pound man down on a six-foot drop, Jack still smashed the back of his head on the concrete, giving him his second concussion in just over two weeks and leaving him with momentary loss of feeling in his limbs. With a setup like that, Pro Wrestling 101 says to just replay the bump over and over so fans will see Jack as a sympathetic character to get behind. Instead, an overblown backstory was created, in which Jack had amnesia, was locked up in a mental institution (which resulted in tons of angry letters sent to TBS from viewers who felt WCW was making fun of the mentally ill), believed he was a sailor who repaired bicycles for children (!!!), and was hunted down for weeks by a bogus news reporter.

Foley truly hated the amnesia angle. When he came back to the ring, he attempted to salvage things by claiming this was all part of an elaborate ruse to play mind games with Vader. However, even after he said these things on TV, the announcers continued to play up his amnesia. This despite him saying that he didn't have amnesia. Contradictory storylines such as this would soon become commonplace in the company.

Even though *Lost in Cleveland* (a mini-movie based on the amnesia angle) was a flop, WCW felt they were onto something, and set forth plans for their next cinematic epic. This one was for *Beach Blast*, in which Davey Boy and Sting were slated to take on Vader and Sid. Standard wrestling booking says that to promote a tag match with the biggest heels in the company facing the good guys, you'd film the bad guys beating the crap out of the babyfaces in the ring. This sets up a scenario in which Sting and Davey would be seeking revenge, but they'd appear to face insurmountable odds in getting it. After all, they'd just been laid out by the guys they were confronting, so how could they possibly win?

Instead, fans were "treated" to Sting and Davey Boy playing volleyball with orphans on an island—and this is a direct quote—"somewhere in the Gulf of Mexico." Vader and Sid showed up to crash the party (on a war boat, no less!) and challenged the good guys to outdo them in a clambake. No, just kidding, they challenged them to a match at *Beach Blast*. In the meantime, an evil one-eyed midget named Cheatum (yes, as in "cheat them") planted a bomb on Sting's boat and blew it to smithereens as the heels had a good laugh.

Let's look at the two scenarios we've presented. Scenario one, in which the heels beat up the faces and leave them sprawled out in the ring, would have cost approximately $0 extra to film. Scenario two, the amazingly well-produced but equally amazingly poorly written and performed orphans/war boat/one-eyed midget/boat explosion route, wound up costing $80,000 (more than double the $33,000 PPV live gate). Both would likely have garnered the same results, as the buy rate for *Beach Blast* received no bump from the prior show, achieving a mere 0.5. There was so much negative feedback on the one-eyed midget skit that all replays were immediately canceled (the bigger story here is that there had been replays scheduled in the first place), as were all future episodes of *Lost in Cleveland* with Mick Foley.

Things had gotten so bad by June that Ric Flair's first TV match back in WCW, teaming with Arn Anderson to take on Brian Pillman and Steve Austin at *Clash of the Champions* drew just a 2.6 rating in 1.5 million homes, by far the least-watched and lowest-rated *Clash* of all time. As will be noted numerous times throughout this book, when wrestling is hot you can make all sorts of mistakes and it'll take a long time to sink the ship, but when wrestling is cold you can do all the right things and it doesn't necessarily make any difference.

Having lost so much money, WCW was looking for someone new to take the reins. Who better than third-string announcer Eric Bischoff?

"They wanted to get away from wrestling people," Bischoff noted in 2014. 'They wanted someone to run the company who understood the entertainment business that wasn't so entrenched in wrestling they were sucked into the politics of it. So I just threw my name in the hat."[6]

And that's how he became the boss. Well, he was kind of the boss. Since day one, unlike in the WWF with Vince McMahon, WCW never really had a boss. Bill Watts was "the boss," but he really wasn't the boss because it wasn't his company, it wasn't his money, and there were people above him who could have pulled the plug on him at any time; he was merely hired by a higher power to try to steer the ship in the right direction. All of this got worse after he was removed from power. A corporate structure was set up consisting of, no joke, nearly a dozen different people, and then they set up a booking committee that consisted of considerably more than a dozen people. Bischoff was the one who got the role of executive producer of WCW, and since WCW was largely about television and television ratings for Turner, he ended up the most powerful person in the day-to-day hierarchy—"the boss," so to speak.

In later years, this would be something commonly brought up by those who watched WCW's collapse; that there was no main boss. There was no "Vince McMahon" who was the final voice, who had veto power, who was the overall leader of the company.

Note we said "later years." When WCW was at its height, everyone knew who the boss was; it was Bischoff. However, after things started to collapse, this became a common theme, a recurring excuse: the "fact" that there was no one main boss.

Which begs the question . . . what happened to the leader that was there before?

But we're getting ahead of ourselves.

Bischoff had been in the industry for just a handful of years and had, in fact, been turned down for a job by the WWF in June of 1990. He'd learned the business from Verne Gagne, the man behind the American Wrestling Association, which, in its day, was a huge power in the pro-wrestling business, operating primarily out of the Midwestern region of the United States. The company, around since the 1960s, had become so established that they eventually were able to ink a television deal with ESPN, which gave them a daily show that reached millions of viewers.

The American Wrestling Association played host to countless wrestling stars, but not unlike Ole Anderson, Verne made sure the spotlight always shone brightest on himself and a handful of his closest friends. Eventually, that wound up biting him in the ass, as the unthinkable happened—he got old. So did his chums. Tired of their geriatric antics, fans made it clear that they wanted to see some fresh faces. Verne was stubborn, though, and stuck to his guns, allowing men such as Hulk Hogan, Jesse Ventura, and the Road Warriors to slip right through his fingers. Even on the rare occasion that a newcomer was able to break through, said newcomer was usually a relative of one of the old guys, notably Curt, Larry Hennig's son, and Verne's own son, Greg—a scrawny beanpole no one wanted to see in main events.

By the time Bischoff arrived in the AWA, the promotion was on its deathbed. Attendance at shows had dipped so badly that Gagne opted not to run any more live arena events, taping his shows in an empty warehouse instead. Seeing the writing on the wall, Verne's top stars fled for other promotions. Bischoff stuck with the promotion until nearly the bitter end before getting far enough behind on pay that he left to try out as an announcer for the WWF. He didn't get the job.

He had, though, developed a taste for the business, and had learned much under Gagne's tutelage. After Vince showed zero interest in him, he turned to WCW and was eventually given a shot as an announcer on lower-end shows. Like a sponge, Bischoff soaked up every bit of wisdom he could—not only from the wrestlers and the booking team, but also from the production people. Bischoff was smart enough to realize that there was more to wrestling than just what went on inside the ring. This paid off for him big-time; following the departure of Bill Watts, the company was looking for a new head honcho. At the time, many believed that the next boss would be Tony Schiavone, WCW's lead announcer at the time. Schiavone had, after all, been with the organization since before it was even known as WCW. He'd worked for Jim Crockett, not only as a wrestling announcer but also as a baseball play-by-play man. If anyone was a lock for the job, many reasoned, it was him.

But it didn't happen. Instead, Turner reps liked what they saw in Eric Bischoff. He was young, he was handsome, and he was aggressive. He had new ideas. And, perhaps most importantly, he also seemed to have a more corporate mentality to him, with an understanding of marketing that they found very appealing. In short, he knew more than just pro wrestling, and he was a far cry from the crotchety old ring warriors who had preceded him. Ole Anderson would start yelling at a moment's notice . . . but Bischoff? No way. He was far too levelheaded, and perhaps for that reason more than any other, he was given the ball and told to run with it.

Despite the artistic and commercial failures of the mini-movie ventures, Bischoff saw the value of having more control over the product he was presenting on-screen. Therefore, the decision was made to forgo most of the arena television tapings and instead begin to record shows at Disney-MGM Studios, a theme park in Orlando, Florida. This would have the twofold effect of lowering costs (as they could tape several shows at once) and allowing the promotion to "demonstrate" to fans at home who was really popular and who was really hated in its ranks. To that end, WCW began to screen the crowds at these tapings, specifically filtering out any hardcore wrestling fans, since they would likely have their own opinions on different characters, opinions that wouldn't jive with what the company wanted to present. For example, Marcus Bagwell was a babyface many hardcore fans didn't care for, so they'd boo him on his way to the ring. WCW didn't want any of that, so they had signs to instruct folks when to cheer or boo, just like a standard television show.

And just like a "normal" TV show, they were taping months in advance. To Bischoff's credit, the tapings likely saved the company many thousands of dollars, which no doubt pleased his bosses in the Turner regime. However, this also forced the company to plan in advance, because they would tape three months' worth of shows at a time. Therefore, any title changes the company had, such as those at live pay-per-view or live *Clash of the Champions* specials, were to be factored into the production of the show. For example, when the tapings began, Barry Windham was the NWA champion, but later in the tapings, Ric Flair was the NWA champion. The match where the belt switched was not filmed since the title change was planned for later on at the *Beach Blast* event. Not only that, but the tapings also made it clear that Flair would drop the title shortly after winning it to Rick Rude. This made for some major headaches for WCW, such as when news of the changes was leaked to the fans. That happened, of course. However, since the internet was in its infancy, the only way fans really knew what was going to happen was through insider newsletters, and WCW didn't consider that a big enough issue to be of real concern.

No, the major dilemma was that once the filming was done, WCW more or less had to follow through with their title changes. They had done this once before, in the early months of 1991, when matches were taped with the Fabulous Freebirds wearing the tag belts despite the fact they hadn't even won them yet. In fact, the 'birds lost the belts to the Steiner Brothers, all before they'd even actually won them in the first place! It didn't matter, because things would play out in order on TV.

Since that scenario had turned out fine, WCW felt that the Orlando tapings would as well, but there were some major issues. One of the biggest was that the National Wrestling Alliance found out about upcoming NWA title switches at the tapings. Since the formation of the NWA, the main governing body had to vote on all upcoming title changes and approve them, so if a promoter wanted to put the NWA title on, say, Ronnie Garvin, the board would vote and say no, unless they'd lost their minds.

In 1993, WCW was still officially an NWA member. If you'll recall, in 1992 there was a big legal battle over the NWA title belt after Flair was fired from WCW without dropping the championship and the belt itself subsequently showed up on WWF TV in the hands of Bobby Heenan. It came out during the NWA versus WCW court battle in September 1993 that around that time, Bill Watts managed to convince the current NWA President, Seiji Sakaguchi of New Japan, to sell the physical belt to WCW for $28,000. During the sale Watts and WCW were also granted intellectual rights to the NWA name. Apparently, most everyone else in the NWA was completely unaware of this, so when they tried to take WCW to court over their booking of the NWA championship in 1993, WCW balked. The NWA's claim was that selling the intellectual rights to the NWA name was something that should only have occurred via a vote amongst the board of directors, which never happened. WCW ultimately broke all ties with the NWA on September 1 and continued booking the belt as they deemed fit. However, they had footage of Rude with the NWA World championship belt bantering back and forth with Flair that they somehow had to factor into their programming. Since they could no longer promote the NWA World title by name and all they had was this big gold belt, they just started promoting matches for the "Big Gold Belt."

Imagine a judge with no knowledge of pro wrestling attempting to make sense of all this.

Another snafu caused by the tapings involved the WCW Tag titles. The Hollywood Blondes, Steve Austin and Brian Pillman, were to drop their titles to the Horsemen, Arn Anderson and Paul Roma. At the tapings, it was revealed that the Blondes would do this at the **Beach Blast** show, but at the last minute, WCW decided to keep the belts on Pillman and Austin. They could do this because there was still a live **Clash of the Champions** event at which WCW would have the belt change hands. All great in theory, until Pillman was injured prior to the bout and couldn't work the show. A makeshift "championship" team of Austin and Steve Regal (who had never worked with Austin before and had no ties to the Tag belts) defended—and lost—the belts to the Horsemen.

For all the problems being created, everyone felt as though the pendulum was on the upswing, especially with the biggest show of the year, *Starrcade*, on the horizon. The event was to feature a match that had never been presented before, one that fans were looking forward to and were therefore willing to pay for the right to view: Vader versus Sid Vicious, with the WCW World title on the line. Again, the MGM tapings revealed the course of events: Sid, with the belt around his waist, was portrayed as a hero.

This time, though, things really fell apart. During a tour of the U.K., a fight broke out between Sid and Arn Anderson following a confrontation at a pub. Both had been drinking, and Vicious became boisterous. He started bragging that by threatening to not lose to Sting at *Halloween Havoc* he'd forced the company to give him a $100,000 raise to approximately $600,000 per year over the next four years (and imagine signing someone with Sid Vicious' reputation to a four-year deal). Meanwhile, he cackled, Arn's salary had been cut about $100,000 in a renegotiation with Watts before Watts was let go. He said this was fitting, because it was time for guys like Flair and Arn, the old dinosaurs, to step aside so guys like himself could get the spotlight and make WCW great. Arn was good friends with Flair at the time (in later years they had a falling out), and the argument escalated and almost came to blows. It was broken up and both men were sent back to their rooms. A little later, Sid went to Arn's room and a fight broke out. Exactly what happened and who started the fight depends on whose side of the story you want to believe. What is known is that in the brawl, Arn had a pair of blunt-tipped scissors and Sid had the broken-off leg of a chair. Arn claimed Sid used the chair leg first. Sid ended up stabbed a few times, they got into a wrestling match, Sid got hold of the scissors, and he then proceeded to stab Arn head to toe. When it was broken up, Anderson was a bloody mess with stab wounds everywhere, including very close to one of his eyes. The walls were destroyed and covered in blood, and glass was broken everywhere; it was a horrible mess. The incident got press all over the U.K. (although in most reports the men were listed as WWF wrestlers) and a little bit in the U.S. and Canada. Sid had been scheduled to wrestle against and win the WCW title from Vader at *Starrcade*, but due to his injuries that plan was scrapped, and ultimately, due to the belief that the whole thing was Sid's fault, the decision was made to fire him.

In a cruel irony, because WCW had taped so much TV in advance, while they were suspended in real life both Sid and Arn were on television most weeks, with Arn, no joke, constantly talking about having been STABBED IN THE BACK by the heels.

And just like that, Sid, the man who was to lead the promotion into 1994 as champion—and who had already been taped doing so!—was history. A mad scramble ensued to determine just who would wind up with the main-event slot at the biggest show of the year against Vader, with Cactus Jack, Sting, and Rude at the top of the list. In the end, the company listened to the crowds at the WCW events: "We Want Flair." Billed as a match after which he'd retire forever if he lost, an emotional Flair beat Vader before 8,000 fans paying $65,000 in Charlotte's Independence Arena to regain *his* title. Yes, despite being "too old" for Jim Herd three years earlier, and of no further use to McMahon or the WWF, Flair was once again the man.

The Flair versus Vader match was one of the most memorable in the history of WCW. Flair did some of his best-ever work on the mic, and the PPV itself, a one-match show if there ever was one, was built entirely around the main event. The PPV actually opened with what would today be likened to a UFC *Countdown Special*, where they showed images from Flair's childhood, adolescence, and college, interviewed him at home with his family, spoke to the other superstars as they arrived at the building, and more. The match was brutally stiff and hard hitting, with Flair taking an epic beating (well, they both did) before finally clipping Vader's knee and schoolboying him to win the championship. It remains one of the greatest moments of Ric's career. It was also the last major angle overseen at least to a degree by Dusty Rhodes, as after three years he resigned as booker shortly thereafter.

Overall, it was a pretty good time for all within the company. For whatever reason, the ratings started to turn around, after hitting an all-time low, for Flair's return tag match at the *Clash*. In August, they not only rebounded but did a 3.4 rating and 8.7 share for an episode of *WCW Saturday Night* featuring a Flair versus Sting forty-one-minute NWA title match, the best numbers for any pro-wrestling show in the U.S. all year (that includes *Raw*), and the best for WCW in several years. The year

While Bret Hart (pictured) and Hulk Hogan would not battle in the WWF as originally planned in 1993, they would eventually meet up in WCW. Sadly, the company would book it so no one would really even notice. [GEORGE NAPOLITANO]

even ended on a great note as Ted Turner, for the first time ever, called a meeting to address all the wrestlers and front office staff, making it clear that TBS was going to support WCW across all of their various platforms; he loved wrestling and as long as he was around WCW would never go out of business. Everybody was very bullish heading into 1994.

The happiness was short-lived, however, as Turner officials decided to look at the books to see just how well the company had done under Bischoff's leadership in the past year. No doubt his new style of promoting, along with his money-saving measures—like filming the bulk of WCW programming at MGM—would pay huge dividends when the financials came out.

But they didn't. Although TV ratings had increased slightly year-to-year comparing November 1992 to November 1993, both house show attendance and revenue had dropped a staggering 70 percent with your average live event drawing around 300 fans. The company was still losing money, a lot of it, and this was something Bischoff didn't want to be a part of; after all, if he could be the first man in WCW to actually turn a profit, he'd likely get even more power and money to do with as he pleased. They were close, so close, and he wasn't about to let *his* company slip away.

After a week or so of intense soul-searching, Bischoff decided that the one thing WCW lacked was mainstream media attention. If they could just be accepted as the WWF's equal, the company would be set. Have we lost money? Yes, Mr. Turner, we have. But we can make it back, tenfold. We just need a bit more time, a bit more money. We need to capture the attention of the casual fan, and I've got just the guy to do it. You've probably even heard of him: Hulk Hogan.

Now *there* was something Ted could buy into: the biggest star the business had ever seen. With Turner's blessing, Bischoff, with a major assist from Ric Flair, who knew Hogan from their WWF days together and who had taken over as booker after Dusty resigned, set out to catch the biggest fish in the pond and bring him home to Uncle Ted. The timing was perfect, because Hogan had left the WWF earlier in the year, following a blowup with Vince McMahon over the way he was being booked. Hogan felt that he should still be the focal point of the company—the champion. McMahon disagreed, preferring to focus on younger guys such as Bret Hart and Shawn Michaels, believing they would connect with a "new generation" of fans. The two got into a bitter argument following Hogan's title win at *WrestleMania IX*, as McMahon wanted Hogan to drop the belt to Hart and "pass the torch" in the process. Hogan, stuck in his 1980s mindset, refused, saying Hart was way too small and wasn't in "his league." Instead, he put over the enormous Yokozuna at that year's *King of the Ring* PPV, then disappeared from the company to pursue acting and wrestle the occasional big show in Japan.

But there was room for Hulk Hogan's star to shine in WCW—if he wanted to be the top dog in the promotion, well, that was just fine. Hogan had, after all, drawn more money than anyone else in the history of the business. Just ask him; he'd tell you so. The only stumbling block was that Hogan wanted *so much* money—a contract larger than any contract WCW had ever offered before, including $300,000 per match, 25 percent of PPV revenue above the WCW average, 25 percent of house show revenue for any show he worked (which wouldn't be many), and a whopping 65 percent of all merchandise revenue. Not only that, his WWF release stipulated that Vince McMahon had the right to match any offer Hogan was given from another wrestling company. In other words, in order to ensure Vince didn't interfere with this deal (which was important given WCW was pushing Hogan very hard on TV, almost to the point of making him the centerpiece of the promotion, before he'd signed any sort of deal), they'd have to offer him a lot of money. A lot as in a lot lot LOT. But Bischoff didn't care. It was Hogan or bust, and after convincing higher-ups in the company—namely Ted Turner himself—of this, he got his wish.

Despite Hogan's signing, the "new WCW" still managed to find ways to be the old WCW, such as when they aired the wrong Control Center segment on the **Sunday Main Event** TV show. Doesn't sound like a big deal. Except in this case, the wrong one was actually the one scheduled to air a week later after the next **Clash of Champions**. Thus before the **Clash** took place, the Control Center revealed, among things, that Ric Flair had beaten Sting to become the Unified Heavyweight champion (consisting of the WCW title and the "Big Gold Belt"). Oops. WCW actually acknowledged this snafu during the opening moments of the **Clash** show later in the week. They essentially claimed that Flair had doctored a tape and somehow, perhaps via Bobby Heenan, gotten it to play on TV to mess with Sting's head. Really. They did not explain how Flair, in doctoring this tape, also managed to predict all the other finishes that were given away as well.

WCW's Hogan era began on June 11, 1994. His arrival was celebrated with an elaborate parade (complete with confetti!), and sure enough Hogan was booked as the number-one contender and set his sights on current WCW champ Ric Flair (who, not surprisingly since he much preferred playing the bad guy, immediately began booking a slow heel turn for himself the moment he took over from Dusty Rhodes). Hogan easily conquered Flair at *Bash at the Beach*, selling out the Orlando Arena and doing a colossal 1.02 buy rate for the company, its biggest since 1991 and one of its largest ever. Going in, with the exception of Bischoff and a small handful of others, virtually every single person in the wrestling industry thought the idea that WCW could do a 1.0 buy rate with Hulk Hogan was completely preposterous. It was also very reassuring for the company as Hogan had not moved TV numbers at all prior to this PPV. The show where he debuted with the confetti parade did the same rating as a show a few weeks earlier had done with Flair versus Ricky Steamboat, and his live debut at the *Clash of Champions* on June 23 saw that show do the fourth-lowest *Clash* rating of all time.

Upon Hogan's arrival, WCW had an entirely different look. The old Center Stage Theater—the longtime taping location for **WCW Saturday Night**—had been completely renovated. According to a source who worked for WCW at the time, "Center Stage used to be a rathole in the grossest part of Atlanta. Then, the first day Hogan came in, they put purple curtains up everywhere so you couldn't see how shitty it was. That very same day. Went from coffee and water and Gatorade to fruit and all sorts of food. In the old days, when wrestlers walked out, they used to come out under the seats, from the bleachers. You're kind of ducking a little bit to not hit your head. So they put curtains up everywhere to hide things and try to make it look better than what it really was."

Regardless, when the *Bash* buy rate came in, Bischoff breathed a sigh of relief. His investment had paid off (the company needed a 0.75 or so to break even on Hogan's new deal and they easily exceeded that), and the fans were really starting to buy WCW as a true alternative to the WWF. It certainly helped that the week WCW debuted Hulk Hogan, WWF debuted—wait for it—a FAKE UNDERTAKER played by Brian Lee, a gimmick that died a death, no pun intended. With this promising start, maybe, Bischoff thought, he could catch Vince. No, no maybes about it—he WOULD catch Vince, and even surpass him. Confidence was buoyed when the August 24 *Clash of the Champions*, headlined by the first-ever free Ric Flair versus Hulk Hogan match on television (they never did a singles TV match in WWF during the early '90s), did a 6.7 rating and 4.126 million households for the main event, the all-time cable TV viewership record for a professional wrestling match in any company in U.S. history.

With TV and PPV success, Hogan was able to convince Bischoff that he held the key that would take WCW to the top of the mountain: his friends (all of whom, coincidentally, needed big paydays). So Randy Savage, Jim Duggan, "Earthquake" John Tenta, Honky Tonk Man, Jimmy Hart, and countless others were brought into the fold.

In the years after this picture was taken, Steve Austin would lose three things: his hair, his job, and his wife, Jeannie Clark, pictured here. Thankfully, she stuck around long enough to tell him to drink his tea before it turned "Stone Cold" . . . and the rest is history. [GEORGE NAPOLITANO]

Longtime WCW employees like Steve Austin, Vader, and Mick Foley were thrown into the background so as not to steal the limelight from Hogan and his pals.

"I was thrilled to be there, don't get me wrong," recalled John Tenta. "Hulk really went to bat for me. But I was amazed by just how much money that company blew. Hogan would tell me about how he and Bischoff would go out for sushi, and spend $1,000 in a single evening. They didn't care. It wasn't their money, it was Turner's."

And then there was Ric Flair, the man who had done everything he could to repair WCW following his stint in the WWF. Bischoff quickly realized that there was no way Hogan and Flair could coexist at the top of the WCW mountain. Flair was a heel and Hogan was supposed to be the tippy-top babyface, but Hogan had made appearances in "Flair Country" and been booed out of the building, which was not what the company wanted. And it wasn't just in the mid-Atlantic area; in "neutral cities" such as Oakland, CA, the response was about 50/50 for both guys. Flair was asked (well, told) to job to Hogan one more time in a "retirement" match at *Halloween Havoc*. At the time the idea was that Flair would "retire" for a while, maybe a year or so, and then they'd shoot an angle for his return. From WCW's perspective, the retirement was never supposed to be permanent; first and foremost, it was done to try to hotshot a giant buy rate for *Havoc*, which would help boost revenue so that when the books were examined at the end of the year, all of the big-money acquisitions, not the least of which was Hulk Hogan, would look like a wise investment.

Flair did not want to retire, but when the idea was proposed he claimed—and this is hilarious in hindsight here in the twenty-first century—that if he did this retirement angle, that was it, he was done, and he was never coming back to wrestling.

Halloween Havoc, with the Flair versus Hogan, retirement-versus-retirement cage match stipulation, plus appearances by Mr. T and

Muhammad Ali, was a cautious success, drawing a live gate just under their all-time record set at *Baltimore Bash 1989*, and another buy rate around 1.0. There were definite grumblings, however, that it only did roughly the same buy rate as *Bash at the Beach*, as there had been those in the cable industry predicting a 1.5 or better, and a few WCW higher-ups predicting even higher, perhaps a 2.0. The show also drew less than 9,000 paid in the 21,000-seat Joe Louis Arena, certainly not befitting what was billed as one of the biggest matches of all time. But even with Hogan's cut it wasn't a money-loser, and it helped pad revenues for 1994.

With Flair gone, WCW needed a new challenger for Hogan. This was set up in a post-match *Havoc* beatdown following the big Legdrop of Doom on Flair. Hogan's old buddy and longtime lackey Brutus "The Barber" Beefcake, Ed Leslie, teamed up with the former Earthquake, John Tenta, to lay out the Hulkster and set up Hogan versus Beefcake—now the Butcher—for *Starrcade*.

But something funny happened on the way to the event. The fans, who had been so hot for the Hogan-Flair showdowns, suddenly lost interest in what Hogan was doing. And when the buy rates came in for *Starrcade*, the company was stunned. At 0.6, it was 40 percent lower than what they'd done for *Havoc* just two months earlier. About the only good news was that the live event sold out, the first WCW sellout in years. But with Hogan's PPV cut and a 0.6 buy rate, while still not a money loser, *Starrcade* became a financially unsuccessful event for the company.

Obviously, Ed Leslie was no Ric Flair.

Also on the show, another former WWF star made his live debut. "Macho Man" Randy Savage, one of the biggest stars of the '80s and a legitimate mainstream name, appeared after the Butcher match and teased attacking Hogan. Instead, the two teamed up and ran off all the heels before posing together in a celebratory manner. Savage, who had parted ways with WWF earlier in the year, had been Hogan's opponent at *WrestleMania V* on April 2, 1989 in Atlantic City, New Jersey. The Hogan versus Savage storyline was among the best long-term storylines not only in WWF history, but in the history of wrestling, and after a year-long build that saw the Hogan and Savage MEGAPOWERS tag team EXPLODE leading to their title match, *WrestleMania V* had become the single most lucrative event in wrestling history. At the time of Savage's debut, the record still stood. Obviously, the long-term idea was to relive the glory days of the '80s with another Hogan versus Savage feud, this time in WCW.

While on the surface it appeared WCW was doing nothing but signing old men, the reality was that a lot of '80s WWF fans had lost interest in wrestling during the early '90s, and suddenly, in 1995, they slowly began to discover that the stars they grew up on were back in wrestling again—just not in the WWF.

It was also shortly around this time that a young wrestler named Jean Paul Levesque decided to leave WCW and join the WWF. He would be renamed Hunter Hearst Helmsley . . . and eventually the heir apparent to WWE upon marrying Vince McMahon's daughter, Stephanie.

WCW continued to rebound in the opening months of 1995. They had barely made it to January when plans were put into motion to bring back the man who a few months earlier said that when he retired he was never, ever coming back, the Nature Boy Ric Flair. Hogan was moved into a feud with Vader. It just made sense, since Vader had been the top heel of the company for the better part of the previous three years. The feud was a big business success, both at the house shows and on PPV. The two battled it out at *SuperBrawl*, which was the first WCW live event to draw over 10,000 paid fans since 1989 (0.96 buy rate, DQ finish,); at *Uncensored*, a goofy card featuring all gimmick matches (0.96 buy rate, foolish finish where Hogan beat Vader in a strap match by dragging the now-unretired Ric Flair to all four corners . . . not kidding); at *Slamboree* (0.57 buy rate, Hogan and Savage beat Vader and Ric Flair in a tag match where you'll never guess whooooo did the job); and at *Bash at the Beach* (0.82). It should be noted that the *Bash* show took place on a real, live, honest-to-goodness beach, which resulted in a real, live, honest-to-goodness gate of zero dollars.

The good news was that *Bash at the Beach*, with all those thousands of beachgoers there watching pro wrestling in the sand (estimated attendance was about 10–12,000 at the peak, so WCW claimed, get this, "HUNDREDS OF THOUSANDS"), made it a news highlight on all the local Huntington Beach, CA, TV stations. The bad news was most of them referred to it as a World Wrestling Federation event.

While WCW was spending more than ever on talent, there was still pressure to cut costs in other areas. A number of longtime execs were fired, including Jim Barnett (who ended up back with the company a few years later as a "talent scout") and Bob Dhue, leaving Bischoff the number-one go-to guy in the company under the new head of the division, Harvey Schiller. Don Sandifer, who booked buildings and worked as a promoter, was also fired and replaced by Gary Juster and Zane Bresloff. Bresloff, a former concert promoter who had worked for the WWF before jumping to WCW in 1993, would end up an unsung hero of the company during the glory days, becoming one of the best local promoters in the history of the business. He died tragically on June 20, 2003, in an automobile accident.

"On a business level, [Zane] had a lot of great ideas," Bischoff told Alex Marvez shortly after his passing. "When it was rolling, I think we talked no less than ten times a day. He had very good instinct. Often when I wanted to try something, I would use Zane as a sounding board because I could trust him and know he was not just telling me what I wanted to hear."

Despite the cuts, there were financial positives as well, not the least of which was the decision early in the year to move to nine PPVs annually and raise the price to as much as $32.50 the day of the show, up from

$24.95. The price increase was an immediate success as it made WCW *Uncensored*, which drew a 0.96 buyrate, the biggest-money show in WCW history. At the time the question was whether too many PPVs would oversaturate the market. At the end of the day, and this is still the case in the twenty-first century, the optimum number of PPVs has been one per month, no more, no less, and increasing the number in the mid-'90s ultimately resulted in both WWF and WCW making significantly more money than they ever had before. In fact, moving to monthly full-priced PPVs (they had started with discounted, two-hour *In Your House* events) was what first took WWF from losing $4.4 million in 1994–1995 to becoming financially solvent a year later.

With business once again looking promising, on June 5, 1995, Bischoff and Turner had yet another meeting, and this time Ted had a question. Why, he wondered, was *WCW Saturday Night* not beating *Monday Night Raw* (the shows were very close in the ratings at the time) if they had Hogan, Savage, and all the other top stars? Bischoff said that *Raw* aired on Monday nights, a better television night than Saturdays (which was funny since wrestling had a long and storied history of excellent viewership on Saturdays), and had the benefit of sometimes going live. Turner, who was already pissed off at McMahon since Vince had been sending him letters for the past year telling him his promotion was an embarrassment to him and he should shut it down, immediately told a supervisor to give Eric one hour of live programming every Monday night on TNT.

In other words, WCW would be competing directly against the WWF's flagship show, *Monday Night Raw*.

Bischoff was elated. He had just been given the go-ahead to fight Vince McMahon mano a mano, and now he had to deliver the goods.

"At the end of three years," he said in a press conference a few weeks before the *Nitro* debut. "I'll be standing alone."

Within the industry, most thought Bischoff was insane to try to run head-to-head with *Monday Night Raw*, which was, despite WWE's financial difficulties, the number-one pro-wrestling show at the time. But Bischoff believed something that few others did: WCW could beat McMahon by changing wrestling forever.

Which is pretty much exactly what *WCW Monday Nitro* did when it debuted on Turner Network Television the night of September 4, 1995—a week in which *Raw* was not-so-coincidentally preempted. The years-old formula of wrestling shows consisting primarily of squash matches flew right out the window. In its place were big-name versus big-name showdowns, something reserved for pay-per-views in the past. Shocking happenings, such as Lex Luger suddenly defecting from the WWF, began occurring on an almost weekly basis. Fans soon learned that if you missed *Nitro*, by God, you could miss a lot, and it became *the* show to watch on Monday nights.

Luger jumped the WWF ship for *WCW Monday Nitro*'s first episode. Although it had been known by those within wrestling that he'd negotiated with WCW a few weeks earlier, the belief was that he could not come to terms with the company only offering him a $1,000 per-shot guarantee. Still, one would have thought that Vince McMahon would have either attempted to sign him to a new deal or refused to book him in a prominent position on his TV if he did not have a contract. But McMahon did neither and Luger made a deal with WCW. They kept the deal a secret and hid Luger backstage during the first *Nitro*, so that when he walked out in the middle of the Hulk Hogan versus Big Bubba Rogers main event, wrestlers within both companies were stunned.

Luger, it should be noted, was not brought in by Eric Bischoff, but rather his best friend: "Sting brokered the deal. We were having a casual conversation, and he asked me how much time I had left on my contract. I said, 'I don't have one,' and he said, 'What are you talking about?' I gave my ninety-day notice back in December of the prior year [1994]. I told him I was basically week to week or month to month right now. He said, 'You've gotta be kidding me!' So he contacted Eric, and Eric Bischoff at the time wasn't a real big Lex Luger fan ['I thought he was an arrogant ass,' Bischoff noted[7]], but I guess he felt I had enough of a name that maybe I could have some momentum for *Monday Nitro*. I had a conversation with Eric who decided to go ahead and reel me in. Unfortunately, he had a stipulation that no one could know except for he and I and Sting. And I had a problem with that, because I was raised to professionally give at least a two-week notice. [But] Eric really wanted this to be a surprise. I literally finished up [in WWF] on Sunday night at a house show in a tag match against Shawn Michaels and Razor Ramon. And the following night, I flew home to Atlanta, got right on a plane and flew to Minneapolis that afternoon. They hid me in a hotel, then they brought me to the building with a towel on my head. About an hour before I was going to go out, they brought me out to the position to go on TV from a side door. And no one knew I was going on until the moment I was standing at the go position, and then I was watching Hogan in the ring. It was a pretty wild turn of events over two weeks, especially those last few days."[8]

September 11, 1995 was the real beginning of the Monday Night Wars as it was the day that *Raw* and *Nitro* went head-to-head for the first time. The belief among many was that there was a finite number of wrestling fans, and that if the two shows aired on the same day at the same time the audience would split, with a portion continuing to watch *Raw* and another portion choosing to watch *Nitro*.

But that's not what happened.

Instead, *Raw* and *Nitro* did 2.2 and 2.5 ratings respectively. Not only were more people watching pro wrestling on Monday nights than at any point in the past several years, but *Nitro*, the upstart television show encroaching on WWF's established Monday night territory, actually won the head-to-head ratings battle. Furthermore, although Turner had only authorized one hour live, he'd actually given the company two hours of programming. A *Monday Nitro* replay drew a 0.9 rating. In other words, despite *Raw* having established a very successful foothold on Monday nights, the very first time the companies battled it out *Nitro* was seen by significantly more viewers.

LESSON NOT LEARNED: One important point that was completely ignored fifteen years later when TNA Impact Wrestling tried to go head-to-head with **Raw** is that it's not like this WCW audience sprung up out of nowhere strictly due to the fact that wrestling was going head-to-head on Monday nights. In fact, WCW had several successful weekend shows at the time, and in fact on the week of September 11, 1995, **WCW Saturday Night** had done a 2.3 rating and **WCW Main Event** a 2.0, numbers that destroyed WWF weekend programming. Impact had nothing approaching these numbers when they decided to run head-to-head with **Raw** in early 2011, nor did they have anything approaching WCW's level of talent or financial resources. Perhaps most importantly, WWE wasn't asleep at the wheel in 2011 like WWF was in 1995.

In the beginning, both WWF and WCW had completely different mindsets about what it meant to go head-to-head. McMahon's WWF had traditionally built a bubble around itself, not acknowledging non-WWF promotions, champions, wrestlers, etc., with only very rare exceptions (the most notable being when "The Real World Champion Ric Flair" jumped to WWF in 1991, but even then there was no acknowledgement of the NWA, WCW, etc.). Although they were now going head-to-head with WCW on Monday nights, they decided to operate as if they were not going head-to-head, there was no competition, and that it was business as usual.

Eric Bischoff, on the other hand, was out for blood. Since the September 11 *Raw* show was a taped show where Shawn Michaels beat Sid, Eric flat-out revealed to the *Nitro* audience that you shouldn't bother turning the channel because *Raw* was taped and Shawn Michaels "beats the big guy with a superkick" that wouldn't have earned him a green belt at the local karate school. He talked about how Lex Luger had jumped ship from WWF nine days earlier and that he was tired of competing in the bush leagues and wanted to be where the big boys played. While there had been bitter head-to-head territorial wrestling wars in the past, nothing like this had ever been done on national television before. And this was only the beginning. Bischoff installed a monitor under his announcing desk so that when the two shows went head-to-head live, he could actually watch *Raw*, see what was happening, and book *Nitro* changes on the fly.

Four days after the first-ever head-to-head meeting, WCW fired one of their performers who had been on the DL with a torn triceps. The Hogan clique hadn't been a big fan of this guy, because he had a high-paying deal that they felt was unjustified; he was a good worker but didn't have any particular special charisma. His name was Steve Austin.

In hindsight, September 1995 was one of the most pivotal months in the entire history of pro wrestling, as three things happened that helped change the course of the business forever. *Nitro* debuted, which ultimately led to the Monday Night Wars and the greatest worldwide boom period in wrestling history. WCW also fired the performer who, more than any other, was ultimately responsible for the rebirth of the WWF, the turnaround in the wrestling war, and the creation of Vince McMahon as a certified billionaire with the resources to keep his company alive for decades to come. And, that very same month, it was announced that Turner Broadcasting was merging with Time Warner to create the single largest media conglomerate on Earth. While some in WCW will confuse the impact this had on the fate of WCW, the reality is that this merger, and that with AOL a few years later, ultimately turned WCW into a company that needed to carry its weight financially, something it had never had to worry about before, and when it couldn't, that did, in fact, lead to its demise.

With the wrestling war picking up, Vince McMahon called a meeting with talent to introduce a new company booker—Bill Watts. Yup, same Watts. Watts buried WCW, talking about how the corporate structure within the company made it impossible to get anything done, and predicting, shockingly accurately as it turned out, that the Time-Warner merger would ultimately result in Ted Turner losing the power to save WCW, and that TBS would drop the company. McMahon said WCW made a stupid business decision going head-to-head with *Raw* as opposed to putting the show on a different night of the week, and said WWF didn't have the resources to go live like Turner's company did. He brought up a talking point that he would stick with for years—that this was a personal battle between himself and Ted Turner, a billion-aire with significantly more assets, which stemmed from the fact that Turner had tried to buy the WWF ten years earlier and had been turned down. While McMahon overstated the issue between the two, largely because by making Turner out to be an evil billionaire trying to take out the mom-and-pop WWF business he painted himself as a sympathetic babyface to his talent, there were some personal issues there, but they more than likely stemmed from a letter McMahon wrote to Turner a few years earlier telling him that his wrestling company was a joke and he should be embarrassed and ashamed and shut it down.

Watts, it should be noted, lasted three weeks before calling it quits. Vince had told Watts he would have creative control and wouldn't be overruled on his decisions. Vince proceeded to immediately overrule him, and that was all she wrote.

Going into October 1995, *Raw* and *Nitro* were at a dead heat. Forgotten in history is the fact that, at least for a while, WWF was airing a *Raw* replay on Thursday nights. Adding in the rating for that show, *Raw* was being watched by more people, but it was an unfair head-to-head comparison. Ultimately the replay was dropped, because at the end of the day the only numbers that anyone really cared about were those head-to-head on Monday, and the feeling was that by eliminating the Thursday show it would convince people to watch on Mondays in-stead. Over the next fifteen years, as *Raw* became the flagship show in professional wrestling, they never aired a full-length replay out of fear that it would erode the audience. In the '00s and '10s they aired *Raw* on Saturday mornings, which was only one hour, and their Hulu feed of the show was also edited down to ninety minutes from the original three hour airing.

Ratings remained head-to-head throughout October despite WCW booking an angle where a mummy debuted, bursting forth from a giant block of ice in a *Nitro* main-event segment. It helped that on the other channel, Diesel, the WWF champion, was being booed unmercifully despite McMahon's efforts to make him the new 1980s-style Hulk Hogan babyface champion.

Speaking of Hulk Hogan, he lost his WCW title at the *Halloween Havoc* PPV in a match with a young newcomer named Paul Wight. Wight, who was named the Giant, was a legitimate near-seven-footer who, at the start of his career, was billed as the son of Andre the Giant. This was his first-ever match on national television, and what a debut it was. Hogan was leaving to film a movie, so they needed to get the title off of him, but he was Hulk Hogan and the idea that he would lose clean or put someone over was preposterous. So the stipulations for the match (kind of, more later) was that the belt could change hands via DQ, which is exactly what happened after interference from Jimmy Hart. The match itself was set up with an angle earlier in the show that we are not making up. The PPV took place at the Cobo Arena in Detroit, Michigan. Prior to the Randy Savage versus Lex Luger semi-main, Hogan and Giant had a MONSTER TRUCK BATTLE on the roof of the building. It is believed the idea was that they would have a sumo match in these gigantic, and we mean GIGANTIC, monster trucks. Of course, it's pro wrestling, so they ultimately got out of the trucks, started fighting, and in the melee the Giant—get ready—was PUSHED OFF COBO HALL, falling to his apparent death. One would assume this would have resulted in no main-event wrestling match taking place. But one would be

Sting and the Giant would become friends in WCW during the nWo era. We like to think that perhaps Sting rescued the big guy from Lake Michigan. [GEORGE NAPOLITANO]

incorrect in that assumption. In fact, Giant came out for his match with Hogan none the worse for wear. You see, although Cobo Hall was planted smack-dab in the middle of a cement parking lot surrounding it on all sides, the claim was that Giant had fallen off the roof INTO LAKE MICHIGAN, and thus he survived and made it back inside twenty minutes later for his match. You'd think if you were going to book an angle so preposterous you'd at least make sure Giant came to the ring sopping wet, but no, he was dry. Then they had their match. After it was over, the guy in the mummy outfit ran in. This man, Ron Reis, was called the Yeti, which Tony Shiavone pronounced "YET-AY!" for some reason. A yeti, for those unaware, is an abominable snowman, the Bigfoot of the Himalayas. Why he was dressed up as a mummy is anyone's guess. He then proceeded—and if you think this visual is preposterous, we're telling you that the real thing was even more ridiculous than your imagination suggests—to bearhug Hogan from behind while Giant simultaneously bearhugged him from the front. They double-humped him. Don't blame us—we're just reporting the facts. That's what happened. Hogan was left in a heap, understandably. And the Giant won the title.

At least until the next week on *Nitro* when it was ruled that he was no longer the champion: the storyline was that Hart, who had turned on Hogan, had put a stipulation in the contract that if Hogan lost via DQ he lost the title, therefore Giant was to get the WCW title. But WCW's storyline (and real-life) attorney Nick Lambros claimed WCW wasn't recognizing this stipulation. However, instead of recognizing Hogan as champion again, he just said the belt was vacant pending an upcoming *World War III* PPV battle royal. Although the storyline was that WCW never recognized the title change, every single title history in existence plus wrestling lore lists Giant as winning the title in his first-ever match. Not that any of this matters much. Randy Savage ended up winning the title in the battle royal.

December was notable for being the first time that either company booked a television overrun period. *Nitro* ran Savage versus Luger for the title on December 4 and the show ran ten minutes past the top of the hour. Because a rating always grows during a match, and because you're invariably going to get a bump due to people tuning in to see whatever show is scheduled to air next, you can inflate your rating with an overrun. *Nitro* was up 0.2 as a result, tying their record 2.6 rating and beating *Raw* (although barely, as viewership for both shows was creeping up). From that point forward, *Nitro* booked an overrun virtually every week. Overruns became an accepted part of Monday night pro wrestling to the point that WWE still does an overrun today despite *Raw* having zero head-to-head wrestling competition and the show already being three hours long going in.

While most would consider what happened on December 18, 1995 just another shocking angle in the Monday Night Wars, in reality it was another pivotal day in the history of pro wrestling. On *Nitro*, Debrah Miceli, who had been working in WWF as Alundra Blayze and was, in fact, their Women's champion, showed up on *Nitro* with her title belt, tossed it in a garbage can live on air, and said that was what she thought of the WWF and their championship belt. She said *Nitro*'s tag line was that this was where the big boys played, but as of today it was also where the big girls played. Vince McMahon was shocked. Why he was shocked is anyone's guess given that her contract had expired a week earlier and they hadn't bothered to take the title off of her. The move led to a bitter lawsuit between the two sides that ultimately played into Vince McMahon's decision-making during the Montreal Screwjob years later, a night that changed pro wrestling forever.

"I was under contract [with WCW] and was told to do what I had to do, and if not, you're fired and would have no income coming in," Miceli noted. "Eric Bischoff told me that I had to put the WWF Women's title in the trash on television or that was it . . . it was put down as if it was totally my fault. However, people don't want to see the other side, and that it was pure entertainment. If I was asked how I felt, and if I would have done it by my own choice, the answer would have been 'No.'"[9]

On *Raw* that same night, Steve Austin debuted as The RingMaster. When people state that this was a golden era in wrestling, this is why. Nearly every Monday night had something that would have fans talking throughout the week.

And as you can see, the battle lines had been drawn. But the war had not yet started in earnest.

Things were about to get a lot more interesting.

And a lot more ugly.

CHAPTER
★ ★ ★ TWO ★ ★ ★
1996:
THE WAR BEGINS

From the time WCW and WWF first emerged as the two major leagues of professional wrestling, fans had debated who would win in a show-down between the two. Many knew that the whole business was in fact predetermined, but it was still fun to contemplate the awesome match-ups that would take place should the two companies ever compete under one banner. In fact, many wrestling magazines seemed to stay in busi-ness by publishing at least one article detailing interpromotional "dream matches" each month. Every fan hoped to see, once and for all, which of the two organizations was truly superior.

"From the day you first watch wrestling and see all the amazing char-acters, it's natural to dream about cross-federation matches, champion versus champion," notes legendary wrestling magazine writer Bill Apter. "When I worked for the magazines full-time we took it one step further and made the dream match seem more like a reality. Everyone loved it and that showed by the mail we used to get each time we published one."

So when Scott Hall appeared on *Nitro* for the very first time, it should have come as no shock that the fans suddenly sat up and took notice. His debut certainly was unique. In the past, promotions typically released video packages to detail a wrestler's imminent arrival. These would establish just who the character was, what his motives were, etc., to create a "buzz" before he ever stepped foot in the ring. With Hall, however, WCW concluded that everyone knew who he was, since he had been an integral part of the WWF's upper card for the better part of the past three years. Therefore, no packages were produced, and nothing was ever mentioned. No, Scott Hall just showed up on *Nitro* one night and grabbed the promotion by the balls.

The night was May 27, 1996, a night that, for many reasons, was a turning point in the history of wrestling. It just happened to be the week that *Nitro* made a huge jump, expanding from one hour to two. Since *Raw* ran from 9–10 p.m., Bischoff decided to run *Nitro* from 8–10, giving the show one full unopposed hour to build up the second hour as a must-see. Turner was happy because the show in the 8–9 slot, *Thunder in Paradise* (which, ironically, featured Hulk Hogan in a leading role), was doing miserable numbers. In exchange for the programming, Turner agreed to pay WCW $2 million per year for the added hour. Because attendance at WCW live events had started taking off months earlier due to a Randy Savage versus Ric Flair feud (yes, Ric Flair, who was not only unretired again, but had, shockingly, briefly won the World title twice in the prior six months and actually pinned Hulk Hogan for the first time since their feud began five years and nine million matches earlier), this additional revenue meant that the company had reached a new milestone: for the first time in history, it turned a profit.

It was on this occasion, as *Nitro* expanded to fill its new time slot, that the Scott Hall deal unfolded. During the midst of a mid-card match featuring Steve Doll and "The Mauler" Mike Enos (that's right, and for historical purposes it should be noted that, aside from Hall's appearance, this show totally blew), Hall jumped the rail from the stands and grabbed

Randy Savage and Ric Flair brought their great matches from the WWF to the WCW. The two had previously been in a World title match at *WrestleMania VIII*.
[GEORGE NAPOLITANO]

a microphone. It looked for all the world like a completely unscripted event, and immediately fans began to think something was up—after all, here was this big WWF star invading *Nitro*! Those fans were even more suspicious when Hall made his way to the ring and began to speak.

"Hey, you people know who I am. But you don't know why I am here. Where is Billionaire Ted? Where is the Nacho Man? Where is Scheme Gene?" The mystery continued to build as Hall hunted down the announce team, including Eric Bischoff himself. "Bischoff, you got a big mouth. You started it, now we're going to finish it!" He also mentioned that he wasn't alone, and that he'd have a "big surprise" for all of WCW the following week. "You want a war?" Hall asked. "You got one!"

WCW got one all right. A real-life war with the WWF that resulted in a real-life lawsuit filed by McMahon's company on June 20. The suit cited, among other things, unfair competition (with regard to WCW's portrayal of this as an interpromotional angle—ironic, given WWF's portrayal of Ric Flair in 1991), trademark infringement (Hall looked and spoke too much like Razor Ramon for their tastes), unfair competition (WCW had allegedly claimed on its 900-hotline that WWF was ready to file for bankruptcy—a stretch, but this was the year in which WWF was closest to going under in its entire history), and defamation and libel (for an incident in which the power went out at *Nitro* and Bischoff implied that "the competition" might have had something to do with it). And this was only the latest legal volley from the McMahon side—earlier in the year he'd filed a long complaint to the FTC Bureau of Competition citing everything from alleged contract tampering to the "unprecedented" act of starting *Nitro* a few minutes early and ending it a few minutes late, all efforts by WCW, he believed, to kill WWF and create a monopoly over U.S. pro wrestling (ten years after McMahon largely did the same, though that fact wasn't mentioned in the complaint). Long story short, his goal was to have Time Warner investigate WCW and the fact that it had lost over $40 million since being purchased by Turner in 1988 with the hopes that, to avoid merger headaches, everyone involved would just opt to drop the wrestling division. This would have signaled a much earlier Death of WCW. The great irony was that at the time Vince lodged his complaint, WWF was actually having somewhat of a business turnaround, having done a great buy rate for *Royal Rumble* and good house show business both domestically and internationally. The biggest difference between the two promotions was that Eric Bischoff was touting how WCW had turned the ratings war around. Funny, in the six weeks prior to the complaint being lodged, *Raw* had won three weeks and *Nitro* had won three weeks. In addition to that, prior to the *Raw/Nitro* war and Bischoff going on and on about ratings, the reality is that nobody in wrestling really cared about ratings at all, and there were very often periods, particularly in the early '90s, where WCW's ratings were consistently better than WWF's. In those days, though, it didn't matter, because business success or failure was determined by house show numbers and pay-per-view buy rates.

The week after the June 20 lawsuit, Hall delivered on his threat as Kevin Nash, who had competed as Diesel in the WWF, made his debut. Not only was Nash a former WWF champion, he was also the man around whom McMahon had developed his most recent marketing campaign, the "New Generation," the idea being that Nash was fresh, while the guys in WCW like Hogan and Savage were yesterday's news. Like Hall, Nash began to berate Bischoff and WCW as a whole.

"You've been out here running your mouth for six months!" Nash bellowed. "This is where the big boys play? What a joke!"

The implication was clear: Bischoff had taken shot after shot at the WWF on *Nitro*, pulling stunts like announcing the results of the taped shows and mocking their top stars. Now, here were two of the WWF's biggest names confronting Bischoff about his actions and threatening to dismantle WCW to its very core. In a stroke of what can only be

"This is where the big boys play? What a joke!" Kevin Nash would soon ride rough-shod over WCW . . . in more ways than one. [GEORGE NAPOLITANO]

described as genius, the words "WWF," "Razor Ramon," and "Diesel" were never mentioned. Indeed, the loudest words were unspoken. On top of all this was the irony of WCW throwing around references to the WWF's entire series of "Billionaire Ted" parody skits. The skits, in which elderly actors played knock-offs of Hogan ("The Huckster") and Randy Savage ("The Nacho Man"), did little more for the WWF than further stir interest in the WCW product.

Everything led to the *Great American Bash* PPV, an event so shockingly great from both in-ring and booking standpoints that many fans at the time went as far as to call it the greatest U.S. pay-per-view of all time. Right before the main event, Hall and Nash showed up again and interrupted the proceedings to a bigger reaction than almost anyone else on the show. In fact, the crowd began to chant "Diesel! Diesel!" Amazingly enough, neither man had even been named by the promotion at this point.

After berating Bischoff once more, Hall and Nash made their demand clear: a three-on-three match for the upcoming *Bash at the Beach* PPV. Bischoff agreed, and Hall asked who WCW's three men would be. Bischoff wouldn't say, so Hall punched him in the stomach, doubled him over, and sent him into the waiting arms of Nash. Nash then lifted Bischoff high into the air and powerbombed him off the stage and through a table below.

The crowd went absolutely crazy. Armageddon had arrived: the WWF was here, and they were taking out WCW from the very top!

Before we continue, it must be said that the manner in which WCW initially booked Hall and Nash was nothing short of phenomenal. The whole idea behind drawing money in wrestling is actually pretty basic: create a match that fans want to see and, more importantly, one that they're willing to pay to see. If fans perceive that one side has zero chance of winning, they won't want to see the bout. After all, the outcome of such an encounter would be predetermined (which is ironic, since all pro wrestling is predetermined). It's also crucial that the two factions are perceived as equals: if a main-eventer takes on a lower-card guy, fans will likely reject the match. When Hall and Nash made their debuts, they were treated as something very out of the ordinary; in fact, they were made to look absolutely dominant. They were a huge threat, not only to this wrestler or that wrestler, but also to the entire company of WCW as a whole.

Never before had two men simply come into a company and acted like it was their personal playground. It was called an "attempted hostile takeover," and by God, that's just what it was. During matches in which they weren't involved, the announce team would talk about them, fearing what might happen when they showed up. These "outsiders" were such a threat that not only was everyone on the alert, but at one point the announce team even had armed guards to protect their positions. It's one thing to KO a guy in a wrestling ring—it's another altogether to be so dominant and intimidating that security guys with GUNS are required.

LESSON NOT LEARNED: Over the years, countless "invasions" have happened in the world of pro wrestling. These have all paled in comparison to the original WCW debuts of Hall and Nash. And the reason is almost always the same: the incoming force is treated as a true threat for a week or two, then is portrayed as the same as everyone else on the roster. For instance, they will have theme music . . . that sounds just like the ones heard on the show for years prior. They are given entrances that look the same. They give interviews at the same times during a show as all others. When Hall and Nash debuted, they were different, they were unique . . . and they were kept that way until they were more established. And once established, their music was radically different, their entrance was different, EVERYTHING was different. And they were immediately programmed with the top guys in the company. End result: they were taken very seriously, and led the company to its greatest success.

This was a threat WCW took very seriously. The only way to fight guys who were the top stars in the WWF was to use their own main-eventers. In fact, on the very first night that Hall showed up, none other than Sting came out to defend WCW's honor. It made sense, as Sting was often viewed as the promotion's franchise player. Unlike nearly everyone else in WCW, he'd never left the company and had remained true to WCW through all of its ups and downs. If anyone could block this WWF onslaught, it would be the Stinger. But he'd definitely need backup, and in this case, he got it in the form of two of WCW's other top stars, Randy Savage and Lex Luger.

So Team WCW was set, but leading up to *Bash at the Beach*, one question remained: who would Hall and Nash (now dubbed "the Outsiders") have as their mystery partner? Indeed, one of the biggest selling points of the PPV was the chance to see just who the third guy was. Although "mystery partner" angles almost always turn out to be complete flops in wrestling, the fact that WCW had delivered two monumental surprises in the appearances of Hall and Nash convinced fans that WCW would unveil another huge name. Right up until the ring introductions, the question remained: who was the third man?

There were several schools of thought as to just who would wind up as Hall and Nash's mystery partner, both in the minds of fans and behind the scenes. Since Hall and Nash had just jumped ship, and it appeared that McMahon was having problems holding on to his talent, one theory had yet another WWF main-eventer jumping ship: Bret Hart. And since it was known that Bret was unhappy with his current position in the WWF hierarchy, he seemed a likely third man. In reality, Bischoff wouldn't begin negotiations with Bret until months after the **Bash**, so it was never going to be him.

As the crowd craned their necks toward the entrance ramp, Michael Buffer made the introductions. But something wasn't right—only Hall and Nash made their way toward the ring. The announce crew immediately cried that this was unfair, and this really said something—after all, shouldn't the WCW announce crew have been happy that it was now

The Outsiders, Scott Hall and Kevin Nash, would help propel WCW into the stratosphere. [GEORGE NAPOLITANO]

PART I THE BIRTH

a handicap match? Apparently not, as Tony Schiavone, practically in tears, screamed, "They've got to tell us who the third man is right now!" His announce colleague, Bobby Heenan, countered, "They know what they're doing. They're keeping us on the edge of our seats and making our palms sweat!" They sure were; they had the entire crowd and all those watching at home antsy about what the hell was going on.

Gene Okerlund made his way to the ring and demanded to know where the third man was. Hall, channeling the Puerto Rican accent he had used as Razor Ramon, retorted, "You know, Scheme Gene, you know too much already. All you need to know, little man, is that he's here and he's ready." Nash followed up and proclaimed: "He's here all right, Gene, but we're enough to handle it here right now."

He was right. Nash and Hall began a complete dissection of the WCW crew, knocking Luger out of the match almost immediately. This furthered speculation that perhaps Luger would reemerge as the third member. That wasn't in the plans, however. And just in case fans at home hadn't caught on that Nash and Hall were bad news, the announcers began to beg for a third guy to come out, so that team WCW would once again have a three-on-two advantage! They needed the help, too, as the Outsiders beat the ever-loving crap out of Sting and Savage. Note to wrestling promoters: *this* is how you book strong heels. Finally, Sting was able to make the tag to Savage, and the crowd went insane. One low blow later, though, Savage was once again down.

Just as things began to look most bleak, WCW's biggest star hit the aisle: Hulk Hogan. As he came down the ramp, the fans cheered—WCW was finally saved!

Hogan surveyed the ring. Hall and Nash had dropped to the floor, leaving Randy Savage alone in the ring, flat on his back. Hogan looked around the ring nervously and glanced momentarily at the crowd. No doubt, Terry Bollea had serious reservations as to what his wrestling persona was about to do. For the first time in over a decade, and for the

Was Lex Luger the third member? No. WCW had someone MUCH bigger in mind . . .
[GEORGE NAPOLITANO]

first time since he had taken the nation by storm as Hulk Hogan, he was about to become a heel.

The third man had arrived.

Hogan dropped the leg across Savage's throat. Sting came back in to make the save, but was promptly thrown out. Again and again, Hogan nailed Savage, stopping only to high-five his new friends. The wrestling world had its new number-one heel. And WCW was about to take off into the stratosphere.

Gene Okerlund hit the ring once more to find out what the hell had just happened. Hogan launched into a tirade: "Mean Gene, the first thing you need to do is to tell these people to shut up if you want to hear what I got to say. The first thing you got to realize, brother, is that this is the future of wrestling. You can call this the New World Order of wrestling, brother!" And thus the group had its name.

What about its motives? "These two men right here came from a great big organization up north. And everybody was wondering who the third man was. Well, who knows more about that organization than me, brother? I made that organization a monster. I made people rich up there. I made the people that ran that organization rich up there, brother! And when it all came to pass, the name Hulk Hogan, the man Hulk Hogan, got bigger than the whole organization. And then Billionaire Ted, he wanted to talk turkey with Hulk Hogan. Billionaire Ted promised me movies, he promised me millions of dollars, and he promised me world-caliber matches. As far as Billionaire Ted, as far as Eric Bischoff, and as far as the whole WCW goes, I'm bored, brother!"

Fans began to get irate and hurled trash into the ring. What began as a paper cup here or there had become a flood of garbage that washed over Hogan, Hall, and Nash. In fact, the entire area was becoming less like a wrestling ring and more like a landfill confined by ropes and turnbuckles.

Hogan continued: "As far as I'm concerned, all the crap in this ring represents these fans out here! For two years, for two years, I held my head high! I did everything for the charities, I did everything for the kids, and the reception I got when I came out here, you fans can stick it, brother! Because if it wasn't for Hulk Hogan, you people wouldn't be here! If it wasn't for Hulk Hogan, Eric Bischoff would still be selling meat from a truck in Minneapolis! And if it wasn't for Hulk Hogan, wrestling wouldn't be here!"

Tony Schiavone concluded the telecast with these words: "We have seen the end of Hulkamania . . . Hulk Hogan, you can go to hell! Straight to hell!"

At this point, the New World Order name was here to stay, despite commentator Larry Zbysko's best efforts to call them the New World Odor. That Larry, he was a damn clever man.

The angle was a culmination of many things that had happened in both companies over the past year. For Hall and Nash, they left a company that had lost $4.4 million in the 1994–1995 fiscal year to jump to a company which had, for the first time since Turner bought them in 1988, finally turned a small profit in 1995. Hall went from an upper mid-carder to a main-eventer, and Nash went from a failed WWF champion—a guy who, while they tried to push him as the new Hulk Hogan, ended up being (up to that point) the worst-drawing champion in company history—to a tippy-top main event superstar in WCW.

For Hogan, fans had grown bored with the goody-two-shoes image that Hogan had used for so many years. Indeed, a handful of fans had already been booing Hogan in his appearances leading up to the turn, and now they were given carte blanche to scream their lungs out against the guy. Hogan, having seen his popularity decline, was truly at a career crossroads. Being a bad guy wasn't something he wanted to do, per se, but Bischoff had made an excellent argument: as a babyface, Hogan had

Goodbye red and yellow, hello black and white. Never before, or since, has a color shift meant so much in professional wrestling. [GEORGE NAPOLITANO]

worn out his welcome, but as a heel, he would be at the top of the cards once more.

It was a good argument, but Bollea was still undecided. He had strong reservations about leaving behind what was a secure (though not as profitable as it had once been) role as wrestling's number-one good guy. He was already starting to wane as a babyface . . . what if he flopped as a heel? Bad guys didn't sell T-shirts, and they didn't take starring roles in movies. In fact, as a heel, Hogan had never main-evented wrestling shows, either. Although none but the hardest of hardcore fans knew it, Hogan had started his national career as a heel for the World Wrestling Federation in 1979, wrestling under the tutelage of evil managers like Fred Blassie and taking on fan favorites like Andre the Giant. In fact, his first babyface turn came by accident, as he was supposed to debut for Verne Gagne's AWA on August 9, 1981, as a heel, but for whatever reason, the fans went wild for him.

By the middle of 1996, Hogan had few options. His WCW contract would be due after two more PPVs, and he had no leverage left. He had tried one of his usual tricks months earlier, and it had backfired. The NBA playoffs were coming up, so he left to film a movie. Of course, the playoffs wreaked havoc on *Nitro*'s ratings, and his plan was to come back and say the reason they were down was because he was gone. There was a flaw in his plan, however. He was gone too long, and when the playoffs ended, *Nitro* returned and started doing better numbers than when he'd been main-eventing every week. So, less than two weeks before the *Bash*, Hogan decided to take the gamble and turn heel.

The gamble paid off. Hulk Hogan, bad guy, along with Hall and Nash, became the talk of the wrestling industry. His career was instantly rejuvenated, giving WCW a huge shot in the arm. Fans who hadn't been following the business suddenly wanted to know just what could have caused such a catastrophic turn of events. The following night on *Nitro*, Hogan launched into yet another tirade, echoing his sentiments from the previous night and adding that if the fans didn't like what he had to say, they could "stick it."

Anyone involved in wrestling—especially promoters and bookers—should take note that even when things appear to be taking off, nothing happens overnight. All the angles that WCW booked in mid-1996 certainly increased casual fan interest in the product. This interest, however, did not immediately turn the company's fortunes around. In fact, despite all the awesome hype leading up to **Bash at the Beach**, the show actually did **fewer** buys than the same PPV the year prior (0.71 versus 0.82). **Nitro** ratings were up, but that was slightly deceptive, partially owing to the addition of an unopposed first hour. And house show business, legitimately up a whopping 125 percent, was the result of the Flair versus Savage feud that had started earlier in the year and had nothing to do with the nWo.

With Hogan, Hall, and Nash running roughshod over WCW, it became apparent that the entire promotion would begin to rally together as a group to fight this invasion. The Giant—WCW World champion at the time—stepped up to the plate to defend WCW's honor, in addition to the title. This was a major turning point in the early formation of the angle, since the Giant had been a heel right up until Hogan's heel turn.

And indeed it was all of WCW against the New World Order, as the invaders began to assail anyone and everyone within the company with a series of sneak attacks, spray-painting their victims with an "nWo" tag. One such attack saw the near–seven foot Kevin Nash launch five-foot-two Rey Mysterio Jr. into the side of a truck like a lawn dart. Arn Anderson of the Four Horsemen was also injured during the beatdown, showing that the nWo didn't care who was a face or heel on the WCW side of things; all were enemies to them. Everyone, from legends like Ric Flair to opening-match guys like Brad Armstrong, stood united against the nWo's onslaught.

To stand up to such numbers, it was clear that Hogan, Hall, and Nash would need to bring in more members. And so came *Hog Wild*— an annual PPV event emanating from the Sturgis motorcycle rally. The matches took place in the middle of a field of thousands of drunken bikers, whom WCW did not charge to attend the event. In other words, the gate was zero dollars. Despite this lack of revenue, the company would hold the event over the next several years, primarily due to the fact that Eric Bischoff was such a huge motorcycle enthusiast. On this occasion, commentators Dusty Rhodes and Tony Schiavone opened the program proclaiming that WCW had stumbled upon new evidence that the nWo was growing, and that their numbers would increase by at least one man by the end of the evening.

The show itself was rather boring and bland, aside from a women's match featuring Madusa (Deborah Miceli, formerly known as Alundra Blayze), who had made quite a name for herself a year or so earlier when she showed up on *Nitro* and threw the WWF Women's title into the garbage. On this night, Miceli took on Bull Nakano from Japan. Nakano was quite the sight, a 200-plus-pound brute of a woman with hair sticking up two feet from her forehead. She looked like the world's most brutal Japanese porcupine. But she was a fantastic in-ring competitor, and the two had some really good matches. Miceli and Nakano had previously had a heated rivalry in the WWF when Miceli, hoping to boost the status of women's wrestling (which had never been taken seriously in the U.S.), urged McMahon to bring in some of Japan's top stars. McMahon, however, thought Miceli would be better served by taking on the 350-pound Rhonda Singh, whom he dubbed Bertha Faye, queen of the trailer park. Madusa was more than happy to get out of the WWF when she had the chance.

Playing to the xenophobic nature of pro-wrestling crowds, especially those containing thousands of (likely inebriated) bikers, the *Hog Wild* encounter saw the two fight for the right to smash their opponent's motorcycle. It should be noted that Bull's manager was the diminutive walking Japanese stereotype, Sonny Onoo, who would later file a lawsuit against WCW for racial discrimination. This despite his claim that he'd ride his bike "like a kamikaze" during this match. Anyway, despite the best efforts of Nakano and Onoo—who unfortunately did not attempt a suicide mission with his Honda—Madusa got the duke and took a sledgehammer to the bike to the cheers of the crowd.

Heading into the main event, the New World Order had yet to reveal any new members. At least not officially. During the Outsiders matchup against Sting and Luger, it looked as though Luger would get the submission victory over Hall. However, referee Nick Patrick accidentally-on-purpose clipped Luger's knee, allowing Hall to roll him up for the pin. This would lead to a loooong angle during which Patrick would become the "official" official for the group. However, at this point, Patrick was not officially a heel, and the nWo still hadn't bolstered its ranks.

Again, in the main event, it looked as though Giant had things in hand, until Hogan walloped him with the title belt, leaving the big guy flat on his back for the next fifteen minutes. They must have replaced the gold with lead. Metallurgic inconsistencies aside, the win gave the nWo their first championship, and Hogan took the spotlight atop the card once more. Out came longtime Hogan lackey Ed Leslie, the man of a thousand horrible gimmicks. Fans had last seen him as The Bootyman, a character who shook his ass at the camera to the delight of no one and used the high knee (get it, as in "hiney"?) as his finisher. Since the *Hog Wild* event fell on Hogan's birthday, Leslie, in an effort to suck up to the Hulkster, brought out a cake. Hogan thanked Leslie, then proceeded to have the Outsiders beat the crap out of him. What an ingrate. They then proceeded to spray-paint the World title belt with the initials "nWo" as the announce squad once again cried foul.

It was around this time that the New World Order began to air vignettes on WCW shows. These were filmed entirely in black and white and featured bizarre camera tricks and sound sampling. They looked as though someone had filmed them with a half-dozen shaky handheld cameras, all of which had faulty zoom lenses. At the end of each of these segments was a black-and-white message that simply read: "The preceding announcement has been paid for by the New World Order." It was completely unlike anything the wrestling world had ever seen, very cutting edge, and so out there that fans immediately paid close attention.

LESSON NOT LEARNED: As we noted previously, ratings don't change overnight. Countless wrestlers' main event pushes were given up on due to the fact that upper management has no patience. Look no further than the Nexxus angle in 2010. The group, consisting of Wade Barrett, Skip Sheffield (who would become Ryback), Daniel Bryan, and others, debuted in June and was pushed to main-event status, destroying Vince McMahon, Ricky Steamboat, and several other legends before entering into a feud with John Cena. Scant weeks later, the group had not only been defeated by Cena but were forced to disband.

Patience, Steph and Hunter. Even Eric Bischoff had it once upon a time.

In fact, fans paid close attention to just about anything the group did at this point. They did interviews in which they'd say things that almost appeared to be shoot (or "real-life") comments, which no one else in the industry was doing. They interrupted matches, threatened announcers, and basically had the entire promotion on the run. More than anything, though, they did exactly what they said they'd do. They'd claim they would win belts, and then they did. They'd say they'd beat people up, and then they did. And, most importantly for the company, they were adding viewers. With the nWo invasion as the focal point of the promotion, the ratings for *Nitro* began to pull away from *Raw*, generally beating the competition by a full point. They were nearing 4.0 at the time—far and away the best ratings *Nitro* had ever achieved.

Seeing that the New World Order had fans on the edges of their seats, it was decided that the time had come for them to add more members. Following an attack on his stablemates in the Dungeon of Doom, Giant came down to the ring, apparently looking for revenge against Hogan and his crew. However, in a moment that made absolutely no sense from a storyline standpoint, Giant turned on his team and joined up with the nWo (the reason this made no sense was that Davey Boy Smith was supposed to be the fourth guy, but the day he was scheduled to jump ship from the WWF, he instead re-signed a five-year contract). Even though the members of the nWo were technically the heels, fans cheered like crazy for the Giant turn, mostly because the four so-called "bad guys" were overcoming incredible odds and were on their way to destroying eight top WCW names.

During the Giant's official induction into the group, Scott Hall, acting on a goofball impulse, asked if Andre the Giant was really this Giant's dad, referring to a pathetic angle a year earlier in which WCW had claimed that as fact. Visibly upset at Hall's sudden ad-lib, Giant shot Hall a deadly glare and replied, "Don't go there."

Shortly before Giant's turn, Ted DiBiase had shown up at *Nitro*, sitting in the crowd. He would eventually act as a mouthpiece of sorts for the New World Order. This storyline made a bit more sense. Furthermore, since DiBiase's character in the WWF was that of the Million Dollar Man, it was explained that he was the benefactor who enabled the group to bring in high-priced talent and air commercials on WCW television. The group had member number five.

Member number six turned out to be a very shocking turn, as WCW's number-one guy turned against his company: Sting. But it wasn't really Sting, and it was the beginning of a tremendous angle that would set the stage for the most successful PPV in WCW history.

Ironically, though, the very first angle they shot in this storyline was such a turn-off for fans that approximately 700,000 people immediately switched channels.

The angle began on the September 9, 1996, *Nitro*. The nWo's familiar black limo was waiting in the parking lot as Lex Luger chased after the group. Out of the car and into the murky night came Sting, who, with the help of the rest of the group, proceeded to pummel Luger. This made little sense, as Sting had been the most vocal against the invaders and had, in fact, begged Flair and Anderson to join himself and Lex Luger to take them on in the upcoming War Games match at *Fall Brawl*. Team WCW seemed to be in a shambles. After all, if Sting was now on the other side, who would defend WCW's honor at War Games?

Aside from the War Games match, the most notable aspect of *Fall Brawl 1996* was the incredible number of outstanding matches on the show.

Not only did Chris Jericho make his WCW PPV debut against Chris Benoit in a fantastic bout, but Juventud Guerrera, Chavo Guerrero Jr., Super Calo, Rey Mysterio, and Diamond Dallas Page all had incredible outings as well. It proved to be a formula for which WCW PPVs would become known: fantastic undercard matches followed by main events featuring big names that weren't so great as far as wrestling action was concerned. And when Sean Waltman—in the WWF as the 1-2-3 Kid—joined the nWo as Syxx (you know, because he was the real sixth member since Sting hadn't really joined), the group found itself with a talented worker to help carry the load in their main-event matches.

Waltman was actually set to debut at **Hog Wild** after the WWF agreed to give him a release from his contract. However, WCW's plans to debut him kept being thrown into disarray when the WWF repeatedly "forgot" to send him his release papers. Strangely, his journey back to the WWF years later would also be due to his getting stuck in the middle of a political game.

While the main events were largely bad in the ring, it would be a mistake to say they were lacking in drama. Never mind that the drama often made absolutely no sense. Indeed, the War Games match had everyone glued to the action, with the question now reversed: who would team with Flair, Luger, and Arn to take on the nWo? The question was seemingly answered in an interview immediately prior to the War Games main event, in which the real Sting appeared before his former teammates and pleaded innocence. "All I've got to say is it's not me, it wasn't me, Lex!" It was never explained why Sting waited six days to have this talk with his pals as opposed to calling them immediately to explain that it wasn't really him who attacked them. Luger, Anderson, and Flair didn't believe him, and so, like total idiot babyfaces, the group headed down to ringside by themselves to take on Hall, Nash, Hogan, and their partner, who turned out to be . . . Sting.

But of course, it wasn't the real Sting, it was the imposter. The crowd picked up on that fact immediately, even though the announce crew didn't. Minutes later, the real Sting hit the ring, and the announce crew figured it out. However, the rest of Team WCW just stood back and watched the real Sting go to work, apparently stunned by his actions. After laying out the entire nWo, he turned to Luger and yelled, "Is that proof enough for you right there?" He then proceeded to flip Luger off and leave the ring. Stunned by the real Sting's departure, Luger fell prey to the bogus Sting, and the New World Order scored yet another win. To cap off the night, Randy Savage—another good guy who was supposed to be getting the next title shot at Hogan—was completely obliterated by the nWo, giving the impression that he had no chance.

As for Sting, a storyline in which he felt that he had been betrayed by both WCW and the New World Order was developed. He changed his look entirely, trading in his trademark Sgt. Pepper–style ring jackets for a long black trench coat. Gone too was the spiky blonde hair and the outgoing demeanor. In their place was a silent, almost ghostly figure who closely resembled the lead character in the movie *The Crow*. He would hang out in the rafters and silently observe the proceedings. Each week, the commentators would question his loyalties, using such clues as the color of his makeup to indicate whether he was nWo or not. He didn't do interviews, and he didn't wrestle, yet he remained arguably the company's hottest commodity.

It should be noted that the fake Sting didn't just appear on WCW television . . . he appeared in videogames as well! In what many argue is the best wrestling videogame ever made, the Nintendo 64 classic WCW vs. nWo World Tour, the WCW roster had Sting, while the nWo team had "Sting." Yes, "Sting," complete with quotation marks so players would know the difference.

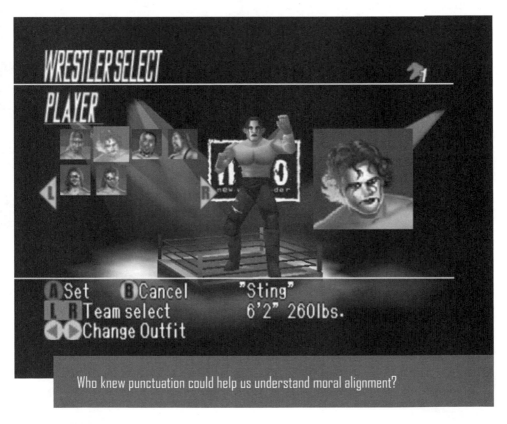

Who knew punctuation could help us understand moral alignment?

Not only did ratings soar, but events also took an almost entirely different direction. Throughout the fall, WWF and WCW became engrossed in the biggest bidding war in wrestling history over the services of Bret Hart. WCW wanted him to come in as the savior of the company for huge matches with Hogan and his cronies. The WWF did not want to lose him. Both sides made huge offers virtually unheard of in the industry: WCW put a three-year, $2.8 million contract on the table, while the WWF offered him a twenty-year deal worth an estimated $12 million total. Ultimately, he signed what he figured was going to be the last WWF contract of his active wrestling career.

This was not the only major signing. Hogan re-signed a lucrative three-year deal with WCW after claiming that WWF was willing to offer him $5 million per year to jump ship. Nobody really believed it except those who were in a position to call his bluff. Roddy Piper also signed a deal to come in and re-create his mid-'80s feud with Hogan. While he could barely move after having undergone hip surgery, it was a smart move by WCW since the *Nitro* audience skewed much older than *Raw* and drew an audience that remembered all these big stars from when they were younger.

During the early days of Piper's WCW tenure, he was able to move the needle in both ratings and buy rates. The one thing he never understood, though, was the concept of a battle between the two companies. "Joe's Bar and Grill was run better than that company, and they've only been open a week. WCW, the 'war.' I never figured it was a war. I wasn't mad at nobody. I just come to fight the guy in the ring. But these guys, the egos got into it . . . I was like 'stop!'"[10]

Sadly, Joe's Bar & Grill could not be reached for comment.

And that audience was growing. On August 26, *Raw* was preempted for the U.S. Open tennis tournament, and *Nitro*, built around the Sting angle, did an unopposed 4.3 rating, by far its biggest number in history. Things were starting to happen.

It had been five months since the beginning of the New World Order angle, and they were on an absolute tear. WCW was made to look totally inept, as Hall and Nash won the tag belts and Giant won the United States title—all in short order. At *Halloween Havoc*, a show with a record-setting $94,000 in first-day ticket sales, WCW put Savage up against Hogan in an effort to regain the WCW World title. But, unlike their encounters in WWF (which were phenomenal), this time the match pretty much sucked, likely due to the fact that both guys were starting to get up there in years, and it showed.

And speaking of Father Time, he appeared in human form as "Rowdy" Roddy Piper to end the show.

"So you're bored, are you?" Piper began. "I've come here to break your monotony! I am not here to represent the WCW, the NWA, the SPCA, the SOB—although I can be one SOB when I want to be! I'm just as big an icon in this sport as you are, Hogan! Do you know what bothers you? I am the only guy you've never been able to beat."

Although that wasn't entirely true, the stage was set for *Starrcade 1996*: Hogan versus Piper. But before that could take place, Eric Bischoff came out on *Nitro* and stated that, for reasons he could not get into, the Hogan versus Piper showdown would not, in fact, take place. Quizzed by the announcers as to the reason, Bischoff stormed off the set. Bischoff claimed that despite his best efforts, Piper was not returning his phone calls or emails asking him to sign the contract to face Hogan. Something wasn't adding up. Soon enough, Piper cornered Bischoff in the ring. The nWo then jumped Piper and revealed its newest member: none other than Bischoff himself!

There were several reasons why Bischoff became the on-screen leader of the nWo. The first, and most important, was that **Raw** had moved an hour earlier to an 8–9 p.m. time slot. Knowing they now had to promote a killer hour of **Nitro** to keep fans from tuning in to **Raw**, Eric's idea was to split the show in half: hour one would be an nWo show, and hour two would be the WCW show. People were reacting more to the nWo at all the shows, so Bischoff figured nWo versus **Raw** would be better than WCW versus **Raw**. He also wanted to make sure that he was on the air doing commentary at the same time Vince McMahon was, because he took great delight in driving Vince crazy week after week from thousands of miles away. And, of course, being a TV star with the hottest heel group in wrestling sure sounded like fun.

Bischoff the character was given leadership in the storylines of the New World Order. From that perspective, it made sense, as who else could orchestrate all these ex-WWF guys coming in or give the invaders so much leeway to get away with things that they reasonably had no right to do? And make no mistake about it—Bischoff was excellent in his role. His smug, arrogant attitude had already alienated some wrestling fans, and he now had the opportunity to be as all-out annoying as he wanted to be.

His first order of business was to give WCW wrestlers a chance to join the most prestigious and elite organization the wrestling industry had ever seen, via a membership drive for the New World Order. Effectively, he was telling the entire roster that they were either with them or against them. This led several WCW mid-carders—Big Bubba, Scott Norton, Michael Wallstreet, and others—to jump ship and join the heel conglomerate. It could—and will—be argued that this was the first huge mistake Bischoff made with regard to the booking of the New World Order storyline. Before, the nWo consisted of top-tier guys in the industry. Now, it was being watered down considerably as wrestlers who had been nowhere near the top of the card gained easy entry into the previously elite group.

The next PPV, *World War 3*, featured an overbooked and confusing sixty-man, three-ring battle royal. On the show, Hogan and Piper had yet another confrontation in which Hogan informed the world that Piper was really just an old man with a plastic hip, going so far as to lift Piper's kilt and show the entire world the scar from his hip-replacement surgery. After dubbing Piper "Pegleg Pete," Hogan signed the contract for the *Starrcade* match, a contract that, according to storylines, Piper himself came up with. Keep that in mind; it's important later on. Then the nWo beat the crap out of Piper once more, although this time Piper was able to regain his feet and hobble to the back on his own. The rest of the show was rather uneventful, with Giant winning the battle royal for a shot at Hogan at some undefined point in the future.

The contract signing set up *Starrcade*, which had traditionally been WCW's biggest show of the year. And, much like the PPVs that immediately preceded it, it had really good mid-card action from the usual suspects like Dean Malenko, Chris Benoit, and Eddie Guerrero. In one of the first wins for WCW since the formation of the New World Order, Lex Luger pinned the Giant after Sting snuck down to ringside and whispered something in Luger's ear. He also left behind his now-trademark baseball bat, which Luger used to waffle the big guy and score the pin.

The main event, of course, was the lure of the show. Despite the fact that both guys were way past their physical primes, Hogan versus Piper had tremendous appeal, especially to more casual fans of WCW. Those fans likely remembered their wars from years past—namely the first *WrestleMania* and the various MTV bouts they had leading up to it—so the nostalgia factor was kicking in big-time. And, to be fair, the booking leading up to the match was very strong as well, with both men playing their roles to perfection: Hogan was really beginning to peak as an insufferable bully heel, while Piper did a super job as the never-say-die babyface.

While the build up was good, the match itself was not. It was becoming apparent to even his most ardent supporters that Piper's best days in the ring were long past, and Hogan, despite the novelty of his being a bad guy, didn't look much better. The two men hobbled around the ring as best they could, trading slaps like a couple of sissies. Piper finally cut loose with a comical punch-kick offense, and Hogan countered with scratches. Suffice to say this was a far cry from what fans had witnessed earlier in the evening from the superb mid-card action. The crowd fell silent following the inevitable nWo run-in, but Piper was able to get rid of the Giant and locked Hogan in a sleeper, the oldest of old-school moves. Hogan's arm dropped three times, and referee Randy Anderson called for the bell.

The crowd was stunned. How long had it been since someone had won a match with a sleeper hold, for God's sake? It didn't take long, however, before they realized that Hogan had been beaten, and they leapt to their feet. As the crowd celebrated, everyone waited for the gold to be strapped around Piper's waist. It never happened, though, because the match was inexplicably a non-title affair. Since Piper himself came up with the contract (we told you that would be important), we hereby nominate Roddy Piper as the dumbest babyface of 1996. But we also must decry WCW for promoting a match that was clearly designed to look like a title affair. WCW had given its fans a bait and switch on their biggest show of the year; one that some would remember right to the bitter end.

Booking aside, the show would have to be considered a complete and total success. It drew a 0.95 buy rate—higher than any other show the entire year—and it nearly doubled the buy rate of *World War 3* just one month prior. The company also celebrated yet another victory in the Monday night wars, demolishing *Raw* by a margin of 3.51 to 1.64—an amazing accomplishment considering that on the first Monday night of the year, they had lost the battle 2.61 to 2.52.

There was absolutely no denying that the company was on an incredible roll, delivering buy rates and ratings WCW had never seen before. Bischoff had the formula, he had the stars, and, perhaps most importantly, he had the one matchup that everyone was dying to see. And he was going to make them wait to see it for an entire year, building up not only the anticipation, but also the inevitably enormous buy rate.

Yes, he had the whole world in his grasp, and as hard as it was to believe, 1997 was only going to get better.

★ ★ ★ ★ ★ PART II
THE RISE

"Hulk has control over what he does. We don't mind,
because obviously he is doing it right. It helps us . . . we need help."

—Terry Taylor, Booking Committee Member, 1997

CHAPTER
★ ★ ★ THREE ★ ★ ★
1997:
THE WAITING GAME

If 1996 taught Eric Bischoff anything, it was that the New World Order was the future of his company. That much was made clear from the ratings and the buy rates, both of which had skyrocketed following the launch of the angle. The numbers did not lie. Attendance was up 43 percent over 1995, gates were up 87 percent, and buy rates for PPVs—where the company made the bulk of its money—were closing in on that. In fact, the very first *Nitro* of 1997 drew 10,034 paid—a brand-new record—and this came a week before the Chicago show shattered that number with over 17,000 fans paying $189,206. The nWo had brought them to the Holy Land, and nowhere else would the spotlight shine brighter than this.

No longer was WCW beneath Vince McMahon's mighty World Wrestling Federation. No, now they were on more or less equal ground, and having come this far, there was no way they were turning back.

Although the New World Order was a strong contingent, the fact remained that they were a bunch of bad guys. And in wrestling, bad guys are only draws if they have a strong babyface to confront them. Although the rest of WCW was often made out as a bunch of buffoons, one guy had not yet been booked to look like a total idiot: Sting. The man who had been the franchise of the company from almost the moment it became WCW, Sting was viewed by fans as the one guy within WCW who could conceivably compete with and defeat these invaders.

To Bischoff's credit, he knew that in order to maximize revenue from the inevitable battle between Sting and Hogan, this could be no ordinary feud (in those days, feuds generally played out over a couple of months). The plan was to make this one of the slowest-building feuds ever—a long, drawn-out affair lasting over a year. By building the feud up to December's *Starrcade*, WCW's biggest show of the year, fans would be lined up to pay to finally see Sting take down Hogan. The only remaining question was whether Bischoff would actually stick to his guns and keep Sting out of action for twelve months, or if he'd get antsy for the big payday and rush the match to pay-per-view.

In order to allow the matchup he wanted, Bischoff felt he had to focus the company almost entirely on the New World Order. Never was Bischoff's game plan more obvious than during the first PPV of the year, *Souled Out,* or to be more precise, *nWo Souled Out.* This show was designed to be a showcase for the group; it wasn't promoted on-air as a WCW event, but as a New World Order event in which WCW wrestlers would show up and get their asses kicked. The idea was to see if a pay-per-view could be marketed and successfully sold solely under the New World Order name. If this could be done, it stood to reason that at some point in the future, Bischoff could begin to run more than one PPV a month, thereby doubling the revenue these events generated. It seemed well worth the gamble to give it a try.

The show opened in a manner most bizarre, as Bischoff, Sean Waltman, Scott Hall, Kevin Nash, and the rest of the group circled the arena riding atop garbage trucks. Say what you want about him, but even the most jaded skeptic has to give Bischoff points for originality: certainly no pay-per-view in the history of pro wrestling had begun in such a manner. Even the set pieces on the show were unique. The standard bright and gaudy WCW sets were vacant, and in their place was a dark, industrial look from which it appeared no color could escape. The entrance was black, the ring apron was black, the ropes were black, and the turnbuckles were black. Aside from a few white nWo logos splashed around the arena, everything was black. In addition, the group's trademark camera tricks were in full effect, with static blacking out the picture at random intervals. The bizarre camera angles likely had first-time viewers wondering if they were watching wrestling or an old episode of the '60s *Batman* TV show. It was totally bizarre and completely different from anything else the wrestling world had ever seen. This was definitely not your ordinary, run-of-the-mill wrestling pay-per-view event. This was new; this was different. This was a New World Order pay-per-view.

If anyone needed evidence that the nWo was starting to become severely watered down at this point, they need look no further than the **nWo Souled Out** PPV. Hogan, Nash, and Hall, the original nucleus trio of the group, had been joined by Waltman, DiBiase, and Bischoff shortly thereafter. Rounding out the ranks were Buff Bagwell, Scott Norton, Masahiro Chono, Mike "Virgil/Vincent" Jones, Ray Traylor, Elizabeth, a fake Sting, and about twenty other scrubs, all of whom tried to push each other out of the way in a vain attempt to occupy more of the television screen. It was almost an omen of what would come later in the year.

In addition to the matches, the show also featured a Miss nWo contest, as middle-aged women straddling Harley-Davidson motorcycles proclaimed their love to the New World Order. It was neither erotic nor comical, but more like what would happen if your mom had a pageant with her friends and they all said they wanted to grope Kevin Nash. Doesn't sound like a good time, does it? The fans in the arena weren't amused and immediately began to chant "Boring," as Bischoff himself began to mack with the scag biker chicks onstage.

In between his make-out sessions with the skanks, Bischoff, taking center stage on a podium above the entrance ramp, began to preach the message of the New World Order to the crowd. His statement was clear: WCW sucks. It was a familiar rallying cry, one that was repeated over and over again to the point that no one watching the show could miss it. And even if they did ignore Bischoff's rantings, the presentation of WCW at the event would certainly sway their opinion. The WCW wrestlers who were not on the show were shown sitting in the crowd like common fans, a band of outcasts who couldn't cut it with Bischoff's rogue coalition. Even the handful of WCW wrestlers who participated in the show looked like losers: they had no music, no pyro, and they were introduced by a monotone voice in a very mocking manner. The nWo, meanwhile, were given grand entrances with music and lighting as the announcer declared their superiority. The point was clear: the WCW guys were pathetic, and they were no match for the New World Order.

Despite the fact that the angle had given the promotion new life, the fact remained that the New World Order, as cool and hip as they might be, were supposed to be the bad guys in the story. All the mockery of WCW seemed to sap the very life out of the crowd, as they sat quietly throughout the majority of the show, seeming neither upset nor particularly thrilled by the outcome of any of the matches. Of course, those outcomes involved the New World Order winning almost every bout, generally with the help of evil referee Nick Patrick. The few wins WCW was able to rack up were generally due to match stipulations in which the referee didn't come into play, such as a ladder match in which Eddie Guerrero (billed as the Mexican Jumping Bean by the ring announcer—a line that surely wouldn't offend anyone) was able to yank down the U.S. Heavyweight belt suspended above the ring. The atrocious main event saw yet another nWo debacle, as Hulk Hogan pinned the Giant (who had joined and then left the group in the span of less than six months) following a beatdown by nearly every member of the group.

Was the *Souled Out* experiment a success? In a word, no. The buy rate was a mere 0.47, the lowest since the start of the New World Order angle. The show took place in Cedar Rapids, Iowa, before a crowd of around 5,000—yet another sellout, but since the building was so small, the take was under $70,000, and a major disappointment. In short, everything was about half of what the previous pay-per-view, *Starrcade 1996*, had generated.

The company decided to go back to the successful *Starrcade* formula for the next show, *SuperBrawl 7*, this time pitting Hogan against Piper in what was very clearly billed as a World title match. To promote the event, Piper was filmed in a bizarre series of vignettes in which he was locked away inside Alcatraz. Following the conclusion of the main event, fans probably wished that they too had been locked in solitary confinement.

To be fair, however, the company had once again gone back to the blueprint they had followed to make *Nitro* a must-see show: they'd feature great matches prior to the blockbuster show-selling—albeit generally bad—main events. Bouts featuring men like Dean Malenko, Eddie Guererro, Sean Waltman, and Chris Jericho opened the show, bringing the fans to life. The undercard was as solid as ever, due primarily to the fact that Bischoff continued to spare no expense when it came to bringing in talent. Through raids of either the WWF, ECW, or Japan, Bischoff had brought in an amazing array of outstanding talent from around the globe. From 1996 to 1997, newcomers like Jericho, Juventud Guerrera, Rey Mysterio Jr., and countless others tore up the ring.

WCW would need the fresh young talent, as it was slowly becoming apparent to everyone (save those in charge) that guys like Hogan and Piper just couldn't deliver in the ring as they once could. Try as they might, the two stumbled through yet another horrible main event. This time, Piper once again appeared to win the belt, but this was overturned when Randy Savage turned his back on WCW and put Hogan's foot under the rope, thus negating the title change. As all this was going on, Sting just watched silently from down the entrance ramp, then slowly turned and walked away. The slow burn would continue.

Despite the bad main event, the show was able to rebound slightly from the depths to which *Souled Out* had taken the company, scoring a 0.75 buy rate and drawing almost $200,000 at the door from the 13,324 in attendance. It was a move in the right direction.

WCW immediately took that money and spent it, announcing that they had just signed a huge star for *Uncensored*, their next PPV: Dennis Rodman. It didn't matter that Rodman wouldn't be able to actually wrestle on the show due to the fact that it was the middle of the NBA season. Bischoff knew that with the media covering the basketball bad boy at his every turn, WCW would get instant exposure, and a ton of it, if he could somehow sign him to do a couple of shows. It was also rumored that Vince McMahon was looking to do the same, so it should come as no surprise that Bischoff was willing to do anything to once again stick it to Vince and the WWF. McMahon had offered the "Worm" $1 million for two dates, so Bischoff outbid him to the tune of nearly $2 million for three dates.

Uncensored once again epitomized the company at the time, with young guys like Ultimo Dragon coming in for great matches with Mexican luchadores like Psicosis. For once, though, the main event of the evening was actually pretty good, largely due to the fact that they crammed nine guys into the ring in a three-way, which the nWo obviously won when Rodman and Savage interfered. In the storylines, this win gave Hogan's organization the right to challenge for any title anytime they so desired. However, as the group celebrated, Sting rappelled from the ceiling, baseball bat in hand, and lay absolute waste to Nash, Hall, and Savage. As the crowd went nuts, Sting slowly raised his bat and pointed it at his target: Hogan. Finally, Hogan got into the ring, and

Sting obliterated him as well. It was unquestionably the biggest response any WCW star had gotten since the birth of the New World Order, and it seemed impossible to believe that Bischoff could hold off on delivering this match on PPV for another nine months.

The buy rate, though, showed that Bischoff was on the right track, as it wound up at just under 0.9 (which WCW trumpeted far and wide as having beaten that year's *WrestleMania*, which scored a 0.77). It was apparent that Bischoff could and would hold off, as the following PPV, *Spring Stampede*, featured neither Sting nor Hogan. Instead, the main event was a showdown between Savage and Diamond Dallas Page. The event was largely forgettable, and largely unwatched, drawing a low 0.58 buy rate. However, even with a weak lineup, the company was still hot enough that it sold out in advance, drawing 8,356 fans paying $107,115. Indeed, selling out shows in advance was becoming a trend—a trend, ironically, that would end up hurting the company in the long run.

To his credit, Bischoff didn't panic and hotshot the Sting-Hogan showdown to the next show. Instead, he continued to do *Nitros* in which Sting would silently and methodically stalk Hogan and the New World Order from the rafters. In a business that is well known for getting the big payday as quickly as possible, it is absolutely amazing that Bischoff stayed his course. Indeed, even after the next show, *Slamboree*, did a similar 0.60 buy rate, as did the follow-up to that, *Great American Bash*, Bischoff was resolute in his plan. In short, his was precisely the type of patience the company would not show in subsequent years—and this would eventually cost them dearly.

By this point, business was really starting to pick up. Tickets went on sale in April for the June 9 *Nitro* at the Fleet Center in Boston and set a new first-day record with 10,000 sold for $170,000. House show business was also through the roof. In fact, by mid-1997 they were doing *triple* the business they had done in 1995. It didn't seem to matter what anyone did; everything the company touched was turning to gold.

Randy Savage forces DDP to feel the madness. [GEORGE NAPOLITANO]

One of the primary reasons that WCW house show business was so hot at the time was due to the awesome work of Zane Bresloff. Bresloff not only promoted WCW events, he was also the man behind the promotion of **WrestleMania III**, for which the WWF claimed to have jammed 93,173 fans into the Pontiac Silverdome. Years later, Bresloff himself would admit that the actual number was 78,000.

The next show featuring Hogan was *Bash at the Beach*, which had become something of a gala event for WCW. Hogan had not only made his debut at *Bash at the Beach* in 1994, he'd also done the legendary heel turn to form the New World Order there in 1996. The 1997 version of the show was also going to give the fans something memorable, as Dennis Rodman would not only be present at the event, but *wrestle* as well. Because basketball season was over, the Worm now had the green light to actually get in the ring, and he would team up with Hogan to take on WCW mainstays Lex Luger and the Giant.

WCW certainly couldn't be blamed for focusing the promotion of the event on the Rodman match, as he was all over the place in 1997. He had just won the second of three consecutive NBA World titles with Michael Jordan and the Chicago Bulls, he was just about to release a bestselling autobiography, *Bad as I Wanna Be*, and he was a constant media magnet due to his bizarre behavior both on and off the court. In short, Dennis Rodman was a hot property.

A hot property and, because of his real athletic ability, Rodman was a surprisingly decent wrestler in his very first real match. Some even went as far as to call him the best wrestler of the four that evening. (This was not high praise; the other three in the tag match were Hogan, Giant, and Lex Luger). Hogan did most of the in-ring work, if you can call stalling for the first five minutes of the showdown "work." After about seven minutes, Hogan finally tagged in Rodman, and the crowd held its breath to see just what the Worm would bring to the table. Rodman strutted around the ring, sunglasses on, and eventually locked up with Luger. And then it happened: he armdragged Luger! Yes, he was able to execute one of the most basic maneuvers in the history of pro wrestling. The announcers went hysterical, acting as though a successor to Frank A. Gotch himself had finally been discovered. Rodman posed for the crowd, took off his sunglasses, polished them, and then put them right back on. Fortunately for WCW, Luger was somehow able to regain his breath, and not only arm-drag Rodman twice, but also Hogan twice for good measure as well. The pro-WCW announce team celebrated, proclaiming, "Welcome to WCW, where the big boys play!"

Hogan and Rodman weren't foiled yet, however. Rodman once again locked up with Luger and threw him into the ropes. As Luger came toward him, Rodman—get this—leapfrogged him. Though this exact same sequence of maneuvers had been done in almost every single match of the last twenty years, the announce team nearly had a heart attack: "That's no rookie we're watching! He's been tutored by the best!" Tony Schiavone even claimed that Rodman was showing, and this is a quote, "flashes of brilliance." Despite the "brilliance" of such high-impact moves as leapfrogs and armdrags, the nWo was defeated when Luger managed to get a submission win over Hogan.

Although the Rodman match was a total and complete fiasco from a technical wrestling standpoint, the show did a decent number: 0.78 with a $150,870 gate. It wasn't the number WCW was hoping for, but the momentum was definitely building. The ratings for *Nitro* continued to move upwards as Luger's chase for Hogan's championship took center stage. The night after *Bash at the Beach*, *Nitro* scored a 3.5 rating. Three weeks of promotion later, a three-hour *Nitro* special (it was the 100th episode) scored a whopping 4.34, and the title bout, in which Luger dethroned Hogan, scored an amazing (for the time, at least) 5.2 rating. Obviously, the success of the show inspired Bischoff to present more three-hour programs in the future.

The Luger win set the stage for the next pay-per-view, August's *Road Wild* (a lawsuit filed by Harley-Davidson forced them to drop the "Hog"), the annual money pit from Sturgis, South Dakota. Not only did the event once again produce its famed zero-dollar gate, it also had to be somewhat of a disappointment, as the buy rate came in at 0.65. This was well below expectations, especially since the Luger-Hogan feud had been generating such good numbers in the Monday-night ratings.

But there may have been an even more damaging effect on the company in this show, although one much less noticeable than could be computed by tallying gate receipts and buy rate numbers. This was the simple fact that, when push came to shove in big matches, the New World Order never lost. At *Road Wild*, this was proven during the Steiners versus Outsiders (Hall and Nash) match for the World Tag

The nWo and their newest member, Dennis Rodman, celebrate their nefarious antics. [GEORGE NAPOLITANO]

championships. The Steiners had been around WCW for years, and even though they'd had a brief run-in the WWF, they were considered true "home team" talent. The pair had been babyfaces during their entire time as a tag team, and so they, along with Sting, were seen as the saviors of the company. The number of wrestlers that fans bought as being on equal ground with the New World Order was slim, with only Luger, Sting, the Steiners, and maybe the Giant viewed as guys who could legitimately hang with Hogan and his cronies. In order for this belief to be perpetuated, however, these men eventually had to be given wins over their adversaries.

In Luger's case, such a win happened, albeit very briefly. The Steiners didn't even get that much. Despite the fact that they had been chasing Hall and Nash for almost a year, they left *Road Wild* without the tag belts yet again. Keep in mind that not only had they been feuding with Hall and Nash all this time, there was even a vignette filmed in which the evil duo ran the Steiners' car off a road. Rick and Scott didn't file charges because in the wacky world of pro wrestling, the only way to get true revenge for attempted vehicular manslaughter is to take your opponent's title belt.

The Steiners were scheduled to take the belts, but in the end, it didn't happen. Hall and Nash went up to Bischoff backstage at the PPV and said the frequent title changes were hurting the drawing power of the belts. Therefore, they argued, they should retain against the Steiners. Bischoff assented. The irony of all this was that Luger, who had just won the WCW title six days earlier at *Nitro*, didn't get to retain, and dropped the belt instead to Hall and Nash's good buddy Hogan. The next night on *Nitro*, Luger was hardly mentioned at all. This upset more than a few of the boys in the back.

It wasn't just Luger and the Steiners—others were being held down as well. The Four Horsemen, led by Ric Flair—the man many fans considered to be the very epitome of WCW—were also made to look bad at every opportunity. Despite having been made out as Hogan's whipping boy since his 1994 arrival at WCW, Flair still commanded the respect of many loyal WCW fans, specifically in the Carolinas, a longtime hotbed for the company. Hogan and Nash didn't particularly care for Flair or for the reaction he was garnering from the crowds there, so at seemingly every live *Nitro* that took place in the region, they would take shots at Flair and how old he was, or better yet, they'd simply leave him lying in a broken heap. To make a long story short, since Hogan, Nash, and Hall basically had total say on their characters (Hogan had complete creative control written into his contract), they made Flair look like an idiot time and time again in front of his hometown fans.

And never did Flair or his Horsemen look more like total idiots than during the *Nitro* that took place on September 1, 1997. A week earlier, the *Nitro* in Columbia, South Carolina, had destroyed all previous ratings records (thanks in part to *Raw* being preempted for the U.S. Open tennis tournament), doing a 4.97 rating for a show built around area legend Arn Anderson's announcement of retirement due to serious neck surgery. The plan for the following week was pretty straightforward. The show would be presented as a tribute to Arn, but halfway through, the nWo was going to do a skit making fun of Arn's tremendous speech the week before. All the fans would be outraged. Then, at the end of the skit, the Horsemen would run out and clean house as Anderson stood smirking on the ramp.

This never happened. Instead, the nWo did the parody, and there was no retaliation, as Nash got the whole Horsemen run-in nixed. Flair, outraged, refused to go out for an interview later, saying it would kill the Horsemen off even more to do so without having attacked the nWo earlier. Arn was so upset he nearly quit the company, not so much because of the content of the skit, but because of the fact that his family watching at home was devastated by it (the skit touched on Arn's alleged alcoholism, and his reaction to this was made worse by the fact that his mother had died of the disease when he was very young).

The parody set up *Fall Brawl*, which took place deep in the heart of Flair Country: Winston-Salem, North Carolina. Before a crowd of almost 12,000 rabid Horsemen fans, Flair was once again booked to take the loss, as new member Curt Hennig (who had been nominated by Arn as his Horseman replacement just weeks earlier) turned on the group and gave yet another win to the New World Order. At this point, it was beginning to appear that no one could ever compete on even ground with the nWo.

Bischoff didn't care about the backstage squawking of men like Flair, since business was going through the roof. *Nitro*, which at the beginning of the year was averaging ratings in the low threes, was suddenly and consistently in the fours. The September 8 show was a huge success, doing a 4.27 to *Raw*'s 2.15 (the biggest margin in history up to that point). Shows were selling out left and right (the weekend of September 4 was the first in history in which the company grossed over $1 million on house show revenue alone), and PPV buy rates were climbing. *Halloween Havoc*, in particular, was a massive success. Despite the fact that the show was headlined by yet another horrendous Piper-Hogan match (the third in the last nine months), it drew a gigantic 1.1 buy rate, drawing 12,457 fans, and a $297,508 gate. On the bright side, the Rey Mysterio Jr.–Eddie Guerrero mask versus title match (which Rey won, although he had been scheduled to lose until just minutes before the show started) was WCW's best match of at least the past five years. As good as business was for that show, the next PPV, *World War III*, was even better, drawing 17,128 fans and $407,831 at the gate.

Who the hell cared about wrestlers pissing and moaning when WCW was making this much jack?

Not only were they making money, but Bischoff was about to stumble upon yet another success, one that would ensure the health of WCW for years to come: Bill Goldberg. The former Atlanta Falcon turned Power Plant trainee debuted on the August 22 *Nitro* in a 2:24 win over

Hugh Morris. Afterwards, he simply held up a single finger, as if to say, "That's one." He didn't say a word, and in fact wouldn't for almost a full year after his debut. By the time the show was over, most had probably forgotten the match—ironic, given that he'd soon become one of the company's most unforgettable stars.

WCW had everything going for them, and it was about to get even better: Bischoff would soon sign the hottest free agent in the history of wrestling. And when he did, it would no doubt be the final nail in the coffin of Vince McMahon and the WWF.

Although Bischoff had amassed the greatest array of talent the wrestling world had ever seen, there was one guy he'd been after for years and had been unable to get: Bret Hart. Bischoff had badly wanted to bring Hart in during the summer of 1996; he knew that if he could somehow grab not only Hall and Nash but also Hart, it would truly appear that every top star from the WWF was coming to WCW. Unfortunately for Eric, McMahon was able to convince Bret to stay, and signed him to that twenty-year deal mentioned previously.

There were a lot of questions regarding that contract, most specifically how could McMahon afford to pay it? Bischoff knew—beyond a shadow of a doubt—that the WWF was in severe financial straits; the company had lost $6 million in 1996, and things weren't looking to improve that drastically for 1997. Pushing WCW castaways like Steve Austin and Mick Foley, who'd been unceremoniously discarded by Bischoff himself, he figured the WWF didn't stand a chance.

As if he needed any more proof to support his theory, the rumor mill had once again begun to rumble about problems developing between McMahon and WWF champion Hart. Those rumors were confirmed when Hart, with the blessing of McMahon himself, contacted Bischoff to see if the possibility existed to accept the contract he'd declined a year earlier. Bischoff no doubt trembled with glee as Bret told him the story: McMahon claimed he could not afford to pay the promised monies to

Hart. In fact, Vince had told Bret that the company was in "financial peril." In Eric's mind, this translated to "Bret Hart is once again a free agent, and the WWF is dead."

This was a joyous moment for Bischoff. By signing Hart, not only was he getting one of the greatest wrestlers of all time, but he was also taking away one of the few remaining WWF draws. Just as he had been able to do with Nash and Hall, he would leave fans' jaws on the floor by bringing Bret to *Nitro*. After all, he wasn't just a huge star for the WWF—he was their WORLD CHAMPION, for God's sake. At this point, Bischoff realized that as bad as he thought things were going for Vince, they had to have been much, much worse than even he could have ever possibly dreamed.

One of the provisions of Bret's twenty-year contract with the WWF was that he had "reasonable creative control" of his character. Therefore, as champion, he had the right to decide whom he'd lose the belt to and when he'd do so. For months, a very real rivalry had developed between Bret and one of McMahon's other favorite performers, Shawn Michaels. Michaels, who also had a great deal of power backstage, seemed to take delight in pissing Bret off at every turn. One time, he even went so far as to allege—on air, no less—that Bret was in the midst of an extramarital affair with popular WWF diva Sunny. This infuriated Hart (not to mention his wife), and it led to an infamous backstage fight between the two men that ended with Shawn temporarily quitting after a huge chunk of hair was pulled out of his scalp.

As Bret's WWF contract approached expiration, and his WCW debut loomed ever nearer, he and Vince began to discuss scenarios to get the title off of him. The next WWF PPV was the *Survivor Series* in Montreal, and Vince suggested that Bret should drop the strap to—you guessed it—Shawn Michaels. Shawn had first won the belt from Bret a year earlier in a sixty-minute Iron Man match at *WrestleMania*, and injuries (both real and fake), fights, and other problems kept the big rematch from ever taking place. At first, Bret exercised his creative control and refused, stating that he'd rather "blow his brains out" than lose to Shawn. One of his main gripes was that, several weeks earlier, Shawn had told both him and McMahon that he wasn't going to do any more jobs to anyone else in the promotion, and that included Bret.

If that was going to be Shawn's attitude, Bret figured he'd just "return the favor" and refuse to lose to Shawn. On the Wednesday before the Montreal *Survivor Series*, Vince called Shawn up and once again asked if he'd lose. Shawn got to talking about it with his good buddy Hunter Hearst Helmsley (Triple H), and Hunter was appalled, arguing that Shawn would be a fool to agree to lose to a guy who was on his way over to the competition. So Shawn called Vince back and said losing the match was a no-go. As soon as Bret heard that, he said if Shawn wasn't going to lose to him in Montreal, then he wasn't going to lose to Shawn anywhere under any circumstances.

A few days later, Bret changed his mind. That Friday, his lawyer sent the WWF a letter stating that Bret was willing to drop the belt to anyone in the company as long as it didn't happen in Canada. Since his WCW contract didn't start until December 1, there were several places where he could lose the belt, including the house shows the following week in Youngstown, Ohio, on November 13, in Pittsburgh on November 14, or at Madison Square Garden on November 15. And, he said, if Vince wanted to do it on PPV, he'd drop the belt in a four-way at the December 7 show in Springfield, Massachusetts.

Vince noted that Bret's WCW deal started on December 1. Bret said that wasn't a problem, and convinced Eric to hold off on his WCW debut until December 8. Upon hearing this, Vince said fine, Bret could win via DQ (thereby not making Shawn look bad) in Montreal, then lose the belt in the four-way in December. But then Vince changed his mind *again*, saying word had gotten out that Bret was leaving, and it was therefore imperative that he lose the title before *Nitro* the night after

Survivor Series. After all, Vince reasoned, even though Bret couldn't show up on *Nitro* until after December 1 for legal reasons, if Bischoff went on TV and even *mentioned* that he'd signed away his champion, the WWF would be dead.

Bret said he'd call Bischoff and get him to hold off on the announcement. Unfortunately, Eric was off hunting in Wyoming, and Bret couldn't reach him. Vince suggested he drop the belt at the house show in Detroit the night before Montreal. Bret again refused, saying that the match between himself and Michaels was too big to trivialize, and that to do it right, he had to go into Montreal as the champion. If Vince wanted him to lose it later that week at a house show, he reiterated, that would be fine.

Sunday was fast approaching, and nobody could decide on a finish, which had Bret on edge. Vince argued that it wasn't fair for him to refuse to lose. Bret said it was fair, as Vince himself had put the creative control clause in his contract. They argued about what the "reasonable" part of "reasonable creative control" meant. Finally, just hours before the PPV, they met backstage. Vince asked Bret what he wanted to do. Bret said he wanted to leave with his head held high, and then the next day on *Raw*, he'd vacate the belt and, without burying the company (i.e., making Vince or the WWF look bad) in any way, he'd tell the fans that he was leaving. Vince acquiesced, and the plan was set for Shawn to lose via DQ that night when Degeneration-X (Shawn's group) and the Hart Foundation (Bret's group) ran in.

During the match, Shawn put Bret in Bret's own finishing maneuver, the sharpshooter. Bret was told beforehand that he would reverse the move, which would lead to another series of near falls. This never happened. Instead, referee Earl Hebner—a longtime close friend of Hart's who had actually sworn on his children's lives before the show that he wouldn't fast-count him—simply called for the bell. The timekeeper, who wasn't in on what was going to transpire, was initially confused about what to do. Thankfully, McMahon himself came down to ringside to offer the following helpful advice: "RING THE FUCKING BELL!" And so Shawn was now the champion, and Bret, as he'd later state countless times, was "screwed."

It became known as the most famous double-cross in wrestling history. Bret had been with his former employer for fourteen years, missing only two shows in that time, and he'd done everything he could to help the WWF. Callously, they'd turned their backs on him. It was a moment that would live forever in the minds of all those who saw it; a memory reinforced by the footage replayed over and over on WWF television in an effort to make fans believe that Vince had done the right thing.

This should have helped WCW (since Bret was about to be all over both programs), and hurt the WWF, which had blatantly screwed over a very popular star. But the wrestling business is a uniquely peculiar world. As it turned out, McMahon—who really just hoped the whole story would die, having no desire to play a major on-screen role—suddenly became the biggest heel on WWF television. This ultimately led to an everyman versus everyboss feud between him and the company's biggest babyface star, Steve Austin. This rivalry turned out to be a springboard for the company's fortunes, which subsequently skyrocketed to the point that Vince became a certifiable billionaire.

And what of Bret Hart? Heading into WCW with such momentum, it seemed absolutely impossible that the company could somehow screw this up. There was no question that something huge would be lined up for Bret come the next big PPV blockbuster, *Starrcade*.

Spoiler alert! Bret Hart, years later, would have this to say of his WCW tenure: "What does make me angry is how poor WCW used me. They couldn't have done a worse job. And the scary thing is what they were paying me . . . all I can say is that it was like a lunatic asylum. I think of Eric Bischoff, who I like as a person, and I sympathize maybe with whatever he was going through . . . but Eric Bischoff was a lot like that 'Wizard' in **The Wizard of Oz**. He really had no idea what he was doing. They never came up with one idea for me, and any time I came up with an idea it was usually turned away. It was the most screwed up place I ever worked for."[11]

Bischoff counters: "When Bret got to WCW, he was not the Bret Hart we had watched in the WWF. I think the incident with Vince McMahon took a tremendous toll on him. Or perhaps Bret never really felt at home in WCW.

You can have the best-written screenplay, with the best director, the best soundtrack, the best supporting cast, and if your lead actor doesn't feel the part, chances are that movie is never going to be what you want it to be. I think in some part, that was the problem with Bret. Regardless of how we used him, there was never the passion and the commitment to the role that could propel him."[12]

As you read through what WCW gave Bret to work with, we will let you, the reader, decide if he was given **Gone with the Wind** or **Ready to Rumble**.

Spoiler Alert! We may have just given that away too.

But prior to that event, Bischoff had something else to take care of. He decided to try doing another show entirely based around the nWo. Apparently nothing had been learned from the *Souled Out* fiasco in January, so serious thought was now being given to handing *Nitro* over to Hogan and his heel contingent. In early 1998, plans were on the drawing board for a two-hour Thursday-night show on TBS, and Bischoff's grandiose idea was to eventually split the company so that there would be a WCW show and an nWo show, thereby making the WWF—get ready, because he really believed this—the number-three promotion in America.

Thus, *nWo Nitro* got a trial run, with results that were either shockingly disastrous or shockingly predictable, depending on your viewpoint. The show opened with the nWo b-squad's arrival and their immediate demand that the production crew tear down anything with the WCW logo on it. Every sign, every banner, even the gigantic metal "WCW" were all laid to waste. In their place were custom-designed *nWo Nitro* banners and set pieces. Just to show that this wasn't designed as a one-time shot, a spiffy new video opened the show. Everyone involved was to be aligned with the New World Order, from the wrestlers to the announcers, right down to the ring crew.

Although the entire group glad-handed each other and went on about how wonderful they all were, the night truly belonged, of course, to Hulk Hogan. The majority of *nWo Nitro* was less of a wrestling show than it was a celebration of the life and times of Terry Bollea, complete with a twenty-minute segment in which Bischoff gave Hogan presents like giant banners and motorcycles featuring his image. He even dropped down to one knee and placed a ring (in the shape of the WCW World title) upon his finger. It looked for all the world like he was going to propose to the Hulkster.

Although all this posturing no doubt pleased Bischoff and Hogan, those watching at home didn't share the love. With *Starrcade* (set to deliver arguably the best-promoted match in the history of the company) just days away, you'd have thought that this *Nitro* would have drawn incredible ratings, possibly the highest-ever for the company. Not only did that not happen, but the show actually dropped almost a full point from its average, and the original plan to air *nWo Nitro* on a weekly basis was permanently scrapped. The elaborate sets, the shirts, the video production—it all amounted to nothing more than a colossal waste of money.

To Bischoff, though, it was just a failed experiment. Sure, they had lost a few bucks on the sets, and the ratings had sagged slightly. But wasn't it worth the risk? What if it had worked? And really, what did it matter? The biggest show of the year, *Starrcade*, was coming up, and it was the one show that every single wrestling fan in the country was going to line up to see. Not only would Sting versus Hogan finally happen, but Bret Hart would also be making his first ever appearance on a WCW PPV as a special referee for an Eric Bischoff–Larry Zbyszko match.

Huh?

In a move that was puzzling to, well, everyone (including Bret himself), the hottest commodity in pro wrestling was not going to appear as an in-ring competitor, but rather, as a referee. The bout between Zbyszko and Bischoff was to determine the fate of *Nitro*: should Larry win, *Nitro* would remain under the control of WCW. If Bischoff took the bout, the world would be "rewarded" with *nWo Nitro* each and every week. The big question leading up to the match was whether Bret would side with the nWo or with WCW. In other words, Bret Hart, the man who was WWF champion until less than two months earlier, the man the company was paying almost $3 million a year, the man who had just competed in the most shocking and noteworthy bout in decades, was nothing more than a pawn in the never-ending WCW versus New World Order battle. It was the start of what would be a long, confusing tenure for Hart in his newfound home.

Much of Hart's difficulty had to do with career politicians like Hogan and Nash, who played Bischoff like a fiddle, getting out of doing jobs to protect their spots high atop the card. And when Bischoff wouldn't cave in to their demands, they'd simply take their ball and go home. Such was the case at *Starrcade*, when Nash was scheduled to take on—and lose to—the Giant. However, that afternoon, Nash, suffering from indigestion, called the office and said that he seriously believed he'd had a minor heart attack. Nobody backstage believed the story, since Nash had been saying he wouldn't lose to Giant for months, and it had become a running joke. Fans instead saw Scott Hall trash-talk the Giant; then he took a chokeslam during an interview. Yes, not only did Nash get out of doing the job, but the obvious replacement match, featuring Hall against the Giant, also didn't take place!

Shockingly (or not, considering the men involved backstage) almost none of the nWo members lost their matches at *Starrcade*. Even career scrubs like Mike "Vincent/Virgil/Whatever" Jones went over top WCW guys like the Steiners. Lex Luger, WCW champion just four months earlier, wound up on his back for a three-count in a losing effort to Buff Bagwell. It was all very strange, because this had been built up as the ultimate WCW revenge show, the show in which the New World Order would finally get their comeuppance from the good guys.

In fact, one of the only bouts in which the nWo was defeated was in the co–main event of the evening, the Bischoff-Zbyszko contest. Yes, on the biggest PPV in the company's entire history, Bischoff booked his match as one of the main events. To show he was a team player, however, he wound up losing when Hart decided to side with WCW, thereby saving the world from repeated viewings of *nWo Nitro*. And even in that match, Bischoff wasn't pinned, nor did he submit—Bret just kind of awarded the bout to Zbyszko due to . . . well, no reason in particular.

It could, of course, be argued that all of the goofiness on the show really didn't matter, because at the end of the day, the fans were really there to see the match WCW had been building for over a year: Sting versus Hogan. Sure, those fans may have been let down by the evening's proceedings, and maybe they'd even lost some faith in WCW. But it didn't matter, because now, finally, Hulk Hogan would get his ass kicked by Sting.

However, this being Hogan, that didn't happen.

Hogan strutted down the ramp in his usual cocky manner, playing his air guitar and eventually ambling over to confer with Nick Patrick, the evil referee assigned to the bout. The two chatted for a moment in a manner far removed from the standard overt pantomimes of the wrestling business. In fact, it almost looked as though Hogan and Patrick were double-checking to make sure they had certain spots laid out within the match itself. Weird.

After having descended from the rafters in a breathtaking manner for the better part of the past eighteen months, this time Sting simply walked down the aisle, stopping to glance at the crowd momentarily, then resuming his journey. He then slowly climbed into the ring. It was as if this were just another run-of-the-mill match on another run-of-the-mill show.

Nick Patrick stood between the men and explained the rules. Hogan and Sting locked eyes, and then it happened: Hogan shoved Sting. Sting responded by slapping Hogan in the face. It was on. Hogan slowly circled Sting, and the two locked up. The crowd came to life, chanting "Hogan sucks." It was obvious they were desperate to see the Stinger KO this arrogant asshole once and for all.

And the crowd kept waiting for that to happen.

And waiting.

And waiting.

It never happened. In fact, Hogan began to dominate the bout, with Sting only scoring a few minor moves here and there. A headlock spot was worked for over two minutes as the life began to drain from the crowd. Hogan took Sting outside the ring and worked him over, throwing him into the guardrail and then choking him out with his boot. He threw Sting back in, cupped his hand to his ear as he had done so often in his career, and bounced off the ropes, landing his signature finishing move, the Legdrop of Doom.

Hogan covered Sting. Patrick dropped down and started his count.

One.

Two.

Three.

Sting didn't kick out.

No, he did not kick out. The man who had stalked Hogan and his evil band for over a year had just failed miserably in a match one year in the making.

Patrick raised Hogan's arm in victory as the once-rabid crowd sat in stunned silence.

The WCW announcers scrambled for an explanation. They claimed that Patrick had issued a fast count and that Sting hadn't really lost. Problem was, it wasn't a fast count. For years it has been debated what

Hogan and Sting would battle many times over the years, but none meant more than Starrcade '97. [GEORGE NAPOLITANO]

happened in this match—how can you screw up the biggest spot of your career, the pivotal fast-count in the biggest match in the history of WCW? Did Patrick just forget? Did he get a double-top-secret pay-off from Hogan to do a normal count so as to not make Hogan look bad? What happened? For whatever it's worth, Patrick's claim was—get this—that although in hindsight it was a perfectly normal three-count, at the time he thought he was counting really fast. Yup.

Following the phantom fast-count and the perfectly clean defeat of Sting at the hands of Hulk Hogan, Bret Hart ran down to ringside and grabbed the ring announcer. Over a muffled house mic, Bret claimed, "This isn't going to happen again" (in reference to the infamous Montreal finish where he himself had been screwed out of the WWF title). Most in the crowd didn't even hear what Hart had said, and they looked angry and confused. And Sting, the savior of WCW, was still flat on his back in the ring. After a brief skirmish, Hart flattened Patrick and tossed Hogan back into Sting, who had finally come back to life. Sting nailed Hogan with a Stinger splash; then he locked on his finishing maneuver, the dreaded Scorpion Deathlock. The crowd waited for Hogan's hand to slap the mat, the so-called "tap out" that would signal his submission. It didn't come, and instead, Bret Hart told the timekeeper to ring the bell, the story being that Hogan had said "I quit" (a fact that no microphones picked up). The belt was awarded to Sting as WCW wrestlers filled the ring in a joyous celebration.

And as the wrestlers and the fans celebrated, so did Bischoff. All his hard work, all his patience, it had all paid off big-time. *Starrcade '97* was, without question, the biggest money-maker WCW had ever produced.

17,500 fans.

A $543,000 gate.

An incredible 1.9 buy rate, meaning nearly $6 million in revenue.

And the beginning of the end.

CHAPTER
★ ★ ★ FOUR ★ ★ ★
1998:
MOMENTUM IS MONEY

The March 9, 1998 edition of *Monday Nitro* was the ninth consecutive sellout for World Championship Wrestling. In addition to those nine sellouts, the company had already sold out the following eleven shows in advance as well. Never before had they sold out twenty venues in a row.

That was not the only good news. Business, as compared to 1997, was through the roof. Attendance in January averaged 8,023 paying fans per show, an increase of 49 percent from the year prior. Gates averaged $157,019 for the month, an increase of almost 150 percent. And the *Souled Out* pay-per-view in January, which drew just a 0.47 buy rate the year prior, pulled a 1.02, an increase of over *173 percent*. That, of course, meant a revenue increase of over 173 percent as well.

The company was skyrocketing. However, the lesson of the year was not learned until much later; sadly, many in wrestling have yet to learn it to this day.

The lesson is that when things are hot in pro wrestling, promoters can do no wrong. Booking can be horrible, matches can suck, storylines can make no sense, TV shows and pay-per-views can be letdowns, wrestlers can be falsely advertised, and none of it matters. Because it's hot, fans are going to spend money on the product. Of course, any damage done during this period eventually takes its toll, but to promoters who live only for Tuesday-morning Nielsen television ratings, the only thing that matters is the moment. Unfortunately, a few years later, WCW would learn the other half of this lesson: when things are bad, promoters can do nothing right.

There has always been a theory that the wrestling business is cyclical. A superstar or an act takes off and gets incredibly hot for a period of time, then things cool off, and eventually things get really hot again. It seems that no one ever has bothered to stop and ask why; it has just been accepted. Today, the explanation is fairly obvious to anyone *outside* the wrestling industry.

First, a wrestling star catches fire. There is not necessarily any rhyme or reason as to how or why this happens. Sometimes a guy comes along and the company knows from day one that he's going to be it; the Rock was a perfect example of this. There were WWE officials who predicted that he would be the biggest star in the business by the year 2000 after his very first professional match. He actually beat that estimate by a couple of years. There are also guys nobody saw coming who got over because they just happened to be in the right place at the right time with the right gimmick. "Stone Cold" Steve Austin, probably the biggest star in wrestling history in terms of drawing money, was a good example of this.

If a star really takes off, he can turn an entire company around. In fact, Austin turned the World Wrestling Federation around to such a degree that they went from losing $6 million in 1996 to grossing $456 million a few years later and going public, making Vince McMahon a legitimate, honest-to-God evil billionaire. But, as the old saying goes, nothing lasts forever.

Eventually, even the brightest star starts to cool. There is absolutely *no* avoiding this. Sure, he might still be popular, and if he's a big enough star, like an El Santo in Mexico, he may become iconic. But he's not going to sell millions of dollars worth of tickets and pay-per-view buys forever, especially against the same old foes he's wrestled a hundred times before. Worst-case scenario, if he's pushed too hard for too long, the fans may actually turn against him, making him more of a liability than anything else.

In a perfect world, the company would use the still-super-hot star to create another huge superstar, a successor of sorts. Unfortunately, to do this correctly, the successor has to be booked in such a way that he appears to be a true successor. That means he has to win a lot of matches, and eventually decisively beat the big star.

Perhaps you can see the dilemma.

Promoters have rarely been able to bring themselves to replace their bread-and-butter before it's too late. They see him making extraordinary amounts of money for the company, and they cannot fathom tinkering with the formula in any way.

LESSON NOT LEARNED . . . OR IS IT?: One need only look to the John Cena era of WWE in recent years to see this situation. He is the biggest star the company has, a true ratings and merchandise mover, and thus there is a natural tendency to avoid changing a status quo that has proven to be a money maker. It has led to a product that many fans feel is stale, yet the company views as safe. The idea to do something different with Cena, such as turn him heel, has been bandied about for years, but is always rejected due to their need to maintain this status quo . . . and their fear of losing their largest merchandise mover.

In many ways, wrestling promoters are notoriously shortsighted; as noted earlier, they live for the moment—for the sound of the cheering crowd, for the following day's ratings, for the next buy rate. They don't have the long-term vision to see that unless things stay fresh, the decline in fortunes can be just as swift, and sometimes even faster, than the ascent.

There is an old saying, popularized by Bret Hart in Paul Jay's excellent documentary *Wrestling with Shadows*, that promoters ride a wrestler like a horse until he can't go any more; then they put a bullet in his head. Inevitably, they ride that horse until he's long past the point of drawing big money, and then, when things start to decline, they panic. The panic breeds inept and hotshot booking, the decline speeds up, and it finally gets to the point where the company is so cold that, in the eyes of the fans, it can do nothing right.

Of course, to those inside the wrestling business, especially those who've booked their promotions into a cold period, this is absurd: wrestling is simply cyclical; there's no reason for it. And if there *is* a reason, well, it certainly has nothing to do with anything they have or have not done.

Once the decision was made to create *Nitro* to go head-to-head with *Raw*, Eric Bischoff created a winning formula that helped the company take off. He put huge marquee matches such as Hulk Hogan versus Lex Luger on free TV to build the audience. He bought all the big-name talent available and put them on TV as often as possible. He used working agreements with promotions in Japan and Mexico to bring in talented performers from around the world and expose them to a new audience. The show basically had it all: big names, great talent, and good matches. If you wanted to see established superstars like Hogan and Sting, you could watch *Nitro*. If you wanted to see great wrestling matches with mat technicians like Dean Malenko and Chris Benoit, you could watch *Nitro*. If you wanted to see crazy highspots from Mexican luchadores, you could watch *Nitro*. It was the best of all worlds, and the company caught fire.

Things were clearly reaching a peak in early 1998. However, for every dollar made, it was as though WCW made another stupid mistake.

And for every million they made, they made one huge mistake that would help cost them everything in the end.

The biggest mistake of all was that nothing changed. Ever. At first, that doesn't sound so bad; they made more money in one year than the money they'd lost in all the previous years put together—why change anything?

The answer, of course, is that nothing is forever. Those big stars? Some of them were old. Plus, those who were old in 1995 were now three years older. Some couldn't wrestle a good match to save their lives, and some, sadly, could barely even move. The nostalgia was gone, and now that all the big marquee matches had been used up, fans were anxious for something new. That something new, you'd think, would come from the guys on the undercard, who were having all those great matches three years earlier.

The good news is that those guys were still having great matches. The bad news is that they were having the same great matches with the same guys they were wrestling in 1995. As great a match as Rey Mysterio versus Juventud Guerrera was, fans could only see Rey give him a huracanrana so many times.

In essence, *Nitro* looked the same in 1998 as it did in 1995. When you have several hours of first-run television every single week, three years might as well be three decades. And anyone who follows the television industry knows that no weekly television program featuring the same characters—no matter how hot it is at the peak—lasts forever.

And make no mistake about it; there was plenty of talent that just never got a chance, and it was taking its toll. Konnan: "I don't think you ever heard anyone say they liked WCW, even the guys making millions of dollars. Even though we were all being paid a lot of money to shut up, we were all being held back. There were drugs everywhere. I never had to use drugs before I got to WCW. Never even thought I would use them. And I thought anyone who did use them was a loser. Everybody was pissed off, everyone was depressed."[13]

Chris Jericho: "The social aspects of WCW were disheartening . . . Hogan and Savage had their own dressing rooms and didn't really talk to anyone else . . . guys like Scott Steiner, DDP, Paul Wight, and Booker T later became my friends, but within the WCW environment they seemed uptight and defensive. Booker even balked at working with Dean, Eddie, and me, complaining, 'I ain't no Cruiserweight,' as if he would get leprosy from touching us."[13]

In early January, two major television changes took place, both ultimately for the worse. First, after internal pressure from TBS, WCW created a new two-hour program to air every Thursday night, *Thunder* (originally, it was going to be an nWo show, but that idea went out the window when *nWo Nitro* bombed). Bischoff was vehemently against the idea, realizing that not only would it likely oversaturate the market (which it eventually did, though not at first), but it would also possibly take a chunk out of *Nitro*'s numbers. The estimated $12 million TBS paid the company for the show helped to change his mind.

The downside to the addition of *Thunder* from the boys' perspective was that, all of a sudden, they had fifty-two more dates on their schedule for the year. One of the perks of working for WCW back in the day was that you could make better money than in the WWF and work fewer dates. Now, with another TV program and more house show dates, the road schedule was getting harder, and the guaranteed deals meant that the wrestlers were pretty much doing those extra dates "for free." This didn't exactly go over too well.

Amazingly, no one in charge of WCW had any idea whether the debut episode was going to be two hours or three until just a few days prior. It ended up going three hours and fifteen minutes, which threw the rest of the TBS schedule into disarray. Although it was more of a laid-back show, compared by some to **WCW Saturday Night**, it ended up drawing what was alleged to be the highest debut cumulative rating in cable TV history: a 4.0. To give you an idea of how hot WCW was at the time, the

January 15 **Thunder** drew a 3.7 rating despite the fact that a satellite malfunction destroyed the picture quality and caused the entire show to be virtually unwatchable (as opposed to years later, when the show was unwatchable regardless of whether the picture was good or not).

The second major change took place on January 26, as *Nitro* was also overhauled and given an additional hour, making it a three-hour program. If four hours of WCW weekly weren't enough, fans were now given *five*. Over at *Raw*, the WWF was building toward *WrestleMania XIV*, and appearing in some capacity on television most weeks was the man who would be the guest enforcer in the Shawn Michaels versus Steve Austin WWF title match: Mike Tyson. As a result, once *Nitro* ended, many viewers were jumping over to *Raw*. Instead of moving the two hours head-to-head (*Nitro* was airing from 8–10 and *Raw* from 9–11), the decision was made to have *Nitro* go an extra hour permanently (they'd experimented with a few three-hour shows in late 1997), therefore keeping the high unopposed first-hour rating to add to their cumulative total.

Alongside all the additional television time, the year started out with yet another new record: 26,733 fans and a $510,610 gate for a January 5 show at the Georgia Dome. It was highlighted by a classic interview between Bret Hart and Ric Flair, in which Hart said that if Flair (who was still the top ratings draw in either company) had a problem with him calling himself the best there is, was, and ever will be, he could do something about it. Some thought it was too early to be booking this match, but the crowd was clearly clamoring to see it.

Hart versus Flair took place at the first PPV of the year, *Souled Out*. The event, largely considered a success, drew a sellout 5,087 fans to Dayton's Hara Arena to witness Luger beat Savage in a horrible main event. Worse yet, they had a chance to have a great headliner with Hart versus Flair, but at the last minute, this match was moved up to the semi-main position. The reason Luger and Savage went on last was that Hulk

Hogan did a run-in afterwards, and of course, he couldn't do a run-in on a semi-main. The buy rate for the show ended up being on par with many of the Hogan-headlined shows, largely due to the hype for what ended up being an excellent Flair versus Hart match.

And how did WCW reward these two men for having such a great match, drawing such great ratings, and popping such a great buy rate? They ended the feud cold turkey and took Flair off TV for several weeks. The reasoning was that too many people were cheering for Flair, and they wanted him to be a bad guy. If the people couldn't play along and boo him, then they would be punished with his absence. (Ironically, later in the year, when Bret was getting a strong babyface reaction despite being booked as a heel, he too was removed from television. Yet another lesson not learned.)

In addition to the horrific main event, there was almost another disaster at the PPV as Giant landed on his head after Nash attempted to give him a powerbomb. The two had done the spot successfully in February 1997, but a year later Nash was physically weaker, having suffered a knee injury. Giant had put on what looked like about 100 pounds through various means, most of which involved consuming massive amounts of pizza and milk. Nash got him about halfway up, then dropped him right on his neck. Thankfully, Giant was OK. WCW Commissioner J.J. Dillon later announced in storyline that because of the incident, the powerbomb was now banned. Of course, the ban affected everyone in the company except Nash, who used it regularly and began to get over as a rebellious babyface because of it. At first, he'd be "fined $150,000" and "arrested" every time he did it, but eventually the bookers completely forgot about it, and the angle was dropped.

Hogan was all over TV. Some found this strange, since he allegedly was not under contract at the time. The belief of many backstage was that this was the latest political move by arguably the most brilliant strategist in wrestling history. Hogan, making around $5 million per year, knew WWF wouldn't offer him anything close to that, especially since they were already investing millions in Tyson for *WrestleMania*. So, using the creative control written into his contract, he booked himself on TV until he was pretty much indispensable, then started to float rumors around that he was about to jump ship to the opposition. It worked, and not only did he get re-signed for his $5 million, but he got a $1.5 million bonus as well. Some would argue that, from a business perspective, WCW would have been foolish not to re-sign him, as an untelevised January 31 house show that he worked against Sting drew 18,759 fans and $325,154 at the gate, a new company record.

As if anyone needed a sign of just how hot the company was at the time, Sin City Productions began work early in the year on a porn video called **Nude World Order**. When the porn industry takes note, you can be sure you're onto something.

Not only was the company doing incredible numbers at the box office, but the ratings continued to soar as well. In fact, the ratings war seemed more futile than ever for the WWF as the February 2 *Nitro*, headlined by Hogan versus Savage for the nine millionth time, did its second-highest rating in history, a 4.93 to *Raw*'s 3.45. This was the most impressive number of all time up to this point, because the previous record, a 4.97 on August 25, 1997, was set on a week in which *Raw* had been preempted for tennis, giving *Nitro* full access to the entire wrestling audience.

Speaking of impressive numbers, Hogan did an interview on the show that showed great attention to detail, as he talked about the $50,000 fines Nash would be paying for executing the powerbomb. The announcers never bothered to note the $100,000 discrepancy in his tale. It didn't help that a few days earlier on *Thunder*, J.J. Dillon had added to the confusion by talking about the $5,000 fines that were being levied. It was just the latest in a string of storyline inconsistencies that would soon become WCW's trademark.

In the midst of all these incredible numbers, tragedy struck. On February 14, Louie Spicolli (Louis Mucciolo), who had just turned twenty-seven and was starting to get a push in WCW as a Chris Farley–like nWo lackey, died of a drug overdose. Spicolli, who took as many as thirty soma pain pills daily, had washed down twenty-seven with some alcohol. He was found dead in his home at 8:55 a.m., facedown in his own vomit. It wasn't his first overdose; in fact, in 1996, while working for the WWF, he'd collapsed after taking fifty-five somas and was in critical condition for two days. Disturbingly, he'd told friends just days before his death that he was concerned that the drug use in the company was getting out of control. The following Monday, **Nitro** opened with a tribute for him. His close friends on the show weren't allowed to mention him at all. The only person who did bring him up was Larry Zbyszko, with whom he'd been feuding. Zbyszko said that there were a few things he'd like to say, but out of respect for the family, he'd keep his mouth shut. Yes, a guy really died, but because there was a wrestling war to fight, WCW wouldn't even allow Zbyszko to get out of character to acknowledge it. Backstage, there was some shock and sadness, but overall, it was business as usual. In fact, to show just how brazen some wrestlers in WCW were, Dr. Joel Hackett, who had prescribed the pills to Spicolli, was flown into San Francisco for that weekend's **SuperBrawl** PPV.

Before 12,620 fans at the Cow Palace, the *SuperBrawl* PPV was yet another sellout with yet another sub-par main event. Sting beat Hogan to win the held-up WCW title, but he'd been killed so dead by the *Starrcade* booking that it was way too little way too late. Worse, he couldn't even make it a clean win, as Randy Savage had to hit Hogan with a spray paint can prior to the finish. Once again, Sting came out looking far inferior to the almighty Hulkster, and fans were starting to catch on to that fact. If that wasn't bad enough, the usually great undercard wasn't so great, although DDP versus Benoit and Chris Jericho versus Juventud Guerrera were both very good. The latter match was the subject of a lot of controversy. Guerrera, real name Anibal Gonzalez, was the son of famous Mexican wrestler Fuerza Guerrera. In Mexico, the pro wrestler's mask (a symbolic take-off on the masks worn hundreds of years earlier in Aztec rituals) is considered almost sacred, and to lose it is normally a very big deal. The biggest superstar in the history of the culture, El Santo, never unmasked after he took on that persona, and he was even buried with it on. Because of the long tradition, which started when Salvador Lutteroth's family opened up the Empresa Mexicana de Lucha Libre (EMLL) promotion in 1933, major mask versus mask or mask versus hair matches continue to sell out huge buildings such as Arena Mexico.

WCW, however, didn't care about all that tradition stuff. After all, this was the United States of America, where wrestlers did not hide their faces. Guerrera, Bischoff explained again, just wasn't marketable with the mask on. When Guerrera was first approached about losing his mask, he—along with his father and all the other luchadores—was appalled by the suggestion. Bischoff swore that they would make a huge deal out of it, building it up over a long period of time with a series of major angles to make the match really mean something. The big push ended up with a loss to mid-carder Billy Kidman, a win over lower-mid-carder El Dandy, a loss to Jericho at *SuperBrawl*, and, ultimately, the sale at the merchandise stand of his and Mysterio's masks a year later.

It wasn't like the luchadores were the only upset mid-carders. Eddie Guerrero, frustrated with both the mask situation and what he saw as a complete lack of upward mobility, tried to quit. Bischoff not only told him no, but yelled at him for even considering it. Later, Eric apologized. He was not sorry enough, however, to give Eddie his release. Dean Malenko wanted to know when Bischoff was going to keep his word and let him book a Cruiserweight tournament. Bischoff, tactful boss that he was, replied that Malenko, Guerrero, Juvie, Mysterio, Benoit, and the like were all great workers, but none of them put asses in the seats.

Their unhappiness was of no concern to Bischoff, who, on the morning of February 17, was overjoyed to learn that the previous evening's *Nitro* (which ran unopposed as the Westminster Dog Show preempted *Raw*) had done a 5.10 rating—yet another brand-new record. Better yet, it was widely considered to have been a great show, despite the fact that the booking was headache-inducing, and Hogan's old buddy Ed Leslie—now known as "E. Harrison Leslie"—was introduced as the newest nWo member, further watering down the once-elite faction. Not only was *Nitro* again breaking its own records, but Eric also had a great card in mind for the *Uncensored* pay-per-view on March 15 in Mobile, Alabama: Hogan versus Savage in a cage, Sting versus Scott Hall for the WCW title, Luger versus Scott Steiner, and Giant versus Nash. Sure, it was the same old largely horrible workers on top, but it didn't matter—it was considered a top-billing marquee.

The same day that **Nitro** set this record, Randy Savage was named Real Man of the Year by the **Harvard Lampoon** for exuding "universal manliness." Welcome to 1998.

The next week, *Raw* and *Nitro* drew a combined 8.60 rating for shows that saw, on one side, the "baddest man on the planet" Mike Tyson join the cutting-edge Shawn Michaels–led Degeneration X (DX) faction and, on the other side, the 100 zillionth nWo run-in DQ. Fans were anxious for WCW to do something dramatically different and creative like, say, a clean finish, but WCW saw no reason to do that. After all, their show did a 4.81, and Vince's show only did a 3.80. They beat the WWF by a *whole point.*

There was no reason to change anything.

Backstage, things continued to spiral out of control. The luchadores, suddenly informed that they would no longer be able to take bookings in Mexico on their off days, were more upset than ever. Most had been making good money collecting paychecks from both WCW and independent groups south of the border. Once the decree was made, some ignored it and took bookings anyway, while others began to trade ideas on ways to get fired.

The company's deal with New Japan Pro Wrestling also fell apart. For years, the two sides had been trading talent back and forth. Usually, it was to WCW's advantage. New Japan would send over one of their big superstars like Masahiro Chono, while WCW would send over talent like Robby Rage, who was unknown not only in Japan, but also in the U.S. Obviously, the international talent spiced up WCW television, and in fact, Keiji Muto (as the Great Muta) was one of the company's huge stars of the late '80s.

The deal fell through mostly because Eric went on one of his now-trademarked power trips. New Japan had an nWo stable, and Bischoff decided to enforce a contract stipulation between the two sides that enabled him to choose who could and who could not be considered a member. Keep in mind that there wasn't one casual fan in the United States who would have had any idea who was and was not in New Japan's nWo stable. The point was that Bischoff had the power, so he was going to use it. As if that wasn't bad enough, he started trying to enforce which guys could even *team up* with nWo guys. It also didn't help when word got out in Japan that Bischoff had gone behind New Japan's back in an attempt to strike up a deal to send wrestlers to a show run by its competition, All Japan Pro Wrestling.

That was hardly Eric's only power play of the month. Back home, he was having problems with Hall and Nash, who were upset that they were being moved down the pecking order in favor of Hogan and his new best friend, Randy Savage. Bischoff decided to show them who was boss in a very brash manner: he fired, via overnight courier, their best friend in the company, Sean Waltman, a.k.a. Syxx. Worse, Waltman was on the shelf at the time, healing a broken neck. Amidst quite a bit of fanfare, he ended up quickly signing a deal to return to the WWF. To fans watching at home, it appeared that a big WCW star had suddenly decided that the WWF was really the place to be. To disgruntled WCW wrestlers, especially the smaller guys, it suggested that if they jumped ship, they might also get a big push right out of the gate. Waltman was given a raise of almost $100,000 more than what he had been making in WCW, and this sent the message that the WWF was willing to pay top dollar to be competitive.

Hall and Nash, meanwhile, were outraged over the firing and wanted to quit. Eric reminded them that they were under contract until 2001 and couldn't appear anywhere else before then. So they stayed, but that didn't stop them from going on TV and acting unprofessionally. In one interview, Hall told fans that he was no longer allowed to say "Hey Yo!" On another occasion, he told Giant, "That's your cue" over the house mic. He was not reprimanded, and he took note of this fact. Later that week, Nash got into a loud argument with Hogan backstage, actually telling him to his face that he wanted his spot. Hogan said he wasn't giving it up, brother.

While Bischoff was likely stressed about everything, his worries only ran so deep. *Nitro* did a 5.7 quarter that week for a Sting and Savage and Giant versus Hogan and Hall and Nash match, killing *Raw*, which did a 3.3 for a quarter built around Austin and Tyson. Better yet, the following week the show aired unopposed again and did a 5.58 composite, destroying the previous record of a 5.10. The final quarter, featuring Sting and Luger versus Hogan and Savage, also crushed the previous week's record with an enormous 6.6. Eric felt like the king of the world.

At least, until *Uncensored*, which you'll recall had that great big marquee lineup. The undercard was again below average, although Jericho versus Malenko and DDP versus Benoit versus Raven were very good. Giant versus Nash sucked. Sting versus Hall sucked. And Hogan versus Savage was an atrociously bad cage-match—even by WCW standards—that included run-ins by Sting and E. Harrison Leslie and didn't even have a finish. To the amusement of some hardcore fans, *Uncensored* at least lived up to its reputation of being the worst PPV WCW presented each year. But the issue that was becoming clear to anyone but those running the company was that, in spite of the sold-out crowds, record-breaking ratings, and amazing buy rates, they were putting on bad show after bad show.

WCW was so hot in 1998 that it affected world commerce. When THQ announced that they would no longer produce WCW's wildly successful video games, their stock dropped $8 per share on the Nasdaq. Amazingly, a full 25 percent of THQ's titles had been WCW-related.

The March 23 *Nitro* was notable for being the true dawn of the Bill Goldberg era, an era that should have set the company up for long-term success since he was about to become the company's most popular wrestler. The idea, devised by announcer Mike Tenay, was incredibly simple: Goldberg did not lose, and the commentators would play up his winning streak. Not only did this ensure that his eventual first loss would mean a great deal (and it did, but unfortunately for all the wrong reasons), but it also gave fans something to keep track of—a statistic of sorts in a fake sport that really didn't have any. In fact, fans got into it to such a degree that signs featuring simply a stat, "76-0," for example, began to appear on *Nitro*. The fragile egos backstage definitely took note of his increasing popularity.

In addition to Goldberg, WCW also had another star tailor-made for success, ironically as the result of an in-ring tragedy: Buff Bagwell, who had been injured earlier in the year taking a top rope bulldog. The injury was so bad that when it happened, everyone broke character and rushed to his aid. Doctors later told Buff that he was just three inches away from that worst-case scenario, and that he'd nearly died twice due to complications. After undergoing double fusion neck surgery the next day, in a near miracle, he was told that he'd probably be able to return to training within six months. In his return to **Nitro**, Bagwell came out in a wheelchair for a face-to-face meeting with the man who broke his neck, Rick Steiner. He told Rick that it was an accident and forgave him for what happened. The people cheered. The other half of the former Steiner Brothers tag team, the heel Scott, then came out and hit his brother with a chair. Bagwell stood up, apparently to make the save, but then jumped Rick and tore his shirt off to reveal, that's right, "nWo." In that instant, not only was the next potentially huge babyface star flushed down the drain, but a real-life neck injury was turned into a cornball wrestling angle. What should have been a new birth for Bagwell's major-league career ended up being the beginning of its end.

But it was something outside the company that month that changed WCW's fortunes forever. On March 29, Steve Austin beat Shawn Michaels to win the World Wrestling Federation championship at *WrestleMania XIV*.

Still with the taint of the black spray paint of the nWo, Bill Goldberg was arguably the company's last chance to save its biggest title. Despite his mighty might, those in charge would make sure his crusade would fail. [GEORGE NAPOLITANO]

Austin's rise to the title immediately affected the ratings war. The crowning of Austin would lead the WWF into their biggest glory period ever, a period that would ultimately result, just three short years later, in the end of WCW. Every wrestling promoter alive today and who ever lives should strongly consider the fact that no matter how great things might be at any given moment, it really can turn around that fast.

And it was turning around VERY fast. Despite winning handily in the ratings war just weeks earlier, *Nitro* was barely able to edge out *Raw* the following evening, 4.19 to 3.79. In fact, had *Nitro* not taken the lead in the last half hour, *Raw* would have won. The WWF's show was built around Sean Waltman's debut as a member of DX. In a pretty revolutionary segment, he ran down Hogan and Bischoff before he added, "And I got something else to say. Kevin Nash and Scott Hall would be standing right here with us if they weren't being held hostage by World Championship Wrestling. And that's a fact, Eric Bischoff!" With that one interview, DX was pushed over the top as being more revolutionary than the now-stale nWo that, over the past few months, had added such prestigious members as mid-carder Brian Adams and everyone's favorite flabby geriatric, Dusty Rhodes.

The devaluation of the nWo with various members certainly did WCW no favors. What was once a tightly focused group, with just three men, had ballooned out of control. That would have been bad enough, but over the years, in both WCW and WWE, various incarnations of the group appeared. This is a (likely in)complete list of all the various groups sporting the nWo name or some variation thereof:

nWo

The unrefined article. Formed in 1996 with Scott Hall and Kevin Nash as its pillars, the group would begin a run of popularity and prosperity after Hollywood Hogan became the centerpiece. Most of WCW's success over the next two years was hinged on this ever-expanding group, whose expanse would peripherally cause the company's downfall.

nWo Japan

Also known as "nWo Typhoon," the group did not, in fact, feature the services of Fred Ottman. Instead, it was an offshoot group meant to take over New Japan Pro Wrestling. NJPW icons like Masahiro Chono, the Great Muta, and Hiroyoshi Tenzan populated the faction, along with American B-Teamers like Buff Bagwell and Scott Norton.

nWo Wolfpac

The first group to secede from the nWo, which many point to as the beginning of the end of the effectiveness of the group. The group featured the likes of Nash and "Macho Man" Randy Savage being tired of Hogan's politics (this probably wasn't a stretch from reality), and introduced a red-tinted rebel version of the Order. Lex Luger and Sting would join this decidedly heroic group, whose catchy theme song by imprisoned rapper C-Murder was quite popular.

nWo Hollywood

Hogan carried on as leader of the remaining nWo members who weren't quite old/ undignified enough to look silly sauntering out to Deep South hip hop, baring their varicose veins. Hall stayed, but was often incapacitated by his own undoings. Bret Hart was another major member, though he had a habit of turning face on **Nitro** and back to heel on **Thunder**. Don't ask us, it's WCW.

Latino World Order: LWO

A frustrated, coffee-stained Eddie Guerrero formed his own offshoot version of the nWo, which was comprised of the hard-working luchadores ignored every week by Eric Bischoff. They performed heinous acts as well, like standing around while Guerrero cut angry promos, and then standing around some more while Guerrero berated Rey Mysterio Jr. Gripping television.

OWN

The nWo-parallel that was run by the (faintly ultimate) Warrior, who was hounding Hulk Hogan upon his 1998 return to the spotlight. The group consisted of two members:

Warrior and a sexually spellbound Disciple (Ed Leslie/Brutus Beefcake), who was often seen in some random submissive position while Warrior spoke. WWF **Raw** won a lot in this time frame.

nWo Elite
Forged together by the "Fingerpoke of Doom," which made WCW look like a stuck-in-the-mud, idealess self-parody, Hollywood Hogan reigned again as WCW champion and fearless leader after a fake retirement, aligning with Nash, Hall, Luger, Scott Steiner, and everyone vaguely interesting from the Wolfpac and Hollywood, to the delight of few.

nWo Black and White
Whomever wasn't absorbed into Elite was left to kick around in this fearsome squadron. Stevie Ray would be the odor-eater-wielding kingpin of such luminaries as Vincent, Brian Adams, Scott Norton, and Horace Hogan. The group had no purpose, except to provide fodder for a series of hilarious satires on the old ScoopThis.com website.

nWo 2000
Vince Russo was now in charge of a dying WCW, and decided to make the nWo his centerpiece heel group, since the Corporation had worked in WWF. That's a joke, by the way. Bret Hart turned heel to lead the charge of the Outsiders, Steiner, and Jeff Jarrett. The idea was that Goldberg would be the new Stone Cold, and combat them, but injuries ruined everything.

nWo, WWE version
After Vince McMahon had botched the WCW/ECW invasion, he needed another popular concept to ruin. In early 2002, McMahon rehired Hogan, Hall, and Nash to run a hostile takeover of his increasingly stale WWF shows. By this point, the cool factor was gone, as evidenced by the t-shirts for the guerrilla warriors bearing a highly visible WWF logo.

The following week, the ratings battle was even closer, with *Nitro* doing a 4.61 to *Raw*'s 4.43. Head to head, both shows did an 8.99

combined rating, a brand-new record. And the segment in which Austin, as WWF champion, came out on *Raw* to confront Vince McMahon did a 5.6, another new record. In the same quarter, *Nitro* did a 3.9. In fact, of all the quarters, *Raw* won four, *Nitro* won three, and one was basically a tie. Bischoff was sweating.

And then, the next week, everything hit the fan.

For the first time since May 27, 1996, *Raw* beat *Nitro* in the head-to-head ratings battle, ending an epic eighty-three-week winning streak. *Raw*, built for two hours around a supposed McMahon versus Austin singles match that never ended up taking place, drew a 4.63 to *Nitro*'s 4.34. The final few minutes also did a 6.0 quarter, the highest in history for *Raw*.

Bischoff went nuclear.

Frustrated beyond belief, he was looking to take his anger out on someone, and that someone wound up being Ric Flair, the man fans identified with WCW more than any other. Flair, who hadn't been used on TV for months, missed the *Thunder* event on April 9 in which he was supposed to re-form the Four Horsemen. He claimed that he'd given the company plenty of advance notice that he was going to attend his son Reid's AAU freestyle wrestling championships at the Pontiac Silverdome that same day. Unfortunately, advance notice was useless in WCW because the shows were often booked literally at the last minute (the term "literally" is not being used facetiously—there were times when the shows were still being written *while they were on the air live*). Flair never knew he was supposed to be at *Thunder* until three days before the show, at which point he wasn't about to change his plans.

LESSON NOT LEARNED: Despite having a full-blown writing staff headed by no less than Stephanie McMahon-Levesque, there have been times recently where **Raw** was also being written as the show was on the air. Actually, "written" is not correct; the show is generally written several days in advance and then given to Vince McMahon to give it final approval. Often, approval is not given, and rewrites are ordered. And then rewrites of the rewrites are ordered. And **then** rewrites of those rewrites are ordered.

Is it any wonder the average tenure of a new WWE writer is about six weeks?

Bischoff came completely unglued, verbally tearing Flair apart in a backstage meeting at *Nitro* on April 13 (which, ironically, had been deemed Ric Flair Day by the city of Minneapolis), then filed a $2 million lawsuit against him for "playing havoc with the script of the wildly popular productions" and "disrupting WCW's ability to introduce its planned storyline, causing significant loss of time, money, and effort by WCW."

On the bright side, Reid won first place in his division.

The big pay-per-view of the month was *Spring Stampede*, which was one of those rare cards that looked horrific on paper, but ended up being, perhaps because expectations were so low, pretty dang good. Both Raven versus Dallas Page for the U.S. title and Chavo Guerrero Jr. versus Ultimo Dragon were excellent. The main event saw Sting lose the WCW title to Randy Savage, who became the very epitome of a "transitional champion" when he dropped the belt to Hogan the following evening on *Nitro*. Savage was not the only transitional champion, as Raven, who won the U.S. title from Page in their match, immediately dropped the belt the following night to Goldberg, who was starting to catch fire not only as a ratings draw, but as a merchandise seller.

In many ways, Goldberg was WCW's greatest ace in the hole and, in hindsight, was their last best chance at salvaging the company. His segments on *Nitro* were becoming the most highly rated, and his merchandise sales were beginning to skyrocket as well. It appeared that they truly had a fresh, hot commodity that fans were willing to pay to see.

In their efforts to push Goldberg to the moon, however, WCW made some critical mistakes. Ever since the announcers had mentioned that he was 60-0, fans with way too much spare time had begun to keep track of his winning streak. These fans were so hardcore that they even kept track of his untelevised house show wins. It was fun to see fans so interested in a character, especially one that WCW had created from the ground up. Of course, since WCW created it, they also had to kill it. One week, announcer Schiavone's number didn't jive with the number the hardcores had. Then, the next week, it was even farther off. As it turned out, in a lame effort to make his streak appear more meaningful, the company had started to add imaginary numbers to the total. This had the exact opposite of its intended effect, as once fans figured out that the streak number had become fiction, all those signs fans had been bringing to the arenas trumpeting Goldberg's record disappeared. Worse yet, WCW was so happy to hear fans chanting Goldberg's name that they decided to pipe in some fake "GOLDBERG!" chants to make it seem like the fans were making even more noise. For whatever reason, though, the *Nitro* TV directors apparently weren't clued in to this, because soon shots began to appear of the crowd sitting there with their mouths closed amidst loud "GOLDBERG!" chants. Again, once fans figured out the chants were being piped in, they stopped chanting so much.

Nitro the following week was in Norfolk, Virginia, at the Scope, just a half hour away from *Raw*, which was running in Hampton. Unfortunately, *Nitro* was bumped to a horrible post-midnight slot, so *Raw* not only broke another ratings record, but broke it by a full point (5.71) to become the most-watched wrestling show in the history of cable. The most memorable part of the show was a series of DX vignettes where they actually went to the Scope before *Nitro* started and "invaded." Their invasion, which should have been seen as an omen of sorts for the future WCW invasion of the WWF, consisted of them asking fans if they thought WCW sucked and banging on the outside doors trying to get in. There was one great line where Waltman screamed that he wanted Bischoff to come out and tell him to his face why he was fired. It was the kind of renegade, in-your-face incident that most fans found hilarious. Plus, it was "real," and if fans believed one thing about the fake business of pro wrestling, it was that WWF and WCW really hated each other.

There was no traditional burial of Ric Flair this week, because Flair was still being sued for $2 million for his fatherly behavior weeks earlier. There were many who thought this whole thing was a work despite the various signs pointing to it being a stark reality (including settlement talks, which don't happen in fake lawsuits). Fans on the internet were outraged. WCW's website actually took advantage of this by posting the following ad in late May: "Ric Flair merchandise now on sale in the Pro Shop!! GET IT BEFORE IT RUNS OUT! The WCW Pro Shop now features selected Ric Flair merchandise at a reduced price!! Internet Fans, don't read anything into this!"

But they did. There were fans who tried to organize *Nitro* boycotts, which never worked; fans who tried to start letter-writing campaigns, which never worked; and fans who voted for Flair online in the *People Magazine*'s Fifty Most Beautiful People in the World poll. Shockingly, that one actually *did* work, and Flair came in second only to Hank the Angry Drunken Dwarf from Howard Stern with 17,145 votes. What was more impressive was that Hank was actually among the available choices while Flair was a write-in candidate.

WCW had a problem at the Augusta, Georgia, house show on April 30. The main event was scheduled to be Flair versus Hennig, but with Flair out indefinitely and Hennig, well, just not there, fans were very upset. So upset, in fact, that hundreds of them demanded refunds. After thinking over several scenarios, the decision was made to do a last-minute change and have Chris Benoit beat Booker T to win the TV title. It worked; the fans were overjoyed. So the decision was made to do it again the next night. And then again, and again, and again. The belt changed hands four times in four days at the house shows, going from Booker to Benoit to Booker to Benoit to Booker again.

Every night, the fans went crazy as they watched something special happen right there in their hometown. But then on Monday, when Booker T showed up to lose the belt to Fit Finley on TV, the announcers never mentioned anything about the house show title changes. They just ignored them, and to all the casual fans watching around the nation, it was as though nothing had ever happened. It also sent a very strong message to all those previously overjoyed fans in Norfolk, Greenville, North Charleston, and Savannah: you don't count, and if anything happens in your little hick town, it won't be acknowledged on TV because it's not important. If they hadn't already done enough to kill business in those areas, this was another nail in the coffin.

May was the beginning of WCW's House Show Tour From Hell. They booked thirty-one—yes, THIRTY-ONE—house shows during the month. Because the company was still on fire and the previously mentioned mistakes had not caught up with them yet, this was possible. To make life easier for everyone, they split the crew in half so nobody would have to work every single show. Guys still weren't happy, though, as the once very easy road schedule of WCW was now a complete nightmare.

But Bischoff wasn't really concerned about any of these small issues; he was still too obsessed with conquering the WWF in the weekly ratings war. By this point, word of Bischoff's alleged increasing mental instability had reached Vince McMahon, who decided to have some fun by doing everything in his power to drive Eric completely over the edge. He had his hooligan group DX "invade" the Norfolk Scope where *Nitro* was being presented. Of course, the WWF guys couldn't get into the arena, so the invasion merely consisted of them talking to fans and telling WCW to "suck it." A week or so later, the WWF sent DX and a film crew to Smyrna, Georgia, for another "invasion," this time of WCW headquarters. Unfortunately, WCW headquarters were private property, so Nick Lambros called the cops and actually claimed that "twenty-five guys" were "attacking" their offices. The cops showed up and told DX to hit the bricks. Their next stop was CNN Center, where they claimed they wanted to interview Ted Turner. The problem here was that the camera crew was now terrified and wouldn't film anything except them standing around in the lobby doing crotch chops and chatting with fans. This was even lamer than the previous invasion, but, once again, fans wanted reality, and that's what they were getting.

That evening on *Nitro*, Bischoff hit the ring to reveal his master plan for revenge. It was ingenious in that mad-scientist-losing-his-mind sort of way. He entered the ring literally shaking with rage and recited a speech that he'd given many times in the past, almost word-for-word, to folks backstage:

> Vince McMahon, this is for you. I'm coming to your backyard this Sunday. That's right, Worcester, Massachusetts. Got a little PPV thing going on, and I got a hell of an idea, just a hell of an idea. You want me? I'm going to be in your backyard. Consider this an open invitation, Vince McMahon. You show up at *Slamboree*, it'll be you and me in the ring. How about it, Vinny? But I want to warn you people right now. If you think Vince McMahon has got the guts to show up, don't buy this PPV, because I guarantee you he's not man enough to step into the ring with me. But I'll be there, Vinny Mac. I'll be waiting for you. And I'm going to knock you out. See you there!

The fans in attendance, understanding the reality of the challenge, cheered Eric as a babyface. The WWF's response on *Raw* two hours later was to have announcers Jim Ross and Jim Cornette cry about it and to have Waltman come out and tell Eric to suck it. A few days later on WWF. com, Vince issued a statement calling Eric's move a cheap ploy to increase PPV buys. "Therefore," he wrote, "I will not appear at Turner's next PPV as invited. However, if Mr. Bischoff is hell bent on fighting me, then such a fight can be arranged at any time, in any parking lot in the country; void of television cameras, photographers, and public announcement."

Eric wasn't finished. That Thursday on *Thunder*, he cut not one, but *two* promos challenging Vince. He also read a real-life legal letter that Vince's attorney, the famed and terrifying Jerry McDevitt, had sent to him, threatening him for what it claimed was a cheap bait and switch to try to get fans to order the PPV. In a true story, McDevitt claimed that when Bischoff told the fans that the match wasn't going to take place he was actually insinuating that it was, because in wrestling, when a person says something isn't going to happen, it's usually a sign that it is. Sadly, this never went to court—it would have been very interesting to see a judge and jury's reaction to that statement. They also aired a Bischoff training video on *Thunder*, which was comical because he was really training quite hard for an imaginary fight.

And imaginary it was. To seemingly everyone save for Bischoff and Hogan. Bischoff noted in his autobiography, *Controversy Creates Cash*, that Hogan had convinced him that Vince would definitely be there "to kick your ass." "I fully expected Vince to show up," Eric wrote. "We had security waiting at all the exits. I was fully prepared to get my ass kicked. I didn't think I would—my kickboxing skills were still there, and I thought I could work the ring."

Yes, this is what the man in charge of WCW was doing at the time: honing his martial arts skills for a match that was never, ever going to take place.

Bischoff came to the ring at *Slamboree* and had Michael Buffer introduce Vince. Of course, there was no Vince. So Bischoff had the referee count the imaginary Vince out and award him the match. The deal had more than run its course, so it came off as incredibly stupid.

The only other major angle of note at *Slamboree* saw Hall turn on Nash and cost them the tag titles to Sting and Giant. Neither wanted to do the turn, but Eric insisted, so they half-heartedly went along with it. It ended up being the usual WCW brilliance as Hall immediately left to attend rehab for six weeks (which was known well in advance, so they could have changed booking plans), and then Nash never did one interview acknowledging the situation.

Ric Flair, meanwhile, had gotten himself into great shape sitting at home doing nothing and wanted to work somewhere. However, because of his treatment, that somewhere was not WCW. He filed a countersuit that he hoped would get him out of his deal and allow him to go back to the WWF for a top heel run against Austin. Bischoff, aware of this, made it known that if he wanted to come back, he'd drop the lawsuit and forget the whole thing ever happened. Flair's attorney said they could talk about it, but he had a list of contract restructuring demands a mile long. So the man who just months earlier was the biggest ratings draw in either company remained on the sidelines instead of helping WCW.

LESSON NOT LEARNED: You'd think that following the disaster that was the entire Eric Bischoff–Vince McMahon non-match, the days of publicly making challenges that would never be accepted would be over. Think again. In 2006, following yet another D-Generation X reunion of Shawn Michaels and Triple H, Road Dogg Jesse James and Billy Gunn decided to challenge their old partners. Sadly for the latter duo, they now competed in TNA Wrestling, and had changed their name to the Voodoo Kin Mafia, which may have been the stupidest name for a tag team ever. But wait! They did so because abbreviated it became VKM . . . the same initials as Vincent Kennedy McMahon! How clever! For weeks, the pair came out on national television, badmouthing "Michael Hickenbottom" and "Paul Levesque" (Shawn and Hunter's real names, so you knew it was a shoot!), offering to fight them anytime, anywhere. They even went to WWE house shows attempting to get attention. Their challenges, of course, were completely ignored. In an effort to elicit some kind of reaction, they offered $1 million to their WWE foes for the fight. Again, ignored. They told Shawn to fight them at the Alamo (really) and showed up there (REALLY!). Ignored. Finally, the TNA guys just claimed victory. During said promo, in which they noted how much they hated their WWE rivals and how Shawn and Hunter were "cowards," they got serious and told

Paul (Hunter) they legitimately hoped his torn quadriceps would get better soon.

You know, because all that other stuff was fake.

Amazingly, all these words and actions did not keep both men from returning to WWE in 2013 and even getting a run with the Tag Team title. Wrestling, everyone. Wrestling.

Just weeks after the whole childish "Vince McMahon versus Eric Bischoff" program took place, WCW took their complaints a step further by filing an unfair business practices countersuit against the WWF, a suit almost identical to the one the WWF had filed against them in 1996 after Hall and Nash jumped ship. The suit, like that of the WWF, was mostly frivolous, claiming that Vince and his crew had done mean things like saying all their wrestlers were old (and this was hilarious, because on several occasions when announcer Jim Ross made such claims, elderly men like Gerald Brisco, Pat Patterson, and Vince himself were involved in matches as he spoke). They did have one good point, however: that the WWF had falsely claimed on several occasions that WCW was giving away free tickets, when in reality the shows in question were legitimately sold out. When DX invaded the Scope, the WWF even went so far as to digitally insert a graphic on the marquee claiming that tickets to the show were still available (yes, they went to these absurd lengths for a corny skit). "In the professional wrestling business," the suit read, "the giving away of free tickets to an event on the day of the show is a response to a failure to sell out the venue, and it reflects badly on a promotion, suggesting that an insufficient number of fans were willing to pay to see the show." Coincidentally, on *Nitro* that evening, Schiavone claimed the *Raw* show in Hampton was not sold out when, in fact, it was.

At the time of the latest WCW-WWF lawsuit, the company found itself being sued by one of its workers as well. In June, prelim wrestler Bobby Walker filed a lawsuit against the company claiming racial discrimination, saying WCW told him point blank that he was being hired as a token black man and that he always had to lose. Never mind the fact that there were ten times the number of white guys who were asked to always lose by WCW. Another one of his points was that he made a lot less than many of the white performers, including—he actually said this—Ric Flair. The suit was eventually thrown out. As absurd as this whole thing sounds on the surface, another suit filed by Sonny Onoo dragged on for five years, and numerous minority wrestlers jumped on the bandwagon. When Onoo's suit was finally settled by Time Warner (long after WCW had ceased to exist), it was said that the guys filing suit "made out like bandits."

In the midst of all the lawsuits and childish behavior, WCW signed three big names: Dennis Rodman and Karl Malone would help generate mainstream interest, and the artist formerly known as the Ultimate Warrior would help to launch them into another universe. Rodman was a friend of Hogan's, and Dallas Page was in tight with Karl Malone. The idea was to bring them in for a match at the *Bash at the Beach* PPV in July in an attempt to generate mainstream publicity—hopefully similar to what Mike Tyson's appearance at *WrestleMania* had done for the WWF. It worked better than anyone had likely imagined. Rodman first appeared on the June 8 *Nitro* after skipping out on a Chicago Bulls practice session without bothering to tell anyone, for which he was subsequently fined $10,000. Keeping with his bad-boy persona, he teamed up with Hogan as Rodzilla to put the boots to Page, setting up Page and Malone versus Hogan and Rodman for the PPV. The angle got tons of publicity nationwide, as many of the major sports shows and evening newscasts aired footage of the incident.

More Hogan fun was on display on June 14 at the *Great American Bash* pay-per-view. He teamed with Bret Hart to beat Roddy Piper and Randy Savage in a horrible match, which led immediately to an equally horrible match where Piper—wrestling with two fake hips—beat Savage with a figure four. The main event saw Sting beat Giant in a match that was memorable mostly because Giant came out smoking a ciga-rette to play off an interview Sting did the week before where he yelled at Giant for smoking too much. None of this could even approach the worst match on the show, however, which saw the incredible Juventud Guerrera, as part of the "big push" he was promised after agreeing to drop his mask, beat Ron Reis. Juvie, at the time, was about 5'5" and 160 pounds, and Reis was a legit 7'2", almost 400 pounds, and, best of all, could not wrestle to save his life. Juvie's superhero babyface performance consisted of him being destroyed forever, then getting the win with a messed-up huracanrana after Van Hammer clonked Reis with a chair. Juvie probably wanted his mask back more than ever at this point, just to hide his shame. By far the lowest moment of the day, however, actually took place backstage when someone with inside knowledge of the Hart family called Bischoff and told him to tell Bret that his father Stu had passed away. As it turned out, it was a hoax, but everyone was greatly disturbed by it and nobody ever found out who made the call.

The *Bash* show was actually not even a focal point for Eric, as his eyes were on the big *Nitro* coming up at the Georgia Dome in Atlanta. By early June they'd sold over 20,000 tickets and were closing in on a $1 million gate. As the date drew nearer, Hogan the wily veteran came up with a plan. Aware that all the Turner bigwigs would be at the show, he offered to take Goldberg on in a non-title, non-televised match in which Goldberg would get the win and send the folks home happy. All the com-pany execs, seeing the huge house, would obviously assume that Hogan drew it, and his standing as WCW's top dog would be cemented.

As the show approached, however, the decision was made to change the Hogan-Goldberg match to a televised title match. This was due almost entirely to the fact that *Nitro* had been losing the ratings war, and Bischoff was obsessed with beating McMahon, even if only for one week. With Hogan taking on Goldberg, there was absolutely no way he could lose the night.

Make no mistake about it: July 6 should have been a pivotal day in wrestling history. It was on that day that Bill Goldberg—less than one year into his professional career—beat Hulk Hogan clean in the middle of the ring to win the WCW World Heavyweight championship. Internally, the sense was that this was the beginning of a new era for the company, and that Goldberg could be the answer to Steve Austin as a super draw. The ovation he received when he won the belt was among the loudest anyone had ever heard. The TV rating spoke volumes as well, as the quarter-hour for the title change set a cable wrestling record: a 6.91 with 5,054,000 homes tuning in, helping *Nitro* win the night 4.93 to 4.0. And Bischoff no doubt smiled widely on Tuesday morning when the ratings came in.

But something was lost in that ratings win: money, and lots of it. The first-ever Goldberg-Hogan match, which could have drawn millions of dollars on pay-per-view, was aired free on *Nitro* instead, owing almost entirely to the fact that *Raw* had kicked their ass the week before. Instead of showing patience, as he had with the Sting-Hogan bout, Bischoff allowed very lucrative business to be pushed aside because he wanted to brag that *Nitro* had won a week in a ratings war that he cared about more than any of the fans watching at home did. The title change, also a last-minute decision, effectively put the kibosh on several storylines that Hogan had been involved in that could have led to lucrative matches with Bret Hart and Kevin Nash.

There was actually worse news than that, too. WCW drew 41,412 fans—the biggest crowd in its history—to the Georgia Dome to see the match. At the time, it was the fourth-largest crowd ever to watch a wrestling show in the U.S. You'd think that WCW would brag about this, and likely even add to the figure, as it had always been common practice in the business to slightly exaggerate attendance numbers. Instead, however, they inexplicably *subtracted* 1,500 fans, announcing 39,919. Yes, WCW became the first promotion in wrestling history to claim a less impressive number than what they actually drew. It gets even worse than that. When they first announced Hogan versus Goldberg locally, they only sold about 2,000 extra tickets. Realistically, the company was still hot enough at this point that very few, if any, of the wrestlers could actually be considered ticket-sellers. Instead, the name "WCW" itself sold tickets, usually on the very first day, before a card was ever announced. The mainstream wasn't aware of this, however, so Hogan decided to manipulate it so that it would appear that he did, indeed, sell tickets pretty much on his own. Therefore, he suggested the idea of doing the match live on TV and switching the title. After all, if the match was televised, it would look like he drew the house, whereas if it wasn't, someone else would get credit for the new company record. And that would be completely unacceptable.

LESSON NOT LEARNED: The sheer amount of money WCW lost in rushing Goldberg-Hogan to free television cannot be understated, but it hasn't stopped anyone from hotshotting various angles and matches in an effort to pop what is essentially a worthless one-week rating. While it had nowhere near the ramifications of the Goldberg title win, the unmasking of Kane in 2003 comes to mind as another perfect example of something that could have been built up for months for a pay-per-view big money match. In Mexico, matches in which a competitor is forced to show his face upon being defeated have drawn money for decades. Of course, these are generally done with a proper build. Instead, one week on **Raw**, it was casually announced that Kane would be battling Triple H for the title. If he lost, he'd lose his mask. He lost. With no real build, the show didn't even gain viewers, doing the exact same rating as it had the prior week. And then he just put the mask back on years later, again with no real explanation. Oops.

Hogan had one major demand: that when "the time was right" to beat Goldberg, he would be the guy to do it. Because he agreed to drop the belt with a clean pinfall loss in the first place, there weren't any problems with this scenario. He also, as usual, had a few diabolical tricks up his sleeve, to be revealed over the next several months.

At the time the Goldberg-Hogan *Nitro* went down, no one really examined Hogan's motives or the long-term impact the title bout would have on the company. Instead, everyone was looking ahead to *Bash at the Beach 1998*, in which Hogan and Rodman beat Page and Malone after E. Harrison Leslie interfered. The show was a shining example of the good and the bad that go along with using celebrities. On the bright side, the match got WCW a ton of mainstream publicity, with everyone from *Sports Illustrated* to *USA Today* sending reporters to cover it. Plus, Rodman and Malone proved to be successful draws, as the show did the best WCW buy rate since *Starrcade*—an estimated 1.5 for almost a $7 million gross. For promoters who only look at the bottom line, that number alone was enough to convince them that they'd made a great decision.

That's where the good news ends, however. Malone was very professional, and for a guy in his very first pro-wrestling match ever, he was more than acceptable. Rodman, on the other hand, showed up in the infamous "no condition to perform." You could argue that at least he showed up, because he'd blown off basketball practice to attend *Nitro*, and blowing off a wrestling show to attend, well, a party or something probably wouldn't have shocked anyone. In fact, he had disappeared for several hours the day of the show, and when he showed up in whatever condition he was in, the company was actually thrilled because they thought he wasn't going to be there at all. He got in the ring and was beyond horrible, screwing up moves left and right and actually falling down on several occasions. Then he tagged out, stood on the apron, and put his head on the turnbuckle, seemingly falling asleep. Luckily, that was the best role for him. Hogan had also demanded *forty-five minutes* for the match—approximately forty-four minutes longer than any of the four, with the exception of Page, could realistically have wrestled and remained entertaining. Everyone, from the fans to the sports reporters who may or may not have ever watched a full wrestling show in their lives, knew it was an in-ring disaster. It should probably also be noted that despite no-showing the last *Nitro* before the PPV, showing up in a questionable state of mind, and doing nearly nothing in the match, Rodman still later sued the company for $550,000, claiming they defrauded him in contract negotiations.

In light of all the publicity Rodman had been generating, WCW started to go overboard with celebrities, adding Kevin Greene (actually a pretty decent wrestler given his level of experience) to the semi-main event. The idea was to tag him with Goldberg to face Hennig and Giant. There was no logical reason for doing this, other than to waste a bunch of money on a guy who wasn't going to add one single buy to the show. Of course, this would be neither the first nor the last time *that* happened.

There was a backstory to the Hennig versus Goldberg match as well. A few weeks earlier, an idea was batted around where Hennig would attack Konnan while he was having a match with Goldberg, and as a result Goldberg would be declared the loser via DQ. Of course, this would have brought the win streak to an end. By the grace of God, Bischoff axed that one, much to Hennig's chagrin. Looking back, it's frankly amazing that WCW didn't screw up the Goldberg push a lot earlier than they did.

And Flair? Still on the sidelines, with WCW unwilling to bring him back to help in the war. Despite this, Flair suddenly found himself ranked number one in the online *Time* Magazine Person of the Century poll, ahead of Adolph Hitler and Jesus Christ, among others.

On July 17, the company came to terms with their next huge mainstream superstar, Jay Leno of the *Tonight Show*. Yes, *that* Jay Leno. If that wasn't sufficiently absurd, Bischoff spent an estimated $75,000 to construct a mock *Tonight Show* set so he could act as host of his own "talk show" during *Nitro* and bury Leno. The first time they did this segment, it was so successful that it caused thousands of viewers to immediately switch channels to *Raw*. Eric, perhaps noting that Rodman and Malone meant nothing for TV ratings but did huge PPV numbers regardless, decided to keep doing the segments despite their enormous turn-off factor. This resulted in a string of some of the worst first hours of *Nitro* in history. The original plan was to bring Leno, a huge motorcycle fan, in for a match at the annual *Road Wild* biker rally pay-per-view in Sturgis. So not only were they bringing in a non-athlete to compete in a worked athletic event, but they were also spending all that money to bring him in for a free show, meaning they wouldn't be making hundreds of thousands of dollars at the gate to help offset the cost of bringing Leno in. Obviously, they were hoping that all the free *Tonight Show* publicity would result in thousands of new viewers buying the PPV.

In July, the one-year anniversary of Bill Goldberg's first-ever win, the one that launched the famous streak and catapulted him to stardom, took place on **Nitro**. To commemorate the occasion, Goldberg—the company's World champion, remember—never once appeared on the show. The same show also featured the final match for several years of Ultimo Dragon, who after a botched operation by a WCW-appointed surgeon was forced into retirement due to serious nerve damage in his left arm. He destroyed one of his students, Tokyo Magnum, in a match that was given "a trillion stars" by **Figure Four Weekly** and long considered the greatest squash match of all time. In second place, by the way, was a match a year later featuring Chris Benoit and David Flair. Dragon went on to form his own training school and cult wrestling promotion in Japan, Toryumon, and over the next few years he turned out some of the most exciting wrestlers the country had ever seen.

Both shows set a new ratings record the following week, with *Raw* doing a 4.84 and *Nitro* doing a 4.72 for a combined 9.58 rating in 7,060,000 homes, meaning that approximately 10.5 million fans were watching wrestling at some point during that evening. This was the only good news for WCW, as Schiavone announced that their show, which actually drew almost 20,000 fans to the AlamoDome, had drawn only 13,000. Meanwhile, the *Raw* show, which drew 12,000, was billed as

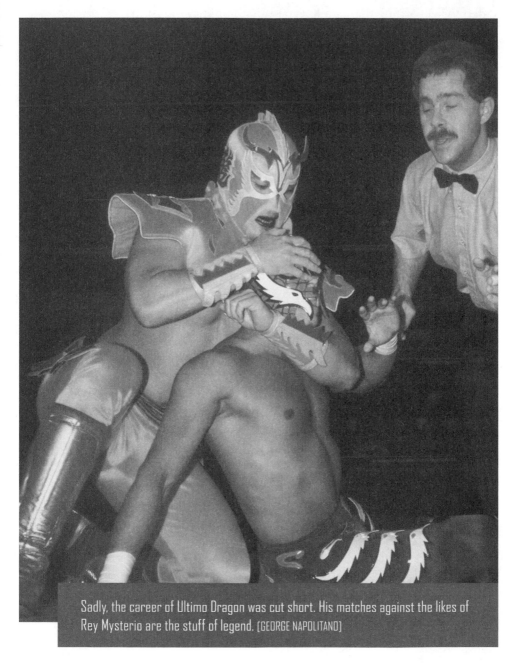

Sadly, the career of Ultimo Dragon was cut short. His matches against the likes of Rey Mysterio are the stuff of legend. [GEORGE NAPOLITANO]

having drawn 18,000 by Jim Ross, so everyone figured the WWF had the better night. To make matters worse, those who watched *Nitro* witnessed one of the most atrocious shows in its history, a show in which, over the course of three hours, exactly nineteen minutes were devoted to actual in-ring pro wrestling. In fact, there was one match in the entire first hour, which ran less than two minutes. Meanwhile, Bischoff did another *Tonight Show* segment that went almost twenty. At the top of the hour, starting the head-to-head battle with *Raw*, WCW presented a true mat classic, Scott Norton versus Jim Neidhart, which went sixteen seconds. No, that's not a typo—sixteen *seconds*. Come to think of it, though, it was superior to those two going sixteen minutes. They replayed the entire horrible Page and Malone versus Hogan and Rodman match from the PPV, essentially telling everyone who bought it that they were stupid for doing so and had wasted their thirty bucks. At least the match got a good rating. Hogan also cut an amazing promo where he threatened to "ride DDP's butt," then "ride him hard and hang him up wet." Hall beat Sting. The nWo came down and destroyed Sting outside the ring. Instead of DQ'ing Hall for the interference, the ref counted Sting out as he was being pounded on. The highlight of the show, sadly, was a tasteless angle with Steiner and Bagwell. Steiner pushed his buddy through the curtain in his wheelchair, then stopped on the ramp to flex. As he turned his back, the wheelchair rolled down the ramp and crashed into the ring. The look on Bagwell's face was priceless. Of course, he got right up and started flexing for the fans. The main event was Page beating Hogan via DQ when–YES!–the nWo ran in. Still, Bischoff argued, the bout served its purpose by pushing the *Road Wild* PPV.

In legal news, Scott Hall was arrested for allegedly getting intoxicated and groping a fifty-six-year-old woman outside a hotel in Baton Rouge, Louisiana. Time for a pop quiz. WCW was so outraged by Hall's behavior that they:

    (A) suspended him without pay;

(B) suspended him with pay;

(C) turned the entire thing into a long-running angle in which Hall would come out on TV "pretending" to be drunk, stumble around in the ring, crash cars (in real life, he crashed five that year), and throw up on people.

Hopefully, after reading this far, you won't be shocked to learn that the answer was C.

The build toward *Road Wild* continued on the July 29 *Tonight Show* when, during a skit with a fake Hulk Hogan, the real Hogan and Bischoff showed up and "took over the broadcast" for a minute or so. Leno finally returned with security and, coincidentally, Dallas Page, who helped run off the bad guys. Page then asked Leno to team with him to take them on at the PPV, and Leno said OK. None of this hype ended up meaning a thing for WCW's ratings yet, but on the bright side, Leno was totally kicking David Letterman's ass.

Even though the two non-wrestlers in the match, Leno and Bischoff, were hardly in the same universe athletically as Malone and Rodman, the pay-per-view match was significantly better than anyone had any right to expect. The main reason was because Hogan did not ask for forty-five minutes this time, plus he and Page figured out that the best course of action was to have the non-wrestlers do almost nothing. Sadly, "almost nothing" did not mean "absolutely nothing," and in a moment that is best forgotten, Hogan and Leno squared off with Leno actually getting the best of it. Leno locked an armlock on the Hulkster that had old-timers claiming the business as they knew it was dead forever. On the plus (?) side, there were probably five matches on the show worse than this one, though that's partly because those five matches were among the worst five of the entire year from any company worldwide. Steve "Mongo" McMichael versus Brian Adams in particular almost set new standards.

One could have argued that at *Bash at the Beach*, it was OK for the

World champion to work second-to-last, because the semi-main was a huge media event. However, Goldberg ended up working second-to-last on this show as well in a nine-man battle royal that absolutely nobody cared about. While logic would suggest that Goldberg would be eliminated by a new challenger for his belt, he not only won, but won decisively, last eliminating Giant in dominating fashion with a spear and jackhammer. There he was, the WCW World Heavyweight champion, standing there with no challengers, no future programs, and playing second fiddle to—that's right!—Hulk Hogan.

The celebrity magic was gone as the show only did in the 1.0 range, just slightly higher than what most pay-per-views from both companies had been doing. You would think that perhaps WCW would have learned a lesson from this, that A-list celebrities are only valuable when used sparingly. You would be wrong.

And there was another lesson that should have been learned, but wasn't. WCW didn't have a full card for this pay-per-view until six days prior to the show. Normally, cards were announced far in advance so there would be several weeks of television that could be used to promote them. Perhaps the mindset was that the company was so hot that they didn't need to announce anything other than a main event involving Hogan. It became a trend; the card wouldn't be announced until a week before the PPV, and the buyrate would be low. This continued for months and months and nobody internally seemed to put two and two together.

The stupidity wasn't taking its toll on business yet, however. For July, the company grossed $4.3 million over nineteen house shows, which made it the most successful month for any American wrestling company in history. Part of the reason that house shows were still doing so well was because many of the big stars were still working on them, including Goldberg, and WCW was doing their best to try to make the fans who bought tickets happy. In fact, when it was discovered that Bill wasn't going to make it on time to compete at the August 16 show in Providence, Rhode Island, WCW did something that was revolutionary—they told the fans that the show was free. That's right, they blew off a $146,000 gate, saying fans could either get a refund after the show or save their ticket to use the next time WCW came to town.

On August 17 in Hartford, Connecticut, right in the middle of WWF country, former WWF champion the Ultimate Warrior made his WCW debut, pretty much out of nowhere. Actually, literally out of nowhere: his gimmick was that he could appear and disappear at will in a cloud of smoke. Before we continue, we need to note that none of the following is being made up. This all actually happened, presumably because someone theorized that it would make fans buy tickets and PPVs.

Prior to his arrival, WCW couldn't hype up Warrior's return like they probably wanted to because they were tied up in a legal battle over what they could call him. It was pretty clear that "Ultimate Warrior" was out of the question, since the WWF had that one trademarked (and you should have seen Eric's face when, on the August 24 *Nitro*, Hogan accidentally said "Ultimate Warrior"). Just plain old "Warrior" seemed to be OK, though, mostly because that's what Jim Hellwig, the man who played the Warrior character, had legally changed his name to. The WWF didn't even want him to wear his face paint, but he claimed he'd worn it when he worked in Texas as the Dingo Warrior at the start of his career.

At the Hartford show, he was scheduled to talk for six minutes, but he ended up rambling on in a pretty much incomprehensible manner for almost twenty, and the entire show had to be rearranged live as a result (not that this was anything new for *Nitro*). It should be noted that the aforementioned ramble was by far the best interview of his entire career. The gist of his speech was that he was back, and he wanted to face Hogan again in an epic rematch from their first battle at *WrestleMania VI* in 1990. In a comical moment, Warrior said that beating Hogan was no big deal, which kind of made one wonder why he would want to have a rematch with the Hulk. The interview was, as expected, a huge ratings draw: nearly seven million fans lost eighteen minutes of their lives watching it.

Warrior allegedly signed a $1 million deal to work roughly three shows per month, which of course had the locker room in an uproar as nearly everyone else was making a hell of a lot less to work a hell of a lot more. And everyone but Eric Bischoff seemed able to predict exactly what the future held: Warrior would have a shelf life of about, oh, five or six weeks, and then it would be all downhill from there. These people were sadly mistaken. His WCW shelf life was actually about three weeks.

Nitro that evening also featured one of those only-in-WCW angles where you had to have a translator to make heads-or-tails of it. Eddie Guerrero came out and ranted and raved about Bischoff, then finished by pouring a cup of coffee on himself and saying he was saving Eric the trouble. You see, months earlier Eric had gotten really mad backstage and thrown a cup of coffee against the wall by Eddie's head. What this had to do with wrestling and how anyone in the audience was supposed to know what he was talking about, was never determined. A few months later, Eddie formed a stable of disgruntled Mexicans called the Latino World Order, or the LWO for short. Presumably, this was supposed to be his way of getting revenge on Eric for throwing coffee at him. Since the Mexicans had always been treated as total losers on TV, fans hated it with a passion, booing loudly even as Guerrero ran down Bischoff and Hogan in promos. Many in the WCW hierarchy, however, honestly felt that it was a stroke of genius. This was the same company that had made over a million dollars in one week.

The week of August 24 was the stuff of legend. The two shows set a new combined ratings record: 9.72 in 7,169,000 homes. Meanwhile, on ABC, the debut of **Monday Night Football**, featuring a Green Bay Packers versus Denver Broncos preseason Superbowl rematch, did a 9.5. Realistically, because network TV is in more homes than cable, football actually beat wrestling 9.3 million homes to 7.2 million. However, it soon became "common knowledge" (read: "urban legend") that pro wrestling was so hot that it was regularly beating **Monday Night Football** in the ratings. Even at its peak, this was never really the case.

But wrestling was legitimately hotter than a lot of other sporting acts and concerts, as evidenced by folks who tried to sell tickets to these events in classified ads over the summer. In the San Antonio market, for example, 75 percent of fans used **Nitro** or **Raw** in their bold headlines. "WCW **NITRO**," the ads would begin, and then underneath it would read: "Yes, Elton John."

The TV trend continued for the umpteenth week: *Raw* was great and *Nitro* was horrible. On August 24, for example, the main event saw Goldberg and Nash beat Hogan and Giant when Goldberg speared and pinned Curt Hennig, who wasn't even in the match. Also on the show, Chris Jericho went to a "ten-minute draw" with Hennig in six minutes, and then three nights later on *Thunder,* he beat Alex Wright in twelve minutes of a match with a ten-minute time limit. Sadly, nobody complaining about *Nitro*'s quality could even fathom at the time that the following year it would get significantly worse.

Short-term, Warrior was generating numbers. And it was beginning to look like another major ratings draw was coming back too, as Ric Flair, after being gone nearly six months, would likely return at the *Nitro* show in Greenville, South Carolina, on September 14. The WWF hadn't made him a serious offer due to their legal battles with WCW, plus some within the company had been very vocal in expressing their belief that Flair was too old to come in and headline against Austin.

Among those who argued against bringing Ric Flair back to the WWF was a young man by the name of Hunter Hearst Helmsley, who said outright in a radio interview that Flair should just retire. This was the same Triple H who, five years later, would end up best buddies with the still-active Flair on WWE television, and would, in fact, write the foreword to Flair's autobiography.

With *Raw* preempted for the annual U.S. Open tennis tournament, WCW's good fortune continued: *Nitro* drew a 6.03 in 4,485,333 homes, setting a new record for cable. Never mind that nearly seven million people witnessed yet another installment in a seemingly endless series of hideous programs, this one headlined by Sting and Luger beating Hogan and Hart via countout. Afterwards, Warrior appeared in his cloud of smoke, a cloud now capable of making horrible wrestlers like Ed Leslie and Brian Adams faint, and good wrestlers like Bret Hart vanish into thin air. Let us reiterate that this was designed to be compelling, not comical. Goldberg, the World Heavyweight champion, again worked the semi-main, successfully defending his title against Kevin Nash's original tag team partner, a man named Al Greene who hadn't wrestled in what seemed like decades. Exactly how Al Greene became the number-one contender to the World championship remains to be ascertained.

September 14 saw a battle of the ages, as both sides put on pay-per-view-caliber television shows with marquee matches and major character turns. From a wrestling standpoint, WCW presented one of its best TV matches of the year with Billy Kidman winning the Cruiserweight title from Juventud Guerrera. From a marquee standpoint, Goldberg's first-ever bout with Sting was a hugely anticipated matchup. On the other channel, the WWF turned both Rock and Mankind babyface, Undertaker made a strong heel turn, and Steve Austin faced Ken Shamrock for the first time ever in a WWF title defense. All of it, though, paled in comparison to the highlight moment of the year: the return of Ric Flair.

His segment, which did a strong 5.4 rating going up against Mark Henry versus Chyna and X-Pac (now that's some competition), opened with Arn Anderson coming out and cutting a great promo detailing the history of his career and that of the Horsemen. He called out Steve McMichael and Chris Benoit, then introduced Dean Malenko as the newest member of the group. At that point, he teased that the segment was over, and boy, were the fans ever unhappy about that. Truth be told, the whole thing almost fell through over the weekend, but Flair and WCW came to a new agreement on Sunday and everything went forward as planned.

"Oh, what a goof," Arn suddenly blurted. "What a goof. You know, I get accused of getting racked in the head a few times and have a little touch of Alzheimer's. My God, I almost forgot the fourth Horseman. RIC FLAIR, GET DOWN HERE!" It was the perfect setup. When Flair came out, he got an ovation that rivaled, and probably exceeded, any other ovation in the history of wrestling—an ovation that nobody watching will ever forget. After finally composing himself, Flair cut a promo talking about his appreciation for the fans, his life in the past few months, and finally, Eric Bischoff. Eric showed up just in time to hear the following emotional outburst:

> You're an overbearing asshole! You're obnoxious, overbearing—abuse of power! You . . . abuse of power! Cut me off! Abuse of power! You suck! I hate your guts! You are a liar, you're a cheat, you're a scam! You are a no-good son-of-a-bitch! Fire me! I'm already fired! Fire me! I'm already fired!

And then they cut to a commercial, right in the middle of the speech that the majority of wrestling fans wish they could have personally cut on Eric.

Thankfully, Flair's promo was so great that it took the minds of many fans off the previous night's *Fall Brawl* pay-per-view, yet another horrible show that the company actually charged fans money to view. There was one good match on the show, Saturn over Raven, and the main event was so atrocious that if you made a list of the very worst major main events in the entire history of this business, it would probably rank in the top five or ten. Dallas Page beat Hogan, Bret, Stevie Ray, Warrior, Piper, Sting, Luger, and Kevin Nash in a double-cage War Games match. It seems unlikely that with so much impressive talent in the ring a match could be this bad, but it was. Technically, there were two teams working against each other, but you wouldn't have known this to see it. Hogan came out with a device known as a slapjack (which looked for all the world like an old dirty sock) and knocked out everyone except Stevie. Neither man bothered to pin anyone, however—they just stood there looking at all the corpses. Warrior then appeared in his magical cloud of smoke. Hogan tore his jacket off, but then the smoke rose again, and when it cleared Warrior was gone, and Hogan was left just holding the jacket. Warrior then ran out from the dressing room. Yes, they went to the trouble of hiring a fake Warrior (the artist formerly known as Renegade) just to do this cartoonish spot. Hogan, with help from Ed Leslie, escaped from the cage and locked Warrior in. Despite magically appearing and disappearing just moments earlier in his magical cloud of smoke, Warrior was now unable to get out of the cage. So he got angry, growled, and finally kicked his way out of the cage. They began to brawl in the aisle, and during this short melee, Warrior, despite having displayed no athletic ability whatsoever in this brawl, somehow managed to both twist his ankle and tear his biceps. Once everyone in the ring emerged from the smoke-induced coma, Page pinned Stevie with the diamond cutter. The crowd's reaction to this whole match took the form of intense and deep-seated hatred.

"WHAT AN EVENT!" Tony Schiavone screamed as the show concluded.

Not only was the action in the ring becoming atrocious, so was the television production. In particular, the *Thunder* prior to this show featured one of the most unintentionally hilarious screw-ups ever. Chris

Jericho had been spoofing Goldberg by going to the ring for his matches accompanied by fat security guards (one of whom was a real-life ring crew worker who would go on to minor fame as "Ralphus"). The storyline this particular evening was that Jericho got lost trying to find his way to the ring and ended up locked outside the building. Unfortunately, the door didn't really lock, so when he pulled on the handle, it opened right up. He quickly closed it and pretended it was locked, pounding on the door and screaming to be let inside. Apparently, someone inside thought he was really locked out, because a door about ten feet away opened, and this dude stuck his head out. Jericho had to pretend like he didn't see him. It gets better. His opponent, Wrath, got sick of waiting in the ring and ran backstage to find Jericho. They did a chase scene outside the building. Finally, they figured the camera was shut off, so Jericho stopped, and Wrath ran past him. Then they both turned and nonchalantly started walking back toward the camera. Problem was, the camera wasn't off, and this whole fiasco was broadcast to millions.

Referee Billy Silverman was also having problems on *Thunder*. One week, he counted three during a Psicosis versus Saturn match when it was supposed to be a two. Since the show was live, millions of fans witnessed Saturn and Psicosis looking at each other in complete confusion, then just giving up and walking to the back. A week earlier, Jericho was supposed to beat Jim Neidhart with his lion tamer submission. He tried to roll Neidhart over, but it just wasn't working. Neidhart said he gave up. Silverman didn't hear him. So Neidhart, in great discomfort, rolled out of the hold. Jericho, irate, told Silverman to ring the bell. Silverman actually said *he couldn't ring the bell because he hadn't heard Neidhart submit yet.* So Jericho said something along the lines of: "Wrestling is fake, you jackass, now ring the bell!"

The string of horrible programming continued the next week on *Nitro*, with an angle in which Warrior, using his magical cloud of smoke, not only kidnapped E. Harrison Leslie, but instantly teleported him from the ring to the rafters. To accomplish this feat, they had Warrior in the rafters hugging a blow-up doll dressed like Leslie—one of the more surreal visuals fans would ever see. It was never explained how any of this was intended to sell tickets. Later, to further hype the Hogan versus Warrior match planned for *Halloween Havoc* the following month, Hogan was brutally attacked—by E. Harrison Leslie. The rest of the show featured only slightly more logical yet ultimately inexplicable booking. It was said that the man partially responsible for all this Warrior malarkey was former child star Jason Hervey of *Wonder Years* fame, who had become good friends with Bischoff. The next week wasn't as bad overall, but they did present one incomprehensible segment where Billy Kidman, who seemed to be a superstar on the rise following his Cruiserweight title win over Juvie, lost to Scott Hall clean in a totally one-sided match.

Scott Hall was arrested again the following week for allegedly causing $2,000 in damage by keying a limo outside the Diamond Mine strip club in Orlando during a drunken fit. This led his ex-wife, Dana, to post a message on an nWo fan site, basically taking WCW to task for still employing him when he obviously had some serious issues to deal with. WCW was so outraged by Hall's behavior that they continued to portray him as a drunk on TV.

As nonsensical as all the previous Warrior segments had become, however, nothing could compare to the October 5 *Nitro*, which showcased quite possibly the most absurd angle in wrestling history. The idea was that Hogan couldn't find Leslie, so he was searching for him throughout the building. He ended up in Leslie's dressing room, and in the mirror he imagined that he saw the Warrior. As he was screaming at this vision, Bischoff walked in. He could not see Warrior, however, and thought Hogan was going crazy. This is all fine and dandy, except for the fact that *viewers at home could see Warrior in the mirror.* Of course, this would mean that Hogan was not, in fact, crazy, but that Bischoff was.

Or Bischoff was right, and the fans were crazy too. But then, to confuse matters, the Warrior in the mirror disappeared, but Hogan could still see him, which basically meant that everyone involved, from Hogan to Bischoff to the fans, was crazy. In the end, it didn't matter if they were crazy or not, because fans in the arena were booing like crazy.

LESSON NOT LEARNED: You just read that paragraph about Hogan and Warrior and the magic mirror, right? Did you ever think anyone would want to bring that magic mirror skit back? Unbelievably, WWE did just this in a Randy Orton versus Undertaker feud in 2005. Not only did Orton see Undertaker in a mirror (as did everyone else at home!), but his father, Bob Orton Jr., also began bleeding for no reason. So in addition to bringing back a horrible WCW gimmick, they also reenacted an awful WWF one as well, as voodoo master Papa Shango did the same thing to the Ultimate Warrior in the early '90s.

In all honesty, we're not sure which is worse.

Or why WWE decided to bring the magic mirror back ONE MORE TIME in 2014 as John Cena saw a sheep mask (presumably Erick Rowen) in the mirror during a feud with Bray Wyatt . . . which then miraculously disappeared.

Again, all this was done in WCW, and it was horrible. And it's never been good since. Why this bit continues to be recycled will forever remain a mystery.

And this was becoming a very bad trend. Instead of the "good heat" that the nWo had generated a year earlier, this was "bad heat," the kind of heat that results in fans feeling ripped off, angry, and annoyed. Some crowds even began to chant "*NITRO* SUCKS!" Seemingly everyone knew that the ship was sinking at this point with the exception, of course, of those steering it.

The next week, fans witnessed the continued rise of a new star—Judy

Bagwell, Buff's mother. They'd flown her in months earlier to do cameos with her son, and everyone soon learned where young Marcus got his ego from. The week prior, she'd gotten a huge pop dragging Bagwell to the backstage area by his ear, and, apparently, superstardom went to her head. This week, she'd gotten a total makeover and considered herself part of the show. Unfortunately, she didn't realize that her part in the show was to act sad when Scott Steiner turned on Buff and dropped him neck-first over the top rope. Instead, she laughed, right there in front of the camera.

On the October 19 *Nitro*, Chris Jericho did an interview basically challenging Dallas Page to a match, which most astute fans found confusing since in the weeks prior he'd been gunning for a match with Goldberg. As it turned out, Goldberg, being very green to the business, was taking advice from the wrong people, namely men like Hogan and Nash. He was told point blank that Jericho was way too small to feud with, and if he did so it would kill his credibility. He told Bischoff to nix the program, and that was the end of that. At the moment, it was just another example of WCW putting the brakes on the ascension of someone who could potentially have become a major breakout star. It was even worse over the long haul.

Wrestlers were often told the sky was the limit, but young guys would start a climb toward the top, and then, right when they were starting to get hot, something would happen and their rise would be derailed. Guys referred to it as hitting their heads on a glass ceiling. Jericho, frustrated with hitting his head time and time again, refused to re-sign his WCW deal and jumped instead to the WWF. Despite being smaller than the guys Vince McMahon traditionally pushed as superstars, he was given the main event treatment on his very first day, sparring head-to-head with Rock in a tremendous *Raw* moment. But then a few months later, following a feud with Triple H, he was back to hitting his head on another glass ceiling, this time in the WWF. Years after that, when Goldberg first arrived to the company, Jericho, who hadn't forgotten about their WCW program getting axed, confronted him about it and they got into a brief altercation backstage. Jericho, son of hockey star Ted Irvine and a former hockey player himself, grabbed the much-larger Goldberg in a front facelock before everything was broken up. Because Goldberg liked to talk about his mixed martial arts training and had a reputation as a tough guy, and because so many people were bitter about the money he was making, Jericho became a hero to much of the WWE locker room.

Nitro's main event that evening was interesting. Konnan and Luger and Nash were wrestling Hall and Stevie Ray and Norton. If you'll recall, fans were more than fed up with *Nitro* matches ending abruptly when guys ran in to interfere. So WCW had the ingenious solution of ending this match abruptly without anyone running it. That's right, they were having the match, and then the bell just rang and it was over. Again, fans were outraged.

But don't forget this chapter's early lesson: when things are hot, a promotion can seemingly do no wrong. A few weeks after this debacle of a show, they put tickets on sale for December's Astrodome and TWA Dome *Nitro*s. As vocal as fans were in their dislike for most *Nitro*s, they still purchased 16,000 and 18,000 tickets respectively on the first day they went on sale.

Halloween Havoc the following Sunday just about set new standards for everything. It almost felt as if the company was trying to see how bad a show they could put on that people would still pay to see. The Hogan versus Warrior rematch was so far beyond atrocious that it actually made their War Games match look like a Ric Flair versus Ricky Steamboat classic. The bout went on for nearly fifteen minutes, and it's no exaggeration that these two forty-plus-year-old men could realistically only go about fifteen seconds. Without question, the highlight of the match was a truly ridiculous spot that looked as though two kindergartners were on the playground. Remember when you were in preschool and you learned how to do the log roll? The one where you lie on your back and just roll over and over sideways? Well, Hogan tried to drop an elbow on Warrior, but Warrior log-rolled out of the way. Hogan decided to try again, and again, Warrior log-rolled out of the way. Suddenly—and I can only imagine the time and effort that went into plotting this spot backstage—Warrior reversed direction and began to *roll toward Hogan.* You'd think that Hogan would have several options at this point: step to the left; step to the right; or, perhaps, jump. Instead, he seemed stricken with fear, because he just stood there as Warrior rolled right into his legs, making him fall down.

Before he'd agreed to do the job to Hogan at **Havoc**, Warrior had also demanded that a new contract pick up where his first one left off. WCW used him on TV less than a handful of times afterwards, so they basically paid him $1 million to agree to lose to Hogan and kill this feud off.

If that wasn't bad enough, a spot was planned for later in which Hogan was supposed to throw fire at Warrior. In wrestling, fire is created by lighting a piece of flash paper. In the corner, Hogan poured his fire-making paraphernalia out of a Ziploc baggie. Warrior came at him. The audience, surely on the edges of their seats, then witnessed Hogan throw a piece of flash paper at Warrior. You read that right: he forgot to light it on fire. The fans, who had been chanting "WARRIOR SUCKS!" and cheering Hogan earlier, booed loudly. Hogan tried again. This time, the paper lit on fire, but it ignited in his hand and burned out. Hogan looked terrified. Warrior was terrified, too, and didn't know what to do.

Finally, Hogan's real-life wrestler nephew Horace ran in and hit Warrior with an incredibly weak chairshot, which Warrior sold like he'd been shot with a handgun. Hogan dove in to get the pin. Afterwards, he told Horace that he'd "passed the test," which begs the question: how bad could the match have been if he'd failed?

LESSON NOT LEARNED: After bringing his nephew Horace in and it being, well, not so grand, you might think that Hulk Hogan would avoid being associated with other members of his clan on national televison. Instead, in 2012, his daughter, Brooke, showed up on TNA Impact as the "Executive in Charge of Knockouts." This role consisted of standing approximately three feet taller than any other woman (and many of the men) on the roster, being involved in top storylines with the lead characters in the company, and being unable to deliver lines properly or contain her laughter when things went wrong on air. Which was pretty much weekly.
Say what you will about the Hulkster, but he is nothing if not a family man.

Much more damaging than the Warrior-Hogan fiasco, however, was the fact that WCW had decided—just a few days before the pay-per-view—that they were going to go three and a half hours instead of the usual three. Fans at home were not alerted to this fact and grew concerned at about the two-hour and forty-five-minute mark, as Hogan and Warrior were still in the ring, and it didn't appear that Goldberg versus Page for the WCW title was going to happen anytime soon. To make matters *significantly* worse, nobody bothered to tell *the cable companies*, because at 11:00 p.m. EST, 25 percent of the folks who had purchased the show suddenly found themselves looking at a blank screen. Local outlets were flooded with angry phone calls and had to struggle to come up with some sort of offer to placate the fans, most of which demanded full refunds. When all was said and done, it's estimated that WCW lost almost $1.5 million in pay-per-view revenue because of this simple miscommunication.

In a dilemma about what to do, WCW decided to air the Page versus Goldberg match for free on Nitro the following evening. The cable industry was not cool with this because a replay of the pay-per-view was scheduled to air Tuesday night, and they figured airing a match on free TV would kill Tuesday's buy rate. WCW agreed not to air the Warrior versus Hogan match for free—possibly the smartest thing they'd done in ten years of business. Despite having aired the *Bash at the Beach* main event three months earlier on *Nitro*, announcer Tony Schiavone, who was losing credibility with the fans on a weekly basis, claimed that this would be the first time in history that a PPV match was ever shown on free TV.

Goldberg versus Page went shockingly well, not only in the ring, but also in the ratings. Its quarter hour on *Nitro* set yet another new cable viewership record, a 7.18, beating out the Hogan versus Goldberg match from the Georgia Dome in July. The rating helped win the night, as *Nitro* did a 5.06 to *Raw*'s 4.48, which, despite the loss of $1.5 million the night before, no doubt made Eric Bischoff very happy.

Hype began for their next PPV, *World War III*. Having learned nothing from past mistakes, they announced no matches save for one that bombed every year previously, a three-ring, sixty-man battle royal. It was somewhat fitting for WCW to run a PPV using three rings.

In early November, former wrestler and commentator Jesse Ventura was elected governor of Minnesota. Hogan and Ventura had been professional rivals for years, and now, Jesse had finally accomplished something that Hogan could only dream about. Hogan, however, was undeterred and announced on *Nitro* that he was running for president of the United States. The show ended up being crushed by *Raw* with the WWF's biggest winning margin in history, a 5.03 to a 4.06. Worse, Hogan's segment was beaten 4.3 to 4.1 by *Raw*'s Val Venis versus Steve Blackman in a battle of lifetime mid-carders. This was a super big blow for Hogan, because he didn't attend the prior week's show and it was beaten in the ratings, and he wanted to convince people that his absence was the reason for the decline. This sure put an end to that theory in a hurry.

Things were starting to implode fast. *World War III* was coming up, and on the last *Nitro* before the PPV they announced . . . zero new matches. All that was known was that there was going to be the traditional horrible three-ring battle royal and a Scott Hall versus Kevin Nash match. Apparently, nothing else was important. Zero had changed on the TV, meaning it was still horrific most weeks. The same old guys were on top having the same horrible matches. Actually, that's not entirely true, there was one new superstar that was pushed right to the top—Judy Bagwell became one-half of the World Tag Team champions with partner Rick Steiner. No, we're not lying. *Raw* clobbered *Nitro* in the ratings, 5.50 to 4.25.

Nitro had settled into a pattern of finishing a point or so behind *Raw* every week. As you can imagine, Bischoff was not pleased and decided that changes needed to be made, and fast.

Unfortunately, these changes had nothing to do with fixing the atrocious shows the company was presenting. No, a completely different plan was in the works: the "time was right," he believed, to beat Goldberg.

Actually, that had been the plan for a long time: Hogan would drop the strap to Goldberg at the Georgia Dome; then he'd win it back at *Starrcade*. But somewhere along the way, there was a change in plans. Perhaps you're thinking that the change in plans was for Hogan not to beat Goldberg after all. Perhaps you're thinking that Goldberg was such a good ratings draw, house show draw, and merchandise seller that it would have been foolish to take the belt from him and put it back on Hogan, whose drawing power had waned over the past several months.

You would be wrong.

The change of plans was to have Goldberg drop the title not to horrible wrestler Hogan, but to horrible wrestler Kevin Nash. Nash had just been named new head booker for the promotion, and once this happened everything backstage went into disarray. It went into disarray for fake reasons, however—not real reasons. Confused?

Basically, Nash, Hogan, and Bischoff came up with a scenario to work all the boys. No, not to work the fans in an effort to make money, but to work the boys in, well, an effort to make them not so miserable. You see, pretty much everyone on the undercard hated Hogan. They saw him as a guy who was past his prime and needed to step aside to make room for new stars. Nash, however, was such a great politician that everyone liked him. In fact, no matter what he did, you'd be hard-pressed to find a person backstage who didn't think he was a really cool guy. So the plan was to give Nash the booking position, and Hogan, "outraged with his loss of power," would pretend to quit. He'd disappear for a while, Nash would make everyone happy, and morale would improve. Of course, the long-term plan was to eventually bring Hogan back and put the belt on him again.

Also, Hogan needed time off to film *Muppets in Space.*

Yes, of course we're serious.

So Nash got the book, and, as most bookers do, he began to write storylines designed to make himself the center of attention. His main idea was to set up his own big win over Goldberg for the belt at *Starrcade*. Step one was to put himself over in the three-ring number-one-contender battle royal at *World War III*, a show that ended up better than expected seeing as it was expected to be the worst ever. Step two was to book himself as a man who ended win streaks. Coincidentally, there was a man on *Nitro* who had been on a win streak lately and was starting to get over. His name was Wrath. He fell to Nash in 4:45 the next night. That was the end of him getting over. Step three was to build Goldberg up as a monster. After all, there's nothing cool about beating a nobody; if you're going to beat someone, you might as well beat a monster. That was accomplished by a 1:34 victory over Giant on *Nitro* the next evening (which was also done because everyone figured Giant would jump to the WWF when his contract expired in February). Step four was to start to write wacky storylines for many of the mid-carders, stories that might not always play out, but that would at least make the guys feel like they were being utilized.

Not all the mid-carders were happy though. A few whose contracts were coming due and hadn't yet re-signed were booked to lose left and right on TV. Nobody was safe, it seemed, except two men—Rick and Scott Steiner. For whatever reason, they were booked in a positive manner on television all the way up until the last *week* before their contracts came due. In the long run, it didn't matter, because they re-signed. But internally, the belief was that they weren't booked to lose constantly because nobody had the nerve to go up to them and let them know. Scott in particular had become super scary, somehow having managed to develop a Herculean physique despite the constant travel and always seeming on the verge of bursting into a violent, unscripted rage.

In fact, the following week Steiner was in court on charges of making "terroristic threats" against a Georgia Department of Transportation worker named Paul Kaspereen. Seems Mr. Steiner was driving his F-150 down the road one day and came upon a closed lane. He told Kaspereen he wanted to go. Kaspereen said no. So Steiner said if he didn't get out of the way he was going to run him over. Kaspereen refused, so Steiner bumped into him twice with his vehicle. That was the dreaded terroristic threat. Even the judge found this absurd, though he didn't like Steiner's courtroom attitude and pulled an early plea-bargain bid. Steiner ended up pleading guilty, and in March 1999 was sentenced to ten days in prison, $25,000 in fines, seven years probation, and 200 hours community service. It is tough to imagine what sort of community service Scott Steiner did.

Part two of Hogan's long-term two-month plan was to go on the *Tonight Show* and simultaneously announce that he was running for president and retiring from wrestling forever. Apparently, he was of the understanding that the American people would not want a man in office who devoted several days per month to having horrible matches on WCW television. It would only be the third time he had retired forever from wrestling, which isn't too bad when you consider guys like the legendary Terry Funk who retired and un-retired so many times that they eventually lost count. Hogan was asked a few hardball political questions, like whether he was a Democrat or a Republican, and he had devoted so much time and research to his campaign that his answer was: "Right now, I'm right in the middle."

"What kind of a lame answer is that?" Leno asked.

Most saw Hogan's "retirement" for what it really was: a carefully orchestrated political maneuver that would benefit exactly one person in the long run: himself. Say what you will about Hogan, but few in the history of wrestling have proven so many times over how adept they are at playing the game. Hogan had taken himself off TV at many times when it was pretty clear the ratings were about to drop (for example, earlier in the year when *Nitro* was being preempted for the NBA playoffs). Obviously, he'd later state that the reason things tanked was that he was gone, thereby increasing his perceived value.

In late November, WCW finally figured out why buy rates had been dropping over the past several months and took steps to rectify the problem. They had the small "Wrestling Online" website shut down because the site owner had been doing PPV play-by-plays on IRC. Strangely, buy rates did not return to previous levels.

The November 30 *Nitro* once again told the story of why the company was about to fall off a cliff. They were still able to sell tickets, that wasn't an issue; in fact, *Nitro* drew their second-largest crowd ever, 32,076 to the Astrodome in Houston, which between gate and merchandise made them almost $1 million. And what did they give those 32,076 fans who paid almost a million bucks? You guessed it—a horrible show. There were two main events, Steiner versus Hall and Goldberg versus Bam Bam Bigelow, and neither took place. Fans were outraged and pelted the ring with garbage after the show. WCW probably didn't see this for what it was; they likely assumed it was the "good heat" that the nWo got, oh, two years prior. Plus, who cared if the fans were mad? They made a million bucks, and their two upcoming events at the TWA and Georgia

Domes had near-$1 million advances. The good times were obviously going to last forever.

Bischoff was as positive as ever. The following week he called a meeting and said there was something that would happen in early 1999 that would change the company's fortunes. As it turned out, he was right, but not in a good way. Speaking of, tickets went on sale for the January 4 Georgia Dome *Nitro*, and, no joke, Gene Okerlund immediately went on the WCW Hotline and told fans in Atlanta not to bother buying tickets because WCW wanted 60,000 in the building, and there would be comps everywhere.

The highlight, or lowlight, of *Nitro* on December 14 was Ric Flair having a fake heart attack that they tried to pass off as real. It started with an interview setting up the match he was set to have at *Starrcade* with Bischoff, playing off the real-life lawsuit that the vast majority of fans really didn't know a thing about. Bischoff came out and Flair chased him away from ringside. Flair, who had actually been running really fast, came back looking none the worse for wear or even out of breath, but then began clutching his chest. Nobody believed it was real, so the company went far more out of their way than usual to convince folks that it was. It was never made clear what the point of doing it was except to suggest that Bischoff was going to have the advantage in their match. The most tasteless part of the whole thing was that they tried to pass it off as real backstage, once again working the boys, and both Doug Dillinger and referee Charles Robinson, a long-time Flair mark, were crying thinking that he might die.

Because Flair's health was supposedly in jeopardy, he didn't appear on *Thunder* that week. You'll never guess where *Thunder* emanated from. Oh, yes: Charlotte, North Carolina. The big angle on the show was Eric confronting Flair's wife, Beth, and giving her a big smooch on the lips.

The following week, the company dropped a bombshell. According to Bischoff, a deal had been signed with NBC to air two prime time

WCW specials in 1999, coincidentally running up against WWF's *St. Valentine's Day Massacre* PPV in February and *WrestleMania* in March. Strangely, everyone from the WWF to NBC denied that any such thing had been signed. Eric, however, was insistent that it was a done deal.

On December 20, *Wrestling With Shadows*, the Paul Jay documentary highlighting the final year of Bret Hart's WWF run, aired on A&E. This was the culmination of a long court battle between Jay's High Road Productions, TBS, and the WWF. The WWF didn't want the movie to get out, and especially wanted all Montreal-related footage cut. They refused to turn over many of the release forms and such that were required by their contract, so High Road was prepared to take them to court. Then Turner decided they wanted to air the movie, since Bret was now working for them, and WCW could obviously promote the movie like crazy on *Nitro*. Once WWF got wind of that, they agreed to turn over everything (including all future royalties) as long as Jay agreed not to sell to Turner.

Even though the film wasn't airing on a Turner station, WCW still had the option of promoting it like crazy. That would make sense, of course, since Hart was portrayed in the film as the ultimate babyface, a hardworking guy who gave his all to a company for over a decade, only to be blatantly lied to and screwed over on his last night in. With nothing more than a few TV plugs, WCW would be on their way to making Hart a babyface star of such magnitude that he'd more than pay off his multi-million dollar contract.

But that's not what happened. You see, Bret was a bad guy on WCW TV. If they plugged *Wrestling With Shadows* and fans watched it, they might start cheering him. While it was never clear why the company found it so imperative that Hart remain a heel, the decision was made to not mention the film at all. In fact, to make sure nobody accidentally made reference to it in an interview, Hart was also taken off television completely.

Flair, despite suffering that horrible heart attack, was back on *Nitro* the next week at the TWA Dome, which drew nearly 30,000 fans and broke the company gate record with $914,389 in ticket sales. He returned to an enormous pop and cut one of his ten million all-time great promos, literally crying while hyping up for a final time his match with Bischoff at *Starrcade*. Tony Schiavone on commentary said it was clear he never had a heart attack. The original plan, as stupid as this sounds, was to claim that Eric poisoned him the week before. Of course, when you look at wrestling angles post-1995, this would have been in the minority as far as total absurdity is concerned.

Starrcade was considered a far better show than anyone expected going in. The opener, Kidman versus Rey Mysterio Jr. versus Juvie in a three-way for the Cruiserweight belt, was one of the best matches of the year. Flair versus Bischoff was decent only because Flair, at forty-nine, was still one of the best workers in the world when he had to be. Of course, even as great as he was, Flair still lost the match after Curt Hennig ran in and gave Bischoff a pair of brass knux to KO Flair behind the ref's back.

And then there was the main event. Goldberg destroyed Nash for a long time until both Disco Inferno and Bam Bam Bigelow ran in. Both were slaughtered. Then, as both Goldberg and the referee were distracted, Scott Hall snuck in and zapped Goldberg with a cattle prod. You read that right, a *cattle prod*. Nash delivered a formerly banned powerbomb and got the pin.

The streak was over—in more ways than one.

When Kevin Nash beat Bill Goldberg to end the legendary win streak, there were basically two schools of thought. The vast minority, consisting of Kevin Nash, his close friends, and immediate family, thought that it was a great idea. To the majority, however, it was really stupid. At the time, however, nobody grasped it for what it really was: the beginning of the end of WCW.

"When they ended Goldberg's streak, it was the biggest mistake that company ever made," recounted WCW announcer Bobby Heenan in an interview years later. "The fans weren't tired of him—they were buying tickets to see him, buying his shirts, chanting his name. But some people didn't care about that."

Kevin Sullivan agreed: "It was like the Titanic hitting the iceberg. I can tell you the exact night [WCW died]. Goldberg getting beat by Kevin Nash. Goldberg, his matches, they looked semi-real. We drew a [near] million dollar house on free TV, 43,000 people there. I went to Eric and said, 'Please do not beat him.' He said, 'People are going to get sick of him winning and they're going to turn against him.' I said, 'We got a million dollars out there!' And they showed that tape over and over again. We had the golden goose and we strangled it."[15]

The beginning of the end for WCW was like the beginning of the end for King Kong. Planes were swarming everywhere. He was teetering there on the edge of the Empire State Building, and he'd just put the girl down. Though his immediate future was not looking good, at the moment, everything was fine. Then he got hit with the first bullet. Then he was bombarded with multiple bullets in a very short period of time . . . and that was all she wrote.

Goldberg losing the belt was that first bullet.

And another barrage of bullets was about to hit the company in a very short period of time.

★ ★ ★ ★ ★ PART III
THE FALL

"The biggest mistake was that they had leadership where all the generals were guys who had never been in a battle. They never had anybody who knew what they were doing. There's nobody who ever understood wrestling or the minds of wrestling fans. They never understood the nature of the business."

—Bret Hart, WCW Wrestler 1997 to 2000

CHAPTER
★ ★ ★ FIVE ★ ★ ★
1999:
GAMBLING ON A SAVIOR

On the surface, 1998 had been a hugely successful year. Although WCW made every stupid mistake that could possibly be made, attendance was up 47 percent over 1997, ratings were up 56 percent, buy rates were up 18 percent, a whopping 49 percent of house shows had sold out, and the average house show gross was up 90 percent. It's not difficult to see why those on the inside thought there was nothing to worry about.

But the sins of 1998 began to take their toll in 1999. Even worse, 1999 was the year that WCW made some of their most horrendous decisions yet, decisions that, instead of turning things around as hoped, actually sped up the company's decline. Consider this: just two years earlier, WCW was the number-one wrestling company in the entire world. In the 365 days of this year, they managed to lose no less than $15 million—more money than any promotion had ever lost in the history of the business.

In a way, it was shockingly similar to the way Jim Crockett Promotions had booked itself into oblivion exactly ten years earlier. They hired a booker (Dusty Rhodes in the mid-'80s, Nash in 1998) who put himself and his friends over at the expense of all the other talent; they booked screw-job after screw-job, run-in after run-in, show after show, until it drew the infamous "wrong kind of heat," the kind that drives fans away; they put all the old, stale talent on top and pushed them hard despite the fact that the ratings made it clear that fans wanted new blood; and all that exciting, young international talent that Bischoff had scoured the globe for in 1996 had been booked so far into oblivion that they were pretty much unsalvageable. At least with JCP, the wrestlers worked hard and did their best even as the ship sank. But in WCW, things were so bad by mid-year that virtually everyone—from talent to the office person-nel—had mentally given up.

As the year began, however, Bischoff was anything but ready to sur-render. He opened the year with another crew meeting, in which he dropped a major bombshell: WCW had struck a deal with NBC, a deal that would give them six prime time specials over the course of the year. This was largely due to an NBA strike going on at the time that had opened up prime time slots, and those within NBC thought that while it would not be an even swap, it would be an acceptable one. Not only that, those specials would compete directly against WWF pay-per-views like *WrestleMania* and *SummerSlam*. It would be like the old days of the *Clash of the Champions* specials, giving WCW a huge advantage over the WWF. He claimed that WCW got it because the network wanted nothing to do with the WWF due to the raunchy nature of their programming. He said that while all the swearing and insanity might benefit the WWF at the moment, in the long run it would work against them. Bischoff was right in the end, but unfortunately for him and many others it worked not only against the WWF, but also against the wrestling industry as a whole. The first special was to air on February 14.

Seemingly rejuvenated by the news of the deal, Bischoff came up with a master plan to restore WCW to its former glory. He would revolutionize wrestling just like he'd done in 1996 by—yep, you guessed it—doing everything he'd done in 1996 all over again.

The scene was the Georgia Dome in Atlanta (or, as it appeared on WCW business cards that year, "Altanta"), home of the now-legendary Hogan versus Goldberg bout. The date was January 4, 1999. And, as Bischoff had hoped, WCW truly revolutionized the wrestling business on this date. Unfortunately, it wasn't a positive revolution, but a new example of just how quickly a formerly successful wrestling promotion could fall.

In hindsight, this show was probably the single most destructive *Nitro* in the history of the company. Yes, other shows were far worse, but this was the one that, more than any other, started the ball rolling toward the company's inevitable doom. It's a cliché, but this program was a disaster of epic proportions.

Nothing much happened in the first hour. Then, just as *Raw* was about to start, some cops showed up and announced that they had a warrant for Goldberg's arrest on an unspecified charge. Goldberg didn't even ask what the charge was. Off he went. So all the fans at home suddenly saw half of the main event they'd so eagerly anticipated (Goldberg versus Nash in Goldberg's first shot at regaining the WCW title he'd lost at *Starrcade*) being escorted to jail just as *Raw* was about to begin. As it turns out, he was accused of the "aggravated stalking" of the now-heel Miss Elizabeth (originally, she was to accuse him of raping her, but Goldberg put the ixnay on that one immediately). Nash, still trying to be a good guy, came out and told Ric Flair, who had become storyline president of the company, that Hulk Hogan must be behind this, and that he therefore wanted a "warm-up" match with him prior to the main event. Hogan, who hadn't been on TV in some time, just happened to be in the building that evening. He came out and said that he'd planned to announce his retirement as well as his running mate that evening (yes, he was still on the president kick), but now he was appalled at what that "sexual deviant" Goldberg had done, and he wanted to beat up that "spoon" Kevin Nash for accusing him of being behind it. Yes, those were his actual words.

Back at the police station, Liz changed her story multiple times, and finally, after being threatened with perjury, she admitted to having made everything up. So the race was on: could Goldberg make it back to the Georgia Dome in time for his main event? The unintentional comedy here was that, earlier in the show, it had been revealed that the police station was across the street from the arena.

Goldberg was somehow unable to get back in time, even though he had thirty minutes to walk several dozen feet. Perhaps the crosswalk light was broken. Regardless, Nash and Hogan came out for their epic encounter. About one minute into the match, Tony Schiavone bellowed, "This is what World Championship Wrestling is all about!" Truer words have perhaps never been spoken. Hogan touched Nash in the chest with one finger, and Nash took this enormous bump like he'd been hit with a cannonball. On the bright side, it was probably the biggest bump Nash would take all year. Hogan covered him and won the belt. Afterwards, Hogan and Nash hugged, revealing that it had been a setup all along. Goldberg finally arrived and laid waste to everyone in the ring until being attacked by his newest foe—the old, immobile, washed-up Lex Luger.

Fans had paid a record $930,735 to see this show. To say they were outraged by what transpired would be a strong understatement.

If everything that happened in the ring wasn't bad enough, Bischoff also made a huge miscalculation in commentary. As you'll recall, early in the war Bischoff had done something unheard of—he gave away results of taped *Raw*s on live *Nitro*s. The reasoning (aside from this being an attempt to be cutting-edge and cool) was that this would convince fans that there was no reason to watch the opposition. Since this was Bischoff's 1996 revisited, he went back to that strategy by having Tony Schiavone reveal to the fans that in the *Raw* main event, Mick Foley was going to beat Rock to win the WWF title. Worse, he had Schiavone bury him, saying a man like that holding a world title was a complete joke.

The problems here were twofold. First, Foley was greatly respected by hardcore fans, so many of them switched channels to *Raw* not only to see him win the belt, but also to stick one to WCW. Among casual fans, Foley was a big babyface hero, and they really wanted to see him finally win what they felt he'd deserved for a long time. They switched channels as well. Final tally: *Raw* did a 5.76, a brand-new ratings record, to *Nitro*'s 4.96. The biggest gap, not surprisingly, immediately followed Schiavone's announcement that Foley the Joke would win the belt, as *Raw* hit a 6.2 opposite *Nitro*'s 4.1. In total, Schiavone's announcement, designed to keep fans from jumping to *Raw*, effectively led almost half a million of them to immediately do just that.

After the fact, Foley actually called Schiavone and left a message; he was "sickened" by what Schiavone had said on the air. He also noted that the words probably were fed to him by someone else, and left his number in case Schiavone wanted to call him back. Sure enough, Tony did call Mick back scant hours later and his wife, Collete, answered, telling Mick that Tony was on the line and he "sounds so sad." Foley tells the story of the call: "As I had thought, the feelings were not his own, but had been forced upon him by his superior. Schiavone's words not only haunted him that night, but for weeks, months, and even years later. Signs started popping up in every arena we went to that disproved WCW's theory, [signs reading] MICK FOLEY PUT MY ASS IN THIS SEAT."[16]

In other bad news, that week Eddie Guerrero was involved in a serious car accident that almost killed him, both at the time and later down the road. He fell asleep at the wheel on New Year's Eve and crashed in a scene so horrific that EMTs on the scene couldn't believe he'd survived. He did recover, but rushed back to the ring way too early and ended up in tremendous pain. This pain led to an addiction to painkillers that resulted in him later being fired from the WWF. He finally checked himself into rehab, cleaned himself up, and was hired back. For a period, he was one of wrestling's great stories of beating addition, and he credited the company with saving his life. Sadly, his life was cut short by a heart attack, dying at the age of 38 in 2005.

The first PPV of the year was *Souled Out* on January 17 in Charleston, West Viginia. Recall the lesson: when wrestling is hot, a promotion can seemingly do no wrong. As horrible as things had been the previous year, this event was a sellout, with 10,255 fans in attendance. Unlike at the Georgia Dome, at least these fans got a good show. The Kidman versus Rey Mysterio Jr. versus Psicosis versus Juventud Guerrera match for the Cruiserweight title was exceptional. They even had a rare good main event that saw Goldberg—who was underrated as a performer even back then—beat Scott Hall in a ladder match where the idea was to climb up and grab a taser hanging from the ceiling. In commentary, it was teased that Goldberg wouldn't be able to make it as they'd shot a video before the show of him screaming in his locker room and holding his knee. Tony Schiavone theorized that he'd been attacked by someone.

"Or maybe he just fell down," Schiavone added.

At this point, Bischoff was willing to do anything to unseat *Raw* in the ratings, so he continued the very dangerous practice of giving away matches that fans likely would have paid to see. Case in point: the following evening's *Nitro* had Ric Flair challenge Bischoff to a match in which the loser would get his head shaved bald. Flair versus Bischoff had been done numerous times, but with the proper build, a hair match between the two would theoretically have drawn some money on PPV or at least popped a rating on TV. After all, in his entire career, Flair, famous for his bleached-blonde hair, had never shaved his head, and most people really hated Eric and would have loved to see him humiliated. WCW, however, had different plans. Instead of properly building the bout, Ric's oldest son, David, came out and demanded the match; then he got the win a few minutes later, and the Horseman shaved Eric bald.

David Flair was nineteen, and despite being the son of arguably the greatest wrestler to ever lace up a pair of boots, he never had much interest in stepping into the ring. He actually wanted to become a state trooper, but shortly after being convinced to do the **Nitro** show, he decided that wrestling wasn't so bad after all. The large paychecks probably helped. He decided to start training with WCW at the Power Plant, unaware of the curse of being the son of a legendary wrestler (nine times out of ten, the father's boots are way too big to fill). WCW, in their infinite wisdom, decided not to bother waiting until he'd trained for a while. They just kept putting him in the ring.

David Flair is doing . . . something . . . here. Selling, we think. Was always hard to tell exactly what was happening in David Flair matches. [GEORGE NAPOLITANO]

Even with giving away huge matches, WCW saw the ratings gap widen. Therefore, Bischoff decided to change directions. The latest idea to turn everything around instantly was to emulate the WWF as closely as possible. Prior to the February 1 *Nitro*, booker Nash called a meeting and announced that there would be some programming changes, most notably a move toward a more *Raw*-like program with lots of taped backstage vignettes. Therefore, everyone was going to have to show up on time so they could film their segments. On the very same night the speech about the pre-tapes was given, an angle was shot in which Flair sentenced Bischoff to sit over a dunk tank as his enemies threw baseballs at him. During the course of the two-hour broadcast, virtually none of the ball-throwers managed to even hit the target. Worse, they did an angle where Rey Mysterio Jr. put his mask on the line again. How, you ask? The culmination of a long feud with another stellar lucha performer? Nope. He and Konnan challenged the very non-lucha Lex Luger and Kevin Nash, and Rey said if either of the huge guys pinned him, he'd unmask. Luger and Nash accepted, laughing, and said they'd put Miss Elizabeth's hair on the line as well. Then she laughed. You can imagine, with compelling programming like this, how many fans suddenly rushed to their telephones to order that PPV.

Other changes were made to give the shows a more "entertainment" feel. For instance, Stevie Ray had suddenly and mysteriously become a major part of **Nitro** (despite the fact that he wasn't a great worker by any stretch of the imagination). Not only was he given inordinate amounts of time in the ring, but he was also given tons of interview time. His promos were, well, interesting. He once identified Barbarian and Meng as "two fish-eating chumps from **Gilligan's Island**." Later, he would call Scott Steiner both "synthetic" (seemingly an accusation of steroid use) and a "sad, sack-ass fruit booty" (seemingly an accusation of . . . you know, we've had 10 years to figure that out, and we're still stumped).

The pre-tapes were in full effect on the February 8 *Nitro*. However, there was an additional change: for whatever reason, it was decided that only fans at home would "see" the pre-tapes. The announcers, who had monitors sitting right there in front of them, were commanded to act as though they didn't see any of the stuff going on backstage. The fans were already conditioned to think that WCW announcers were morons, and this didn't help matters. The show was once again atrocious, but because *Raw* was preempted by the Westminster Dog Show, it did a 5.67 rating—almost a new record. Of course, the bad news was that this meant over eight million fans witnessed yet another horrible show. Instead of easing into the taped segments, it was total overkill to the point that, when it was over, it seemed like there had been more vignettes than wrestling matches.

Perhaps, though, the vignettes were better than what happened that night in the ring: Bret Hart lost the U.S. title to Roddy Piper in a terrible match after interference from Will Sasso. No doubt many of you are asking just who the hell Will Sasso is. He was a fat guy from a program called *Mad TV*, a show on which Bret had done a comedy skit a few weeks earlier. During said skit, Bret "went crazy for real" and "attacked" Sasso, using such "real life" fight moves as a sharpshooter leglock. So Sasso's "revenge" was to come to *Nitro*, somehow end up ringside, and cost Bret the match. Piper, who could barely move due to two bad hips (one of which had already been replaced), had to work almost thirteen minutes in great pain. And why did the nearly crippled Piper become U.S. champion? The plan was for Bret to wrestle Hogan at *Halloween Havoc* in October. Nash, however, didn't like Bret and felt he was over-paid, so he had no interest in putting this match together. He wanted Bret to lose the belt to Booker T, because Bret had beaten Booker several times on TV. Bret said he shouldn't be losing to guys right now if they were grooming him for a World title shot. Somehow, the argument ended with the decision to have him lose to Piper. Don't try to make sense of any of this.

It was terribly sad to watch, almost as sad as the look on the talent's faces when February 14 arrived. As you will recall, this was the date Bischoff was trumpeting as WCW's prime time debut on NBC. Despite Bischoff's countless references to the date, it came and went—with no special on NBC whatsoever. To be fair, this was largely due to two things: Turner brass delaying negotiations repeatedly and the end of the NBA strike. Suddenly, WCW was not so coveted by NBC. Still, Bischoff claimed that they were merely "postponed," which was quickly—and correctly—translated by his wrestlers to mean "canceled and never mentioned again."

In the Wasteful Spending Department, the **WCW Latino** show, a show that most fans had zero clue even existed, was canceled. It was a program the company had in development to air on the Spanish-language Telemundo station. It would feature many of EMLL's (Empresa Mexicana de Lucha Libre) top wrestling stars. Bischoff spent $300,000 to create a fancy new set and began negotiations for wrestlers with EMLL promoter Paco Alonso. Shortly before the first taping, Alonso signed a deal with the WWF (which, coincidentally, was for a Super Astros lucha libre show that also ended up going bust) and pulled out all of his talent. The first taping was a disaster, so Bischoff scrapped the entire project. Telemundo was furious and threatened a lawsuit. To avoid any bad press, Turner came up with an idea: they'd air hour-long edited editions of **Nitro** with Spanish voice-overs for the sixteen weeks they'd promised programming. This would have been a fantastic plan if not for the fact that all the Mexican guys on **Nitro** worked their asses off week after week, and ultimately lost to the white guys week after week.

It was probably just as well, as *Nitro* was getting comically bad by this point; it seemed that every week, a new contender for worst-ever pro-wrestling show aired on television. The February 15 show reached a new low. The main angle was an intensely appalling and hideously long skit in which Hogan and the nWo, wearing ski masks, beat up Ric Flair in a field. If you're wondering what this had to do with wrestling, join the club. Fans at home were able to see this because it was all filmed by numerous cameramen, including one in a helicopter. Do not even ask how much money was spent on this. After the beating, the nWo unmasked—which raises the question of why they wore ski masks in the first place—and ran off into the night. Flair was left in the field for one hour. We knew this because there was a cameraman with him, filming his body. The cameraman, however, did not offer any aid or call 911. Neither did the three unidentified friends who had been traveling with Ric in his limo prior to the attack, all of whom were apparently abducted by a UFO because they were never seen again. Finally, a redneck in a turnip truck (don't ask us, it was WCW's angle) picked Flair up and brought him back to *Nitro*. When he finally arrived, stumbling around and wielding an axe handle, Bobby Heenan—who, like all the other announcers, wasn't allowed to see the taped segments—wanted to know if he was drunk. Instead of making a babyface comeback, Flair and all the rest of the Horsemen were treated to another beating.

When the show was over, most involved thought it had been a huge success. But the ratings told a different story. *Raw* did a record 5.90 to *Nitro*'s 3.90—the biggest gap in the history of the war. There was no denying that wacky, skit-laden shows were not what the public wanted to see, and so the very next week, things were back to "normal" (meaning only a few crappy skits and the usual amount of crappy matches). The ratings were also back to "normal," which by this point meant that *Raw* only beat *Nitro* by a million viewers or so.

Still, those in power felt there were other reasons for the 3.90 rating, pointing to guys like Flair, Bret, Benoit, Malenko, Jericho, and Raven who, not surprisingly, also happened to be among the best workers on the roster. Those six, in addition to Kanyon, Bam Bam Bigelow, and Roddy Piper, were singled out in a mid-February booking meeting as guys who needed to be cut off at the legs (not literally, although if Nash could have literally done so, he might have).

Bigelow may have been on the hit list, but interestingly enough, he didn't care. "There was a lot of animosity in that locker room, just with everything. It was getting to be so much bullshit. And there was so much stuff going down that nobody was happy. I was pretty much the only one that was happy because my checks weren't bouncing. I didn't give a shit."[17]

Of course, as WCW kept getting trounced in the ratings, the last thing they really needed to do was continue to push the old stale guys while killing off the younger rising stars. Word spread, and the locker room morale sank lower than ever. Benoit and Malenko were outraged when word got around that Nash had referred to them as "vanilla midgets" (a slang term for small, boring guys), and it seemed more certain than ever that Jericho, their close friend, would get the hell out of Dodge when his deal came due.

Ironically, Jericho could have left sooner than he did: "Even though I'd been working in WCW for over a year I had never signed my contract. I wasn't holding out for more money or having a legal disagreement, I simply never put the pen to the paper and returned the contract to WCW's lawyers. Nobody seemed to realize it and I decided to see how long I could go without signing. It was astonishing that no one in the office had ever followed up with me about it, but this was the same company that once sent me a FedEx with nothing inside, so it wasn't too hard to believe."[18]

Most of the undercard guys were beginning to despise Nash, feeling he was only there to push his close friends and bury the talented workers. Nash, of course, denied this and blamed Hogan. Hogan, he said, had control over all his own storylines, and there was nothing anyone could do about that. It was ruining the shows, he lamented. There was also concern because Bischoff, seemingly having given up all hope himself, was spending less and less time at *Nitro* and more and more time in Hollywood. Everyone figured he knew the ship was going down and was

Believe it or not, without his mask Rey actually looks more like a kid than he does dressed up like Spiderman here. [GEORGE NAPOLITANO]

working hard to make sure he'd have a lifeboat to fall back on when it was fully submerged.

One man who managed to get out of WCW before it all hit the fan was Paul Wight, a.k.a. the Giant, who made his WWF debut at the **St. Valentine's Day Massacre** PPV from Memphis on February 14. He came from under the ring, interfering in a Vince McMahon versus Steve Austin cage match and accidentally assisting Austin's win. The WWF, having had so much success with Andre the Giant, had always had an eye on Wight. McMahon repeatedly ridiculed Wight's WCW run, saying the idiots there had no idea how to book a man as a giant. He then proceeded to spend several years booking Wight (who took on the ring name Big Show) a million times worse than WCW had done on their most inept day. In fact, just weeks after his debut, he was presented as just another big doofus doing a clean pinfall job to Austin.

WCW's burial of their talented workers continued on February 21 at the *SuperBrawl* PPV. Benoit and Malenko beat WCW Tag champions Barry Windham and Hennig in a non-title match to win a title shot against them. The title match took place thirty seconds after the first match and was over in the blink of an eye as Windham hit Malenko with a belt and pinned him. Both Benoit and Malenko ended up looking like goofs. Months earlier, the plan had been for them to win a tournament for the vacant belts. Plans changed. Nash and Hall beat Rey Mysterio and Konnan to win Rey's mask. Rey, unmasked, looked about fourteen years old, but apparently Bischoff felt he was more marketable that way than as a superhero-like luchador whose mask would sell en masse at the merchandise stand.

"In Mexico, when a wrestler loses a mask, it's the high point of the night and maybe the year," noted Rey Mysterio. "There's a moment of pride: the winner takes the mask and treats it like a sacred trophy. It's a matter of respect to the profession as well as to the wrestler. But in America, things are different. Nash and Hall started playing with the mask in the ring. Kevin stuck it on the back of his head. Not exactly a lot of respect for tradition there."[19]

Hall won the U.S. title from an immobile Piper in an atrocious match. And, in the main event, Hogan beat Flair to retain the World title when David Flair zapped his dad with a taser and joined the nWo. This was also the pay-per-view debut of one Torrie Wilson, a former fitness model who would go on to become one of the biggest female stars in wrestling history and eventually appear in one of *Playboy*'s biggest issues ever. In the grossest sight imaginable, she made out with David afterwards.

Despite all the damage they had done with their string of horrific shows, *SuperBrawl* was a huge success: its 1.1 buy rate nearly beat out the WWF's *St. Valentine's Day Massacre* that had featured the Austin versus McMahon cage match. The office was jubilant.

What they did not know, however, was that this would be the last great buy rate the company would ever draw.

Following *SuperBrawl*, Bischoff attempted his latest publicity ploy. Shockingly, however, it had nothing to do with *Nitro*. Instead, Goldberg appeared on *The Tonight Show* and challenged Steve Austin to a fight. Goldberg had never wanted to issue the challenge, rightly feeling that it made him look like a lesser star, but Nash and Bischoff made it clear that he had to. So he did, but with such a lack of enthusiasm that it came off as lame. Then, to make matters worse, after Tony Schiavone hyped it up like crazy on *Nitro*, WCW never showed footage of the challenge or even bothered to mention who had been challenged. The majority of fans at home hadn't watched Leno and ended up with no earthly idea what was going on. The WWF, obviously, never acknowledged it.

One could argue that it was good that WCW never showed footage of the incident because it would have made them look like clowns. That is probably true. The bad news, however, is that WCW had a bad habit of never showing mainstream footage of *anything*—even stuff that would have made them look cool or hip. Whenever the WWF received free outside publicity, they milked it for all it was worth. WCW's unwritten policy was apparently to just ignore it.

"I remember one time Goldberg met Mark McGwire, who was on the verge of breaking the home run record and was in the news literally every day," recalls Bobby Heenan. "McGwire was a huge mark for wrestling. He and Goldberg met up before a game, did some batting practice. Had this happened in the WWF, they'd have filmed everything, probably had Goldberg and McGwire going to Louisville to pick out bats. But we never showed anything. We weren't allowed to make mention of it, because it wasn't WCW's idea."

Around this time, Nash realized just how much heat he was getting backstage and attempted to do something about it. The February 22 *Nitro* saw him put over Rey Mysterio. The idea here was twofold: first, it was a "reward" for Mysterio, as he'd agreed to lose his mask and become "marketable," and second, it was a way for Nash to show the crew that he was willing to do a job for anyone, even someone (almost literally) half his size. Nash went for a powerbomb, but Rey punched him repeatedly in the head, and Nash fell onto his back for a fluke pin. In reality, it meant nothing, but Nash used it for pretty much the rest of his career to point out what a "great company guy" he was.

It should be noted, however, that losing his mask caused Rey all kinds of problems in his native Mexico. For instance, the following week, Mysterio and Psicosis had a very controversial match in Tijuana. The original plan was to bill it as mask versus mask and put Psicosis over clean, since Rey was already going to lose it five days earlier at *SuperBrawl*. Mexican wrestling tradition, however, bars wrestlers from wearing masks after they've lost them (not that this doesn't happen regularly). Rival promoter Antonio Pena of AAA went to the newspapers and ratted out Mysterio, and the Box y Lucha (boxing and wrestling) Commission—a legit commission despite the fact that it oversees a fake sport (don't ask)—refused to let the match take place as planned. So it was decided instead to have Rey put his hair on the line against Psicosis' hair. For unknown reasons, the commission put the kibosh on that one as well. Finally, it was decided to just do a straight match for Psicosis' WWA title, which Rey won. The fans in attendance, all aware of what had happened in WCW, booed Mysterio—formerly a huge babyface— nearly out of the building.

LESSON NOT . . . NO WAIT, LESSON ACTUALLY LEARNED:
Upon his arrival to WWE in 2002, Rey Mysterio showed up wear-
ing his mask. This led to approximately 10 trillion masks being sold and
Rey becoming the top Hispanic star the company has ever had.

Although the *Nitro* featuring the Nash-Rey fiasco was better than the usual crapfest the show had become, WCW got destroyed in the ratings: 4.32 to *Raw*'s 6.32. At the time, the WWF had hit on their own winning formula: big stars (Steve Austin, Vince McMahon, Rock, and Mick Foley) combined with over-the-top raunchiness (half-naked women, transvestites, simulated sex, and more). In fact, things were getting so wild that the mainstream media were starting to take notice, and some of the WWF's own allies were pleading with them to tone it down. One, TSN in Canada, was so outraged that they began to heavily edit the shows (axing both language and entire segments) to the point that some of them in no way resembled the original broadcast.

Bischoff, in a pre-show *Nitro* meeting on March 1, again claimed that the WWF's strategy would backfire because sponsors would pull out within a year (his theory would eventually prove to be correct; it just took longer than he thought). Therefore, the company was going to change its course *again*. He went over a laundry list of things that would now be banned, including crotch-grabbing, talking about hoochies, and lewd dances. He said WCW was going to go in the opposite direction of the

WWF, because even if their ratings went down, if they had sponsors and WWF didn't, they'd win. It was a good theory.

More real-life tragedy struck on February 22, when Richard Wilson, the Renegade and many-time "stunt double" for Warrior during his disastrous 1998 run, shot and killed himself after an argument with his girlfriend. He'd been released from his WCW contract weeks earlier and was said to be very despondent over it. In case you haven't noticed by now, the real-life casualties of this so-called wrestling war were beginning to pile up. By the time the Monday Night Wars ended, Rick Rude and Bobby Duncam Jr. would also be dead, and Bret Hart and Sid Vicious would both have suffered career-ending injuries.

Whether or not Bischoff even believed they had a chance to turn things around is debatable, as his trips to Hollywood were on the rise (his longtime pal Jason Hervey of *The Wonder Years* was shopping him around as—get ready—"The Golden Boy Who Saved Wrestling"), and in early March he took his daughter to France on vacation. This was not a several-day excursion in between major TV tapings; he simply left and didn't come back for weeks. This left Kevin Nash completely in charge of the company.

There's an old belief in wrestling that bookers shouldn't be on-screen talent themselves: it's almost impossible for them to do what's right for business, since what's right for business is usually not them. Virtually everyone in the company believed that Nash was slowly turning *Nitro* into a vehicle to get himself over, and since he was smart enough to understand that Hogan, no matter what, was always going to be around, he buddied up with Hulk and built the show around him as well.

Nash's first move was to present a *Nitro* that featured no wrestling in the first hour. None. Not a single solitary match. You might recall that *Nitro* was a wrestling show. Apparently, Nash thought that wrestling on this wrestling show was unnecessary, and he booked the show like this to prove that they'd draw the same rating if they had zero match-es in the first hour as they would if there were ten. In lieu of actual, you know, wrestling, the infamous hour featured a video of some kids jumping around at a *Nitro* party; one of the Nitro Girls talking about life while sitting on the grass with her dog; a Konnan music video; a video of Hogan making fun of Flair; a skit in which Buff Bagwell and Scott Steiner got arrested and were told by the cops that they could get off the hook if they became cops themselves (Fatty Arbuckle and Buster Keaton did this same storyline, only they did it about seventy-five years earlier, and it was much more entertaining); a skit in which Hogan and Nash watched the video of Hogan making fun of Flair that had aired earlier; a skit in which Hogan, Nash, and Torrie went to a firing range; and a skit in which Torrie, Nash, and Hogan went to dinner. And then, at 9:00, the first thing to air was a skit in which Flair challenged Goldberg and began to do the one thing he didn't need to do: turn heel.

Raw obliterated the show by almost 2.5 points.

The Flair heel turn, though, would prove to be even more damaging in the long term than the lack of wrestling. Make no mistake about it: Ric Flair was one of the all-time great heel wrestlers; he knew exactly how to beg off and bump around to make his babyface opponent look a hell of a lot better than they sometimes really were. He worked this style for years, and fans grew to love him because he really was the very best, night-in and night-out, year after year. In 1999, however, Flair was fifty years old—a true living legend or elder statesman—and no matter how much he wanted to be the Ric Flair of old (and make no mistake, he was still damn good at it), fans had no interest in paying to boo him. Worse yet, he so badly wanted to work heel again that he convinced Hulk Hogan to turn babyface. Hogan was stale on top, and it was prob-ably time to do something about it, but in the list of somethings that might be done to turn WCW around, this double-turn certainly wasn't near the top.

The turn took place at the *Uncensored* PPV on March 14 before a sellout 15,930 fans at Freedom Hall in Louisville, Kentucky. The good news was that it was a fun show with an insanely excited crowd—almost to the point you'd think you were watching a different promotion. The booking, as always, was ridiculous. As usual, the idea of *Uncensored* was that none of the matches were sanctioned because WCW executives were afraid things were going to get wild, and they wanted to wash their hands of the whole deal (in other words, just like real life). Of course, how three titles could change hands at an unsanctioned event was never explained. The main event was scheduled to be Hogan versus Flair in a first blood match for the WCW title with a big stipulation: if Flair lost, he had to retire, and if he won, he got control of WCW forever. Yes, forever. For non-wrestling fans, in a first blood match, two men wrestle, and the first guy to bleed loses. The irony of this was that Turner had clamped down on usage of the word "blood" on TV, so in the weeks leading up to the match, the announcers were unable to utter the "blood" part of "first blood." This is true. So during the match, which took place inside a cage, Flair got gashed in the head with some razor wire and began to bleed. The announcers, confused, couldn't figure out why the match was continuing. They would have been comforted to know that fans watching at home couldn't figure it out either. Then Hogan bled. Then a bunch of people ran out, including David Flair (whose helpful advice to Hogan was "HULK UP!") and Arn Anderson. Finally, Anderson threw a tire iron into Flair, which Flair used to knock out Hogan, get the pin (in a first blood match, mind you), and win the belt. Sure enough, Flair—who'd been telling people backstage that he was *sure* he could pull off this double turn—was roundly booed.

ECW's perennial underdog and former World champion Mikey Whipwreck debuted with the company that night, a night he'd never forget for all the wrong reasons. "I was told four different things when I debuted against Kidman at *Uncensored*," noted Whipwreck. "Jimmy Hart told me I was winning in ten minutes. Kevin Sullivan told me I was losing in eight. Mike Graham told me I was getting DQ'd or something after only five minutes, setting something up for *Nitro*. Finally, Arn Anderson told me to ignore everybody else and put Kidman over in about fifteen. I was there two hours and I already hated the place."

This was not the only first-night hilarity. "I saw Bret Hart at *Nitro* the night after *Uncensored*," Whipwreck said, "and they flew him into Cincinnati for no reason. They had nothing for him. He told me he heard Kidman and I had the match of the night. I told him I thought it was good and was hoping it would lead into something. He looked right in my eyes and said, 'You're probably fucked.' Yep, he was right."

The only exciting thing about the Spring Breakout **Nitro** from Panama City, Florida, on March 22 was that after Rey Mysterio Jr. beat Flair in a title match via DQ, he tossed him into the swimming pool that the ring was floating on. Some observers strongly believe that if a wrestler was thrown into a swimming pool on every single edition of **Nitro**, the company would still be alive today.

The Flair-Hogan double turn didn't help to slow the ratings plunge— it increased it. At this point, *Raw* was really beginning to pull away in the ratings battle, setting a brand-new ratings record: 6.51 to *Nitro*'s 3.51. If that wasn't embarrassing enough, the HHH versus X-Pac (Sean Waltman) *Raw* main event did a 6.47 to *Nitro*'s 2.85, one of the biggest gaps of all time. And what was *Nitro*'s main event? Dallas Page versus the newly turned babyface Hulk Hogan. Hogan, of course, placed the blame on Page, no doubt saying that the rating proved he wasn't a main event–quality star.

Part of the reason for the ratings decimation—besides the obvious fact that *Nitro* had grown so hideous that more and more fans were giving up entirely on the product—was that WCW was foolishly throwing away the perfect opportunity to attract fans. As you'll recall, *Nitro* was three hours to *Raw*'s two. The final two hours were head-to-head, but WCW's first hour was completely and totally unopposed. Instead of using that first hour to, say, build up the rest of the show or present blow-away matches or angles that would compel fans to keep watching, they turned that free hour into a kind of pre-show, a sixty-minute period so forgettable that there wasn't any reason to even tune in. In fact, on the March 28 show, the announcers were instructed not to even talk about that day's events until the second hour began. Keep in mind, they had a full unopposed hour to go all-out promoting the Bret Hart versus Goldberg confrontation set to take place in Bret's native Canada with interviews and history packages. Instead, they aired horrible matches and lame Hogan skits.

After all the banter back and forth, the online accusations, and the radio show interviews, Dana Hall got back together with Scott. Mean Gene was so happy for the couple that he immediately requested fans drop $1.49 per minute to hear the details on the WCW Hotline.

The Bret-Goldberg angle was one of those things that could have led to monster business if anyone in the company had even the slightest clue. The backstory, obviously, was that WCW had dropped the ball on Bret since the day he'd signed his contract. You've surely noticed that since Montreal, very little has been written about Bret in this book, and that's because very little of importance happened. Despite being paid almost $3 million a year, he had been booked into oblivion. In the months leading up to this show, Nash had made it clear that he didn't think Bret was a draw and that his contract was completely unjustified.

LESSON NOT LEARNED: Countless wrestlers have gone to WWE since WCW died, some of whom were paid top dollar, which some in the company felt was not warranted. One such wrestler was a man who went to UFC and became a huge pay-per-view draw: Brock Lesnar. Despite a massive reaction by crowds to his initial return appearance following **WrestleMania XXVII**, he was soon booked to face John Cena on a WWE **B Show**. He lost that match. He then got into a feud with Triple H that lasted most of a year, and by the time that feud was over, so was Lesnar's ability to draw big numbers on pay-per-view.

Of course, that's the catch-22: if you don't believe someone justifies their paycheck and you utilize them accordingly, there's no way they'll ever possibly justify said paycheck. Bret had spoken with Bischoff about an idea he had for an angle that would lead to him actually becoming a main-event player in the company. Nash, upon hearing it, tried to kill it off (when Bret confronted him about this, he claimed he wasn't *really* trying to kill it, he was just working an angle since everyone assumed they had heat). Although Nash was booker, Bischoff still got final say, so in the end the angle went pretty much exactly as Bret had formulated it.

For one day, at least.

Bret, who was a heel at the time, came out for his interview. Since this *Nitro* was in Toronto, he got one of the biggest babyface reactions of the entire year from the crowd. He didn't even bother trying to remain a bad guy; instead, he recited the Canadian national anthem to deafening cheers; then he started to run down various guys, including Goldberg. Fans booed Goldberg's name in a thunderous manner, but since WCW wanted to keep him a good guy, Eric demanded they pipe in the fake "GOLDBERG!" chants louder than ever. Bret, in a line that got him some heat, said it was ridiculous for Goldberg to challenge Steve Austin, seeing as how he (Bret) had beaten Austin every time they had wrestled. Goldberg finally came out and speared him. The crowd did not like that one bit, but you wouldn't be able to tell this from watching on TV due to all the piped-in chants. After the spear, however, both guys just lay there dead. Finally, Bret recovered, turned Goldberg over, and counted his own pin. The crowd went crazy and counted along with him. Afterwards, Bret removed his shirt to reveal that he'd been wearing a steel plate.

"Hey, Bischoff," he growled into the house mic. "I quit!" Then he stormed off.

"When I got home," Bret said, "I actually contemplated quitting for real. It seemed to me that Eric just didn't have enough wrestling smarts to do his job."[20]

Regardless of the ridiculous notion that Bret would come to *Nitro* with a steel plate under his jersey so he could knock out Goldberg, some people in the company actually thought this was real. Part of that had to do with a loud argument between Bret and Eric backstage right after the segment, with no cameras present. Most everyone in the company, however, knew it for what it really was: another lame attempt to work the boys. Bret disappeared from TV for a while, in part because he had to undergo groin surgery that would keep him on the shelf for several months. Ultimately, nothing became of the angle, but for once, Bret's absence wasn't WCW's fault, and this time, the reasons behind it were devastatingly tragic.

On May 23, 1999, Bret Hart's brother Owen died. While any wrestling death is tragic, this one was different. Owen didn't die due to a heart problem likely brought on by excessive steroid abuse; he didn't overdose on the popular combination of alcohol and pain pills; he didn't die by any fault of his own. Owen James Hart died because he was a company man, a pawn in a ratings battle that had already been over for a long time.

The scene was the WWF's *Over the Edge* pay-per-view at Kemper Arena in Kansas City. The time was approximately 7:40 p.m. CST. Owen stood high in the rafters above the ring dressed up in a ridiculous blue superhero costume and hooked up to a harness. Early in his career he'd wrestled as the Blue Blazer, a masked, high-flying good guy. This was 1999, however, and masked high-flying good guys were not cool.

Instead, they were comedy material. Owen, back in character, told children to drink their milk, and because guys who told children to drink their milk weren't cool anymore, he was a bad guy. He was, essentially, a spoof on the babyface Hulk Hogan, and his descent from the rafters was a spoof on the babyface Sting. The plan was for him to descend to the ring for his entrance, but then get "stuck" about ten feet above the canvas and do a pratfall once released. For days, Hart had been nervous about the stunt, but, as a model employee, the closest he ever came to refusing was when he told them he wouldn't do a second practice run-through on the day of the show.

Obviously, a pratfall from above the ring would require a quick-release mechanism. Those who watched Sting's previous descents will probably recall how long it took him to get his harness off once he reached the ground. He had to unhook the main harness, then the safety backup. Neither had a quick-release mechanism.

Tragically, the harness Owen was attached to on this evening was not designed to hold the weight of a 220-pound man; it was actually used on sailboats. As a video of him cutting a promo aired on the TitanTron, the harness released prematurely, and he fell seventy-one feet into the ring. The physicians on hand attended to him; then he was rushed to the hospital, where he was pronounced dead on arrival.

Moments after his body was taken through the curtain, in a moment still debated to this day, Vince McMahon made the decision to continue the show. Nobody involved, from the wrestlers to the announcers to the employees backstage to the fans, can likely remember very clearly much of what happened in the next two hours.

The next day's *Raw* was a strange show, seen as an example of damage control by some and as a beautiful tribute by others. They presented several straight-up wrestling matches with clean finishes, and in between, interviews with the wrestlers. Many of the wrestlers openly broke down and wept when talking about Owen. *Nitro* opened with a graphic and a three-bell salute; then Tony Schiavone offered his condolences to the family.

Hours after the accident occurred, Bischoff met Bret at the airport and chartered him a flight back to Calgary. He told him that he didn't expect him to come to *Nitro* at any point in the future and that he could take as much time off as needed to get through this. Bret strongly considered retirement, feeling he'd never get his passion for the business back, and it would be virtually impossible to ever feign anger toward someone for a wrestling storyline again. Obviously, all plans to do a Bret versus Goldberg program were shelved indefinitely.

Owen's death wasn't the only tragedy to hit the Hart family around this time. On April 5, Bret's brother-in-law Davey Boy Smith lay in the ICU at Calgary's Rockyview Hospital, being fed through an IV. It had been a rough few years for him. First, he suffered multiple knee injuries at the end of his WWF run in 1997. Then, he was so upset with what happened in Montreal that he requested his release from the company. Vince McMahon, generous soul that he is, said sure—but it would cost Smith $150,000 to get out of his contract. Smith paid up after he negotiated this down to $100,000. Things didn't end up any better in WCW, as he took a bodyslam during a match with Alex Wright at **Fall Brawl** and landed right on the trap door that was used to help Warrior magically appear and disappear. He crushed the C-9 and C-10 vertebrae in his back and fractured four other vertebrae. To mask the pain, he was taking a laundry-list of pain medication, including morphine, and when he finally checked into rehab after his wife, Diana, tried to scare him straight by overdosing on 100 Xanax (not the ideal way to try to scare someone straight), he took three weeks to detox instead of the usual five days. On top of all that, he was suffering from a staph infection and was confined to a full-body cast. At the time, many speculated that his career was over, and he was in bad enough shape that there was some fear he might not survive. WCW, obviously deeply concerned, cited the ninety-day injury clause in his contract and immediately fired him via their usual delivery method, FedEx. This caused such an uproar that Bischoff immediately went on the defensive, saying he had no idea what rough shape Smith was in when he made his decision, and for a period of time at least, Davey Boy's checks kept coming.

In late April, the Spanish-language Telemundo opted to pick up *Nitro* for another six months, which was a shock to everyone. After the WCW Latino deal fell through, WCW started sending one-hour edited versions of *Nitro* to the station. Pretty much everyone thought the deal would go bust since the Mexicans in WCW were always promoted as total losers. Surprisingly, however, the ratings were really good. One would think that WCW would have seen the success of the show in the Hispanic community and decide to make their Mexican wrestlers look better on TV to help draw new fans. But that never happened, and later in the year, it would be far, far worse.

Nitro the following week was notable only for a weird snafu in the main event. It was Hogan versus Flair versus Goldberg versus Page in a four-way for the WCW title. Goldberg hit Hogan with the spear and jackhammer. Nash, Hogan's good buddy, was supposed to make the save. Since continental drift is faster than Kevin Nash on foot, he didn't make it to the ring in time. Lo and behold, this caused Hogan to "have to" kick out of Goldberg's finisher. It was a small thing, but all the small things week after week were starting to seriously water down Goldberg.

And that was a common theme; although Goldberg was a top draw, things were starting to collapse for him. In addition to the loss of the feud with Hart, each week it seemed that events, either planned or unplanned, were watering him down. Goldberg's descent continued at the *Spring Stampede* pay-per-view, where he wasn't even booked in the main event that saw Dallas Page pin Ric Flair in a four-way, also featuring Sting and Hulk Hogan, to win the WCW World title for the first time in his career. Page was in his mid-forties but he looked older thanks to years and years of "hanging and banging" at the beach.

From an athletic standpoint, it was no big deal to put the belt on him because he was a hard worker, and he usually had very good matches. The problem was that WCW, over the last two years, had gained a reputation of being an old man's company, and taking the belt off a fifty-year-old and putting it on a guy who looked fifty did nothing to counter that stereotype.

It didn't help that the match was such a mess that most fans didn't even know what happened at the finish. As a result, the crowd reaction to the title change—which would have been disappointing in any case, given that Page was the least popular of all the guys in the ring—was even less extraordinary. Perhaps the biggest news coming out of the match was Hogan's fake knee injury (well, his knee really was hurt, and he did have it scoped a few weeks later, but he didn't get hurt in this match and they overplayed the severity of the injury). Hogan sold it to the point that he even used help to get into the hotel that night during a period where there weren't any fans around to see it. Most knew what was going on here: he realized he was getting stale on top, plus he saw WCW falling apart at the seams and didn't want to be seen as the guy on top during that period.

It didn't matter where Hogan was during this period, he was always working. For instance, he appeared on the *Tonight Show* on April 9, the same *Tonight Show* where he announced his retirement several months earlier. He explained that he never said he was going to "retire"; he just said he was "tired."

Following the airing of an ESPN **Outside the Lines** special that touched on steroid and human growth hormone use in pro wrestling, WCW scheduled a "surprise drug test" before the April 15 **Thunder**. Strangely, Scott Steiner no-showed the event, claiming he had suffered a back injury, and was therefore not tested. Not only had Steiner become so muscular he could barely move, but he had also developed a short temper, seemingly flying into an uncontrollable rage at the slightest provocation, to the point that he had been arrested several times. In a match the following week on **Nitro** (his back seemingly miraculously healed in less than a week), he carried the near-400-pound Scott Norton all the way across the ring before giving him an atomic drop. The crowd, oddly, chanted "STEROIDS!" during the match. Bobby Heenan responded by shouting, "I've never heard a crowd so pumped up before!"

While *Nitro*'s ratings had unquestionably begun a downturn, other WCW shows were in a flat-out freefall. Longtime WCW fans are probably wondering why little mention has been made so far of the company's other television programs, *Thunder* and *WCW Saturday Night*. The main reason is that we decided to give the shows as much attention as WCW gave them, which, as you can see, was essentially zero. *Thunder* was considered an A-show for a week or two, and from that point on, it was just two hours of mostly filler. *WCW Saturday Night* made *Thunder* look like *Raw* at its peak. When you have a wrestling show and you treat it as filler, fans quickly stop tuning in. By this point in the war, *Thunder*, which had been drawing ratings in the 4s just a few months earlier, was down to a 2.0, and *Saturday Night* was down to a 1.7. The *Thunder* rating was especially bad since advertisers had been sold on the show doing a 3.5. Since the show was promised to do a 3.5 and it did a 2.0, WCW had to recoup advertisers with "make-good" ads. This costs money. *Thunder* was consistently so horrible (most weeks, the only entertainment the show provided was unintentional comedy and two hours' worth of bickering between announcers Mike Tenay and Tony Schiavone, who hated each other) that it almost seemed as if WCW didn't *want* the show to get to the 3.5 range, so they were willingly losing money *and* providing horrible programming week after week. This is not a formula for profit.

And now *Nitro* had begun its ratings collapse as well. The April 19 *Nitro* illustrated just how bad things had become. Quality-wise, *Nitro* kicked *Raw*'s ass, but it didn't matter because, as they say in the stock market, *Nitro* was on a downward trend. They did finally put some effort back into the unopposed hour, including an awesome Cruiserweight match and a great interview in which Flair appeared to go insane, but it didn't matter. The damage of all those horrible shows, specifically in the first hour, was done. Overall, *Raw* did a 6.11 to *Nitro*'s 4.08 that night.

The tragically bad shows weren't about to stop, either, as confusing, convoluted storylines were now becoming the order of the day. The "Crazy Flair" interview, in which he stripped down to his boxers, featured the man who was once WCW's top draw ranting and raving about how he was not only World Heavyweight champion, but also president of WCW and president of the United States as well. This led to Roddy Piper managing to convince a mental institution to lock Flair up as a madman upon his son David's request. It should also be noted that three days later on *Thunder*, it was announced that Flair had been released and was president of WCW again. Then, four days after that on *Nitro*, the show opened with footage of Flair "still locked up." (On the bright side, nobody ever watched *Thunder*, so that storyline snafu could be ignored.)

While Flair quite literally danced around the hospital in his underwear with other insane inmates, J.J. Dillon announced that since he was vice president of the company (which was news to viewers), Charles Robinson would be the new acting president until Flair returned. For those who don't know the name "Charles Robinson," he was a referee whose sole claim to power in WCW was apparently that he was a big Ric Flair fan who had bleached his hair blonde like the Nature Boy. Piper then did an interview saying that since Flair was gone, he was in charge. Although the storyline was not likely designed this way on purpose, it drew close parallels with the real-life WCW in that nobody really had any clue who was in charge, and if someone said they were in power for the day, everyone just sort of went along with it because they'd given up long ago.

Piper and Robinson then had an in-ring confrontation that ended in Piper being arrested. This ultimately led to Flair versus Piper being signed for the PPV, the stipulation being that if Piper won, he would

Most would look at this photo and see Ric Flair and Roddy Piper engaged in battle. We look at it and see Charles Robinson, WCW president. Reason No. 1387 we shake our heads at this company. [GEORGE NAPOLITANO]

become WCW president. Perhaps you'll recall that when Flair won the presidency in the match with Bischoff, the stipulation was that he'd be president "for life." There is no such thing as "for life" in wrestling. Flair then ran into Scott Hall, who, as you might recall, had been off TV for some time. It was never explained why Hall was in the mental hospital, and his appearance was never acknowledged by the announcers. Apparently, someone just thought it would be funny to put him in there for a cameo, not understanding that when wrestling fans see something happening on TV, they automatically (and often foolishly, especially in WCW's case) assume that there is a reason behind its occurrence. It wasn't until the following week, in Charlotte, North Carolina, that Flair returned to TV. He explained that Arn Anderson had bailed him out. Bet you never knew that when you're confined to a mental institution, you can leave simply by posting bail. His first order of business was to put a bounty on Kevin Nash's head. Over the course of just this one show, the dollar figure changed from $100,000 to $50,000 to $1,000,000, depending upon who was telling the story. His second order of business, since it was Charlotte, was to get knocked out by DDP in the main event.

If you thought the last three paragraphs were confusing, imagine watching it play out in all its glory on your television set. And this was just your average convoluted *Nitro* storyline from 1998–1999. This is not to say that the WWF was writing great TV; many times, a *Raw* show would draw a tremendous number, and folks would sit there wondering how this was even possible. The WWF writing was full of plot holes and angles that made no sense, angles that often insulted the intelligence of the average human being. But the big difference was simply that WWF's writing *was better than WCW's*. World Championship Wrestling set a standard for bad television in the late '90s that will likely never be equaled (and TNA Impact Wrestling in the '00s tried). There have been countless other bad wrestling TV shows, but they were all bad for other reasons; perhaps they had no real talent (GLOW), or bad production (your typical independent promotion), or the people writing it did so just to get a family member over as a star (TNA Impact Wrestling, though to be honest, most every promotion has been guilty of this).

WCW was different from all the others; they had a deeper talent pool than any other promotion in the history of this business, and Turner owned them, so they certainly had the capacity for tremendous production. The greatest difference of all, though, was what they did with their talent. While some companies tried way too hard to get a family member over as a star, those companies were at least trying to get *someone* over as a star. WCW killed all their talent. They killed the undercard guys by making them out to be bit players, they killed the mid-carders by making it very clear that they were mid-carders for life, and they killed anyone even close to the top of the pack by booking them as goofs or losers or having them alternate between heel and babyface with such rapidity that fans had no idea whether to boo or cheer them. As it turned out, nobody was a star, and worse, when it appeared a wrestler was starting to get some fan support, he was immediately booked into oblivion.

It wasn't just in-ring talent; from a production standpoint, despite having the ability and finances to produce great shows, they had more snafus than one could imagine. Sometimes, when watching *Nitro* and especially *Thunder*, one couldn't help but feel like they were *trying* to screw things up, because it would take a great deal of talent to purposely make a show seem so unintentionally funny. What is most mind-boggling about WCW TV in 1999, however, was that fans who took copious amounts of aspirin to allow themselves to continue watching week after week could never have imagined that just one year later, WCW would get to a point where these storylines looked like Emmy material in comparison.

If it wasn't apparent to everyone by this point that the company was in severe trouble, the Charlotte show offered proof positive. The fact that the show was massacred by *Raw* in the ratings battle by over three points was one thing. More damning, however, might have been the fact that despite always drawing big crowds in the Carolinas, they had to give out thousands of free tickets just to get a respectable crowd into the building for TV.

WCW had no one but themselves to blame for that. Over the years, they had booked Flair, a "hometown hero" in the region, so badly that it had become a running joke that whenever they were about to run a show there something stupid was inevitably going to happen with him. Obviously, having Flair go crazy in a mental institution in a period when heels were supposed to be young and cool was stupid. As entertaining as Flair was, even in roles as idiotic as this, his drawing power was killed in a matter of weeks. This was especially distressing since he and Goldberg were the only two guys in the entire company who had been able to affect the ratings in any way. Well, in any positive way, at least.

Thanks, in the storyline, to Roddy Piper, Randy Savage finally returned to the promotion, and, like Scott Steiner, he came back so muscular it looked as though he'd been pumped full of air at a service station. He brought with him a new girlfriend, Stephanie Bellars, a young blonde stripper who had been dubbed Gorgeous George. The backstory there is that Rob Kellum, an undercard worker known as the Maestro, had purchased the rights to the name from the family of George Wagner, who had used it during his run as the biggest star of the early days of televised wrestling. Then, WCW bought the rights when they signed Savage's brother, Lanny Poffo (formerly the Genius in the WWF), who was planning on going as Gorgeous George. It would turn out, however, that Poffo would never once appear on WCW TV, so they gave the moniker to Bellars instead.

It should be noted that despite his never wrestling a single match for the company, WCW saw fit to pay Lanny Poffo $150,000 per year.

At this point, the company decided that perhaps they could slow the ratings slide by playing "hot potato" with their belts. The April 26 *Nitro* featured no less than three title changes. First, Sting beat Page in an awesome match to win the WCW title, and then, an hour later, Page won it back in a four-way also featuring Nash and Goldberg after hitting Nash with an international (called as such because Turner officials wouldn't allow the word "foreign") object. The latter was, um, not as good as the former. Also, Mysterio beat Psicosis to regain the Cruiserweight belt that he'd lost a week earlier. This was the beginning of the desperation booking of the belts (frequent changes) that led to the belts meaning nothing, which led to fans not caring about them, which led to them being useless as far as drawing ratings or PPV buy rates. Like the Flair storyline, however, it would only get worse as time went on. Coming up short in poorly promoted World title matches week after week was also killing Goldberg's drawing power (and he was the last guy with any left after they'd killed Flair in the mental hospital). The saddest part of this whole scenario was that this hotshotting didn't do a rat's ass worth of good: the show only did a 3.89 rating to *Raw's* 5.99.

LESSON NOT LEARNED . . . THEN LEARNED: During a three month period in the fall of 2011, WWE did a similar antic as they changed the WWE title no less than seven times. This led to no real changes in ratings or PPV buys. What **did** lead to interest, however, was putting the title on CM Punk and having him hold it for 434 days. It established Punk as a legitimate main-eventer, and at the time of this writing he was one of the company's biggest merchandise movers . . . despite not even being on television or on shows due to his decision to leave.

It didn't appear that things could get any worse for the company, but in early May, it happened. The show began a several-week period of preemptions for the NBA playoffs. Normally, whenever one of the two shows was preempted, the other show would gain 20 percent of their audience for that night. On May 10, the first night of preemption, *Raw* gained a whopping 50 percent of WCW's audience to draw an 8.09 rating with 9.2 million viewers, making it the most-watched wrestling TV show in the history of the USA Network since the original *Royal Rumble*. The main event overrun, featuring Rock and Austin and Vince versus Undertaker and Triple H and Shane McMahon, did a 9.17 rating and 10.4 million viewers, another record. Although the war had really been over for some time, this put the exclamation point on it.

At this point, it was clear there was no turning around anytime soon. The entire WCW product—from the matches to the look of the TV to the announcers to the guys on top to the entire promotional philosophy—was old and stale. The only hope for a turnaround was to basically scrap everything and start all over again. Doing so, obviously, would lead to a further decline, and realistically, it would take a long period (perhaps a few years) of reprogramming before new wrestlers would start to catch on. Some decline was inevitable if the company hoped to turn around, but it would have been better to start when the show was in the 4s rather than in the 2s.

Sadly, those in charge at WCW had zero patience. Nobody had a two-year plan to turn the ship around; they wanted to turn the ship around *that week*, by any means necessary. Past history should have made it clear that hotshotting generally does more harm than good, but for whatever reason, nobody internally (at least nobody with the power to do anything about it) could see that, despite the fact that evidence—in the forms of ratings and buy rates—was readily at their disposal.

After having put all their banter, all the online accusations, and all the radio show interviews behind them in order to get back together, Dana and Scott Hall separated again.

The bad TV was killing business so fast that the *Slamboree* PPV at the massive TWA Dome, with three title matches and a "winner gets control of the company" match resulted in just 13,789 fans paying $494,795. It was a respectable crowd that sadly was generated only by giving away almost 7,000 free tickets. Only six months earlier, in the same building, 30,000 fans had paid almost a million dollars to get in. When the momentum shifts downward, it does so very quickly. Part of the problem might have been that the previous week's *Thunder* had ended with the following: "*SLAMBOREE*! TOMORROW, 8 p.m. EST." The problem being, of course, that *Thunder* aired on Wednesday and the PPV aired on Sunday.

Slamboree made no effort to reverse the nonsensical booking trend. Flair beat Piper, after hitting him with brass knux, to retain his "presidency" of the company. After the match, Bischoff, who hadn't had any power in storyline for almost six months since his loss to Flair (and had in fact last been seen on TV working as a janitor!), came out and reversed the decision. Long story short, six months of storylines were tossed right out the window with Bischoff's magical (and totally incomprehensible) return as babyface company owner. In the main event, Nash beat Page to win the WCW title. Since this was the fourth time the belt had changed hands in four weeks, it would be an understatement to say that nobody cared. The show ended up doing a 0.45 buy rate, putting the company, at mid-year, $12 million behind budget in PPV alone.

Nitro was a comedy of errors the following night. Flair, who had supposedly lost the presidency, was back as president because Bischoff apparently didn't have any power after all. Of course, if that was the case, the Nash title change shouldn't have been allowed to stand either, since Bischoff restarted the match after Page had won via DQ. Later, however, Gene Okerlund identified Bischoff as a "powerful executive" in WCW, though exactly what kind of power he possessed was never specified. Then Piper gave an interview saying *he* was president, but later in the speech he revealed that he was the commissioner. By the time the show was over, nobody had any idea what in the hell was going on, and that included both fans at home and the people writing the storylines.

As the ratings spiral continued, the company decided that fresh blood was in order. Unfortunately, they decided that this fresh blood should be in the form of Tank Abbott, and they signed him to a huge three-year deal. Abbott, a big fat barroom brawler from Huntington Beach, California, had made his name in the Ultimate Fighting Championship by knocking out a few guys in devastating fashion and going on to garner the worst record of any professional fighter in the history of that organization (8-10-0). He was charismatic, however, and his occasional knockouts were so vicious that he remained a draw and had some people convinced that he was one of the baddest men on the planet. Keep this in mind throughout the rest of this book as you see his name pop up here and there.

In addition to signing Abbott, they re-signed Dennis Rodman. The same Dennis Rodman who no-showed the final *Nitro* before his last PPV appearance, showed up at the big show in no condition to perform, did nothing in the match, then sued the company for $550,000. WCW's ingenious plan to settle that suit? Offer him a new contract for five more dates. Coincidentally, Rodman's first day was supposed to be the Georgia Dome *Nitro* on July 5. And, of course, he no-showed.

Deciding that they hadn't thrown quite enough money out the window that week, they also signed rapper Master P. Why they decided to sign a rapper, who had no interest in getting in the ring and working, is anyone's guess. Despite this, he was given $200,000 per appearance. Yes, *per appearance*. So over the course of a month, WCW paid Master P around $1 million . . . to not wrestle.

All the signings made no difference. On June 7, *Raw* beat *Nitro* by over 3.5 points, which was complete and utter destruction. The main angle on the show saw a mysterious white Humvee crash into a limo containing Kevin Nash, seemingly killing him. This was a brilliant idea, considering that he was supposed to headline a PPV six days later. Worse, $50,000 was spent to shoot this, and it drew a pitiful 2.7 rating. On commentary, Bischoff hinted that the driver was the WWF's Sable, Rena Mero, who had just filed a $140 million sexual harassment lawsuit against McMahon (years later, she'd go back to work for him and play the role of his mistress—welcome to wrestling). Another angle hinted that it was several different people, including Carmen Electra (yes, *that* Carmen Electra). In the end, the real driver was never revealed.

In a real shocker, Sable actually showed up on *Nitro* two nights later and sat in the front row. The commentators never identified her by name nor was a graphic put up, and days later, when confronted by WWF lawyers, they actually claimed she'd just bought a ticket. Presumably, she also bought front row tickets for all of the security guards surrounding her as well. Later, when questioned about the incident in a *USA Today* article, she spouted the following gem: "I wanted to see if the same level of obscenity was taking place. It was not." WCW, after being threatened with a federal lawsuit, told WWF attorney Jerry

McDevitt that she hadn't signed anything and would not be shown on their TV again until after her WWF deal expired. To their credit, WCW upheld this agreement.

In fact, she never showed up on WCW television again.

As if **Nitro**'s ratings freefall wasn't bad enough, **WCW Saturday Night** had plummeted to a 1.3 rating, its lowest ever. "Ever" meaning "in three decades." So WCW came up with a solution: put old-timer Dusty Rhodes on commentary. In reality, this might not have been the worst idea, because the viewing audience for **Saturday Night** skewed quite a bit older than for **Nitro** and particularly for **Raw** (whose median viewing age was about twenty-four). The problem was that Dusty was far more interested in putting himself over than the product, plus it didn't make any sense for a show viewed by so many middle-aged and older people to be used to debut new talent. The exact opposite held true for **Nitro**; the average viewer of that show was in their early thirties, yet WCW continually built the show around wrestlers in their forties and fifties.

The following Sunday, WCW presented *Great American Bash 1999*, an event that so clearly illustrated everything that was killing the company that it could be considered a textbook example for future promoters of what not to do. The show opened with Tony Schiavone, Mike Tenay, and Bobby Heenan running down the card. You might wonder why they would run down the card on the PPV broadcast that *fans had already paid for*. The reason, of course, was that they had failed to promote any matches in the weeks leading up to the event.

Compare this to, say, McDonald's. You'd never go to the restaurant and wonder what your order is going to consist of. Their commercials run a million times during the day, and in the restaurant itself, you're bombarded with information in the form of giant menus that not only describe in detail what is in each meal, but also feature full-color pictures of the meal in question. If McDonald's only served one item—the McMystery Meal—and you never knew whether you were going to get a hamburger, chicken nuggets, a fish sandwich, or whatever, few would dare to purchase it.

WCW pay-per-views were like McMystery Meals: you never knew what you were going to get. WCW never bothered to run down their cards on TV, fearing that fans would switch over to *Raw* while they were doing this. Ironically, they'd then complain that nobody was buying their PPVs.

LESSON NOT LEARNED: WWE presented a McMystery Meal of its own in the form of ECW **December to Dismember** in 2006. Prior to the event, only two matches were promoted, and there was zero real clue as to what else may appear on the show. The event itself was abysmal beyond belief, largely due to infighting behind the scenes between Vince McMahon and Paul Heyman. "That show was just a wreck," Heyman noted. "I knew it going in."

The show was an unmitigated disaster, drawing the lowest domestic buy rate in company history, which led to not only Heyman being fired, but the ECW brand being completely killed off as well.

Then the wrestling started, and man, was it ever bad. Hammer versus Mikey Whipwreck: horrible. Ernest Miller versus Horace Hogan: atrocious. Ric Flair versus Roddy Piper: abysmal. Rick Steiner versus Sting: miserable—and worse, nobody could figure out who won since it just ended when Sting got attacked by three dogs. Yes, as in actual canines. Finally, in a horrific match, Nash (not dead after all following the *Nitro* Humvee attack) beat Randy Savage via DQ when Sid Vicious ran in. Sid, you might recall, had left WCW about ten years prior on horrible terms after nearly stabbing Arn Anderson to death in a real hotel room–brawl in England. We wish we made this stuff up. The show, taking place during the middle of the biggest boom period in American wrestling history, ended up doing a 0.43 buy rate, the fifth-lowest up to that point in their history.

Former Intercontinental and U.S. champion Curt Hennig would unfortunately not add "country music star" to his resume. [GEORGE NAPOLITANO]

Nitro the following Monday was at the SuperDome in New Orleans before a paying crowd of 15,593. Master P had bragged to the company that his presence would make the building sell out. Considering that the building could hold over 55,000, Master P was wrong. The show was built around him and his crew, the No Limit Soldiers, who repeatedly chanted "HOOTIE HOO!" to progressively louder boos. The idea was that Master P and his crew were supposed to be good guys, taking on the bad-guy group of Curt Hennig and his posse (Barry and Kendall Windham and Bobby Duncum Jr.), who would become known as the West Texas Rednecks. The problem here was twofold. First, there were ten or so Soldiers and four Rednecks, which meant the Rednecks got cheered for valiantly holding their own against tremendous odds. Second, Hennig and his crew wrote a hilarious country song called "Rap Is Crap," and since WCW had its roots in the South, this also got them over as big heroes. "Rap Is Crap" became so popular at one point that several country stations around the nation played it in rotation. WCW, of course, responded as they always did when lucking into something like this: they killed the angle dead. Also on the show, Eddie Guerrero returned and had a lackluster match with Juventud Guerrera. Despite having nearly died in a car wreck earlier in the year, his return was presented as an afterthought.

LESSON NOT LEARNED: Much like WCW with "Rap Is Crap," WWE failed to capitalize on something handed to them. Actually, the situation is arguably worse. After telling their undercard talent that "no one would hand them anything" and that they had to make their own breaks, one man did just that: Matt Cardona, better known as "Long Island Iced Z" Zack Ryder, grabbed a video camera and started a goofy YouTube series known as Z! **True Long Island Story**. In the series, Ryder made fun of himself via a batch of skits with his friends. It started to gain momentum, and to date has had over twelve million views. That's not a typo—TWELVE MILLION VIEWS. Additionally, Ryder has amassed over 1.3 million followers on Twitter, 600,000 Facebook likes, and was listed as one of Sports Illustrated 100 Most Influential Social Media Users in Sports. Could anyone blame the guy for having a belt made to declare himself the internet champion?

Despite this, and despite non-stop chants for him at event after event, WWE decided to keep him chained to the bottom of the card . . . when they decide to book him at all, that is.

The highlight of the following week's show was actually something really cool that almost nobody picked up on. Flair, Anderson, and Charles Robinson were in the ring. Sid came out for a promo. Arn, who had never been approached when the decision was made to bring Sid back, immediately walked to the corner and just stood there as if he wanted nothing to do with anything that was going on. When the interview was over and they were about to go to commercial, Sid turned, walked over to Arn, and shook his hand.

For the week of June 28, not only did *Raw* destroy *Nitro* again, but it set a cable ratings record that will probably never be broken. During the Steve Austin versus Undertaker main event, where Austin regained the WWF title, the show actually hit a 9.5 rating and 17.1 share. The rating meant 10.7 million people were watching, and the share meant that of all the TVs with the USA Network turned on in the entire United States, 17 percent of them were tuned into that match. Overall, it was 6.64 to 3.41 in favor of *Raw*. The war was so over at this point that it wasn't even funny.

Things were collapsing so quickly that wrestlers were actually going out in public and burying the company. Hogan, who had been off TV for months rehabbing his knee, made a bunch of friends when he appeared on the Mancow morning show in Tampa that week and ridiculed WCW and all its wrestlers. He even went as far as to say that he was sick and tired of hearing "Malenko and the rest of the midgets" complain about their roles. He also downplayed Goldberg's popularity, saying anyone could win 20,000 matches in a row. Never mind that when Hogan first made it huge in the WWF, he did so by winning approximately 20,000 matches in a row.

It was obvious that things weren't going to change for the mid-carders, and any of them able to get out of the promotion was doing just that. On June 30, Chris Jericho signed with the WWF. In the six months prior to his contract signing, WCW had made very little effort to retain him. In the last few weeks, they panicked, but to no avail, as his mind had already been made up for some time. The WWF saw real potential in him and even went so far as to say he'd be the next Shawn Michaels. Jericho was willing to take a pay cut for an opportunity that he was absolutely not about to get in WCW; specifically, he had lobbied for a showdown against Goldberg, and despite his having done several interviews setting up the angle, nothing ever transpired.

Many of the wrestlers in WCW were upset, because Jericho was well liked, and they couldn't believe the company wouldn't offer him a good deal while it was throwing money away on limos, Humvees, fired NBA stars and rappers (one of Master P's henchmen, Swoll, a huge guy with no talent, was signed for $400,000 per year).

As if Jericho couldn't wait to get out of the company fast enough, his fiancée went to the store one day and bought a Jericho-Malenko WCW doll set. Strangely, the receipt claimed that she'd purchased a Hogan-Sting package. Of course, that meant that Hogan and Sting got the residual revenue from the purchase, not Jericho. "I once received a royalty check in the mail for zero dollars and zero cents," Jericho noted. "Stamps cost thirty-seven cents . . . what was the sense in even mailing it?"[21]

Interestingly enough, before he left, someone asked Jericho if he could also tag along. The conversation went like this:

"He came flat out and asked me: 'Are you going to work for Vince?'

'Yeah, I think I'm going to give the WWF a shot.'

While we have pointed fingers at Eric Bischoff for losing control of WCW and thus leading it to the edge of a cliff, we also want to make note that he was the mastermind behind its only real run at the top of the wrestling business.

Arn Anderson, Chris Benoit, Dean Malenko, Ric Flair, and
Steve "Mongo" McMichael—The Four Horsemen.
Wait, that's one too many. Which one would you lose?

Being a three-time World champion is something to be proud of, Diamond Dallas Page. The work you've done since your wrestling career ended, in which you rehab former stars back to health, though, is perhaps your greatest achievement.

Sparks and steam flying, Goldberg's entrance was a true highlight that enraptured crowds. Not sure what's more amazing: that WCW killed off all his star power or that they allowed to get him over in the first place.

[GEORGE NAPOLITANO]

Gorgeous George didn't look like THIS in the 1950s. Randy Savage's girlfriend was a bombshell, no doubt. Too bad they had to give her a black eye in yet another ill-conceived storyline.

The hottest free agent in wrestling came to the company just in time for its biggest event ever, *Starrcade '97*. In its wisdom, WCW pretty much just had Bret Hart stand around and do next to nothing upon his debut.

[GEORGE NAPOLITANO]

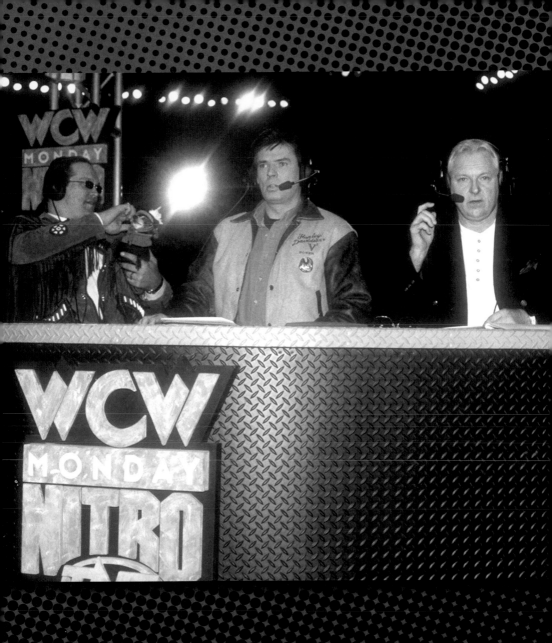

Bobby Heenan looks thrilled to be joined by Eric Bischoff,
Steve McMichael, and Mongo's dog, Pepe. No wonder the guy
admittedly phoned it in during his last years in the booth.

The worm sez: PUT THE MONEY RIGHT HERE!
Dennis Rodman, ladies and gentlemen.

A young Chris Jericho began making a big name for himself in the latter part of the 1990s. Too big, in fact—those in charge were not thrilled when his popularity began to grow without their permission. He'd soon leave for the WWF and become one of their biggest stars. Oops.

[GEORGE NAPOLITANO]

A sometimes overlooked part of early *Nitro*s was the appearance of
the Nitro Girls. Their dance routines kept fans entertained between matches.
It was when it was decided the girls needed to start wrestling
that fans ceased being entertained by their antics.

[GEORGE NAPOLITANO]

The nWo was a legendary force until they started bringing on every
Tom, Dick, and Virgil they could find and wore out their welcome.
Can't blame the big fella for wanting to hide his face.

[GEORGE NAPOLITANO]

Vince Russo liked to pack a lot into every *Nitro* episode.
Here he tells us how many different angles we're about to see
in the next fifteen seconds of the show.

[GEORGE NAPOLITANO]

Sid Vicious looks to be deep in thought about what he may tell us next.
It may take a while; by his own admission, the man has half the brain you do.

Former Ravens cheerleader Stacy Keibler was so stunning she wound up in WCW, WWE, and George Clooney's bedroom. We'll leave it to you to decide which was most impressive.

[GEORGE NAPOLITANO]

"Come on, guys—the main event of *Starrcade '97* was the easiest thing in the world to book! How did you screw it up?" We're with ya, Stinger!

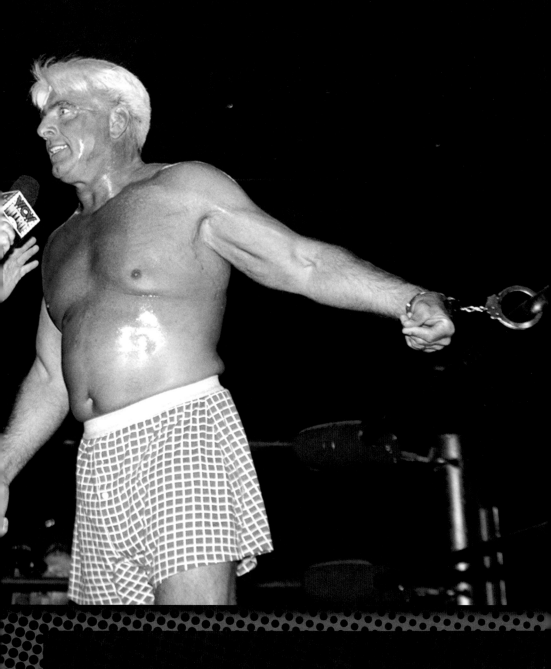

Ric Flair, in his underwear, handcuffed, and unable to help the company.
This pretty much sums up WCW near the end.
Is it too late to change the cover?

[GEORGE NAPOLITANO]

He looked me in the eye and said, 'Can you take me with you?'"

The other party in the conversation? Hulk Hogan.[22]

Nitro on July 5 broadcast once again from the Georgia Dome, home to some of its biggest past successes. Those days were long gone. The show drew 25,338 fans, just over half a house, and $594,745. This was especially bad since the costs of running the show were over $1 million. Don't even ask how it was possible to spend $1 million on a *Nitro*, because nobody will ever figure it out. WCW blamed the low attendance on the holiday weekend. If you haven't already noticed, promoters almost never put the blame for a poor house on themselves. Instead, they blame any outside force they can think of. The crowd is small because it's summer. The crowd is small because it's winter. The crowd is small because it's raining. The crowd is small because it's sunny. By refusing to address the real issue (nobody gives a shit about their show), promoters often delude themselves right out of business.

The show was built around two things; the return of Bret Hart and the return of Goldberg. WCW, in its infinite wisdom, advertised neither ahead of time. They did, for some inexplicable reason, find it fit to advertise an Ernest Miller versus Jerry Flynn kickboxing match that nobody outside Flynn and Miller's immediate families could possibly care about. The show also featured another ingenious angle that further killed off one of their belts, the U.S. title. The champion was Scott Steiner, who had recently undergone a complete transformation to become a 1999 version of 1970s icon "Superstar" Billy Graham. In real life, he had an injured back that required surgery. Instead of admitting this on TV and starting a tournament with all the top guys to crown a new champ, they instead had Ric Flair come out and say that Steiner was so busy pleasuring all of his women that he didn't have time to defend the belt. If that wasn't bad enough, he then awarded the belt to his son David. The irony of this is that word had gotten out that Ernest Miller was going to be the next U.S. champion, and hardcore fans complained long and loud about how that would tarnish the belt. The show ended in typical city-killing Georgia Dome fashion, a 1:27 main event that ended with a hundred guys running in.

Bret's interview began with him saying that WCW had told him to go ahead and talk for as long as he wanted. He basically said that his family had lived for wrestling their whole lives, and now, tragically, they'd also died for it. He said he wasn't sure if he'd ever wrestle again (this was met with a violently negative reaction), and that if he never got a chance to say it to his fans again, thank you. Getting into the ring was obviously a lot harder than he had thought it was going to be, and it was upsetting to him to hear the few hecklers who obviously didn't understand the gravity of what had happened to his family.

"And that's about it," he concluded. "Thank you very much."

The Goldberg return was also epic. First rock group Megadeth came out to play a tune. WCW would soon learn that concerts on wrestling shows are death in the ratings, as the segment garnered a 2.13, *Nitro*'s lowest number in years. The crowd hated the concert with a passion, but then when it was over, an explosion went off and Goldberg emerged from the flames. The crowd went haywire.

WCW responded by immediately cutting to a commercial.

It should be noted that just days after the Megadeth rating came in (the lowest in years, don't forget), WCW contacted KISS and asked them to play at the August 23 **Nitro** for $500,000. Then in late July, they contacted Chad Brock, an obscure country singer, and asked if he'd play a song on the August 9 **Nitro**.

Next stop: the *Bash at the Beach* pay-per-view from Fort Lauderdale— another truly wretched show in a seemingly unending series. The incident with the most far-reaching consequences was a Junkyard Battle Royal featuring Public Enemy, Jerry Flynn, Steve Regal, Horace

Hogan, David Taylor, Brian Knobbs, Ciclope, and Mikey Whipwreck. Though they spent $100,000 to put on the match, which took place in a real, honest-to-goodness junkyard, WCW did not see fit to advertise the match on *Nitro*. Therefore, no one bought the show to see it. Furthermore, Damian, Ciclope, and Whipwreck all suffered serious injuries, as the junkyard was a truly dangerous environment. All three men were out of action for months.

"I suggested shooting the junkyard battle royal the night before to Jimmy Hart," said Whipwreck. "This way everybody could get a spot or two in and they could edit it together to make sense. Instead they shot it live and we all know how that turned out. If you were there live it was awesome. An arena made out of junked cars, fire, explosions, and helicopters flying overhead with spotlights. Real cool visual."

The main event saw Savage and Sid Vicious beat Sting and Nash in a tag match, so Savage won the WCW title. Yes, the belt was on the line in a tag match. It was quite ironic that Savage was given the belt, considering that he'd been involved in a woman-beating storyline the week before that had the brass at Turner outraged. It also had the wrestlers outraged since, in a completely unscripted moment during one of his skits, he had slapped Torrie Wilson across the face. She was so shocked by this that she actually began to laugh on live television. Savage's valet, Gorgeous George, who showed up on TV sporting two black eyes, sat in Nash's corner during the PPV match, but then turned on him at the end to help Savage get the win.

Nitro the next night, despite being built around Hulk Hogan's return and subsequent title win over Savage, was shockingly good. Of course, that's "shockingly good" in comparison to the usual WCW fare. Hogan, because he'd been gone for so long, got a big babyface reaction coming out, and the fact that the main event ended with a babyface winning the belt instead of a hundred guys running in for a DQ made the people very happy. Afterwards, Nash came out and challenged Hogan to a title match at their annual *Road Wild* PPV debacle.

A few days after his title win, Hogan was on WCW's internet radio show, **WCW Live**. Now that he was back and champion again, he did a complete 180 from his Mancow interview the previous month, this time putting over guys left and right (Goldberg, for example, was now "a big star and a dynamic personality"). He also claimed you'd never see him in the red and yellow outfit again.

In mid-July, the booking regime changed again. Head booker Nash was relegated to a minor role behind Bischoff, Hogan, and Dusty Rhodes. They actually put together a very good show on July 19, but you'd never know that from looking at the ratings. *Raw* destroyed them again, 6.28 to 3.33, and the Hogan versus Sid main event did a depressing 2.91. At this point, WCW's best bet would have been to just accept that the war was over and spend some time trying to rebuild the company. And that's exactly what did not happen.

First, they had Sting beat Flair for the 1,404,437th time in their WCW career to "win control of the company." Bischoff's storyline plan was for Sting to give the company back to him, and then he would turn heel and run wild again. Of course, this had been done to death for years, but when you're writing your own TV, you can do whatever you want. There were three ref bumps in this match alone, which made the grand total over the previous two weeks about fifteen (seriously). The main event also had no finish as Kevin Nash ran in. If you think reading about this feels repetitive, imagine having to watch it week after week after week after week. And then think about how the folks in charge had no clue as to why ratings were plummeting. This finish was also quite ironic given that Hogan told the *WCW Live* radio program a few days prior that one of the major problems in the company was that the main events never had a finish.

The July 26 *Nitro* from Memphis was not good. Yes, huge shock. It featured Goldberg's first match back against Curt Hennig, and in one of the most embarrassing moments of the year for the company, the quarter hour rating was doubled by *Raw*, which was featuring a mid-card tag bout with Godfather and Val Venis versus Droz and Albert. The show also featured the famed second-greatest squash match in the history of wrestling, Chris Benoit versus David Flair. A squash match is an encounter where one wrestler just totally destroys the other. The reason this worked so well is that nobody in the world at the time could dish out a more believable beating than Benoit, and nobody in the world looked like they deserved such a beating more than young David. Benoit gave him a chop to the chest so hard that you actually heard people in the stands scream in terror. Charles Robinson then refused to award the match to Benoit after David gave up, and Dallas Page ran in and clonked Benoit with a belt to allow David to get the pin. Perhaps you are wondering why Robinson was allowed to be heel ref when Sting had won the WCW presidency from Ric Flair. Join the club.

Leading up to *Road Wild*, Dennis Rodman finally began to make appearances on WCW telecasts. On the bright side, he showed up every week. The bad news was that his mainstream appeal had vanished; his appearances meant nothing for the ratings, nothing for publicity, and nothing for the matches and angles he was involved in. On top of this, he made claims in public that for the five dates, he was making $1 million, which was probably legitimate, as Master P was being paid this amount, and he had nowhere near the same name recognition as Dennis Rodman.

Meanwhile, Chris Jericho, who had always been told that he was too small, couldn't sell tickets and wasn't a ratings draw, debuted on the August 9 *Raw* in a confrontation with the Rock and helped garner a 6.53 rating to *Nitro*'s 2.37. What is ironic about this is that the *Nitro* segment he destroyed featured Dallas Page, who on his website a few weeks earlier had stated that Jericho had never drawn a buy rate and wasn't a main event–calibre wrestler. Also on *Nitro*, Chad Brock appeared for his big concert, with the good news being that even though the rating tanked, it only tanked to a 2.35.

The WCW storyline that most mirrored real life ("Who the hell runs this company?") continued on August 9 when Sting returned control of WCW back to WCW. Because that plot line hadn't been beaten into the ground already. More specifically, Dusty Rhodes was chosen in storyline to share the duties with J.J. Dillon, who, for whatever reason, had always seemed to have some power anyway. They also continued killing off potential stars, as Hennig, who was really starting to get over with the "Rap is Crap" tune, was given brand-new horrible music. In another lame effort to sell PPV buys, the Hogan versus Nash World title match at *Road Wild* was changed to a loser must retire match.

And so *Road Wild* came, and as you can probably guess, it was atrocious. But little did anyone watching know just how unraveled things had become behind the scenes in the days prior to the event. The event was preceded by the annual motorcycle ride to Sturgis, which saw Jason Hervey and Dustin Runnels crash their bikes, and Goldberg and Rick Steiner get so lost that there was concern they'd been killed in an accident. As if that weren't bad enough, Buff Bagwell and Ernest Miller got into a real fight backstage after Buff complained about the planned finish of their match.

The biggest blowup, however, came between Hogan and Savage. The two had always had an intense love/hate relationship; when they could make money together, they were in love, and when they couldn't, they weren't. Savage, a well-known paranoid who often carried a gun in his gear bag, went insane, screaming at Hogan that he was holding him down, giving the top spot to Sid, and furthermore, he'd killed off the Humvee angle. While he was at it, he should have yelled about being booked to work a match at *Road Wild* with Rodman that involved being thrown into a Porta-Potty. Following the show, Savage walked out and no-showed the next several events.

Master P henchman Swoll was arrested for speeding and was held when they found he was late on his child support payments. This despite the fact that WCW was paying him $400,000 per year.

With tensions mounting behind the scenes, it was certainly no shock when Bischoff finally snapped and blew a gasket in front of everyone backstage. He yelled at Raven for making disparaging remarks about the company in public, at Konnan for saying the word "pussy" on TV, at Rey Mysterio Jr. for making gay references on TV, and at Public Enemy and Bagwell for crying about having to lose matches. He told Raven that if he didn't like things, he could leave right now. Amazingly, Raven got up and left. Bischoff, figuring nobody else would have the balls to do the same, made the same offer to the rest of the crew.

Konnan agreed to leave as well . . . but Bischoff wouldn't agree to his rather unique terms. "Eric went into the room . . . he said to Raven, 'You're always bitching. Here's your contract, I'll give you your release papers if you want them, there's a lawyer right outside.' So Raven said, 'Give me the release papers, I'll sign them, I'm tired of your bullshit.' And he bounced. He said to me, 'Konnan, you had some foul language on the mic, and I'm not going to put up with it and I heard you're always bitching.' And I said, 'How come Rodman can say bad words on the mic?' He said, 'I don't expect any less from him.' And I said, 'If you're going to let Rey Mysterio go, I'll take you up on the offer.' He said, 'No, I'm not going to let Rey Mysterio go . . . but if you stay, I will make your life miserable.' He definitely kept his word on that one."[23]

Whereas in the old days Bischoff could comfort himself with the Tuesday-morning ratings report, they no longer gave him any relief. *Nitro* had drawn its lowest number in years, a 2.92. The KISS concert, as expected, bombed, doing a 2.25 rating. Nothing like spending half a million dollars to get a number like that. Despite the horrific rating, only weeks later, a plan was put into motion to create a New Year's Eve PPV that would feature a three-hour wrestling show followed by a full-length KISS concert at the 70,000-seat Fiesta Bowl in Tempe, Arizona. This would seem to indicate that Eric, under the severe amount of stress, did, in fact, go totally insane.

That would be the only explanation for the next main event feud, which was to feature Sid versus Goldberg. In order to promote the eventual encounter, Sid came out on *Nitro* one week and claimed that he was 55-0. Never mind that he hadn't had fifty-five matches on WCW TV since coming back. Or, while we're at it, the fact that he'd lost several times on TV over the past few weeks alone. By midway through the show, he was at 59-0 despite not having won any matches. Bobby Heenan explained this by saying he'd already beaten up nine men. Nobody was sure how fifty-five plus nine equaled fifty-nine. The next week, despite losing at every house show the company ran, he was suddenly up to 68-0. Then he pinned Juventud Guerrera, Lenny Lane, and Lodi. This made him 70-0. Again, do not ask how sixty-eight plus three equals seventy. Three days later, on *Thunder*, Sid said he couldn't wait to get to six more wins so he could break Goldberg's 176-0 streak. And, ummm . . . yeah. Once he did this, Sid inexplicably added, he was going to "shake all over." In September, Sid, at 76-0, lost to Saturn via DQ when Rick Steiner ran in. On *Nitro* the following Monday, however, he was billed as being 77-0. So yes, losses were now counting as wins in this streak.

If Sid "shaking all over" wasn't enough to entice viewers to continue watching, Barbarian on this same program threatened Harlem Heat by loudly proclaiming in an interview with Gene Okerlund: "How you say . . . WE WILL EAT YOU LUNCH!" Nobody ever figured out what that meant. Some theorized that Barbarian wanted it known that when Harlem Heat showed up at the building the following week, he was going to eat their lunch.

Shockingly, the Sid winning streak didn't stop the downward spiral.

The following week, *Raw* was moved to 11:00 p.m. due to the U.S. Open tennis tournament, which meant *Nitro* had all three hours unopposed. They responded by putting on a horrendous show that actually seemed designed to fail. Final tally: *Nitro*, unopposed, did a 4.0 rating, *losing* to the 11:00 p.m. *Raw*, which did a 4.16. It got even worse, as that Thursday, the WWF debuted their *SmackDown* show opposite *Thunder* and destroyed WCW once again in the ratings, 4.16 to 1.94.

And the hits just kept on coming. September 6 was the special fourth anniversary *Nitro* show from the 16,000-seat Miami Arena. They drew 3,818 paid. Not only that, *Raw* had been preempted for tennis again, and sure enough, they still won 4.38 to 4.12. The *Nitro* show, for the second straight unopposed week, was hideous. There was one good thing on the show: they began auditions to find a new Nitro girl, and after eight weeks, they settled upon a young Ravens cheerleader named Stacy Keibler. Not only would she go one to become one of the biggest female wrestling stars in history, she would also spend a few years dating George Clooney.

Finally . . . finally . . . it was too much for Turner brass to take.

And so Eric Bischoff, the man who led WCW to its most profitable two-year period ever, was "reassigned" on September 9. (Bischoff would later claim that this basically meant he was sent home to Colorado, where he hunted and fished for many months while still collecting huge paychecks.) There really was no other decision the Turner brass could have made, as under Bischoff's watch, WCW had not only grown to never-before-seen heights, but was also now tanking at mind-boggling speed. Turner was so upset with Bischoff that he was banned from all WCW events as well as from the office. On top of this, Turner demanded that no references to Bischoff be made and that no footage of him be used in any future video packages. To the company, the man who once turned it all around had just suddenly ceased to exist.

A strange little man by the name of Bill Busch, who'd started at Turner almost a decade earlier as an accountant, was put in charge as executive vice president. Because he knew virtually nothing about wrestling, TV producer Craig Leathers was put in charge of creative. And who was working under him, doing all the real grunt work in putting the shows together? None other than the three men who had helped get WCW into this mess in the first place: Dusty Rhodes, Kevin Nash, and Kevin Sullivan.

Busch, along with Dr. Harvey Schiller, the Turner representative in charge of overseeing WCW, met with the wrestlers and announced that some things were going to change. The New Year's Eve pay-per-view idea with KISS was canned; a ridiculous contest to give away $1 million (to a lucky fan rather than, say, an inebriated Dennis Rodman) was canceled; the annual *Road Wild* PPV from Sturgis, now an annual money-loser at a time when money could not afford to be lost, was canceled; and a proposed *Nitro* cartoon (seriously, and by a "cartoon" we mean an animated children's program, not just another episode of the show) was scrapped.

Further tragedy struck on September 8, when referee Brian Curtis Hildebrand passed away following a long battle with stomach cancer. Only thirty-seven, he was such a courageous and loveable person that condolences were sent out on Monday night not only on **Nitro**, but on **Raw** as well (where he'd never worked). Like Owen Hart's death, this was particularly tragic as he left his friends and family behind through no fault of his own.

The first post-Bischoff PPV was *Fall Brawl*. If anyone needs evidence of how screwed up WCW was at this point, consider the fact that they'd done such a poor job of planning that there wasn't any card at all a week before the show aired. Even the cable companies finally lost it, and the following ad appeared in newspapers nationwide: "We're the advertising agency and they won't even tell us who's going to be there! For God's sake don't miss it!" Below that, it read: "Sunday, September 12. Insert time here." When the buy rate numbers came out, WCW's incompetence was illustrated quite painfully: the show did a 0.30, lower than any number the WWF or WCW had ever done.

The show, in the 11,000-seat Lawrence Joel Coliseum in Winston-Salem North Carolina, drew 3,347 paid, the result of years of killing Ric Flair and the Horsemen over and over and over and over again in the Carolinas. There was no Flair on the card, and in fact there had been no Flair on TV in months, since he'd had yet another falling out with Bischoff and neither side could agree on terms to return. Perhaps you're thinking that with Eric gone, Flair could come back. Well, you're right, and he returned on *Nitro* the next evening. However, he was actually in Winston-Salem for the PPV, and WCW, per their usual stupidity, didn't use him on the show at all. The main event saw Sting beat Hulk Hogan to win the WCW title. For weeks, the idea had been batted back and forth to turn either Hogan or Sting heel. Hogan didn't want to do it, feeling it was too early since he'd just turned babyface months earlier. So Sting got the gig, and it was his first run as a heel in over a decade. The bad news was that the fans hated Hogan, so when Sting hit him with a baseball bat and got the win, they all cheered.

The biggest event on *Nitro* the following night was arguably Kidman beating Psicosis in a very good mask versus hair match. Bischoff had been wanting to take Psicosis' mask for a long time (you know, because masked guys aren't marketable), and even though he was done with the company, they went through with the angle anyway. Sid, by the way, was magically at 86-0 this evening, and somehow, over the next three days, he won thirteen matches, going into *Thunder* at 99-0. The next week, he was at 120-0, and since he never won at the house shows (not that there were twenty-one during the week anyway), all that could be theorized was that one loss was now counting as five to ten wins.

And then, on October 3, it happened: the beginning of the end.

Well, the latest beginning of the end.

That was the day Vince Russo, after a lengthy meeting with Bill

Busch, signed his WCW contract.

Russo was a longtime wrestling fan and video-store owner who broke into the business in the early '90s by sponsoring a wrestling radio show in New York. Eventually, the WWF hired him, more to shut him up than anything else. He was put to work as an editor for the *WWF Magazine*, and after he wrote a few fantasy storylines that the company liked, they put him in charge of the division. Eventually, he worked his way up to being a television writer, and he had significant input into the late '90s product that laid waste to *Nitro* week after week.

Russo was good. Not at writing wrestling TV, mind you, but at spinning folks into believing that he and his buddy Ed Ferrara, who'd also jumped with him, were the sole reason behind the WWF's success.

In hindsight, it's clear that Russo was a very creative man. However—and many in the WWF expressed this belief long before he ever even started work for WCW—his creativity had to be harnessed by an editor, and in the WWF, that editor was the same guy who'd had final say since day one: Vince McMahon. In WCW, he had no editor, and the results spoke for themselves. Despite anything he might ever say to the contrary, the history of his regime follows in hard numbers and will hopefully settle a few arguments once and for all.

While Russo was in fact deemed WCW's possible savior, interestingly enough, others were also courted. One such person was longtime Southern wrestling promoter Jerry Jarrett. Jarrett, who promoted wrestling in Tennessee and the surrounding states, certainly made sense as someone WCW would make a play to bring in to a position of power. His history included a stint in Memphis where his show wasn't only the biggest pro-wrestling event on television, it was the biggest show in ALL of television in the market. The thirty-plus years he had in promoting wrestling was also a huge plus in his favor. So why didn't it happen? For the very simple reason that Jarrett saw it as a no-win situation: "I refused the job at WCW on five occasions because I would not allow myself to

Masked luchadores? Sorry, La Parka—WCW doesn't have time for that crap!
[GEORGE NAPOLITANO]

be in a situation that was sure to fail." And what did Jarrett think of the Russo-produced WCW? "A horrible hodgepodge. The shows had no form and I could not follow anything as far as storylines. It was like reading a book by someone on LSD. There was no continuity. One can make plenty of excuses about talent cooperation or corporate interference, but there are no excuses for ignoring the basic rules of creative writing whether it's a novel, a short story, or a wrestling program."[24]

Yep, sounds like he didn't like it.

Another Russo detractor would be Jim Cornette: "I had to spend eleven months in the same room with Vince Russo and Vince McMahon, that's where I really got to hate life in general. They put Bruce [Prichard] in the office and put Russo on the writing team. At first, it was sort of like the Donald Pleasence line in the original Halloween, 'For the first six years, I tried to reach him, and then I spent the next eight trying to make sure that he would never escape being locked up. Because what I saw behind those eyes was pure and simple evil.' For the first few months I thought, 'Okay, he is a nice, energetic guy, who doesn't know anything about wrestling, we're going to try to teach him. Then I figured out he didn't want to learn, because he thought he knew what the fuck he was doing and that we were all crazy . . . and that he wasn't ever going to learn anything about wrestling and didn't want to. Then, I made it my life's mission to somehow keep anything that he did from actually seeing the light of day to the detriment of the wrestling business. Finally it got to the point where all we did was argue with each other . . . but Russo's problem, besides the fact that he is from New York and he's the worst stereotype of just an obnoxious Yankee, is that he was not a wrestling fan. He watched wrestling and liked angles and liked gimmicks. He wasn't enough of a wrestling fan to watch and understand that all those things he saw as a child, like Piper hitting Jimmy Snuka with a coconut or whatever, those things happened every few months, and then you followed up on them so they made sense when you did them because you told the story leading up to them, explaining why these people would do these things. All Russo would remember, because he had the attention span of a fucking junkie with a clicker on a morphine drip, were the actual incidents themselves, so he wanted to write a two-hour television show full of people hitting people over the head with coconuts, and he fucking loved the Jerry Springer show and he thought that the wrestling fan's IQ was that of a flea and their attention span was like his, and all they wanted to see was mayhem and carnage. He didn't believe in baby faces and heels, because there is no such thing as good people and bad people, everybody knows that . . . fucking idiot. So, he put matches together where people didn't know who to cheer for; they didn't know whose side who was on. That was the problem—Russo remembered all the highlights, in his little pea brain, that he had seen growing up, but he didn't understand how they were done, why they were done, how they were led up to and how they were followed up on."[25]

Not a fan, obviously.

The October 4 *Nitro* was broadcast from the Kemper Arena in Kansas City, where Owen Hart had passed away several months earlier. The storylines were no better than usual, but this can be blamed on the old regime, as Russo's first day was scheduled to be *Halloween Havoc* later that month. Kevin Nash, who had retired forever months earlier, returned on this show along with Scott Hall, who took his stint in rehab so seriously that he acted drunk during his promo. Hall actually said that Nash was working a fake retirement, and that when wrestling got fun again, he'd return. When Gene Okerlund tried to say it *was* fun, Hall said Okerlund must not have been in the dressing room lately.

There was one very bright spot on the show. Several months earlier, Bret had asked if he could do an Owen Hart tribute match with Benoit on the show. The company agreed, although they nixed his request to let Benoit win, feeling it would dampen the spirits of the crowd. The match was excellent, and went 27:33, making it by far the longest in-ring TV encounter of the year. Although fans had been groomed to only accept short, crash TV–style matches, they responded very well to this and gave both guys a standing ovation afterwards.

Prior to his first *Nitro*, Russo appeared on the *Wrestling Observer Live* radio show to promote himself. He said that, years back, when WCW started *Thunder*, everyone in the WWF had rejoiced because they knew it would lead the company to sink at a rapid rate due to overexposure. However, they clearly didn't learn a lesson from that because they had just recently started their own second two-hour show, *SmackDown*. He said he had been working ungodly hours and was rapidly burning out, so he went to McMahon and asked for a raise, a fifteen-month contract to give him a little job security and the freedom to move out of Stamford, Connecticut. He'd always hated Stamford, but because the WWF offices were located there, he was stuck. McMahon shot him down. Russo said this was ridiculous, because in the real TV business, if you were writing one show and were suddenly asked to write another, you wouldn't be asked to do it for free. He was especially irate when, after saying he never had time to see his three children, Vince told him that he made enough money to hire a nanny.

Almost nothing of value happened on *Nitro* over the next few weeks since they were all lame-duck shows written by a regime that was simply holding down the fort until Russo took over. The most notable thing was that Hogan was absent, supposedly teasing another retirement after getting word that Russo thought he needed to be phased out. In reality, he was in cahoots with Russo for another storyline. A strong Goldberg push also began. Management had decreed several weeks earlier that Goldberg should be the top guy in the company, and Russo believed that he could be the biggest thing in wrestling, but he'd just never been pushed properly.

Although Russo wanted to push Goldberg, he made it clear that there were others he wasn't interested in doing anything with. In an on-line interview with Ben Miller of the website WrestleLine.com, he made the following statement, which he'd live to regret:

I'm going to tell you something right now that you will absolutely not agree with, but I've been a wrestling fan my whole
life and I will live and die by this. It's hard enough, believe me,
I write this shit, it is hard enough to get somebody over. You
will never, ever, ever, ever, ever see the Japanese wrestlers or the
Mexican wrestlers over in American mainstream wrestling. And
the simple reason for that is, even myself, I'm an American and
I don't want to sound like a big bigot or a racist or anything like
that, but I'm an American. If I'm watching wrestling here in
America, I don't give a shit about a Japanese guy. I don't give a
shit about a Mexican guy. I'm from America, and that's what I
want to see.

Russo and Ferrara ended up starting early, on October 18 in
Philadelphia. It was quite the *Nitro:* a three-hour car crash that featured
two or three things happening in each of the sixteen quarters scripted.
To say that this was overkill would be putting it lightly, as by the end of
the third hour, the live crowd was completely burned out, sitting in their
chairs like zombies staring at the ring. Russo had a plan to take care of
that, however. No, it was not to book less "stuff," but to eliminate the
third hour of *Nitro* at the beginning of 2000.

It was a completely different show. Backstage, everyone was handed very detailed scripts, yet as detailed as they were, some still couldn't
figure out whether they were supposed to be good guys or bad guys.
The majority of this was tied to the fact that Russo didn't believe in the
traditional good guys versus bad guys thing; he felt that every character
should be a mix of both, a shade of gray, so to speak.

He also apparently believed that every fan scoured the internet
for insider wrestling news twenty-four hours a day, seven days a week.
Because he'd praised Bagwell in one radio interview, he booked a segment in which Bagwell came out saying that "everyone knew" he was

the chosen one according to the new writers. Of course, not everybody knew that. Worse, he then had a "fake match" with La Parka (yes, a fake fake match) and "took a dive." Afterwards, Bagwell jumped up like nothing had happened, grabbed the mic, and proclaimed: "Hey, Russo, did I do a good 'job' for you?" Of course, "doing a job" means "losing a match" in wrestling.

The point of these angles was never explained. After all, 95 percent of the fans weren't online looking for wrestling news all day, so they had no idea what Bagwell was talking about. And the 5 percent who were aware didn't buy it anyway, so there was no logical reason for it. The longest match on the program went nine minutes, actually a lot longer than many people expected. Also, for historical purposes, it should be noted that the first match of the Russo era went to a no-contest when a third man just sauntered into the ring. The match was Juventud Guerrera versus Evan Karagias, and the third man was Bret Hart. The best part of this was that nobody bothered to clue Juvie and Evan in, so they had no idea what was happening and just stood there looking totally confused.

On the bright side, the show did a much better rating than the week before, jumping 0.7 to a 3.30. Of course, it still lost to *Raw*'s 5.39, but things were much closer for once. Many fans and wrestlers felt this was proof that Russo's formula was the way to go. Others noted, correctly, that the 2.61 rating from the week before had been for a lame-duck Nash presentation that had seemed to stretch about six minutes' worth of thought into a three-hour broadcast. A review of the monthly averages proved there hadn't been a major jump (which media reports at the time pegged anywhere between 25 and 32 percent). July averaged a 3.37; August averaged a 3.27; September averaged a 3.38; and Russo and Ferrara's first three shows averaged a 3.33. Despite the hype, not much had changed.

One of Russo's first orders of business was to poach Jeff Jarrett, the WWF's Intercontinental champion, from the competition. Jarrett had been a colorless heel for much of his WWF tenure and had just started to get over doing an angle in which he beat women. Everything was building toward a PPV match where he would defend his belt against the top women's wrestler in the company: Chyna, a huge female body-builder with an alleged 350-pound bench press. But, for once, it was the WWF who had the problem. The PPV was on a Sunday, and Jarrett's $350,000 contract expired the night before. Vince McMahon was in a quandary. His Intercontinental champion suddenly didn't have any con-tractual obligation to return and could show up on *Nitro* the day after the PPV. Because the ball was in Jarrett's court, the WWF ended up paying him $150,000 to come back and wrestle the one match, losing his belt to Chyna clean in the middle of the ring. Jarrett was especially pleased be-cause earlier in the year, despite the booming business, he'd been forced to take a $100,000 pay cut.

Incidentally, because he held the company up for money (and, given the circumstances of them not taking the title off of him prior to his contract expiring, he had every right to do so), Jarrett was permanently banned by McMahon from ever returning to his company. In the end, it was the pro-wrestling butterfly effect. Because the PPV happened to fall one day after his contract expired, he used that to his advantage, held the company up for money, and was subsequently banned from ever re-turning. So when WCW died, he had no option but to try to put together a new promotion to headline in—the eventual TNA Impact Wrestling. Had his contract come due one single day later, perhaps the future Spike TV wrestling franchise would never have existed.

The October 14 **Thunder** was one for the ages. Since it was the last under the Nash era, he basically turned it into one giant inside joke. He sat in on commentary and did nothing but make shoot comments all night, the vast majority of which were not only too inside for 99 percent of the audience, but also not funny at all. His very first statement was that everyone had accused him of being a horrible booker, but he had outsmarted them all by booking himself in the greatest angle ever: his own retirement. If only that were true.

—————————

Halloween Havoc, Russo and Ferrara's first WCW PPV, took place on October 24 at the MGM Grand Garden Arena in Las Vegas before 8,464 fans. It definitely illustrated a new direction, although it was too early to determine whether or not it would pay off. It was an angle-laden show, and the wrestling itself was largely bad. Some of it just made no sense whatsoever. For example, Goldberg won the WCW U.S. title from Sid on a blood stoppage, but then, in the very next match, Flair bled a total gusher, and the match wasn't stopped. Bret Hart, who was being groomed for the WCW title, lost to Lex Luger.

And then there was Hogan versus Sting, which never took place. The idea Russo wanted to get across was that he told Hogan to lose the match and Hogan didn't want to. So Hogan went out in street clothes, whispered something to Sting, then lay down so Sting could pin him and win the WCW title. Nobody watching had any idea what in the hell was going on, the cameras quickly cut away, and the announcers never bothered to try to explain it. They attempted to explain what was happening in the main event, saying Goldberg versus new WCW champion Sting was non-title. A few minutes later, Goldberg pinned him and was handed the WCW title. The show ended with everyone in a state of utter confusion.

LESSON NOT LEARNED: The insane pace of WCW shows from this era was truly a precursor of what Russo was going to bring to his future employer, TNA. If anything, the 2006–2010 **Impact** shows made **Nitro** look like the slowest moving foreign film your girlfriend ever dragged you to see. Part of this may have had to do with **Impact** being taped in advance, and Russo believing that he could cram more into a two-hour show than the constraints of time allowed. Major championships would be won, but there was no time for celebration; instead, viewers needed to be immediately sent backstage where women were complaining about their makeup. Absolutely nothing was given time to sink in, and therefore, nothing could be taken as an important event. Just how major of an issue was this? The most recognizable catchphrase at the time wasn't that of any TNA wrestler, but of announcer Mike Tenay. His verbiage?

"TO THE BACK!"

The show was also the last decent buy rate the company would ever do. Regardless of what anyone might say about the quality of the show or the style of Russo's writing, the fact is that this PPV did a 0.52 buy rate. Whether it was because they toned down the in-ring product in order to present significantly more angles or ran angles targeted toward a great minority of viewers, the fact is that fans were turned off by the idea of paying to see World Championship Wrestling on pay-per-view. Within eight months, things would get so bad that the company would loudly celebrate buy rates in the 0.19 range.

Going into the October 25 *Nitro*, Goldberg was the WCW World and U.S. champion. However, J.J. Dillon explained that Sting versus Goldberg from the night before was not a sanctioned match, and therefore, the belt had been held up. A thirty-two-man tournament was set up, with the final two men squaring off at the next PPV to determine a new WCW champion. The first tourney match took place in the *Nitro* main event. Bret, on a losing streak, beat Goldberg not only to advance, but also to win his U.S. title. Also on the show, Nash, who had retired forever in August, returned to the ring. What was the big angle to bring him back, you ask?

He was told he had a match. That's it.

Prior to the show there was another major shakedown with Busch going crazy about how upset Turner Standards and Practices had been lately. Their biggest complaint was Flair's juice job on the PPV, which, as you'll recall, had also been a big deal internally because he bled more in his match than the guy did in the match that got stopped because of blood. It was said in no uncertain terms that there would be no more swearing, no more bleeding, no more ref bumps, and no more hitting women without 100 percent authorization given. Busch even went as far as to say that if things didn't change, Turner would consider shutting down the company outright. Later, despite the fact that these decrees should have helped make the product better (fans were sick of constant ref bumps, and it wasn't like swearing and beating up women was going to turn the company around), Russo blamed these limitations for the company failing under his leadership.

Russo's insanity took center stage on the October 28 *Thunder*. They did a skit backstage in which Kidman came across Scotty Riggs and Buff Bagwell having a conversation. Here, printed verbatim, is their conversation:

Bagwell: "You're pinning me? One, two, three?"

Riggs: "That's the finish they gave me!"

Yes, *they were in the midst of planning out their fake wrestling match.*

It gets better. During the match, Bagwell rolled him up with a small package and "refused to let him go." The ref counted two, paused, then grudgingly counted three. Bagwell ran off laughing, having supposedly put one over on those evil writers from up North. Again, insider fans considered it a stupid fake angle, and casual fans had no idea what was happening, so there was ultimately no reason for doing it. But Russo trudged on.

What was also strange was that the November 1 *Nitro*—now operating under the new decrees to the point that they were bleeping out the word "screw"—was widely regarded both internally and by fans at home as a really good show. Of course, "really good show" meant a really good show for *Nitro*, not necessarily a really good show by any other standards. There were production snafus galore, including cameramen giving post-angle cues before they'd cut away, wrestlers blatantly breaking character because

One can only surmise the conversation Buff Bagwell and Lex Luger had before this match. Guessing it was Buff saying, "You're pinning me? One, two, three?"
[GEORGE NAPOLITANO]

they thought the cameras were off, and just plain downright horrible acting. They also continued the World title tournament, which was a booking disaster. Most of the matches lasted about a minute, death in any tournament that you're trying to make seem important. Plus, weird things were happening, like guys advancing to the second round despite never actually having won a match in the first round.

Nitro also introduced a new character, one that would soon be the spotlight of every show: Russo's voice. That's right; he would sit behind a wall, so all you could see was an arm, and he'd talk to guys like Dr. Claw from the old *Inspector Gadget* cartoons. On *WCW Live* later that week, he vowed that his face would never be seen on television.

"NEVER!" he reiterated.

In a strange turn of events, Dr. Harvey Schiller, the man who made the move to can Bischoff, suddenly left Turner to take a job with George Steinbrenner. He was replaced by Brad Siegel, whose name you'll hear quite a bit more in the coming pages.

The November 8 *Nitro* was the exact opposite of the show the week before: this program was horrible on countless levels. Instead of three things happening in each of the sixteen quarters, about ten things happened in each, and none of it made any sense at all. Sid opened the show with a weird promo in which he informed everyone that he was not as stupid as he looked. Madusa, a woman booked into a tournament for the men's Heavyweight championship who had already been eliminated, was reinserted into the brackets . . . and then eliminated again. Probably the highlight of the booking insanity was Brian Knobbs beating Bam Bam Bigelow via countout in a falls count anywhere match. Yes, the falls could count *anywhere*, even, presumably, in another universe, but somehow, Bam Bam Bigelow got counted out. He was fighting with Knobbs backstage, then ran off to help Kimberly. The referee apparently decided that if Bigelow wasn't there, he wasn't anywhere, so he counted to ten, and when Bigelow didn't return, he called for the bell.

The sad thing is that show actually made more sense than the one the following week, which was notable for a skit in which Ferrara went out in front of the live audience and mocked WWF announcer Jim Ross, who had been suffering from Bell's palsy for years. He then introduced his new sidekick, Steve Williams, a longtime friend of the real-life Ross. Williams' task was to run in during a piñata on a pole match with the Mexican wrestlers and beat them all up. He beat them up all right, and put El Dandy, Juventud Guerrera, and Psicosis in the hospital for real.

"For whatever reason, those guys (Russo and Ferrara) were total marks for a pole match," Eddie Guerrero wrote in his autobiography. "They'd put anything on a pole—piñatas, brass knuckles, a crowbar, a leather jacket, Buff Bagwell's mother. My personal pole match fiasco had the Revolution locking Billy Kidman's girlfriend, Torrie Wilson, in a shark cage. Russo and Ferrara had no idea how to save WCW. The backstage politics might have improved under their reign, but the product continued to suck."[25]

Sid, whose interviews were quickly becoming a weekly highlight of the show, said he was twice the man Kevin Nash was, then added: "I have half the brain you have!" Main event was Sid versus Nash in a no-DQ match that ended in a DQ. All of this is true. The show did a 3.07, well below average. Russo, still eyeing that lone 2.61 the Nash show had drawn, continued to insist that things were turning around thanks to him.

It should be noted that **Raw** did a 6.20. Why is this important? Well, besides claiming that he turned WCW's numbers around, Russo also claimed for years that when he left the WWF, things started to rapidly go downhill. In reality, everything across the board—from ratings to buy rates to merchandise figures—increased, in some cases dramatically, and this was during a time when three of the company's biggest stars (Undertaker, Austin, and McMahon) had been off television for months.

And so Russo continued with his wacky skits and matches. Wrestlers retired forever . . . and then unretired days later. Matches ended when wrestlers who weren't in the original match pinned other wrestlers who also weren't in the match. Sid's promos somehow began to make even less sense.

Russo would later tell the *New York Times*: "There is one word that we start and end every conversation with: logic. Once you lose the logic of the situation, then you lose the realism and you lose the audience."

Indeed.

The WCW *Mayhem* PPV, which replaced the annual debacle known as *World War III*, drew 12,119 paid ($313,847 U.S. at the gate) for the finals of the disaster known as the WCW World title tournament. Because Russo's emphasis was on wacky angles instead of in-ring work, four of the matches (Evan Karagias versus Disco Inferno, Meng versus Lex Luger, Vampiro versus Berlyn, and David Flair versus Kimberly—yes, Kimberly) were in the infamous negative-star range, and three (Bagwell versus Hennig, Scott Hall versus Booker T and Goldberg versus Sid) were only slightly better. The crowd in Toronto turned on the show big-time, and some of the seemingly most popular babyfaces, including Goldberg, were booed vociferously (although it made sense with Goldberg since the last time he was in the area, he did the steel-plate-under-the-jersey angle with the super-popular Hart). The fans left happy, at least, as Hart beat Benoit in a good match to win the tournament and the title. Unfortunately, because the tournament had been booked so poorly, and because the title had been devalued so greatly over the past year, he actually won a belt nobody cared about.

Oh, and if you're wondering why Kimberly Page, who created the Nitro Girls, was now wrestling instead of, well, dancing, this would be the reason why: "Russo killed it [the Nitro Girls]. When he showed up there, he didn't want to have the Nitro Girls anymore. From a marketing standpoint we were a jewel, selling calendars and magazines and such.

But he wanted to go in a different direction. He said, 'If the girls are going to stick around, they're going to have to get in the ring. By that point, I was over it.'"[27]

And speaking of titles, Psicosis was suddenly the Cruiserweight champion. Thankfully, WCW.com explained what happened: "Psicosis was awarded the belt after the West Hollywood Blondes angle was dropped."

Nitro the following night, which was better than usual, did a 3.41 to *Raw*'s 5.51. There was one big victory, however. The main events going head-to-head were HHH versus the Acolytes for *Raw*, and Goldberg and Sid versus Hall and Nash for *Nitro*. The *Raw* match dropped from a 5.23 to a 4.73 while the *Nitro* rating jumped from a 3.44 to a 3.99, meaning many fans gave up on the *Raw* main event to watch *Nitro*'s.

Let's briefly backtrack to that week's *Nitro* and look at some of the fun, logical things that occurred during the three-hour period: Sid turned babyface and was immediately pinned in the main event; Evan Karagias, who had just won the Cruiserweight belt from Disco the night before, got squashed by Saturn for no discernible reason in one minute; two Nitro Girls had a horrific match and didn't even show any skin; Dean Malenko beat Chris Benoit in a capture the flag match by grabbing the Canadian flag, even though Tony Schiavone had stated that the only way to win was to grab your own flag; and Curt Hennig, who'd retired the night before to a standing ovation, pinned Buff Bagwell in a match that he wasn't even in (it was Bagwell versus Booker T—don't ask).

Or how about the week after, November 29? Jushin Liger, the presitigous IWGP Junior Heavyweight champion for New Japan Pro Wrestling (identified by Russo as "Jushin 'Thunder' Liger, the IWGP Light Heavyweight" champion), lost the belt to Juventud Guerrera, the Mexican, when Juvie hit him with a tequila bottle; Jim Duggan beat up four men with a foam rubber two-by-four; Jerry Only of the band The Misfits (who were being paid over $4,000 per appearance, despite not being wrestlers) beat Steve "Dr. Death" Williams in a cage match; Scott Hall took a bump into the cage and sliced at his forehead right in front of the TV cameras, but it turned out to be a rib because he wasn't holding a razor and didn't bleed; Hennig officially un-retired, then wrestled a scary Amazon female named Midnight; the Nitro Girls had a food fight; Hall locked Sid in a room with a door that had no hinges, so Sid easily broke free; and Rhonda Singh and Liz had a mud match where the finish saw Roddy Piper, who was not in the match, pin Ron Harris, who was also not in the match.

On *Thunder*, which somehow still existed at this point, Russo made the move to add a new man to the color commentary position—Juventud Guerrera, who spoke almost no English. You see, Russo thought it was funny to hear this guy going on and on for two hours in broken English, making insider comments such as how Lex Luger was on "the juice" (slang for steroids, although Tony Schiavone tried to claim Juvie was talking about apple or orange juice). This was funny for a few shows, but quickly overstayed its welcome, which of course meant Russo had to keep it going much, much longer.

This all led to the December 16 show, quite possibly the worst *Thunder* of all time. It opened with Sid cutting his usual nonsensical promo in which he identified Nash and Hall as "two shoes." He and Benoit were told they had to have a one-on-one match with each other later, and if they didn't they'd be suspended for six months. They never had the match and they never got suspended. Juvie was back doing commentary, and put over the Prince Iaukea versus Karagias bout as the "jabronie match of the week." David Flair somehow managed to go to a no-contest with Norman Smiley in a hardcore match. This caused Juvie to state, in a truly great line: "Now tell me please the point of this match." Jeff Jarrett, perhaps wanting to get a big push like Sid, attempted to outdo him in a promo by telling Dustin Rhodes (whom he called a "hornyacker") that he could bring anything he wanted to their upcoming Bunkhouse match, including a "bay of hail" or a "hail of bay." The main event just kind of ended after referee Roddy Piper was knocked out, which meant in a two-hour show, not one single match had a clean finish.

What did all this horrible booking do to the company? Consider this: from January to March of 1999, average house show attendance was 8,000 per show. From April to June, that dropped to 6,000. July through September, 4,500. And October to the end of the year, 4,200. Yowtch.

"Kevin Sullivan told me it was the **Titanic** and Bobby Heenan told me it was the **Hindenburg**, so get your check on the 15th and 30th of the month while it lasted," Whipwreck said.

But fear not! Russo had a plan.

For weeks there had been talk that he was gearing up for his big angle, the storyline that was going to turn the company around once again. It was originally set to peak at *Mayhem*, but then was pushed back to their biggest show of the year, *Starrcade*. Fans and wrestlers wondered what it could be. Did a major name jump ship from *Raw*? Had Russo, the "insane genius," come up with an idea that nobody in wrestling had ever thought of before? What was it?

It was Montreal.

Yes, again.

Bret Hart beat Goldberg to retain the WCW title after Roddy Piper, playing the role of Earl Hebner, came out and rang the fucking bell when Goldberg was locked in the sharpshooter. It was quite something to see Bret playing the role of Shawn Michaels. Fans had no idea how to react to this, except with hatred. It was a hell of a way to cap off a show featuring thirteen mostly bad matches.

Amazingly, things were about to get worse.

Nitro the next night featured Goldberg damn near ending his career as the result of a stunt gone wrong. The beginning of his match against

Hart was to see Hall and Nash tease-hitting Bret with a baseball bat, but then hitting Goldberg instead to lead to the pin. Roddy Piper would then run down and cover Goldberg's body to save him from further damage. Piper missed his cue, so he covered Goldberg immediately after Hall and Nash hit him with the bat. This caused a problem seeing as how Bret hadn't pinned him yet. So Bret tried to pull Piper off, but since Piper had been instructed to stay on top *at all costs*, he refused to move. So finally, the ref just counted three with Roddy on top, then announced that Bret, somehow, was the winner. Afterwards, Bret, Hall, and Nash reformed the nWo for the eighty-seventh time.

As the show was about to end, Goldberg stormed to the back, vowing to kill every member of the new nWo. He broke many things. One of the things he decided to break was the window of a white limo that supposedly contained the evil scriptwriter, Vince Russo. Russo, of course, was responsible for him not beating Bret at *Starrcade*, and also for causing him to lose to Roddy Piper moments earlier. The original idea was for Goldberg to break the window with a sledgehammer. It was decided that this would not look cool enough. Instead, he was going to break through the window with his bare fist, aided by a concealed piece of pipe. Unfortunately, he dropped the pipe, and since he wasn't done breaking things, he tried to bust through a window with his bare elbow. A shard of broken glass ripped through his flesh, and he began to bleed profusely. The cameras quickly cut away, and guys rushed in with towels, several of which were soon completely drenched with blood. Goldberg was rushed to the hospital to undergo plastic surgery. Later, he was told that he'd lost 31.5 liters of blood (!) and that he'd come within one centimeter of losing his arm.

This dangerous stunt meant zero for ratings, though, as the show ended up doing a 3.20 to *Raw*'s 5.83.

Russo, irate at the negative internet response to the two shows, went ballistic on *WCW Live*, saying none of this was his fault, and the reason ratings hadn't turned around was because Standards and Practices had banned, among other things, angles like Roddy Piper calling Rhonda Singh "fat" and Ed Ferrera mocking Ross' Bell's palsy. Nobody was sure how a fat Rhonda Singh or a poor Jim Ross impersonation was going to turn the company around, but Russo was indignant. He said Turner could either have a squeaky-clean show or ratings, not both. Again, nobody was able to explain why not. As revenge, he said, he was going to repackage Lenny and Lodi as a dork tag team called Standards and Practices. That would show them. It sure would.

The last *Nitro* of 1999 was quite fitting, as the man who told the *New York Times* that he began and ended every conversation with the word "logic" wrote an angle in which Sid was locked in a car, which Bret then ran over with a monster truck. Not only did Sid survive, he was back the following week. The show did a miserable 2.86 to *Raw*'s 5.85. Russo insisted that everyone relax; the turnaround, he said, would take at least six months.

Little did Russo know that he himself didn't have six months left.

"They always say, 'You can't kill this business, you can only bruise it.' But what happened with WCW is living proof that you can kill this business when the people running it know nothing about it."

—Bobby Heenan, WCW Announcer from 1994 to 2000

CHAPTER
★ ★ ★ SIX ★ ★ ★
2000:
EVERYTHING FALLS APART

WCW entered 2000 in poor shape. The promotion wasn't dead yet, but it was certainly very ill. As mentioned in the previous chapter, when all the numbers came in for 1999 the company was found to have lost $15 million. The reasons for that were many, although some simplistically tried to pin the blame on "guaranteed contracts." Many wrestlers were guaranteed huge money, they argued, and this created a tendency to not work as hard. As a result, the product suffered.

It's time to debunk that theory once and for all. The real reason WCW lost so much money had nothing to do with guaranteed deals; in 1996 and 1997, wrestlers with guaranteed deals were making tons of money, and because the company itself was making bank, these wrestlers were actually underpaid. There were a few complaints about guys being lazy, but those who were would have been lazy no matter what kind of contract they had. The problem wasn't the guaranteed contracts—it was that the people in charge failed to elevate or create new main-eventers when they had the perfect opportunities to do so. And when business started to fail, all of a sudden those same guys who were underpaid in 1997 were now overpaid.

Things got worse in 1999 because so much money was spent on stupid things like destroying Humvees and paying rock bands hundreds of thousands of dollars to do 2.13 quarters. In the past, this could easily have been covered, but because the buy rates were tanking, there wasn't enough revenue to make up for those expenses. The good news seemed to be that, under the soon-to-be AOL–Time Warner corporate umbrella, $15 million was merely a drop in the bucket. Plus, it wasn't like there was no hope whatsoever for the company; even in early 2000, it appeared that one good idea could potentially turn everything around. Sadly, the mistakes from 1999 were not only repeated in 2000, but even dumber errors were made. As buy rates continued to sink, the company found itself buried deeper and deeper in debt. By early 2001, 1999 looked like the cheery days of yesteryear.

Going into 2000, however, Vince Russo was confident. The company was rolling into the new century primed for some major ratings changes. Interestingly, the changes had nothing to do with his booking savvy or lack thereof.

In early January, *Nitro* moved from three hours to two. There were a couple of reasons for this. The first was that three hours was just too damn long to run a wrestling show, both for the writers and for the fans (especially a show that had become as ponderous as *Nitro* had). The second was that by cutting out the opposed third hour, the composite two-hour rating would pretty much automatically jump by several tenths of a point.

LESSON NOT LEARNED: In 2012, WWE was commissioned by the USA Network to change **Raw** from a two-hour show to a three-hour version. Obviously, the additional revenue of $150,000 per episode made it an easy decision and, from a financial standpoint, arguably the correct one. Sounds familiar, right? However, note the word **arguably** here . . . as ratings have slowly dropped consistently lower and lower since the change. The exact same thing happened eventually to **Nitro**. One difference to note is that when **Nitro** originally went to three hours, the ratings actually went **up**, not down. Such was not the case with **Raw**. But in the past ten years, things have changed somewhat dramatically for WWE: in the past, PPV buys and house show attendance were the company's largest revenue streams. Today, one of the largest is television rights fees. They have garnered new revenue not only from a longer **Raw**, but also from new shows such as **Main Event** and more. It's definitely more money today . . . but is the short-term cash boost worth the potential long-term damage of consistently burning out the audience?

Time will tell.

Perhaps equally important was the fact that football season was about to come to an end. Historically, wrestling ratings always took a major hit in September, when the season started, and then in January, when *Monday Night Football* ended, they would return to normal. Often, wrestling bookers would try to swerve people by claiming that they were "turning business around" in early January, when in reality, what they wrote had nothing to do with drawing in new viewers. The rating jumped simply because the viewers who had left in September to watch the NFL were returning from their annual hiatus.

Long story short, Russo was about to find himself looking like the company savior.

But all was not so peachy. Taking away an entire hour of *Nitro* meant that the company was also taking away an entire hour of advertising revenue. In order not to lose money, this change meant that *Nitro* had to add one-third of its rating to the other two hours. Since the show was averaging a 3.2 at this point, this meant that the move to two hours and the elimination of football competition would have to bump *Nitro* all the way up to a 4.5 or 4.7. Even those who knew the game doubted that things could change so dramatically.

Ratings aside, business was hardly exploding under Russo. By the end of December 1999, *Nitro* was averaging a miserable 5,000 paid. Worse, the December 14 *Thunder* from Mobile, Alabama, drew only 1,797. Despite what anyone claimed, clearly none of the wrestlers was over with the fans, because merchandise sales, which had been as strong as $10 per head at the company's peak, were now in the $4 range. The buy rate for *Starrcade*, the biggest show of the year, came in at a dismal 0.3, which was especially pathetic since they'd had over a month to build up the quest of their biggest star, Goldberg, toward the WCW title. Russo, again, insisted that a turnaround was going to take time.

The first *Nitro* of 2000, from Greenville, South Carolina in front of only 4,966 fans, looked pretty much like almost every *Nitro* of 1999: that is, it was horrid and illogical on every level. The big angle on the program was the introduction of Terry Funk as the new WCW commissioner. The fans were so excited to see Funk that they immediately began chanting "WE WANT FLAIR!" In real life, Flair and the company were yet again at odds, and in the storyline, he had been buried in the desert. And no, that's not a joke.

The show was built around a tournament for the World Tag Team titles, and for some perverse reason, Russo booked it in such a manner as to make the WCW title tournament look stellar in comparison. The matches themselves were abysmal, and the worst team on the roster, David Flair and Crowbar, beat Nash and Scott Steiner in the finals. The finish saw Arn Anderson, now Funk's enforcer, hit Nash with a crowbar (the physical object, not the wrestler of the same name), leading to the pin. Afterwards, David attacked Arn, no doubt as a way to thank him for helping them win the tag belts. And then Nash and Steiner beat up Funk as well.

If you're wondering why Funk was beaten up on his first day in, the answer is that the show was in the Carolinas. You see, Flair was supposed to be the commissioner, and was therefore scheduled to take the beating, to once again be humiliated in front of his hometown crowd. Since he refused, Funk took his place in the pummeling.

This *Nitro* was the first to be cut to two hours, so everyone eagerly awaited the ratings to see if the show would jump up to the 4.5 or 4.7 range needed to make it worthwhile. Finally, it came in.

3.29.

Yes, the exact same number that they'd been doing at three hours. To say people were appalled and horrified would be quite the understatement.

The ratings weren't the only thing taking a pummeling. On January 4, during a hardcore match with Terry Funk on *Thunder*, Bret Hart took several blows to the head with various objects, including trash cans. Bret had been taking quite the beating over the past few weeks, as his *Starrcade* encounter with Goldberg saw him take a brutal kick to the head that caused a concussion. Figuring it was really no big deal, he continued to wrestle over the course of the next few weeks, and because his brain had swollen, he suffered another minor concussion every time he took a major hit to the head. Shortly after the Funk match, he penned a column for the *Calgary Sun* newspaper. He'd been writing the columns for some time, but had taken several weeks off without explanation.

"A couple of weeks ago, I ended my column by saying that I'd have some explaining to do," he began. "I haven't written since then because I had a lot on my mind and I wasn't sure how to say it."

In detail, Bret described how much wrestling had changed and how he felt the sport had passed him by. He wrote about the superkick from Goldberg at *Starrcade* and how, in the following few weeks, he'd had a very physical match with Chris Benoit, a match with Jerry Flynn in which he got kicked full force in the ribs, and finally, the hardcore match with Funk.

"I signed an autograph for a guy who asked me the ever-present 'Is it fake?' question and I was stunned to realize that I'm not even sure I know the answer anymore. Is what fake? The lump on my head is sure real enough."

He was also outraged about having been asked to drive the monster truck that ran over Sid's car, and about another angle that required him to screech out of the arena in a getaway car.

"I'm flooring it, tearing out of backstage, with no time in the scene to even put on a seat belt, and it turns out an icy rain had coated the ramp. There I am, careening out of control, toward a huge trailer truck filled with television equipment. In the last moment, I was somehow able to swerve to safety."

He said this was made worse by the fact that, on the same night, Goldberg had cut his arm all to shreds on the limo window. In the old days, nothing like this would have ever happened in wrestling.

"I'm a wrestler, not a stunt man," he wrote. "And even a stunt man has time to strap himself in. I'm a professional wrestler and I get paid to wrestle in a ring. What am I doing fighting in the back taking falls on concrete and doing stunts in speeding cars?" He said he was especially appalled to think that he was doing the same sort of thing that had resulted in his brother Owen's death.

"So what's the point of all this?" he concluded. "I'm not sure I know. I just know I've emptied my head and my heart and this is as real as it gets. Maybe the whole wrestling business is pathetic . . . including me."

A week after the *Thunder* match with Funk, Bret went to the doctor. He was diagnosed with a concussion so severe that his doctor banned him from doing pretty much everything, including lifting weights and flying in airplanes. Wrestling was absolutely out of the question. Sadly, it would turn out that after an illustrious twenty-four-year run, Bret Hart's final official match—at least for a decade—was a lame no-contest with Kevin Nash on the January 10 *Nitro*.

Bret immediately called the office and told them the news. Since he was WCW champion and obviously wouldn't be able to defend the belt against Sid (whom he'd had the temerity to accuse of being a "big stupid dummy") at Sunday's *Souled Out* pay-per-view, the decision was made to strip him of the title. The next day, Jeff Jarrett called up and said that he had a concussion as well, suffered when he took a splash from the fifty-six-year-old Jimmy Snuka off the top of a cage four nights earlier on *Nitro*. Right there, the company was out four matches, because Jarrett and Chris Benoit were scheduled for a best-of-three series. The PPV was dead.

LESSON LEARNED: It's hard for us, as authors, to read back through repeated references to Chris Benoit. We understand that you, the reader, may also have issues with this. What may be harder still is seeing how many concussions are noted in these pages. The book is littered with so many tragedies that could have been avoided. Thankfully, not only in wrestling but also in nearly every real sport, head injuries are now being taken very seriously. It may have been painful, but it is a lesson that seemingly has been learned.

As for Benoit, we've chosen to leave him in this book. While we understand why WWE has chosen to whitewash him from their canon, we consider this more of an historical account.

We have also done this for other deceased wrestlers.

We hope you, the reader, can understand why we have done so.

Russo, the "insane genius," came up with a plan, and it truly was insane. There would be a battle royal to crown a new champion at the PPV, and the eventual winner would be someone nobody would have predicted going in—Tank Abbott. The real reason nobody would have predicted this is that nobody was quite stupid enough to think that WCW would make Tank Abbott, the shootfighter WCW had hired the previous year, who hadn't connected with the fans at all, the World Heavyweight champion.

Tank Abbott was a tough, tough man. Sure, he had the worst record of anyone in the history of the Ultimate Fighting Championship, but he'd beaten the shit out of many people for real, and when he was allowed to cut loose on the mic, he was a charismatic guy. The problem was that WCW was not UFC. WCW was a place where Tank Abbott had no idea what he was doing; he couldn't wrestle, couldn't sell, and couldn't cut much of a promo. Worse, for the majority of his wrestling career, he hadn't been booked as a badass killer; he'd been booked as just another guy, and a non-wrestling, no-selling guy who wasn't good on the stick was hardly the type of person that fans would take seriously as champion.

Even Bill Busch, who knew nothing about wrestling, knew it was a stupid idea. This, combined with the fact that guys had been in his ear for months telling him that Vinny Ru was an idiot, led him to remove Russo from his position as head writer. In a move that was probably designed to get him to quit, Busch told him that he could stay on as part of a booking committee with Kevin Sullivan, J.J. Dillon, and Terry Taylor—similar to the committees he worked on in WWF when he actually did help turn the place around. Russo quit, or—more precisely, since he was under a long-term deal—he just went home and continued to collect his checks.

To finally settle any dispute about what Vince Russo accomplished in WCW, let's look at his run from a pure numbers standpoint. The final tally from day one to his departure in January 2000 looked like this:

- *Nitro* ratings went from a 3.08 average to a 3.10, though it was realistically a 2.9 since the 3.10 was for the new two-hour show. Don't forget, this also resulted in the loss of tons of ad revenue, since they deleted the third hour.
- Average attendance fell from 4,628 per show to 3,593 due largely to the fact that the company had failed to create any new

stars and had made their previous draws, such as Ric Flair and Goldberg, look like total idiots.

- Buy rates, the company's main revenue source, plummeted from 0.52 to 0.26. That's not a typo—buy rates actually dropped by half.

Hardly a stellar track record. In all fairness, however, he did help boost *Thunder* from a 2.06 to a 2.32, and if you want to compare his reign with the reign of the men who followed him, well, they were both about equally horrible.

Bam Bam Bigelow: "Russo was the worst. He didn't know what the hell he was doing. I don't know how he flim-flammed WCW by saying, 'Hey, I'm the guy who made Vince McMahon! You have to hire me, I need to run your company!' What a scumbag. Russo's the biggest asshole in the world. He didn't know what the hell he was talking about. He was the worst. Ever ever ever ever ever!"[28]

With Russo gone, everything fell into complete chaos. The company scrambled to come up with new ideas for the PPV, and some of them, quite frankly, were almost as stupid as the Tank Abbott deal. For example, one idea was for Nash to beat Funk and become commissioner, and then, in his very first act, say that Scott Hall was the number-one contender and would face Sid for the belt. Hall, however, would be in Florida drinking (in the storyline—or maybe not, to be honest), and so Nash would announce that the number-two contender was getting the shot. That, of course, would be Nash himself, and he'd win the title. Nash, knowing how unpopular he already was in the locker room, turned it down.

Finally, they decided to give the shot to Benoit. Sadly, there was a flaw in this plan. Benoit hated Sullivan, who was now more or less the head of the booking committee. In fact, Benoit and at least fourteen others hated him so much that they all got together the Saturday night before the PPV and decided to ask for their releases. Their main gripe was that when Sullivan had been briefly in charge of booking the year prior, he'd done everything in his power to keep the mid-carders down, and there was no reason to believe that he'd do any differently this time around. By Sunday afternoon, half of the wrestlers had changed their minds, probably for fear of losing their guaranteed deals without any other concrete offers on the table. The WWF likely would have taken some, but not all, of them, and most were unwilling to gamble their financial security on it. So Benoit, Dean Malenko, Eddie Guerrero, Perry Saturn, Konnan, Billy Kidman, and Shane Douglas all went to Busch as a group and said they wanted out. Busch, totally unprepared for this, told them to please wait a week, and he'd try to handle the situation.

Even though Benoit had asked for his release, they still went with the original plan and had him win the belt from Sid with his crossface submission at *Souled Out,* in Sid's best match since 1996 (which really isn't saying much). Sid's foot was underneath the bottom rope while he was locked in the submission, which, in traditional wrestling rules, should have meant that the hold had to be broken, and the match should have continued. What should have been a ploy to set up future matches between the two ended up being used as an excuse to explain why, eighteen hours later, Benoit was no longer champion.

Before *Nitro,* Busch tried to reason with everyone. He said that if they stayed, he'd take Sullivan off *Nitro* and *Thunder* and put him in charge of only *WCW Saturday Night,* which none of them would ever have to work on. That seemed to be cool with everyone. Then, a few hours later, Busch called everyone except Benoit back into his office and said they were being sent home. When Benoit found out, he said if they were being sent home, he was going as well. Busch, obviously trying to play to Benoit's ego, said the plan was for him to beat three men on *Nitro* en route to retaining his WCW championship. Benoit, wisely seeing the belt as a prop in Busch's plan and nothing more, repeated his statement: if everyone else was going home, so was he. He would, however, drop the belt to whomever they chose on TV before doing so. In their seemingly never-ending quest to destroy the credibility of their World title, they told Benoit to just go home. He left the belt with referee Nick Patrick on his way out.

That night on *Nitro*, the announcers basically told the truth: the title was being held up because Sid's foot had been under the ropes, and because they truly didn't know what its status was, fans would have to tune in to *Thunder* to find out.

One week later, in what came as a shock to many, Busch actually lived up to his word and sent Benoit, Malenko, Guerrero, Saturn, Douglas, and Konnan unconditional releases. Konnan and Douglas did not sign due to the fact that both had bad blood with the WWF from years back (Konnan had been scheduled to be the original Max Moon in a deal that fell apart, and Douglas had left on bad terms in 1995), and they were therefore unlikely to get jobs there.

The big question remains: how were they able to escape—with a completely unconditional release!—when others had tried in the past and been denied?

"We had some ammunition in our pockets that forced WCW to give us full releases," Eddie Guerrero noted in his autobiography. "When we said we wanted out, one of the WCW road agents got pissed off and threatened to 'slice our throats.' He was just talking out of anger, but it allowed us to go to Turner's human resources department and say, 'Look, one of your employees threatened to kill us if we left. Either take out the no-compete stipulation or we'll sue. Needless to say, Chris, Dean, Perry, and I were given full unconditional releases. We were officially free agents."[29]

So, yes, the four were released and found themselves the focal points of the January 31 edition of *Raw*. Most would look at this story as typical WCW ineptitude. But in reality, this was much more significant;

the departure of the four was a huge nail in the coffin of WCW. While they weren't the biggest stars or the most charismatic guys on the roster, they were the heart of the company—four young guys who should have been given a chance to run with the ball in 1997 and 1998 when it was time to create a new generation. All of them, Benoit in particular (considered by many to be the best technical wrestler in the world), were workhorses who went out there every night and did the absolute best they could under what were usually the worst of circumstances. In early 2000, WCW didn't have a lot left. Really, the only thing they could brag about in comparison to the WWF was a strong roster of workers. When they lost these four, they lost those bragging rights and were left with virtually nothing.

Perry Saturn: "I wanted to get out of there at any cost . . . WCW was very unorganized. I can't tell you how many times I would be on the road and they'd forget to buy my ticket home. So I'd have to buy the ticket home and they'd have to reimburse me. Or I'd go to the airport (to go to a show), and there wouldn't be a ticket for me. It was all just so unorganized."[30]

Saturn's complaints about the travel arrangements were not unique, as the company would routinely double- or triple-book travel for talent. One source noted he'd have two or three versions of an itinerary . . . and yes, that meant the guy would have two or three airline tickets. The solution? The airlines would credit the tickets and would say the money could be used for future tickets or, get this, SkyMall credit. Yes, the magazine with the overpriced trinket crap the airlines put in the seat pocket on all flights. Amazingly, the source noted he'd rather use the free credit for family vacations than to buy a life-sized garden Yeti.

Malia Hosaka, who worked for WCW when they started their new Women's division in 1996, confirmed the above with a story of her own. "When they decided to fly me into Duluth, Minnesota to work with Madusa, they sent me to two full-fare tickets; I think they were $2,400 each. I used one to go to the show and traded the other in and used it for about a year to get to other indy shows, and the indy promoters paid me for the tickets to get there. It was one of the few times I can say I actually made money in the biz rather than taking a loss."

Those backstage in WCW downplayed the loss of Benoit and company, saying the four would get lost in the shuffle due to their size and their lack of interview skills. They were just the "Vanilla Midgets." They also had what they thought was an ingenious back-up plan: the reintroduction, or digging-up in storyline, of Ric Flair. Where did it take place, you ask? On a huge, heavily hyped *Nitro* event, perhaps a show unopposed by *Raw*? On the *SuperBrawl* pay-per-view?

Of course not. It took place with no hype on the January 25 *Thunder* from Las Vegas (which was, in fact, where Flair had been buried in the storyline, so for once WCW had some level of continuity). His big role on the show was to go out and say "good job" to Sid for having regained the WCW title from Kevin Nash. The whole process of Sid losing and winning the belt was so convoluted that we won't explain it here for fear of causing serious brain damage to readers.

OK, we will—but be forewarned that it is so baffling, it almost makes the previous year's Flair-Piper insane asylum storyline seem logical in comparison.

After Benoit left, Terry Taylor announced on *Thunder* that there was going to be an nWo versus WCW match on the January 24 *Nitro* for the vacant title. Sid, he announced, was the WCW representative, and the nWo was going to be able to choose whomever they pleased. Nash, the commissioner, chose Jarrett. But, he said, if Sid beat Jarrett, he wouldn't get the belt. Instead, he'd get a match with Nash for the belt. If Jarrett won, Nash would presumably just get the belt via forfeit.

Nitro came, and it was announced that Jeff Jarrett couldn't wrestle yet because of his Snuka-induced concussion. So Nash said that Sid had to beat Don Harris instead in order to win the shot against him for the title later. Confused yet? It gets even more ridiculous. During the Sid versus Don match, Don switched places with his twin brother Ron. Sid pinned Ron. During the commercial break, however—and keep in mind, this was therefore not seen by fans at home—it was announced that Sid had beaten the wrong guy and had to return to beat the right one. He didn't return, so he was counted out. Logically, this should have meant that Don Harris was the new WCW champion. Or Nash was. Who knows? Anyway, since this happened during the break, on TV they pretended that it had never happened. So in the main event, Sid got his title shot against Nash anyway in the most horrendous match since, well, the last time they had a horrendous match, which was at *Starrcade* the month prior. This particular technical classic was highlighted by them screwing up the very first move they tried, which was a bodyslam. Jarrett ran out and accidentally hit Nash with a guitar, allowing Sid to get the pin and become the new WCW World champion.

A mess, to be sure, but at least WCW had an undisputed champion.

Well, actually, they didn't. After all this went down, it was announced on *Thunder* that Sid had, in fact, pinned the wrong Harris twin. So, Nash ruled that he (meaning Nash) was the champion. He then signed a new main event, himself and the Harris twin that Sid hadn't beat (that would be Don . . . well, we think) versus Sid in a cage match for the title. He made sure to note that the only way Sid could win the belt was to pin both himself (meaning Nash, though by this point we wouldn't have put it past WCW bookers to have Sid actually pin himself) and Ron. Sid managed to beat both Nash and Harris, thankfully putting an end to perhaps the most nonsensical and convoluted storyline in the history of pro wrestling.

Or at least in WCW that particular week.

Flair made his return to *Nitro* on January 31, head-to-head with the debuting Radicals (the new team name given to Benoit, Malenko, Guerrero, and Saturn) on *Raw*. Despite the fact that the ex-WCW guys had been portrayed as mid-carders for years and told in no uncertain terms that they could never draw as main-eventers, *Raw* did a 6.59 rating to *Nitro*'s 2.79. Those who argued that *Raw* was just hot and the number had nothing to do with the arrival of Benoit and company were about to be in for a big surprise.

The rest of the *Nitro*, with the exception of Flair's interview and subsequent brawl with Terry Funk, was just as miserable as ever. As a dig on the departed Russo, there was a storyline in which Lenny and Lodi abandoned their Standards and Practices gimmick and Stacy Keibler said she was done playing Miss Hancock. These gimmicks were stupid, they said, and WCW sucked. The few fans that were still watching the shows agreed. Many, however, had heard WCW performers say the promotion sucked for so long that they started to believe it, and then they stopped watching altogether.

On the January 17 *Nitro*, it appeared that WCW had actually happened upon a match that the fans wanted to see. A bout between Dallas Page and Buff Bagwell caused the quarter hour rating to jump from a 2.7 to 3.9. WCW looked at the number—which was higher than any quarter hour they'd drawn in months—and responded by killing the feud instantly, telling both guys that they were instead going to become friends and tag team partners. Why? Who knows, and both Page and Bagwell were stupefied.

Even with Russo gone, the string of stupid storylines continued. One angle featured Big T, who had several years earlier been the WWF's Ahmed Johnson, filing a lawsuit against Booker T claiming that he owned the rights to the letter T. Big T would eventually win the bout (and the letter) in a match that would have been a main event on any episode of **Sesame Street**.

The February 7 ratings war, if you can even call it that, was something else. *Nitro*, which should have seen its ratings increase automatically

Booker T in happier times, when he had the tag belts with his brother. And also a last name. Err . . . letter. [GEORGE NAPOLITANO]

after having eliminated a full hour, instead drew an abysmal 2.66. The only number even remotely in that neighborhood was the final show of the Nash era, which drew a 2.61. However, that show was three hours long, so realistically, this was the lowest number in years. *Raw*, on the other hand, did a 6.49 rating, peaking at an 8.11 for—that's right—the former Vanilla Midgets and DX versus Rock, Cactus Jack, Rikishi, and Too Cool. Not only that, but 25 percent of *Nitro*'s audience switched to *Raw* when the show went off the air. Suddenly, Bill Busch was looking like a bigger fool than ever.

Poor Busch. Besides having to deal with criticism over how he handled the Benoit situation, he also had to deal with the money pit that WCW had become. Hearing that the company had lost more money in one year than in all three years of Jim Herd's reign of terror put together, he decided to cut costs. But fear not, he had a plan. Get this: they'd only fly in the guys who were going to work on a given show. Yes, it sounds incredible, but it's true. Believe it or not, up until this point they were literally buying airline tickets to each event for the entire roster of 160 or so performers, but using only twenty to thirty of them during a show. Now they would only fly in the folks they were going to actually use. Very clever, and truly a revolutionary concept for WCW.

At this point, the company had no clue what to do, so they turned to the man who claimed to have always been their savior: Hulk Hogan. Having been absent since *Halloween Havoc*, Hogan made his big return on *Thunder* for no explicable reason. Even less explicable was the fact that when he returned, he made no mention of *Halloween Havoc*, no mention of why he'd walked out on the match with Sting, and no mention of where he'd been, though he did manage, in the span of two minutes, to say the word "brother" five times, "dude" four times, and "Jack" twice. In this epic speech he also talked about how the "young guys" like Lex Luger (a spry forty-one at the time) needed to go because they thought they were stars. He attacked both Luger and Liz when they came out, giving the latter the single worst atomic drop in the history of wrestling—she sold it by gently patting her own ass.

Amazingly, that wasn't even the worst bump on the show. The company had been building up a new wrestler named The Machine, who was scheduled to debut later in the night against Dallas Page. They had your typical 1980s prelim bout, with Machine climbing to the top rope to do some sort of wacky high-flying stunt. Page, however, bonked into the ropes just before he took flight, so Machine was supposed to crotch the top turnbuckle. Instead of immediately doing so, Machine did the following:

First, he stood up from his crouched position. Then he uttered a scream of terror. Finally, he jumped literally about six feet from the top turnbuckle and crotched himself on the ropes. It is unlikely that anyone who saw this could ever possibly forget it, and Page was said to still be laughing about it months later. And in his big debut that they'd been hyping up all night, Machine got pinned and was never seen again.

In an effort to give the younger guys something to do, Evan Karagias, Shane Helms, and Shannon Moore were dubbed 3 Count and given a boy band gimmick. They would come out and sing and dance to the delight of, well, no one in particular. The highlight of their run came when Karagias said that 3 Count's first album, which was not available anywhere, had somehow gone platinum, and that their next album, which would be even bigger, was going to go gold. (In the music industry, platinum outranks gold, and you'd think Jimmy Hart of all people, who came up with the 3 Count gimmick, would have known that, particularly since in another life he played in the band The Gentrys, best known for the hit song "Keep on Dancing.") While misery was widespread in WCW during this year, not everyone was miserable. Helms years later said that while he found the addition of Tank Abbott to 3 Count kind of goofy, "To be honest, they treated me great."

There was no such comedy the following Monday, as the performers, watching WCW die around them, began to openly lash out at both the company and each other. Scott Steiner cut an unscripted promo on *Nitro* that totally buried Ric Flair (though not literally this time). Steiner went on a rampage, calling Flair, among other things, a "jealous old ass-kissing, butt-sucking bastard." He said that the previous week when Flair came out on TV, everyone watching at home turned to *Raw* to watch Steve Austin, because WCW sucked. He ranted for so long that the format for the show went right out the window, and several pre-taped segments had to be axed. His punishment was to be suspended from *Thunder* . . . with pay, of course.

Steiner wasn't the only one on the warpath that week, as Hogan did an appearance on the *Bubba the Love Sponge* radio show and once again ripped WCW apart. He went after Billy Kidman, saying he wouldn't be able to headline a wrestling show at a flea market. A few weeks later,

Going out on a limb and guessing that DDP had a better bout here against Bret Hart than he did against the legendary Machine. [GEORGE NAPOLITANO]

in another interview, he ripped apart most of the roster, saying nobody under the age of forty could draw.

It seemed that even WCW.com was against Kidman. The website would commonly post "best match" polls every night after **Nitro**. The polls, however, were strange in that if fans voted for, say, Booker versus Kidman, credit would go to Sid versus Abbott instead. Sometimes, the polls were so weird that if you voted for Kidman, a main-eventer would get the votes, and poor Kidman would actually lose votes.

Hogan's interview made clear two of the problems in the organization at the time. First, nobody under forty could draw (and it should be mentioned that Goldberg was under forty and had been quite the draw for a long time before his legs were cut off) because nobody over the age of forty had made any effort to turn them into superstars back when things were hot. Second, nobody over the age of forty was drawing anymore either, because the lack of new stars had led fans to tune out in droves. The worst part about all of this was that when Hogan had signed with WCW, they'd given him a creative control clause that pretty much allowed him to book his own storylines, so the company was resigned to catering to his whims until at least 2001, when the contract expired.

To be fair, it should be noted that too much emphasis was placed (and still is at times) on the chronological age of the wrestlers. The real problem was not their actual age, but their "TV age," or how many times they'd been in a prominent spot on television over the course of a year. For example, in early 2000, with only a few exceptions, all the top stars in the WWF were under thirty-five. Just three years later, though, the newly dubbed WWE was experiencing the same problems WCW had in 1999: the top stars had become stale. It wasn't as if the top stars went from age twenty-nine to forty-nine in the span of three years, though. They were only three years older, but because WWE was putting on four hours of television every single week, the main-eventers had appeared in approximately 300 main events, and in "TV years" they had become just as old and stale as the forty-five-year-olds who were killing WCW's business in 1999. Not only that, but in 1997, WCW's top stars were in their forties, and the company was killing the WWF business-wise. If it was all about age, that shouldn't have happened since the main WWF stars were years, and sometimes decades, younger. Instead of arguing about "old guys versus young guys" or the need to "elevate young wrestlers," the argument should be about "fresh versus stale" and the need to elevate new faces—regardless of their actual age—to the top of the cards.

Never was this more evident than at the *SuperBrawl* PPV on February 20, as Hogan (against Luger) and Flair (against Funk) were both featured in main-event matches. A year earlier, the two of them facing off against each other drew a $550,000 house and a 1.1 buy rate. Just 365 days later, they helped draw a $177,324 house and 0.15 buy rate. If ever there was proof that running with a pat hand for too long was death, this was it.

The **SuperBrawl** main event saw Sid beat Scott Hall and Jeff Jarrett in a three-way to retain the WCW title. In a strange coincidence, Hall took a guitar shot from Jarrett and a powerbomb from Sid and was injured for real. The reason this was so weird was because everyone was sure that as soon as both guys walked through the curtain after the match, Hall was going to be fired. Earlier in the week, on a flight to Germany for a tour, he'd gotten so messed up that he wasn't even allowed to board a plane back to the U.S. (they just happened to get the same flight crew going back as they had going over, and they said there was no way they'd spend another sixteen hours with this man). Consequently, he missed the **Nitro** that aired six days before his scheduled PPV main event.

On top of that, prior to the **Thunder** taping the next night, he claimed he was going to hit Terry Taylor with a guitar during an angle, and because Terry took this as a serious threat, Hall was pulled off the show. Because of this, the program started late, and to kill time, ring announcer Dave Penzer entertained the crowd with horrible jokes for forty minutes. Everyone thought this was it for sure, but because Hall claimed a spinal injury and scheduled an MRI for February 22, he was not fired. It should be noted that, spinal injury or not, Hall thought there was no chance of him ever being fired. He told friends that he was just in "time-out," and that the company couldn't afford to lose him because he was too valuable a witness in the WWF versus WCW trademark infringement lawsuit.

The show also made it apparent that the crutch of using celebrities didn't help matters, either. The third match on the show featured the Wall versus the KISS Demon in what was billed as a "Special Main Event." The Demon was a wrestler Eric Bischoff debuted in 1999 as part of the deal with Gene Simmons in which the band was paid $500,000 for a 2.13 quarter-hour. As part of the agreement, WCW was required to use the Demon in a certain number of main-event matches. In reality, they gave up on the KISS Demon (Dale Torborg) within, oh, one week, leaving him as nothing but a jobber with a fancy ring entrance doing third-match-on-the-card "main events."

A much less costly, but perhaps even more idiotic, celeb miscue happened later in the show. For months, WCW wrestler Ernest "The Cat" Miller had proclaimed himself the Godfather of WCW, dancing to the ring to a tune reminiscent of many James Brown hits. He claimed that he knew James Brown and that he'd bring him out to the ring one day. He did this on a weekly basis, and no one believed that Brown would ever show up. However, Brown did in fact show up at *SuperBrawl*, but since WCW never promoted this, fans at home didn't find out about it until the following night on *Nitro*. Inexplicably, the company kept Brown's appearance a secret, so he was ultimately paid $25,000 to show up, dance, and bring no additional viewers with him.

The only other "highlight" of the show was a match between Tank Abbott and a guy named "Big Al" that no one had ever heard of before (or since, come to think of it). At the end of their leather jacket on a pole match, Tank pulled a knife on Al and screamed, "I could fucking kill you!" He then placed the knife squarely on Al's throat as the cameras quickly cut away. Tony Schiavone, thinking on his feet, came up with a remarkable explanation: Tank, he said, was just trying to shave Al's beard.

Unfortunately for Tony, Al had no beard.

Nitro and *Thunder* were just boring shows for the next few weeks. It's hard to determine whether they were better or worse than Russo's horrible shows, because at least the latter were comically horrible. Fans used to spend those two hours debating whether to laugh or to cry, but now the two hours began to just drag on and on and on.

Actually, there is a business answer to that question. These boring shows were worse. *Far* worse. The February 28 *Nitro* did a 2.57 rating, its lowest in years, versus *Raw's* 6.50. Yes, *Raw* nearly *tripled* their number. At one point in the evening, it was 6.70 to 1.89 in *Raw's* favor. Then, on March 6, they drew 2,236 paid to the Chapel Hill, North Carolina, *Nitro*. Keep in mind that, a year earlier, they had sold out all 16,000 seats in this building the very first day tickets went on sale.

Bret Hart, who had been severely injured in the line of duty, was sent a letter informing him that he'd been on the shelf for so long that they were cutting his pay in half. Not only that, but as of April 15, they could fire him. He wasn't fired, but the pay cut stipulation ended up being a huge source of controversy. The deal, which was written into most of the contracts, was that if you got hurt and were going to be out for a long time, your pay was cut in half until you were able to return. Actual sports stars out in the real world could not believe their ears when they heard this. WCW's argument was that these guys were making huge money, and if they didn't want to work, they could just claim an injury, sit at home, and still make a ton of money. WCW did not realize two things. The first is that, as bad as WCW was, the vast, vast majority of the wrestlers, even those who hated the environment, still loved to perform and weren't going to stay off television any longer than absolutely necessary. And second, the threat of pay cuts did far more harm than good, since it led many guys to return to action way before they were healthy enough to do so, which in turn led to more injuries, more pain pill addictions, and, in a few cases, tragedy.

With business in the toilet domestically, WCW turned to Europe for help. The week of March 13 was actually a spectacular one for the company, because fans across the pond were starved for wrestling. In England, as a result, they drew the biggest houses since their U.S. peak: 11,812 in Birmingham; 10,450 in London; and 16,318 in Manchester. After these tremendous successes, they came back home and made absolutely zero mention of them on either *Nitro* or *Thunder*.

Europe was where the good news ended. The March 13 *Nitro*, the latest in a string of boring, nothing-happening shows, set a new record low: a 2.53 against *Raw*'s 6.28. And then came *Uncensored*, which in years past had garnered the reputation of being one of the worst PPV events of the year. This was no exception. The show was miserable, exposing once again all that was wrong with the company. You'd think that by now, every glaring mistake would have been obvious and the bookers would have made a strong effort to turn things around. You'd be wrong. The first day tickets were made available, WCW grossed about $90,000 in sales. They then did weeks and weeks of horrid television, building up the show and adding wacky stipulations to many of the matches. When show time finally rolled around, they'd sold $97,925 worth of tickets.

Amazingly, all that TV—all those angles, everything—resulted only in approximately *200 additional tickets* being sold. This was the epitome of television writing that sold—almost literally—no tickets. It was one horrible match after another. If you take star ratings seriously, exactly one of the first ten matches broke the two-star mark. Then Hogan beat Flair in the main event in a strap match. The rules of this match were that in order to win, you had to drag your opponent around the ring and touch all four ringposts in succession. The announcers calmly explained this to all the confused fans at home. So what happened at the finish?

Hogan hit Flair with the Legdrop of Doom and pinned him. Then he won a second time by touching all four corners.

Remember, one year and one month earlier, the exact same Hogan versus Flair match (minus the strap stipulation) had drawn a 1.1 buy rate. At *Uncensored 2000,* it did a 0.13, nearly a *90 percent* drop-off in business in just over one year!

Despite the atrocious numbers, it was clear the Hulk Hogan show was starting again. This time, his big feud was against another bright, up-and-coming young star, Sid Vicious, another dude as stale to fans as a bag of moldy bread. On the bright side, he was very charismatic, but certainly not charismatic enough to anyone in the world except the goofs running WCW to be considered a World champion, which he was.

In what can only be described as a miracle, Sid and Hogan actually did a great angle on *Nitro* the following evening. Clips aired of Sid at a press conference. He was happily answering questions when Hogan walked in and started taking over. As the Hulkster yapped away, Sid just stood there smiling like it was no big deal, but you could tell it was a fake smile and he was boiling inside. Of course, this was method acting at its finest, since Hogan really was the sort of guy who stole the spotlight from everyone else, and Sid had to pretend that he was cool with it (the funniest part of all of this, by the way, was that Hogan was supposed to be the babyface). Finally, at the end of the night, Sid snapped. All was not completely well, however. The match he snapped in saw him team with Hogan to take on Jeff Jarrett and Scott Steiner. He went crazy, chokeslammed Hogan, then pinned him. Yes, he pinned his own partner. The referee even counted. Nobody in WCW bothered to explain how this was possible, but it didn't matter because fans had long since given up on trying to find any logic in WCW storylines.

Following this latest debacle, the tables turned again. Brad Siegel, who oversaw the wrestling division, decided to shake up the power structure by bringing Russo and Bischoff back together to head creative. Bill

Busch, outraged, said that if Bischoff came back, he'd quit. Siegel didn't believe him. So Busch quit. This was not good news. Siegel, having seen the $15 million WCW lost in 1999 under Bischoff, made it very clear that Eric would only be involved in the creative side of the company and that he'd have nothing to do with the business. Busch was supposed to handle the business, but once he quit, Siegel ended up having to work twice as many hours to deal with that situation as well. Kevin Sullivan was also sent home.

The return of Bischoff and Russo was pushed as the pairing of the man who had turned the WCW around and the man who had turned the WWF around. (To be fair, Bischoff had actually turned the company around twice, once for the better and once for the worse.) Most in the company figured it was only a matter of time before the two self-destructed; their personalities were such that it didn't seem possible for them to work together for any length of time.

Russo, years later, had this to say about the pairing before it even took flight: "I just knew that because of the differences in personalities, that it was only a matter of time before this experiment blew up in all our faces. But again, I had to go along with it because I had no choice. As long as I was still getting paid, I could handle it . . . or so I thought."[31]

Bischoff noted that he liked Russo . . . at the beginning. Before long, though, things went south in a hurry: "I didn't know how badly Russo wanted to be on TV. He was already a monster in many respects, but the newfound 'celebrity' really got to him. He went off the deep end. Soon, the storyline was reality."[32]

Despite this, the two had allegedly been talking for a while. A month or so earlier, Siegel had asked Sullivan and his crew to come up with a booking plan for the rest of the year, or at least an overview of what they were going to do. Russo and Bischoff, at the same time, decided to submit a plan of their own. Their plan was basically to create a group of young guys headed by Russo to feud with a group of old guys headed by Bischoff. On the surface, this looked like a fine plan; at least it would get the young guys mixed up with the old guys and hopefully, in a perfect world, create some new stars. You all know the dilemma; WCW was absolutely not a perfect world.

On *WCW Live* that week, Russo did what he did best: he talked about himself and why it was everyone else's fault that things had tanked in late 1999. He also spun the numbers something fierce, claiming he took *Nitro* from a 2.5 to a 3.5 in twelve weeks. This, of course, would have made Bill Busch look like a major idiot if true. He said he'd wanted to bring Bischoff back for a long time, but during his first run, nobody went for it. Now, he said, Eric would be back leading the nWo, which would help turn things around. That, plus more emphasis on the Cruiserweight division, would improve the situation. Keep in mind that in Russo's first run, the Cruiserweight division was built around an Oklahoma versus Madusa feud—one of these wrestlers was not a Cruiserweight; the other was not, actually, a man. He said the WWF turned around when DX went to that WCW show with a rocket launcher. Humorously, this was something WWE also claimed years later, mostly because Triple H was involved in that, and he was now married to Vince McMahon's daughter, Stephanie. In reality, that had approximately zero to do with it. He said he wanted *Thunder* moved head-to-head with *SmackDown* (it had been switched from Thursday to Wednesday nights at the beginning of the year in an attempt to boost ratings), and *Nitro* head-to-head with *Raw* for both hours. Last, but not least, he said he wanted to bring Warrior back, because "in all honesty, there isn't anybody out there that wouldn't love to see a Goldberg versus Warrior match." Shockingly, Brad Siegel did not fire him the second this statement came out of his mouth.

The March 27 **Nitro** was a fun little show, mainly because it was the annual Spring Breakout event in which the ring was set up poolside. This was a lame duck show, one of the last before Russo and Bischoff regained power, highlighted by a Hogan versus

Wall feud that built throughout the show. It started with Gene Okerlund interviewing Hogan in mid-ring. As Hogan ranted and raved, a tiny figure in white appeared on top of a building about a mile away. The cameras zoomed all the way in but could barely make out this mysterious figure's identity. Hogan, who wears glasses in real life, immediately identified this person as the Wall. "THE WALL!" he desperately screamed. "IT'S THE WALL, BROTHER!" The tiny figure raised a hand up in the air to signal for a chokeslam. Hogan took this as a challenge and said he'd beat Wall up later. They ended up wrestling in the main event, and the match ended in a no-contest when, after Wall actually kicked out of Hogan's vaunted Legdrop of Doom, Vampiro ran in. Wall got to chokeslam Hogan through a table afterward, but, sadly for him, that was pretty much the end of their program. Also on the show, Sting beat Luger after he backdropped him into the ocean, and the referee counted the pin on the surface of the water.

On April 3, the company ran a taped *Nitro* designed to set up the return of Bischoff and Russo, who had obviously lied months back when he said his face would never be shown on TV. Most mind-boggling was that, in hyping up the event, Tony Schiavone actually said that they were doing it to remind fans of how great *Nitro* used to be. Yes, he outright told viewers that *Nitro* used to be good, but it now sucked so bad that they were going to have to start over. Running a "best-of" program was actually an ingenious little ploy, because the taped, nothing-happening show drew a 1.78, which meant they had quite the number to build on. The show was a mix of factual and fictional history (mostly fictional), and in closing, announced that the teaming-up of Russo and Bischoff was, literally, the biggest news of all time in wrestling.

On April 10 they did their first show, and one thing was very clear: no matter what anyone wanted to say about Russo, he could write a hell of a first chapter. The problem, as would be made clear countless times down the road, was his inability to follow up on that first chapter and maintain momentum.

The show was built around three men: Russo, Bischoff, and Hogan.

The storyline that had Eric heading one group and Vinny Ru another was thrown out in favor of having the two of them team up to lead a group of young guys, the New Blood, against the old dudes, the Millionaires Club. To their credit, they actually got two things to happen that most in wrestling thought were impossible: Flair wrestled his real-life nemesis Shane Douglas, and Hulk Hogan lost to Kidman, the guy who couldn't headline a flea-market wrestling show.

While that sounds all fine and dandy on paper, a distinction should be made between "losing" to someone and "putting someone over." To "put someone over" means to make them look credible—like a real, legitimate threat, an equal of sorts. Ric Flair put a lot of guys over in his career, meaning they beat him, and in doing so, became superstars. The best example of this, obviously, is Sting: at the very first *Clash of the Champions*, Flair allowed Sting to beat the crap out of him throughout their forty-five-minute match. It should be noted that Sting didn't even win that match—it was a draw. Despite this, Flair had done such a masterful job of making Sting out to be an equal that fans bought him as being on par with the Nature Boy. In essence, Flair made Sting a star in one night.

Just losing to a person doesn't necessarily mean anything, and it was clear from the beginning that Hogan wasn't willing to do for Kidman what Flair had done for Sting. In their first match, Hogan beat the hell out of him the entire time, until Bischoff finally hit Hogan with a chair and Kidman got the pin. Even though Kidman "won," the fans saw it for what it was: Hogan getting screwed and Kidman merely being in the right place at the right time. In other words, Kidman didn't get over at all, and it was a waste of a match. Sadly, this trend was only just beginning.

Also on the show, they announced that all the titles were being vacated. This led to one of the most telling moments of the year for the company, a moment they should have learned from, but didn't. Basically,

Eric asked Sid to hand over the World title. Sid said no. So Eric made a crack about how he didn't have scissors. This was, of course, in regard to the U.K. hotel room incident ten years ago in which Sid and Arn got into a real fight and Sid almost killed Arn with a pair of scissors. The announcers went crazy, feigning complete disbelief that Eric would say something like this.

The crowd, however, sat there in complete silence. Eric figured they must not have heard him, so he said it again.

Silence.

The problem, of course, was that 99 percent of wrestling fans did not scour the internet for wrestling news every day, and probably only 5 percent of them, at most, had ever even heard of that story. Russo, however, who lived and died by the internet responses to his shows, was so surrounded by the medium that he concluded that every single fan had heard every single inside story that had ever happened in the business. The simplicity of wrestling booking is that it's fake, so you can make up any story you want, and as long as you push it hard on television and it's even remotely credible, fans are going to go along with it simply because they enjoy suspending their disbelief. The thing is, you have to push it hard on television. This was not the first or the last angle created on the assumption that fans knew way more than they actually did. The *Halloween Havoc* deal with Hogan and Sting, where Hogan laid down for him and then walked out of the building, ended up meaning less than nothing, because in order to get fans to think it was "real," the announcers never mentioned it and never talked about it again. They assumed that every fan knew what had happened and why it had happened, when in reality, virtually nobody did. Instead of being left eagerly anticipating what would happen next, they were instead left utterly confused.

Even more perplexing is this quandary, again in relation to *Havoc*: the finish was booked to fool the insider fans. However, because they're insider fans, they weren't fooled; they knew the entire story by that night or the next morning. Meanwhile, those who weren't insider fans had no idea what had happened and never found out because the announcers never explained it. The angle accomplished absolutely nothing.

On the bright side, Vince and Eric's first *Nitro* was a big success, doing a 3.06 rating to *Raw*'s 6.17. Better, fans really seemed to enjoy it and were excited to tune in the following week. And best of all, there was a very positive team meeting before the show started at which everyone was told that they had a chance to turn it all around if they just worked together for everyone's benefit. The wrestlers left the meeting feeling more positive about the future than at any point in the last several months.

On the not-so-bright side, opening that weekend was *Ready to Rumble*, a WCW-commissioned movie about two of the dumbest human beings on the planet, both of whom ended up being wrestling fans. Critics showered the movie with praise, calling it everything from "moronic and insulting" (*Entertainment Weekly*) to "dumb and clueless" (*TV Guide*) to "spectacularly inane" (*Screen It*) to "the new worst movie of all time" (*Orlando Sentinel*). If that weren't enough, Rey Mysterio also tore his ACL after performing take after take of a frankensteiner for the film. He was out of action for months following this.

There was also turmoil behind the scenes. In yet another effort to recreate 1996, WCW went after some big stars outside the company. Since everyone in WWF was completely locked up, Bischoff and Russo went to ECW champion Mike Awesome and offered him a huge-money deal to jump ship. Awesome verbally agreed. The problem was that Paul Heyman claimed he had a three-year contract with Awesome's signature on it. Both sides went back and forth. Finally, a concession was made: Awesome could appear on *Nitro* as ECW champion (without the belt), do an angle with Nash, and the announcers would hype up his April 13 ECW match in Indianapolis (where he was scheduled to lose the title). WCW said OK, but then failed to mention Indianapolis directly and to let Awesome cut a promo, both of which reneged on the agreement. For a while, it looked like WCW wasn't going to be able to get him after all.

Finally, though, a resolution was reached. WCW paid a reported six-figure settlement to get Awesome out of his contract, and, per the terms of the deal, he was allowed to go back to ECW for that one date in Indianapolis and lose the belt. Despite having lost the belt, Awesome was now one of the hottest topics in wrestling. Therefore, WCW brought him and gave him virtually nothing to do. He bounced around the mid-card, portraying horrible characters such as "That '70s Guy," in which he wore a leisure suit, and "The Fat Chick Thriller," in which he made . . . ummm . . . fat chicks swoon. Neither got over, and in the end, Awesome's booking made his signing just another colossal waste of money.

ECW owner Paul Heyman came up with a scenario he thought was ideal for Awesome to drop the ECW title: the WWF's Tazz, who'd first made his name in ECW, would return and beat Awesome with help from Tommy Dreamer. Heyman felt it would be great to have a WWF guy beat a WCW guy in an ECW ring. Unfortunately, this whole deal did more harm than good. The match went just 1:13, and then when it was over, Awesome simply got up and walked out of the building as if nothing had happened. Because the bout was so short, it neither hurt Awesome nor helped Tazz, but did major damage to the title itself. In hindsight, what was really worst of all was that Awesome's departure ended up being another one of many nails in the coffin of ECW.

The first major PPV of the Russo-Bischoff era was *Spring Stampede* on April 16 at the United Center in Chicago. It was a success in many ways, drawing 8,377 paid for a $272,930 gate and being pretty well regarded by fans. They put the New Blood over strongly, having members of the group win the Cruiserweight (Chris Candido), Tag Team (Shane Douglas and Buff Bagwell—yes, they were considered young guys), U.S. (Scott Steiner), and World (Jeff Jarrett) titles. The downside was that, just like their first *Nitro*, virtually every single match had a run-in or interference of some sort leading to the finish. Despite all that, the match quality was still better than usual, and worlds better than *Uncensored* one month prior.

There was more bad news than good on the April 17 *Nitro*. The show was still built around Hogan, and in one of the main angles, he got revenge on Kidman for "beating him" the week prior when he ran a Humvee into a dumpster that Kidman was supposedly in, apparently killing him in storyline. In one of those only-in-WCW moments of unintentional comedy, the announcers made mention that in the new WCW, there were going to be real winners and losers because the refs weren't going to be calling for DQs. This comment was immediately followed by three DQs in a row. Worse, Sting made his ring entrance by coming down on a cable from the rafters. Nobody in wrestling had done this since Owen Hart died, and in fact, nobody in the NBA had either. Worst of all, Bret Hart was backstage when this whole thing went down.

The rating for the program was dismal: a 2.47 to *Raw*'s 6.75. The final segment, which featured a Hogan-Bischoff confrontation and Bret's return, did a mere 1.73 to *Raw*'s 7.68. Granted, *Raw* had quite the trump card: they announced the return of Steve Austin, who had been out since late 1999 following his spinal surgery.

Thunder the following Wednesday night was a better show, though it did feature the debut of a person no hardcore WCW fan will ever forget: David Arquette, star of *Ready to Rumble*. Keep in mind that a "better show" for WCW still featured such implausibles as Sid beating Harlem Heat 2000 in a no-DQ handicap match via DQ, and clips of the finish of a Sting versus Los Villanos match that, because of an editing problem, aired before the match had actually taken place.

The April 19 **Thunder** also saw Brian Knobbs' last appearance in the world of wrestling as he was doing an angle with Meng in which Meng hit him with a life-sized cardboard cutout of Goldberg (which Knobbs sold). He was then thrown out a thirty-foot window. He didn't really fall thirty feet, but it was in fact the last time Knobbs ever appeared on a nationally televised WCW pro-wrestling event. If you're going to go, you might as well go in style.

Production woes, however, would soon be the least of the company's problems. *Nitro* in Rochester, New York, on April 24 was headlined by DDP beating Jarrett to win the WCW title in a cage match. It was the only thing resembling a good match on the show, but still, it was a textbook example of how to kill off a Heavyweight title. As DDP hit his diamond cutter finisher and was about to win, Mike Awesome ran down and ripped off the cage door—a truly stupid move, because the point of a cage is to convince fans that nobody is going to be able to run in. It was ten times as dumb here, because the main event of the PPV two weeks later was scheduled to be—that's right—a cage match. Kanyon came down and brawled with Awesome, and as he was doing so, Page got the pin. Because so much was happening at once, nobody cared about the title change. Also on the show, Kidman got another "big win" over Hogan. It was a two-on-one match, with Kidman and Awesome teaming up to take out the Hulkster. Hogan beat them both up for what seemed like forever; then Awesome finally powerbombed him through a table, and Kidman got the pin with a legdrop. With each passing week, this angle made Hogan and Kidman progressively less over, the exact opposite of what a young guy versus old guy feud should do. And it wouldn't be complete without something like this: Sting went to a no-contest with Vampiro in a first blood match (yes, a no-contest) when blood fell from the ceiling and drenched Vamp. Inexplicably, the show ended up gaining a half a point to a 3.05 final rating. It was still massacred by *Raw*, however, which did a near-record 7.15.

And then, on *Thunder* two days later, the company made perhaps its biggest mistake ever.

The show was built around Jeff Jarrett being upset with Arquette, claiming he had cost him the title, an odd claim since Arquette hadn't been involved in the *Nitro* match in any way, shape, or form. One can only surmise that perhaps Jarrett had watched *Ready to Rumble* that weekend, and his brain was so fried that he was unable to concentrate on his title bout. Regardless, this led to Arquette and Page versus Bischoff and Jarrett, the stipulation being that whoever got the pin got the belt. Page gave Bischoff the diamond cutter; then Arquette, the movie star, covered Eric and became WCW World Heavyweight champion.

The WCW title, which, in storyline at least, dated back to 1905 and had been the catalyst for huge pay-per-view matches and giant house show gates throughout the company's history, was now dead, buried, and had a headstone resting above it.

The idea, of course, was to get WCW some mainstream publicity and to help rebuild their ever-decreasing audience. To Arquette's credit, he pushed hard not to be given the belt, saying he was undeserving, and, as a lifelong wrestling fan himself, he understood that fellow fans would absolutely detest the switch. Unable to change Russo's mind, he went along with the bout, and sent all the money he made during his WCW run to the families of the recently deceased Owen Hart and Brian Pillman, and also to WWF star Darren Drosdov, who had been paralyzed from the neck down in a tragic in-ring accident on *SmackDown*.

Was Russo's idea of putting the belt on Arquette a success? Not in any way, shape, or form, no matter what anyone might argue to the contrary. Although they garnered a fair amount of mainstream press, including an article in *USA Today* and a mention on *Entertainment Weekly*, all it did was make WCW look like complete idiots because they had an actor winning their top belt. *Nitro* confirmed this, doing a 2.46 rating to *Raw*'s 7.40 the following Monday. The quarter-hour ratings made it very clear that casual fans were irate about the handling of the belt and were, in essence, boycotting WCW.

Years later, Arquette equated his WCW run to "an opportunity to play cops and robbers as grown ups. It was surreal. To be able to be a part of that world and be a fly on the wall and see the workings of the circus, it was a dream come true."

In a way, you could almost say this low rating was good for WCW, because it meant a lot of people did not see just how atrocious the show actually was. It would probably be possible to write one full book about every horrible WCW show from 1996 onwards, but for the sake of brevity, we'll just say that at one point on this program, Arquette pinned Tank Abbott in two minutes—the same Tank Abbott who they'd been grooming for a match against Goldberg. The same Tank Abbott Russo wanted to put the title on, remember? Abbott was dead in the water after that one, and once Goldberg heard about it, he was ready to smash through another limo window.

The compelling Arquette storyline continued on the May 3 show, which was really telling, since by this point the movie had already left most theaters. This was a program where Mike Awesome somehow won a Kidman versus Ric Flair match after getting powerbombed by Kevin Nash during a brawl with Hulk Hogan. It's probably best to not even ask. The idea was that Page and Jarrett would brawl on top of a lighting stand (it was never explained why they would be doing such a thing), and Arquette, in trying to hit Jarrett with a guitar, would accidentally hit Page. This would result in Page falling through a gimmicked part of the stage. Unfortunately, when Arquette came out for the spot, the stage broke early and he fell into the hole. Once Arquette was helped out, Page fell in. Since the show was taped, fans at home ended up seeing Page and Jarrett on a lighting stand, then Page was suddenly lying in a hole in the stage.

All of this fantastic television led to the *Slamboree* show on May 7. Again, this was a mix of good and bad, both from business and storyline standpoints. The bad was that they did a horrible number at the gate: 4,862 paid for $139,202. Keep in mind that, eighteen months earlier, their shows were almost breaking the $1 million mark. Tickets were actually selling pretty well until May 1, when they came to a screeching halt. That was the day, coincidentally, that it was announced that Arquette would defend the title in the main event of the show. The decision to do so also resulted in a buy rate so low that WCW refused to release it publicly (it was rumored to be around a 0.14).

On the bright side, the wrestling was better top-to-bottom, and the main event, a triple-decker cage match with Arquette defending against Page and Jarrett, could only be described as a modern-day miracle. The triple-decker cage, obviously, came from the *Ready-to-Rumble* movie. Arquette got bumped early on, which allowed Jarrett and Page to do most of the work. The only way to win was to climb up to the third cage (they were all stacked one on top of the other) and grab the belt, which was hanging from the ceiling. Arquette got up there first, but he sold it like he was afraid of heights and just laid on his belly. Finally, Jarrett and Page got up there with him, and in the big swerve, Arquette took a guitar and clonked his best friend DDP in the head with it, allowing Jarrett to regain the championship. Afterwards, they did a brawl with Awesome and Kanyon that saw Awesome throw Kanyon off the second cage onto the ramp. Obviously, the ramp was heavily padded, and Kanyon, who had practiced the stunt three times that afternoon, was fine. Pretty much everyone watching just thought it was a really cool bump. Fans live, however, were appalled, as the show took place at the Kemper Arena in Kansas City—the site of Owen Hart's death. Although this wasn't meant to spoof it, it hit way too close to home for a lot of people in the crowd.

Nitro on May 8 was a real sign of the times, as the TWA Dome, which a year and a half earlier had drawn a legit 29,000 paid, had under 3,500 fans in attendance. At least Tony Schiavone didn't downplay it like in the old days and claim, say, 1,500 in the building. The main event saw Jarrett pin Sting after Sting was sucked down into the ring by a mysterious force that later turned out to be Vampiro. He emerged covered in blood and was quickly pinned. In another Vampiro-related angle on

Nitro a few weeks earlier, a big pool of blood had fallen from the ceiling and drenched him. For whatever reason, Sting showed up on *Thunder* a few days later still covered in blood, indicating that he did not, in fact, shower regularly.

There was trouble behind the scenes again, as the May 9 **Thunder** taping saw Buff Bagwell get arrested after an altercation with crew member Darrell Miller backstage. According to Miller, he was trying to get a roll of carpet through a door that Bagwell, Luger, and Liz were standing in front of. A local news report added that the carpet was "taken from the wrestling arena following a match that involved much spilling of a bloodlike substance." Miller asked the wrestlers to move. Bagwell said they were busy. Words were exchanged, and Miller claimed Bagwell—and this is a direct quote from the police report—"punched him upside the neck." He punched him so hard, in fact, that he was left with a "fist-print." Luger and Liz were questioned and claimed they hadn't seen or heard a thing, "because wrestler Goldberg's monster truck was crushing a Buick outside the convention center at the time." Buff was taken to jail and released after posting $500 bail; then Brad Siegel suspended him for thirty days.

The show itself was another comedy of storyline errors. It opened with a brand-new video package, and for whatever reason, there was no footage whatsoever of Ric Flair. This was especially funny given what happened on *Nitro* the following week, when David Flair, Daffney, and Crowbar did an angle walking around New York City. They went into a strip club, and David acted as though he'd never seen a naked woman in his life. Then he asked Daffney, his storyline girlfriend, to marry him. That's all well and good if you want to suspend disbelief and accept that Ric Flair's son had never seen a naked woman before. However, fifteen minutes later, David, standing beside his storyline girlfriend to whom he'd just proposed, cut a promo about his long-legged blonde girlfriend. Daffney, it should be noted, was neither long-legged nor blonde. It seems he was talking about Stacy Keibler, who had zero relationship to David in storyline, but was his real-life fiancée. The idea was to get across that his father neglected him as a child, but that he'd done very well for himself, regardless of that. Clearly, nobody in the crowd had any earthly idea what was happening.

More hilarity occurred later in the program, when Kevin Nash was the target of the dreaded red blood. However, something went awry as the blood was dropped from the ceiling, and it missed him by a mile. In fact, the only people it drenched were the folks who had spent decent money to get front-row seats. Unlike all the wrestlers, the fans did not sell the blood as being poisonous. They showed a shot of Nash looking utterly confused, then cut to a shot of a horrified Vince Russo standing there with his jaw hanging open. Konnan and Juvie, standing behind him, totally broke character and burst out laughing.

Nitro on May 15 began to build toward the next big PPV, *Great American Bash*, with the following lineup (see if you notice a trend): Nash versus Jarrett for the World title; Ric versus David Flair, with the elder Flair having to retire if he lost; Hogan versus Kidman, with Hogan having to retire if he lost; Sting versus Vampiro in an inferno match (a bout in which the ring is surrounded by fire, a gimmick made popular in Puerto Rico); Dallas Page versus Mike Awesome in an ambulance match (in which the loser had to leave on a stretcher in an ambulance); Wall versus Shane Douglas in a tables match; Lex Luger versus Chuck Palumbo in a "Lex Flexer" (one of those weird 1970s muscle-building bendy bars) on a pole match; and Scott Steiner versus Tank Abbott in a fake shootfight. As you can see, Mr. Russo was fond of stipulation matches. It's too bad he had no clue about the point of putting a stipulation on a match; instead, he just added stipulations for the sake of stipulations, and they never meant anything.

The show was better than usual, mostly thanks to Ric Flair, who, in the main event, at fifty-one years of age, pinned Jarrett with an inside cradle to win the WCW title. The fans went crazy, viewers watching at home went crazy, and the announcers . . . well, the announcers just sat there because nobody had alerted them about the title change. They just assumed that the referee must have screwed up. The title change popped an unexpectedly great quarter-hour rating (3.29, up almost a full point from the previous segment), so the decision was immediately made to take the belt off Flair, fast. Presumably, this was part of Russo's long-term plan to make the belts mean more, changing them one to two times every single week. Keep in mind that in years past, the World title belt had changed hands maybe once or twice a year. This helped to give the belt stability and make it appear a worthy prize, something that every wrestler strived for. By switching the belt so frequently, its value as a prop in top feuds became nonexistent.

It got worse. On *Thunder* two days after he won the belt, Flair fell down in the main event and they sold it like he was having a heart attack.

Yes, again. You'll recall that, a year or so earlier, they had tried the same thing, and it went across horribly, mainly because nobody believed it was real (which was good, because it wasn't). They went to such lengths to convince folks—even Flair's closest friends—that it was real that everyone lost what little trust they still had for management. Flair claimed that an inner-ear imbalance threw off his equilibrium this time, but true or not, nobody believed the story.

On the May 22 *Nitro*, to further put over how fake the heart attack was, Russo did a mock funeral complete with a casket, saying that Flair had died of a brain aneurism, and gave Jarrett the WCW title belt. Of course, there can't be a coffin in wrestling without someone coming out of it. That someone ended up being Nash, with great difficulty. He grabbed the belt and ran off. The main event ended up being Nash versus Jarrett for the apparently vacant title. The encounter was a five-minute disaster, the likes of which hadn't been seen since the Black Plague. The finish saw Russo run out, so Nash grabbed him and tried to powerbomb him in the aisle. The evil red blood fell from the ceiling, and once again, it missed. This time, Nash tried to move into its path and managed to get some of it on him and Russo. For reasons never explained, the substance incapacitated Nash but not Russo, and Jarrett subsequently got the pin.

As bad as that all sounds, the rest of the show was worse. The Cruiserweight title also changed hands, going from Crowbar to his girlfriend, Daffney. Don't ask. They did a backstage brawl with Mike Awesome and Shane Douglas attacking Wall. Thankfully, Dallas Page was there to make the save, and he threw Awesome into an ambulance that zoomed off. Then, seconds later, Awesome and Douglas were inexplicably in the ring for the funeral, the result of the previous two pre-taped segments being played out of order. Hogan did another "job," this time to Vampiro, that featured the Hulkster beating his opponent's ass for five minutes, only to have Kidman hit Hogan with a blowtorch to get the fluke pin. It was another perfect example of how to make two guys less over at the end of the match than they were when it started.

Thunder on May 23 in Saginaw, Michigan, was another stellar effort. The World title changed hands again in the main event when Nash won a three-way over Jarrett and Steiner, pinning Jarrett with a powerbomb. The title was so beyond dead by this point that things like this honestly didn't matter anymore. On the bright side, the Cruiserweight belt didn't change hands again as Daffney (a non-wrestling manager who, coincidentally, was also trained in acting) retained the belt over the Artist Formerly Known as Prince Iaukea, who was formerly just Prince Iaukea before Russo showed up and gave him his new wacky persona based on a purple color scheme and a valet named Paisley. Fans continued to not care.

Russo topped himself on the May 29 *Nitro* by featuring not just one, but two world title changes. First, Nash came out with the belt and said since Flair never lost it in the ring, he was giving it back to him. Jarrett came out and said he wanted a title shot. Flair said no. So they showed footage of Ric's son David holding Beth and Reid Flair hostage. Beth and Reid Flair, as you might have deduced from reading their last names, were Ric's wife and son, and also, strangely, David's mom and brother. If you are wondering why David was holding them hostage, then you will likely also wonder why, when Ric saw this, his first reaction was to give Jarrett that title shot he'd asked for. Jarrett won the match when David, who was assigned to be the referee, hit Ric with a guitar, and then Russo ran down and counted the pin for Jarrett. Fans pelted the ring with garbage in anger. And of course, no mid-2000 *Nitro* would be complete without something like Terry Funk and Vampiro managing to go to a no-contest in a hardcore match.

And the company was probably wondering why the show did a 2.98.

It should be noted that Goldberg, after almost six months, finally returned on this show from his elbow injury. Despite the fact that he wasn't scheduled to be medically cleared to return for several more weeks, he immediately challenged Tank Abbott to a match on June 5. Keep in mind that the *Great American Bash* was scheduled for six days after that, and instead of holding it off in an attempt to actually sell some pay-per-views, they aired it on TV for free in order to a get a 2.90 quarter-hour rating.

Goldberg versus Abbott was over in less than three minutes, so all that work they'd done trying to build Abbott back up for his big confrontation was ultimately for naught. In a shockingly good match, Russo (who cut a mind-boggling promo earlier in the show in which he said that he'd been forced out of the WWF eight months earlier to work for WCW, and it had been the worst eight months of his life) beat Ric Flair in a cage. Flair carried him to what was undoubtedly the best match of Russo's career until finally putting him in the figure four. Russo wouldn't quit, and because of a timing snafu regarding more blood falling from the ceiling, he withstood the pain for an absurd length of time. Finally, the blood dropped onto both of them, and for whatever reason (none of this was ever explained), only Flair was incapacitated. David Flair, who wasn't even in the match, then put his dad in the figure four and Russo covered him for the pin. If you think that's stupid, the main event angle saw over ten men attack Nash until Goldberg made the save. The idea was that Nash would be overwhelmed, so Goldberg, in saving him, would come across as an even bigger hero. As it turned out, Nash hardly sold for anyone, so Goldberg's run-in really made no sense.

Following the Goldberg match, Abbott was made into a groupie for 3 Count, WCW's boy band tag team. In all honesty, he'd been booked into such oblivion that it made no difference in his career, and years later, he talked about how much fun he'd had singing and dancing like a total goof. At one point, the company offered to pay for singing lessons. Tank declined, saying that his voice was going to suck no matter what.

Thunder two days later was another classic effort. It opened with one of the announcers identifying himself as Mike Tenay, then suddenly realizing that he was, in fact, Tony Schiavone. Terry Funk was almost killed doing a hardcore match with Chris Candido, as they ended up brawling outside in a stable and a horse bucked him ("You fucking horse!" Funk screamed in an all-time great man versus beast promo. "I'll kick your ass!"). Please do not ask why they were fighting in a stable. Thankfully the horse bucked him in the arm and not the head, so he ended up OK. They did another horrible skit with Ralphus (yes, the same fat ring-crew guy, who would later go on to be fired after he began to develop a movie-star-like pompous attitude—seriously) and Norman Smiley, who in storyline had been fired. They came upon a backyard wrestling group. Smiley asked if the kids knew who he was. "Yeah, Booker T!" one of them said. Even on WCW TV there was nobody who watched WCW anymore. Norman gave the kids a stern lecture, saying they shouldn't be doing pro wrestling in their backyard because it was dangerous. He offered to show them some amateur moves but then shot on the group's champion and pinned him to win his belt. The idea was to bring him back as the World Backyard champion or something equally absurd. Main event saw Nash and Scott Steiner beat Jeff Jarrett and Rick Steiner, so Nash, who got the pin, won a shot at Jarrett's WCW title at the *Great American Bash* PPV the following Sunday.

The show was built around what was promised to be the biggest surprise in the history of sports entertainment, a surprise so big that it would change the landscape of the industry forever. FOREVER, mind you. And shockingly, Russo was telling the truth, because the surprise ended up being a poorly thought-out Goldberg heel turn that probably helped speed up the process of WCW going out of business, something that really did change the landscape of the industry forever.

In reality, though, WCW had a different announcement in mind, and when that fell through they had to come up with a back-up plan. It seemed likely the original plan was to announce a deal for a promotional group called SFX (which handled many major concerts) to purchase the rights to promote all of WCW's live events. Bischoff did an interview on the May 31 *Thunder* where he announced the landscape-changing event, and he did it in such a way as to indicate that it was not just another wrestling angle. As it turned out, SFX had made an offer to outright buy WCW for an estimated $500 million (yes, a HALF BILLION DOLLARS, please keep that number in mind), but Ted Turner quickly shot it down.

It wasn't just SFX Bischoff had been talking with, as both he and Hogan had also been negotiating with FOX. Eric's idea, which he'd had for some time, was to put another wrestling show on the FOX Network, build up the wrestlers that would be sent there, and then eventually do an interpromotional feud (actually, this was very similar to what WWE ended up doing with their *Raw/SmackDown* "brand extension" years later).

The Goldberg turn, helping Jarrett pin Nash to retain the WCW title, was met by a hugely negative reaction which included the fans pelting the ring with garbage for several minutes after the show went off the air. The company had yet to learn that while this was a positive thing in 1996 when the nWo caught fire, by 2000 it was a sign of what it really was, fans throwing garbage at the ring out of legitimate anger. The turn was a horrible idea, mostly because he'd just returned from the injuries suffered in the limo window incident and fans were salivating to cheer him killing bad guys. Ironically, WWE would make this same mistake in 2001 with Steve Austin shortly after he returned from an injury. It bombed just as badly.

To show how badly WCW had killed off their stipulation matches and how little faith fans had in the company upholding any of them, the show, featuring bouts with both Hogan and Flair where they'd have to retire forever if they lost, drew 4,677 paid. On the bright side, WCW at least kept their word because both guys won and thus did not have to retire. The undercard was a mess of run-ins and interference. Most comically, Mike Awesome beat Dallas Page in an ambulance match when Kanyon, who had been in a wheelchair since falling off the triple-tier cage, jumped up and laid out DDP with a diamond cutter. The reason this was so funny is that it was the third straight PPV where Page had lost because one of his friends turned on him. And people wondered why nobody got behind the WCW babyfaces. Fans hate stupid babyfaces, and WCW never ended up learning that lesson.

By far the low point of the **Great American Bash** was a Vampiro versus Sting inferno match. The gimmick was that you had to light your opponent on fire. The torch to be used, however, was at the top of the giant WCW movie screen near the entrance. Both guys climbed to the top, then the lights went out and all sorts of wacky lighting effects started. The reason this happened was because they had to replace the real Sting with a stunt double. The double then lit himself on fire, jumped off the screen, and crashed through a hole on the ramp into a foam pit. It looked spectacular, but nobody in the crowd bought it for a minute. Worst of all, the announcers broke down into the same solemn tone of voice that Jerry Lawler and Jim Ross legitimately broke down into when Owen Hart really fell from the ceiling and died. It was a tasteless move, and one that inspired even more hatred toward the company, hatred they could ill afford.

Despite the garbage being thrown in the ring, WCW trumpeted the show as a major success. And when the buy rate came in, they were right: it had jumped a whopping 25 percent from the previous show. The bad news, of course, was that even with the increase, the show still did a miserable 0.19.

By this point WCW was becoming truly desperate for ratings, even more so than they had been previously. The biggest match on *Nitro* the following evening was Ric Flair and his son Reid versus his son David and Russo. The stipulations were that if Flair's team lost, he had to retire forever (again), and if his team won, Russo would be shaved bald. Now you might be thinking, why not do this match on PPV and try to make money out of it? Instead, it was thrown out on free TV so that they could draw a 3.01 quarter to *Raw*'s 6.67. Ric, after interference from everyone in the world (including his wife, Beth, and daughters, Megan and Ashley, the latter of whom went on to become Charlotte in WWE's NXT developmental system), lost after Megan threw in a towel when he was trapped in David's figure four. They shaved Ric bald afterwards, and it actually looked like the beginning of a hot angle. As it turned out, Flair disappeared later that week to get rotator cuff surgery, and by the time he returned, all his hair had grown back.

The show, despite all the hype, drew a 3.0 rating to *Raw*'s 6.84. Most embarrassing of all was the fact that the Goldberg versus Nash main event did a 3.19 to *Raw*'s 6.42. And what huge match was the WWF presenting at that time? Crash Holly defending the Hardcore title against retired Vince McMahon lackey Gerald Brisco.

LESSON NOT LEARNED: While WCW would eventually kill Goldberg thanks in part to a ridiculous heel turn, they were at least able to maximize his aura in the short term. That's arguably better than WWE's idea of what to do with the big guy, where the idea of him as a more or less silent killer that had made WCW money was ignored in favor of giving him a "personality." This was done by having him meet a "family member" by the name of Goldust, Dustin Rhodes, who wore full body gear and makeup to be completely covered in gold from head to toe. We should also note he was working a Tourette's syndrome gimmick at the time. Goldust met his "relative" and placed a blonde wig atop Goldberg's head. The old money-drawing Goldberg would have no doubt speared the guy through a brick wall. The new, "improved" WWE version told him the wig looked better on Goldust than himself, patted him on the shoulder, and politely asked him to never put the wig on his head again. "Appreciate it," he noted. The segment ended with Goldust alone, noting he'd "soiled" himself and needed to change his pants.

Shockingly, within a year of his debut, such comedic interactions had drained Goldberg's star power completely. He chose to leave wrestling and never return.

On June 15, Russo got mad and quit again. This time, he was upset that management wanted to bring back Lex Luger, Kimberly, and Elizabeth—he'd sent them all home earlier and had no plans to ever use them again. The issue was actually quite complicated. In Luger's case, he didn't want to work with Chuck Palumbo, a young Power Plant guy Luger felt wasn't at his level. There was really no good justification for this; he just didn't want to do it. Kimberly walked out because the company wanted her to do a physical angle with Scott Steiner, who terrified everyone in the company with his short fuse and physically aggressive nature. Liz's problem was that she didn't want to be a pro wrestler. Her $156,000-a-year contract, which was disproportionately huge for the amount of work she did, was for her role as a manager; her contract gave her the right to refuse to get into the ring. Russo kept her around early in his tenure and was constantly trying to get her to strip down to her bra and panties on TV, probably since when he was a wrestling fan growing up on Long Island, she was the biggest sex symbol in the WWF.

Russo, apparently feeling that having Liz in the ring and Luger versus Palumbo was going to help turn the entire company around, said that if those two got away with refusing to do angles, the inmates would soon be running the asylum. He went home, though the betting lines were that he'd be back shortly. After all, he had a big mortgage to pay off in Atlanta, and the WWF, despite what he'd forever claim, was doing just fine without him. Internally, it was said that he was taking a few days off to nurse a concussion.

Nitro, therefore, was written without him. Not so coincidentally, it was generally regarded as a better show, mostly because every single solitary match didn't have a run-in, and also because Booker T was allowed to be Booker T again. Several weeks earlier, Russo had learned that early in his career Booker had wrestled as "GI Bro," so he made the decision to put him in the Misfits in Action "military group" and go back to using that name. This despite the fact that Booker T was one of the few fresh faces that fans had any interest in at all. Overall, the show did a 2.75 to *Raw*'s 5.79. While a 2.75 is about what they had been doing, it was actually impressive to have stayed at the same level since this was the first week they were going head-to-head with not only *Raw*, but the NBA Playoffs.

In mid-June, several employees in the company began making requests to be transferred to other divisions within Time Warner. With internal estimates suggesting that the company was on track to lose $60 to $80 million that year, these people wanted to land somewhere safe just in case the company got sold. As it turned out, they had more foresight than pretty much anyone involved in the wrestling business.

The haplessness continued. Scott Hall, who still had not been fired, cared so much about the company and his job that on the June 13 *Thunder*, when they called his house so he could do a phone interview on live TV with Nash, he wasn't home. This was not grounds for his termination, either. In early July, booker Terry Taylor told Scott Steiner that he was going to have to do a job on *Thunder*. Steiner responded to this by blowing a gasket and threatening to kick Taylor's ass. WCW was so outraged with his behavior that they sent him home over the weekend of July 4 . . . with pay. It eventually became such a joke that it was worked into storylines; a few months later, commissioner Ernest Miller said that if Nash or Goldberg did anything to screw up his show, he'd send them to jail. "I'm not gonna send you home!" he screamed, "Because someone in the office might pay you!"

June 15 was notable for a $50,000 ad that ran in the international version of **USA Today** plugging **Monday Nitro** that evening on TNT.

Sadly, WCW placed the ad so that it appeared in a paper that came out on Thursday.

As for Russo, he actually ended up staying out for the rest of the month, and on the July 3 *Nitro*, neither he nor Bischoff was in attendance. The show was building toward the July 9 *Bash at the Beach* PPV, which was scheduled to be headlined by Jeff Jarrett defending the WCW title against Hogan. The rumors were that they wanted Hogan to do the job, but he was refusing due to his creative control contract stipulation. If only it turned out to be that easy.

This *Nitro* was notable for a few things. First, this was the show where they took the killer Tank Abbott and made him part of the boy-band tag team 3 Count. Yes, the former shootfighter was now singing and dancing in the ring. Also on the show, Johnny the Bull did the dumbest thing some people had ever seen in wrestling. He came up with an idea for a move backstage. He'd get in the ring, springboard over the top rope, and do a legdrop on Terry Funk, who would be laying on the hard floor. A legdrop, of course, requires the person doing the move to land on their ass. He was warned repeatedly that this was not a good idea. He did it anyway, and everyone was right. He ended up—literally—breaking his ass, and worse, Funk refused to end the match immediately and made him work another minute or so before finally pinning him. Johnny the Bull did not return to TV for a long, long time. Also on the show, they debuted Gaylen Chandler, the supposed head of the hated Turner Standards and Practices division. Everyone laughed. Ha ha ha, Gaylen Chandler. As it turned out, the head of the hated Turner Standards and Practices really was named Gaylen Chandler, though the guy playing the role was not the real deal.

The fun and games went right out the window on July 9 at *Bash at the Beach* when Russo booked another one of his beloved shoot angles. Before going into the details of what really happened backstage, let's take a look at what fans saw on television.

Russo came out before the match looking sad. Jarrett and Hogan both came down to the ring and looked at each other. Jarrett then laid down in the ring and Hogan, feigning confusion, put his foot on Jarrett's chest for the pin. Russo threw the belt into the ring for Hogan. Jarrett walked to the back looking irate. Hogan told Russo this was all bullshit, then stormed off himself. Fans sat there wondering what in God's name was happening.

Later, Russo came out and just went off on Hogan. Amidst chants of "Russo sucks!" from the crowd, Russo bared his soul to the world:

"From day one, since I've been in WCW, I've done nothing but deal with the bullshit politics behind that curtain. The fact of the matter is I have a wife, I have three kids at home, and I really don't need this shit. But let me tell you the reason why I did come back. I came back for every one of the guys in that locker room that, week in, week out, busts his ass for WCW . . . I came back for the guys behind that curtain that give a shit about this company! And let me tell you who doesn't give a shit about this company—that goddamned politician Hulk Hogan! Because let me tell you people what happened in this ring here tonight. All day long I'm playing politics with Hulk Hogan because Hulk Hogan tonight wants to play his creative control card. And to Hulk Hogan that meant tonight, even though he knows it's bullshit, he beats Jeff Jarrett. Well, guess what? Hogan got his wish. Hogan got his belt, and he went the hell home, and I promise everybody, or else I'll go in the goddamned grave, you will never see that piece of shit again! And Hogan, you big bald son of a bitch, kiss my ass!"

What really happened? Backstage that night, no one seemed to know. Many had heard that the original plan was for Jarrett to win after Scott Steiner interfered for a DQ. Perhaps this is sounding vaguely familiar to those of you who recall what happened to Bret Hart in Montreal. Everyone saw Hogan storm out of the building backstage as if he was really upset. Some thought it was a shoot, believing (rightfully) that Russo would have to have been out of his mind to go to such lengths just to fool the other wrestlers. Among these people was Kevin Nash, which should tell you something, since he was responsible for some really stupid booking ideas in his day. Others figured it had to be a work. After all, if the Jarrett versus Hogan thing wasn't supposed to happen, why were there conveniently two World title belts in the building that day? Why would they have been allowed to go to the ring in the first place if they hadn't agreed on a finish? Plus, many had heard that Booker was going to end up champion at the end of the show, and that couldn't have happened had the "shoot incident" not taken place.

As it turned out, it was a shoot—and a work. Or, more precisely, a work that turned into a shoot. Even more precisely, it was a half-work–half-shoot that turned into a full-fledged shoot. If this sounds confusing, what's even more confusing is the fact that, as complicated as it was, it didn't draw one penny.

Basically, it's believed that only Hogan, Russo, and Bischoff were in on it. Yes, even poor Jeff Jarrett, Russo's best buddy, wasn't filled in. To this day, if you ask him, he'd probably still insist that the whole thing was real. The idea appeared to be an amalgamation of three different angles: Montreal, *Halloween Havoc*, and the deal Nash and Hogan had concocted in 1998, prior to Hogan's "retirement" on Jay Leno. They'd do the *Bash* angle. Hogan would storm out. Russo would say he was gone forever. Everyone in the locker room would cheer. Russo would become a hero. Then, down the road, Hogan would come back with his belt to feud with whoever the WCW champion was at the time, claiming he was the rightful title holder. Russo would then captain the New Blood team with their champion against Bischoff's Millionaire's Club team with Hogan at the helm.

As confusing as that would have been, it likely would have worked, had it not been for one thing: that little speech Russo gave, the one in which he called Hogan a "big bald son of a bitch." Originally, it was supposed to be a much shorter and much less vicious speech. After Russo was done, Hogan legitimately felt he'd been double-crossed, so when he stormed out of the building in anger, he was really storming out, and he really was angry. In fact, he was so angry that he filed a character defamation lawsuit against Russo. Regardless of what some folks might think, real lawsuits are not filed in real courts over fake angles, especially since a lawyer could be disbarred for doing it. And even if someone did go to such lengths, the lawsuit wouldn't still be going through the courts years after the company where the angle started had gone out of business (because the suit was still outstanding in 2004, Hulk Hogan refused to work for Jerry Jarrett's NWA TNA promotion if Russo was involved).

LESSON NOT LEARNED: Unbelievably, Hogan and Russo did work together in TNA . . . and the results were pretty much exactly what one would expect. Eventually, even Russo had seen enough and decided to leave the promotion. He departed until Hogan and Bischoff left. At the time of this writing, it is rumored he is back working with TNA in a non-contracted advisory capacity.

On *Nitro* the next night, to further ensure that no money was made from this, they barely mentioned anything that had happened, and they gave absolutely no details about the Hogan versus Jarrett match. The show was pretty generic, and that was actually a good thing at this point since it meant that it wasn't filled with mind-numbing amounts of pointless angles, and it featured Jarrett pinning new champion Booker T in a four-way to win a title shot at the next PPV. The show did a 2.58, which should put to rest any arguments that these sorts of shoot angles are money in the bank, or even good for a one-night curiosity ratings pop.

The July 18 *Nitro* was the second strong show in a row. Most of this was attributed to the hiring of John "Johnny Ace" Laurinaitis to book the match finishes. Laurinaitis had been working for years in the very traditional All Japan Pro Wrestling, and his influence was evident pretty much immediately. There was such a marked improvement, in fact, that many began lobbying for him to be given total booking control. Never happened. The show featured a U.S. title tournament that was won by Lance Storm, who had jumped ship recently from ECW. The idea was that he'd bill himself as the Canadian champion in order to attempt to recreate the great success the WWF had in 1997 with Bret Hart's Team Canada group.

In mid-July, the company got some rare great news. They put tickets on sale for a tour of Australia in October and did gangbuster business. The reason, of course, was that Australia was starved for live pro wrestling and hadn't been completely burned out by the WCW product as pretty much every building in America had. Over the years, many promotions learned that they could make great money overseas even when the U.S. market was depressed, either by running shows or selling television tapes to local TV affiliates.

The July 24 *Nitro* was notable for the main event, which saw Booker T pin Goldberg with his uranage (basically a Rock bottom). The idea, obviously, was to try to get both Booker and his finisher over, since fans weren't really taking him seriously as World champion. The problem was in the execution. Goldberg, having learned so much from the oh-so-professional Hogan and Nash, made a power play backstage that resulted in the entire format of the match being changed. As it turned out, Goldberg faced him early in the show and beat him up so badly that Booker's brother Stevie Ray threw in the towel. Referee Ernest Miller then stopped the match and declared Goldberg the winner. However, he added, the title could only change hands on a pinfall or a submission, so Booker was still champ. You read that right, Booker was beaten supposedly to near death, but he couldn't lose the title that way. Then, later, they did the match again. This time, Goldberg utterly destroyed him for several minutes, laid down for three seconds after Jarrett and Ernest Miller ganged up on him, then immediately recovered to spear and jackhammer Booker. It was one of those classic matches where both guys ended up less over afterwards than they were going in (Booker in particular came out of it looking worse than the worst jobber who ever worked worldwide), and backstage, several irate people suggested Goldberg be sent home as punishment.

Nitro, after a few good shows in a row, reverted to its downward slide on July 31. Storm, who had previously won the U.S. (or "Canadian") title and the Hardcore belt, added the Cruiserweight title to his collection with a win over Chavo Guerrero Jr. a.k.a. Lieutenant Loco. Moments after grabbing the belt, Tony Schiavone, who a few years earlier had done commentary for matches when Ultimo Dragon held ten titles at the same time (as the result of winning titles both in WCW and in a multibelt tournament in Japan), asked if anyone had ever held three belts at the same time before. Then, just to make sure the big push of Storm went absolutely nowhere, they had Nash come out and lay waste to him in short order. They also did a Viagra on a pole match with Kidman and Shane Douglas, apparently because someone thought it would be really funny to have a Viagra on a pole match. Main was Booker T, who people still weren't taking seriously, over Sting when the KISS Demon climbed out from under the ring and beat up Sting to lead to the pin. The show did a 2.66 rating to *Raw*'s 6.39.

In late July, perhaps the most underreported story of the year (and maybe in the history of WCW) occurred: Matt Williams quit. It's a name 99.9 percent of wrestling fans probably would not recognize, and for good reason. Matt Williams was director of research for WCW. He spent a year of his life polling fans about what they liked and disliked about the company, and what they felt should be changed to make it a more enjoyable product. He polled not only fans who were still watching, but fans who had long since given up on the product. The results probably would come as no surprise to anyone; the fans wanted more wrestling and less "sports entertainment."

When Mr. Williams presented his findings to WCW, you can imagine the response. The entire study was thrown out, since the writers, obviously, couldn't take seriously the thought that their job was overrated and wrestling fans were more interested in watching—GASP!—wrestling. Williams, outraged, quit for a job in another Time Warner division.

So nothing changed. At the end of July, the internal estimates came back and showed that the company had lost $7 million over the course of the month. One month! Keep in mind that until 1999, the most WCW had lost in an entire *year* was $6 million.

Changes were immediately made. First, almost two dozen undercard guys were cut. This was in addition to the two dozen or so that had been cut over the past year. Then discussions about cutting some of the higher-priced guys began, names as big as Hogan, Goldberg, Luger, DDP, and Bret.

The belief was that these guys were being paid too much on their guaranteed deals, and it was killing the company.

The stark reality was much different: the company was being killed, and therefore the revenue wasn't coming in to pay off those deals. Not only were the big stars making just as much money two years earlier, but they also had 260 guys under contract, some of whom, like Kevin Wacholz and Lanny Poffo, never made one single appearance for the company. Despite this, the company made a huge profit, because they were still making tons and tons of money from house shows, pay-per-views, merchandising, advertising, and so forth. As it turned out, had every single wrestler in the company worked for free in 2000, the company would still have been on track to lose $40 million.

Internally, there was another big management shakedown, and when the dust settled, Bischoff was relegated to being a consultant, and Brad Siegel had put all his faith behind Russo. This was a very controversial decision, since many in the company, unlike Siegel, actually had backgrounds in wrestling and saw Russo for the flop that he was. In fact, a week earlier, an internal memo had been passed around detailing the "Ten Questions Not To Ask Vince Russo." Among them were "How many 'young and hungry employees' does it take to screw up an entire company?" and "What does the second 'W' in WCW stand for?"

Perhaps as a way to get Goldberg to quit, Russo had a meeting with him on August 2 and told him the plans were for Kevin Nash to win a three-way over him and Steiner at the August PPV, and then on the September show, Steiner would pin him. Goldberg was not down with this and walked out. Everyone immediately assumed the whole thing was a work. He was back a week later, but quite unhappy.

The August 7 *Nitro* in Denver featured a Vince Russo interview where he went on and on with his delusional figures about how the company was better off now that he was there, and how WWF was in much worse shape. No one was quite sure where he was getting these numbers, since the WWF went from grossing $251.5 million in 1999 to $379.3 million in 2000, the year after Russo had left. However Russo tried to spin things, hard numbers told a different story. Nobody was sure what the point of doing this interview on *Nitro* was, either. And, in quite the coincidence, the show did a horrid 2.44 rating, well below what it was averaging when he first started. The main angle was Goldberg giving Steiner's valet, Midajah, a jackhammer through a table backstage and

Steiner running to her aid. This should have made perfect sense because guys who beat up women are bad, and guys who run to their aid are good. Problem here was that Goldberg was supposed to be the good guy and Steiner the bad guy.

Thunder the following evening featured announcer Gene Okerlund and Buff Bagwell versus announcer Mark Madden and Kanyon in a truly wretched match. If that wasn't bad enough, because Madden was in the ring, someone had to fill in for him. That someone was Judy Bagwell. Apparently the match was supposed to be a shoot, because when Madden gave Gene a low blow, Gene just stood there, causing Tony Schiavone to scream: "Gene didn't sell it!" The big question is, if this was a shoot, why on Earth would Kanyon have chosen Mark Madden to be his partner?

The following Sunday, prior to the *New Blood Rising* PPV in Vancouver, British Columbia, Siegel called a meeting with the boys to announce that further changes were afoot. The first move was to cut back drastically on production (making Russo irate, since one of *his* first moves had been to greatly boost the production values, convinced this would make the show more competitive with *Raw*), to get rid of two of the three big screens, and to ignite less pyro at the beginning of the show and for the wrestlers' entrances.

The biggest change planned was that, effective in late October, they were going to cancel the *Thunder* tapings and film the show immediately after *Nitro* on Monday nights. Obviously, the idea was to dramatically cut costs, since the *Thunder* shows weren't drawing fans. The downside was that nobody was going to *Thunder* because they did not like *Thunder*, which meant few were likely to stay after *Nitro* ended to watch the second show. Some fans, who watched WCW only for its perverse comedy value, anxiously awaited these tapings since the plan was to film the entire two-show block in three and a half hours with no commercial breaks. This meant that all the pre-tapes would be done earlier, then inserted into the shows. Seeing as how pre-tapes had often been inserted into *Nitro* in the wrong order, the thought of the production crew trying to get things right with this new taping plan appeared to be a disaster in the making.

New Blood Rising was, of course, a horrible show, not only because the production was drastically cut back, but also because the matches were awful and the angles were atrocious. The fans were so clearly sending a message, but nobody was listening. This was another one of those shows where they sold almost 5,000 tickets very early on, and then as soon as they started to announce matches on the television programs, ticket sales stopped dead in their tracks. The message, obviously, was that WCW was booking things fans did not want to see. Instead of learning a lesson from this, WCW went on to attempt to force fans to like what they were presenting, and you can imagine how that worked. As if the message wasn't clear enough, it should be noted that almost 3,000 free tickets were snatched up around the Vancouver area; when the day of the show came, only 1,300 of those folks actually bothered to show up.

Those who showed up left wishing they hadn't. The opener, Jung Dragons versus 3 Count, was good. The main event, Booker T versus Jeff Jarrett, was good. Everything else almost set new standards for bad. Ernest Miller pinned Great Muta in a travesty of justice that Muta, one of the greatest workers of all time, couldn't save. Bagwell beat Kanyon in a below-average "Judy Bagwell on a pole" match (please, don't ask) that despite featuring a run-in by everyone's favorite former WCW champion David Arquette, was actually the third-best of the evening. Kronik versus Chuck Palumbo and Shawn Stasiak versus Mark Jindrak and Sean O'Haire versus General Rection (Hugh G. Rection was his name—yet another Russo high-concept) and Corporal Cajun in a four-way that was overbooked to death. Disco Inferno played heel referee. The finish saw Lieutenant Loco, who was buddies with Rection and Cajun, run down and physically force Disco to count the pin for—yes—Kronik. It probably does not need to be noted that this made zero sense. Kidman beat Shane Douglas in a strap match. Bad. Major Gunns beat Miss Hancock (Stacy Keibler) in a women's match. Horrendous, plus they teased a miscarriage angle afterwards. That's good family fun. Sting versus Demon. Miserable. Storm versus Awesome for the U.S. title. This was a guaranteed good match because Storm, a Canadian, was super over in Vancouver. Russo, however, showed a tremendous amount of talent by figuring out a way to book the match so that everybody hated it by the end. Jacques Rougeau, another Canadian ex-wrestler, was referee outside the ring. Try to follow this. Awesome pinned Storm with a powerbomb. Storm kicked out and the ref counted three anyway, but in the grand scheme of things, that screw-up could be forgotten. Rougeau said no, according to the CANADIAN RULE BOOK (which they actually printed up, and which Storm took home) you could only win with a five count. Awesome put Storm in a dragon sleeper and Storm gave up. Rougeau said no, according to the rule book you couldn't win by submission. Awesome then got a five-count pin after a splash off the top. Rougeau said after a pin, the loser had ten seconds to get to his feet, and if he did, the match continued. Storm got to his feet. Both guys went through a table, and this time the ring announcer said that the first man to his feet at the count of ten would win. This, of course, made no sense, unless the ring announcer was able to see into the future and predict that one man would, indeed, rise to his feet exactly at the count of ten. Well, Awesome got up first, but Rougeau punched him with brass knuckles behind the other ref's back, allowing Storm to stand up for the win. To say this was hated passionately would be praising it too highly. The only good thing about it was that Bret Hart came out afterwards to a hero's ovation and hugged Storm and Rougeau.

Storm recalls: "When the finish was pitched to me, it was pitched in a manner where the office thought all of these restarts would be hilarious, and the match was being booked this way for comedic purposes.

The finish was obviously booked to protect Mike and keep him strong, which would have made sense had they not turned him into a comedy act a week or two later when they made him 'That '70s guy.' The way the match was booked was so absurdly stupid because obviously I was going to be a heavy babyface in Vancouver. I got a monstrous face reaction coming out, the crowd was a sea of Lance Storm signs, so the match was a failure live. They booed every time Mike beat me and then popped every time Jacques restarted the match. Before the match, Bret even pulled me aside, and keep in mind this was the first time we'd met in person, and told me that he thought there was a good chance that after getting beaten this many times the crowd might turn on me. I told him I thought that's why they had him there, figuring no matter how bad they buried me in this match, if Bret Hart came out at the end to endorse me I would be redeemed in the eyes of Canadians. I got the impression that Bret was reluctant to be a part of this angle because if the crowd did turn on me, he would be going out there to endorse a loser that had just gotten beat three or four times in one match in front of his home crowd. I, too, was worried this match would bury me to Canadian fans. I thought doing this match in Canada was astronomically stupid, and WCW was passing up their chance to cement a new Canadian star since Bret's future was in serious doubt after his concussion. This could have been a passing of the torch moment. Thankfully the crowd stayed with me and even popped when I won, and then when Bret came out post-match it was the loudest reaction I've ever heard. Jacques and I had to yell into each other's ear to be heard as Bret made his way to the ring. I suppose I got a little bit of heat in the U.S. out of cheating so many times to keep my title, but to me it killed most of the credibility I had, making my title run purely a joke."

Following the Storm/Awesome debacle, Kronik then wrestled AGAIN, losing to Vampiro and Muto in a Tag title match. Hideous. Finally, in the coup de grâce, Nash beat Goldberg and Steiner to win a shot at Booker T at the next show. This was so bad it was funny. Nash cut a promo before the match saying that Goldberg was claiming to be hurt due to a motorcycle accident in Sturgis (he really did get in an accident, by the way), but was actually faking the injury and wouldn't come out because of it. They played Goldberg's music twice, and sure enough, he never came out. The match started, and a few minutes later Goldberg finally appeared. They had a horrible match. Nash went to give Goldberg a powerbomb, but Goldberg deadweighted him and walked out of the ring. The announcers started screaming about how— this is true—Goldberg wasn't going up for the move and was screwing up the finish. When Goldberg got to the top of the ramp, Russo came out and yelled at him. Goldberg screamed "Fuck you!" and stormed off. The announcers began insinuating that Goldberg was being totally unprofessional and wouldn't do the scripted loss. So Nash and Steiner continued their horrible match. Tony Schiavone, in a direct quote, then said: "If, in fact, the jackknife powerbomb was part of this design, what are they going to do now, improvise?" So finally, Nash pinned Steiner with the powerbomb and the announcers went off about how professional Steiner was for going up for the move. The irony of all this was that it was supposed to be a shoot, yet not even the dumbest hardcore fan could ever believe that Steiner was this much of a professional.

The idea in all of this, which was lost on 99 percent of the people watching at home, was that Goldberg didn't want to lose two straight shows in a row in real life, so they were going to turn it into a storyline. Of course, in order to do so, they had to pretty much state that all wrestling matches were fake. The concept was lost on WCW that even though most fans accept that wrestling is not on the level, they want to get lost in the action and suspend their disbelief for the few hours that they watch. It's just like going to the movies. Everyone knows that what they see in the movies is not real, but they're still able to let themselves go for two hours and "believe" what they see up on the screen. Imagine what would happen if, during a key scene in a movie like Jurassic Park, there was a technical screw-up and everyone suddenly saw the animated dinosaurs on a computer screen running after rendered versions of the actors? Or if, during a key dramatic moment in another film, both actors just started laughing and said they needed to start over again? Suffice to say, the effect would be ruined. It's the same thing with wrestling. Exposing the secrets of the wrestling business on backstage shows on the WWE network is one thing, but nobody wants the secrets to be exposed in the middle of a match.

Storm recalled a story from that weekend. "The week before *New Blood Rising* I was contacted by the merchandise people to finalize the Lance Storm T-Shirt. I asked them if they were going to have them for *New Blood Rising* because it, as well as *Nitro* and *Thunder* that week, was in Canada, and that was obviously the best week to sell Lance Storm merchandise. They said absolutely, that's why they were rushing now to get this done. At *New Blood Rising*, I did an autograph-signing thing before the show and had a HUGE line. I was signing quite a few of these T-Shirts, but before too long a guy came up with a Goldberg shirt for me to sign and I asked him why not a Lance Storm shirt. He said that's what he wanted, but that they were sold out. I thought, 'Holy shit, I'm sold out already!' and got excited about the possibility of my first merchandise check being gigantic, and also hoped they would ship more shirts for *Nitro* and *Thunder*. Well, they didn't have any shirts at *Nitro* or *Thunder*, and better yet, when I got my merchandise check for T-Shirts I did the calculations and I had sold a total of 144 shirts. Yes, they brought twelve dozen T-shirts for a three-show loop through CANADA for the guy who held three championship belts that he had put CANADIAN flags on, which had sold out in the first thirty to forty-five minutes of the first show. When I asked about why they had made so few, they said, 'Well, last time we were in Canada we didn't sell much merchandise.' I asked, 'Did you have any CANADIANS on those shows?' To which they replied, 'I don't think so.'"

Nitro the next night was better than the PPV, but that's like saying a gunshot wound to the foot is better than one to the arm. It opened with another wacky "shoot" segment in which Russo said Goldberg was going to have to face Tank Abbott, and this time, unlike at the PPV, there was going to be NO SCRIPT! This segment's quarter did a 2.0. Jacques Rougeau, who had been central to the Storm storyline the night before, also quit after this show since they asked him to do a job for Ernest Miller on *Thunder* that week. Because he'd started his own promotion in Montreal and had no interest in getting beaten on TV, he'd had it put into his contract that he'd do anything WCW asked except TV jobs. WCW had agreed to this and then attempted to renege on the deal. So he went home. The show as a whole drew a 2.40 rating, which means at this point it was doing well below what the horrible Kevin Sullivan programs had drawn many months earlier. Also, keep in mind that in order to make up for the ad-revenue loss in the move from three hours to two, the show needed to be averaging in the 4.5 range, nearly double what it was doing. Clearly, that wasn't about to happen anytime soon.

If it wasn't bad enough that *WCW Saturday Night* had recently, without any warning, been turned into a taped show after twenty-seven consecutive years on TBS, the few fans who were still loyal to it were shocked to find the program off the air that weekend. Done. Finished. No graphic, no farewell message, nothing. Again, this for a show that had been on the network for over a QUARTER CENTURY!

More people were also fired that week, including every Mexican in the entire company with the exception of Rey Mysterio Jr. and Juventud Guerrera. This certainly did not help WCW in regards to Sonny Onoo's racial discrimination lawsuit. Also axed was Chris Daniels, which was surprising for two reasons. First, he was in his twenties, and the story was that the promotion really wanted to push their younger talent; and second, he was making $75,000 per year, which, in comparison to what some of the deadweight was making and how much the company was losing, was a drop in the hat. By the time the bloodletting was over, they were down to less than fifty wrestlers under contract. That's pretty impressive when you consider they went into the year with 234. A freeze was also put on the hiring of any more new talent.

Russo on *WCW Live* went off on a variety of topics. In particular was his claim that on *Nitro*, as a "total shoot," he was going to offer Bill Goldberg his release from the company. Of course, it was an angle, and the reason everyone knew it was an angle was because Goldberg, who hated WCW and wanted out bad, ripped the "release papers" up. This whole deal made it impossible to believe anything else Vinny Ru said in this chat.

The August 21 *Nitro*, despite being a mess of illogical storytelling, had better than usual in-ring action. The problem was that WCW was so uncool at this point that it would have taken months and months of awesome shows to even start turning a corner. As it was, they'd have a good show one week, then a string of horrible ones, then another good one, and so on and so forth. Occasionally they would have two good shows in a row, and this was so rare that when it happened, it was newsworthy. This show was built around Goldberg and his contract. WCW contracts were a funny thing; they could seemingly not be destroyed. For example, one day Goldberg got mad and ate Scott Hall's contract on TV. Yes, he ate it, like it was a taco. Amazingly, the next week on TV the contract was back, looking as pristine as ever. The storyline on this particular *Nitro* was that Goldberg had a no-cut deal, which was why he was being offered a release. After he ripped up his contract, Russo said if Goldberg laid one hand on him, he would be fired. This, of course, would suggest that Goldberg's contract was not a no-cut deal after all. Then, a few minutes later, Booker T laid several hands on Russo in an unrepentant beating, yet somehow this did not result in him being fired.

The political turmoil of the week involved Kevin Nash, who was lobbying to get the World title from Booker T at the next PPV. His argument was that Booker was not over and that the fans were cheering more loudly for him every week. Truth be told, Booker wasn't getting over like a World champion should, but the reason for that is because he wasn't booked like a top guy, and he was often portrayed as an idiot on television (trusting guys even the dumbest fan knew were going to turn on him, etc.). And in Nash's case, he was getting bigger crowd reactions because he was always pushed harder than almost anyone else, but that didn't necessarily mean he was any bigger of a draw than anyone else. The fact is that nobody in the company was drawing any money, and the belt had been destroyed so far beyond hope that it really didn't matter who was wearing it by that point.

To show how little folks cared about the angles in those days, in late August tickets went on sale for the September 11 *Nitro* in Charlotte, North Carolina. Since it was Flair Country, the big angle the show was being built around was the wedding of David and the supposedly pregnant Stacy Kielber. They sold 700 tickets. On the bright side, when word got out that Ric would be returning on that show, ticket sales surged—to 1,657. And after years of screwing the fans countless times, that's what *Nitro* in Ric Flair Country did as a final number.

WCW got some rare good news as *Nitro* on August 28 did a 3.52 rating, up quite a bit from the week before. Was the company turning around? Did the improved in-ring action from the week before result in an influx of new viewers? No, *Raw* was preempted by the Westminster Dog Show. WCW, knowing this was their chance to hit a home-run show, threw everything they could muster into an attempt to win fans back. The big angle to end the show had Bret Hart return and meet Goldberg in the desert. Don't ask why they were there, or how Goldberg got all the way to the desert within ten minutes of leaving the *Nitro* building. Bret said he wanted Goldberg to kill Russo as revenge for what had happened in Montreal. Truth be told, Russo had zero to do with Montreal, and in fact, he had no idea what a double-cross was at the time. The swerve, of course, was that Bret was actually mad at Goldberg for ending his career at *Starrcade* in December, with the superkick that nearly knocked his head right off his shoulders, so he beat him up. You might wonder why this was booked if Bret wasn't going to ever be able to wrestle again and would therefore be unable to have a money match with Goldberg. Or why Goldberg had initially trusted Bret, who was mysteriously right there in the Las Vegas desert after having been in Canada since January. You'd need to ask Vince Russo.

To give an idea of how much of a joke the company became to even their most loyal followers, one **Thunder** taping in 2000 featured a fan holding up a sign that read "I'M AT A WCW EVENT" while wearing a bag over his head. This wasn't the only sign-related comedy. A man named Peter Goldschmidt sued another man, Robert Catell, for appearing on WCW telecasts holding up various derogatory signs, including "PETER GOLDSCHMIDT LOSER 4 LIFE." Apparently, the two used to be friends on Long Island. Then, one day, Catell asked Goldschmidt to help him move. Goldschmidt supposedly said he was unable to because it was a workday, and the friendship came to a bitter end, leading Catell to travel around the nation and hold up disparaging signs at wrestling events. The number of lives that WCW ultimately affected is staggering.

On August 29, Bischoff resurfaced, flying to Atlanta to talk with Brad Siegel. The hot rumor going around was that he wanted full control of WCW without anyone above him to overrule his decisions. That meant, obviously, that he'd have to purchase the company. He denied it to most everyone who asked.

WCW cut even more costs the following week. Some were noticeable on TV and others were known only to the wrestlers, who were quite unhappy about them. For instance, while a few had it written into their contracts that their hotel rooms would be paid for, most did not. Up until this point, it had always happened, but this week, everyone was told they'd have to start forking over the cash for their own rooms. The guys were outraged, which was funny because the WWF wrestlers had been required to pay all their own expenses, including hotel rooms and rental cars, since the beginning of time.

The September 4 *Nitro* from Dallas was built around the *Nitro* Swerve™, which had been popularized a few weeks earlier. The swerve was that two bad guys would tease turning on each other, but then in the end, they would reveal that they'd planned some horrible deed all along. It got to the point where this swerve was done so often that the only way it would have been a real swerve is if the two bad guys really did turn on each other. This week's bad guys in question were Russo and Nash. They teased turning on each other as participants in a triple-tier War Games match, but, of course, in the end Russo gave Nash the belt and allowed him to escape. Yes, Russo had possession of the belt right before the finish, which meant theoretically, he could have made himself the WCW World Heavyweight champion.

You laugh.

Soon you shall cry.

The September 11 *Nitro* emanated from deep in the heart of Ric Flair country. You know, the one where they promised Ric was going to return and still only drew 1,657 paid? The brilliant storyline idea was to have him arrested and taken off the show. The five straight minutes of "BULLSHIT!" chants would have taught most wrestling companies a lesson. Not WCW. There was another *NITRO* SWERVE™, this time with Steiner and Nash. They teased fighting each other, but then turned on babyface ref Booker T and double-teamed him into oblivion. Nobody was sure why the stupid babyfaces never saw things like this coming after witnessing it week after week after week. And of course, there was the David/Stacy wedding, which, in a swerve, never took place, as Stacy revealed that David wasn't the father of her unborn baby. By the grace of God, the company went out of business before we had to hear her identify Vinny Ru as the dad. The show was doing very well up until that point, well enough to do a shockingly high 3.20 composite rating to *Raw*'s 5.90. The 3.20 was actually the third good rating in a row for *Nitro*, mostly because there had been no *Raw* competition the previous two weeks. Unfortunately, it was not a sign of an upward trend.

Fall Brawl on September 17 was a surprisingly good show with the exception of one very scary moment involving fifty-two-year-old Paul Orndorff. Orndorff was a major league wrestling star in the '80s when the WWF was starting to catch fire nationally. During a run with Hulk Hogan he suffered a neck injury, but because there was so much money to be made touring, he didn't take any time off. He ended up with severe nerve damage, which caused his left arm to permanently atrophy, and he retired forever for the first time in 1987. In the early '90s he made a short return for WCW, but was eventually forced to retire again when the injury acted up and he underwent neck surgery. Leading up to *Fall Brawl*, his main job with the company was as a trainer for their Power Plant wrestling school. Despite his advanced age and physical limitations, he was still able to stay in tremendous physical condition, so when he was asked to come back for another match, he said OK.

The match was a fourteen-person tag featuring Orndorff and Disco Inferno and Big Vito and Rey Mysterio Jr. and Juventud Guerrera and Konnan and Tygress (a Nitro girl) versus Mark Jindrak and Sean O'Haire and Mike Sanders and Chuck Palumbo and Reno and Johnny the Bull and Shawn Stasiak. Orndorff stayed on the apron for almost the entire match. When he finally tagged in, he attempted to give Jindrak his patented piledriver, but their timing was way off. Basically, when giving a piledriver, the person taking the bump has to jump a bit to allow the person executing it to get them up quickly and easily. Because the timing was off, Orndorff had to muscle him up, and in doing so he tore his hamstring. In attempting to compensate, his neck went out and he collapsed into a state of temporary paralysis.

No one in the ring had any idea what to do. So they did the only thing they could think of doing under the circumstances; they kept wrestling. Trainers hit the ring to attend to Orndorff while the wrestlers attempted to perform outside and on the other end of the ring. Finally, after about two minutes of utter confusion, referee Charles Robinson took matters into his own hands and ended the bout. The audience, for once, was well aware that this was a real-life situation and were respectful while he was being worked on. Thankfully, Orndorff ended up being OK afterwards, but he never wrestled another match again.

The rest of the show featured far better than usual in-ring action, although there were a couple horrible bouts (Sting versus Vampiro versus Great Muta springs to mind). The semi-main saw Scott Steiner beat Goldberg in what was actually a tremendous match. Both guys were huge, scary men, and they threw each other around and hit each other really hard and the fans got very much into the drama. After interference from various people, including Russo and Steiner's valet Midajah, Steiner finally got the win after Goldberg "passed out" in a submission hold. It was by far the best match either man had been involved in all year and the best of Goldberg's career up to that point. Most impressive of all was that Goldberg hurt his shoulder minutes into the match and was still able to gut out a great performance.

Sadly, that wasn't the final match as Booker T beat Nash in a boring cage match to close out the show. On the bright side, at least Booker got a chance to pin a main-eventer clean with his uranage finishing move for once.

Nitro on September 18 took place in Canada. The reason that this is important is because Canada is the home of some very rabid and loyal wrestling fans, and they don't care who they're "supposed" to cheer or boo; they just do whatever the hell they want. As a result, the crowd reactions on this show were all over the place. Goldberg, who was supposed to be a babyface, was booed mightily since the Canadians hated anyone who had feuded with Bret Hart and played a role in ending his

career. Heels like Russo and Scott Steiner were cheered, the former because he ran down Goldberg and the latter because he beat Goldberg
the night before. And all the reactions weren't necessarily related to big
Bill; the fans cheered heel Jeff Jarrett and booed babyface Booker T. The
main angle on the show was another one of those WCW specials. It was
Booker and Sting versus Jarrett and Steiner with the winner getting a
title shot the following week. You'll never guess which of the four men
won. You could never guess even if given four tries, because none of
them were the victor. The victor managed to be Russo, who wasn't even
in the match at all.

All of this set up a day that will live in infamy, the September 25
Nitro from the Nassau Coliseum in Long Island. See if you can put two
and two together before you finish reading about what happened. Vince
Russo, creative goof and number-one contender to the World title. His
hometown. Perhaps that was too much information.

Midway through the show, literally with no warning whatsoever, they had a Goldberg
versus Steiner cage match. Keep in mind their previous match was an awesome dramatic affair, so theoretically, they should have been able to draw a bit of money on
PPV by locking the two inside a cage. Instead, not only did they give it away for free on
Nitro, but they gave it away for free with no warning whatsoever. Long story short, they
made zero dollars on pay-per-view to draw a 2.17 quarter. YAY WCW!

The main event saw Russo get his title shot against Booker in the
cage. It should be noted that Russo was so popular in his hometown
that when they announced on *Nitro* that he'd be getting a title shot here,
approximately 200 additional tickets were sold that whole week. The
rules of this match were that you could win by pinning your opponent,
making him submit, or leaving the cage. A hundred million men ran
in, including Goldberg. We'd note that it sort of kills the entire concept of a cage match when folks can just walk in and out at will, but

WCW had already been doing this for years. Finally, Booker moved to escape, but just as he was about to set foot on the floor and retain his belt, Goldberg speared Russo so hard that Russo went through the side of the cage and crashed into the guardrail. The guardrail, of course, was outside, which meant—oh yes!—Vince Russo was the WCW World Heavyweight champion.

Years later, no less than Jim Herd would have this to say about Vince Russo, WCW champion: "Vince Russo was a guy who thought in his own mind only that he was a draw. Give me a break!"[33]

You know what makes us most sad about WCW dying? The fact that we never got to see an on-air team-up of Russo and Herd. That would have been spectacular.

The only good thing about this entire situation was that the visual of Goldberg spearing Russo through the cage was really awesome. Goldberg shared that opinion himself: "WCW . . . the downfall's name was Vince Russo. The only entertaining part [of his time there] was getting to spear him and having his head hit the post. Before I got in the ring, his helmet fell off, and I wasn't going to step foot in that ring until he had it back on because I didn't want him to sue me for killing him."[34]

Booking-wise, this was the final nail in the coffin that housed the WCW World Heavyweight championship, a belt that (in storyline at least) dated back to 1905. Its days of drawing money were over. Well, they were over more than ever. But, storyline stuff aside, there was something else that could have ended up in a coffin: Russo.

Vinny Ru had been getting involved in a lot of matches over the previous few months, and suffice to say, he was no athlete. He was certainly nothing resembling a pro wrestler. Although wrestling is predetermined ("fake"), the fact of the matter is that when an untrained layperson gets involved, he is setting himself up for some serious injury. The human body does not like the idea of falling flat on its back, and learning to do so takes time, sometimes several months. If you land with your weight too low, your head can snap back and bounce off the ring, which, contrary to popular belief, is made of steel and wood and in absolutely no way resembles a trampoline.

Russo had suffered various injuries during his bouts, including a number of concussions. There was a reason that he wore a helmet to the ring when wrestling his later matches, and it wasn't strictly for comedy purposes. His brain was swollen, and like with all concussions, once you suffer one, the likelihood of suffering another increases immensely. Bret Hart knew this first-hand; his career ended for that exact reason.

You can say whatever you wish about Vince Russo as a writer and booker for World Championship Wrestling, but in real life, he was a human being with a family, and going into the ring after having recently suffered multiple concussions was putting his health, and his life, in jeopardy. It was sad to see him doing so, especially in light of the Paul Orndorff, Bret Hart, and Darren Drosdov situations, all of which occurred that very same year.

And what did he get for risking his livelihood? *Nitro* did a 2.87 to *Raw*'s 5.44. Believe it or not, a lot of people were thinking that *Nitro* was going to win that evening. The reason for this is that after seventeen years on the USA Network, the WWF moved to TNN. TNN at the time was The Nashville Network, and the belief was—seriously—that wrestling fans weren't going to be able to find *Raw* after it switched. Now keep in mind that it was still airing Monday nights at 9:00 p.m., and that all fans would have to do was run through all the channels, and if their cable service had TNN, at some point they were going to find it. This did not matter to many. They were sure the WWF was done for. They were wrong. The only thing that was done for was ECW's weekly TNN show, which was scheduled to be canceled on September 22 due to McMahon's Viacom contract stating that his shows could be the only wrestling programming on the network. Vince, however, being the benevolent evil billionaire that he was at the time, mercifully allowed them to stay on by waiving the clause. Ultimately, it didn't matter because he eventually signed ECW owner Paul Heyman to a contract, and the company, which was going to die no matter what because it just didn't have the assets to compete, closed up shop shortly thereafter.

In late September, the WCW booking situation was finally cleared up by Kevin Nash in a radio interview. He said he was never really in charge of booking, because all of his great ideas ended up being shot down by Hogan and Bischoff. What was funny about this was that Hogan always told his friends that he never changed any ideas, he just did what he was told and let Bischoff and Nash run it. And you'll never guess what Eric always told people: he never gave any input, instead putting full booking power in Nash's hands so he could sink or swim. Apparently a mystery man was writing all the shows.

In early October, the first serious rumors of WCW being sold began making the rounds. There had been plenty of talk in the past that Time Warner might be interested in selling and that Bischoff was doing whatever he could to get investors together to make an offer. There were even rumors that offers had been made, but both sides were far apart on numbers. In fact, in the summer of 1999, Mandalay Bay Sports and Entertainment had registered the WCWextreme.com and WCWXtreme.com domain names. This, however, was the first time that anyone was mentioning what they believed was a real time and place—October 23 in Little Rock, Arkansas, the first *Nitro* back after the Australian tour. The story was that Bischoff and Mandalay were teaming up to make a purchase. As it turned out, the day came and went, and no sale was announced.

On the October 2 *Nitro* in San Francisco, WCW World Heavyweight champion Vince Russo announced that he was vacating the title, meaning that not only did he win the belt, but nobody ever would beat him for it. He had two other major announcements. First, he wasn't going to fire Goldberg for spearing him out of the cage last week. Instead Goldberg had to win 176 matches in a row to get a title shot, and if he lost even one, he'd be fired. Many of the fans who'd lived through the Sid win streak strongly suspected that this might not be on the level. Russo also announced a Jarrett and Booker versus Steiner and Sting tag match, with the two winners squaring off for the vacant belt in the main event.

Jarrett and Booker won the match, and the two squared off in yet another Russo classic: the world's first-ever San Francisco 49ers match. Basically, there were four boxes hanging from poles. Inside one of the boxes was the belt. Inside the other three were, well, not the belt. Whoever got the box with the belt in it would be the champion. If Frank A. Gotch didn't turn in his grave after watching the Nassau Coliseum show, he sure did after this. The first box opened contained a blow-up doll. The second contained a photo of Scott Hall, who hadn't been seen in as long as anyone could remember, but was still way more popular than 95 percent of the active roster. The third box contained a glove that you would use for, say, gardening, but it was identified as a coal miner's glove. The finish saw a midget named Beetlejuice from the Howard Stern show give Jarrett a low blow, allowing Booker to open the last box. Unfortunately, the belt fell out of the box before he was able to get it, so ring announcer Dave Penzer had to pick it up off the floor and hand it to Booker for the win. Of course, following the rules to the letter, this should have meant that Dave Penzer was the new WCW World Heavyweight champion, but thankfully Russo wasn't fast enough on his feet to change everything around at the last second.

One week after Russo's steel cage stunt match, Bill DeMott (Captain Rection) did an interview with Alex Marvez and revealed that he'd suffered "six concussions in three weeks" and had been advised by his doctor to quit wrestling. You see, the injuries had caused legitimate brain damage, and simple tasks, like reading street signs and even standing for long periods of time, had become extremely difficult. He was making good money, though, so he vowed to wrestle at least one more year before retiring.

Rumors of the company's "impending sale" grew hotter as October wore on. In fact, things got so out of control that Brad Siegel told Terry Taylor to meet with the boys on October 8 to discuss it. Taylor basically said that four companies were interested in purchasing WCW: in addition to Bischoff's group, there were three others in Japan, France, and Germany. None of the latter three was specified, although months earlier, rumors had spread that one of Japan's major wrestling organizations (either New Japan, All Japan, or NOAH) was interested in buying, though it was never clear which. Taylor said there was no guarantee the company would be sold, but they were entertaining various offers.

Another name that popped up that week as a possible buyer was Vince McMahon. The instigator of this rumor was Antonio Inoki of New Japan, who had a history of making up outlandish tales. Whether he knew more than he let on or not, the fact was that McMahon was interested. Soon, *MultiChannel News* was reporting, through unnamed sources, that the WWF had the right to match any offer for the company as a result of settlement terms of their copyright infringement lawsuit. Both that lawsuit and WCW's countersuit had been quietly settled out of court in September. Since the details were sealed, nobody knew for sure whether or not this was true, but as the weeks wore on it was believed to have been a false story (WWF lawyers even publicly denied it). Regardless, McMahon had serious interest, and talks between the two sides continued for many weeks. By the end of 2000, however, it appeared that McMahon had decided to pass on the deal entirely.

In the midst of all these sales talks came what should have been a highly successful tour of Australia. Tickets had been going like gangbusters since mid-July, and this looked to be WCW's most successful house show run of the year.

Almost immediately, however, things went wrong. Juventud Guerrera, apparently in a drug-induced fit, caused a huge scene at the Brisbane Marriott Hotel. The previous night, at a club, he'd smoked something given to him by an unknown person, and the authorities suspected it had been laced with PCP. He went to bed, and the following morning he went insane near the hotel restaurant where all the wrestlers were eating, tearing his clothes off while screaming that he was going to kill himself. Several wrestlers—nearly all of them much larger than Guerrera—tried to subdue him, to no avail. Cops showed up with pepper spray. Finally, he was tackled, handcuffed, and escorted from the building. Between fines and compensation to several officers he attacked, he was ordered to pay $1,850 U.S. He was also lucky enough to not have a conviction placed on his record, because as a Mexican citizen who traveled internationally, that would have seriously impacted his career. A WCW spokesman, speaking to a local newspaper, said that Juvie's behavior was, among other things, "unexpected"; so apparently him taking all of his clothes off and going insane in a drug-induced rampage was not on the itinerary for that day.

WCW was so outraged by Juvie's behavior that they promptly fired Scott Hall, who as you might recall went crazy on an overseas tour back in February. As you also might recall, he thought he could never be fired because of the trademark infringement lawsuit, and, as coincidence would have it, that lawsuit had been settled a month earlier.

And yes, Juvie was canned too. WCW never bothered to tell him initially, though, and he wasn't aware of it until a bunch of friends called and told him they'd read about it on the internet.

There wasn't much to the Australian shows in terms of content, but, as expected, they all did tremendously well business-wise. In fact, every show drew at least 9,000 paid, and even *Thunder* completely sold out. Of course, since this was WCW, they actually managed to lose money on the tour. Apparently, the company had signed a contract with the Australian promoters saying they'd buy back any unused seats at the shows. Unfortunately, this included seats that could not be sold due to the TV production equipment. Because they ran four shows taped for

TV, the faux pas resulted in WCW losing $400,000 on a tour that should otherwise have been profitable.

And so back to America the company came, and, as usual, they brought their crappy shows with them. The October 5 *Nitro* was one of those horrible shows where everything that could possibly go wrong did. It was supposed to be pushed back a half hour due to a NASCAR race. In the past, WCW had often forgotten to alert viewers that their programming was being moved to a different time or even to a different day, but this time, they made it very clear that the show was starting at 8:35 p.m. Unfortunately, when fans tuned in at 8:35 p.m., the show had already been on for a half hour since the program hadn't been preempted after all. There were a bunch of hideous matches, including Wall versus Jim Duggan, a match so horrible it made one long for a Vince Russo WCW title defense. The Jung Dragons, three great Cruiserweight wrestlers, were all squashed at the same time by Scott Steiner, putting a damper on the whole idea to push the Cruiserweight division. Lex Luger, in an interview segment with Stevie Ray called "Suckas Gots to Know," asked if what he was about to say was just between the two of them. Apparently he was unaware that the program was being broadcast nationwide to several million people. Stevie was apparently unaware as well, since he responded that it was "just between you, me, and 5,000 viewers." Yes, 5,000 viewers. Tony Schiavone tried to make the save by claiming—really—that he meant 5,000 viewers in each house.

The following week, Russo cited brain damage—post-concussion syndrome, to be exact—as his reason for "temporarily" removing himself from the creative process. Even though he'd stayed in the U.S. and faxed all of his storyline ideas to Australia for that series of shows, he suddenly announced that he would not be able to do his job anymore since his doctor had banned him from leaving the house until November 16. Some theorized that his fax machine must have been broken.

While it was unfortunate that Russo had a concussion, at least he got to keep his job. Bret Hart wasn't so lucky, as on October 20, he was released. The termination notice came literally days after he received another letter that said he'd been re-signed for two more years. It was a business decision, as he hadn't wrestled since January due to the head injuries that resulted in him suffering 10 percent brain damage, and he was theoretically the second-highest-paid wrestler in the company, behind Hogan, pulling in roughly $25,000 a week while injured.

"At this point in time," Brad Siegel wrote in his termination letter, "we have been unable to utilize your wrestling services for over nine months and according to your doctor, you remain incapacitated. Based on your ongoing incapacity, WCW is exercising its right under paragraph 8(e) to terminate your independent contractor agreement effective Friday, October 20, 2000. Your contributions to the wrestling business are highly regarded and we wish you only the best in the future."

While it was thought Bret would never wrestle again, he did actually come back to WWE for a "match" with Vince McMahon at **WrestleMania**. We put "match" in quotes, because honestly, it wasn't much of one, just a one sided beating that was designed to make Vince a sympathetic babyface. Amazingly, the crowd did not agree that Vince McMahon was, in any way, shape, or form, a sympathetic babyface. We should also note that despite not taking any bumps or shots to the head, Bret still managed to win and lose the U.S. title.

On October 23, WCW did their first double *Nitro/Thunder* taping. It could have been worse. Surprisingly, the *Thunder* show was much better than *Nitro*, which featured all sorts of insanity, not limited to Kevin Nash doing two interviews revolving around the fired Scott Hall. You could cut WCW some slack due to the fact that Hall wasn't scripted to be mentioned. But then again, you could cut them no slack for not disciplining Nash in any way, not to mention letting him do the same thing again on the same show a bit later. Main event saw Scott Steiner beat Mike Awesome in a good match. This didn't prevent the show from doing a 2.22 rating, its lowest non-taped number in years. *Thunder* main was Goldberg and Sting and Booker T beating Jarrett and Kronik when Sting pinned Jarrett. The original plan was for the bad guys to win, but then—and you may find this impossible to believe—someone remembered that if Goldberg lost, he had to retire. So instead of just ignoring that, like they did with Sid so many times, they actually changed the finish. Ironically, Goldberg, like Sid, magically went from being 7-0 to 12-0 between *Thunder* and *Nitro* despite having not wrestled any matches in the interim.

This all led to *Halloween Havoc 2000*, an event high in the running for the worst pay-per-view of that year. Russo had gone home again, this time citing stress and post-concussion syndrome, and the interim bookers (Ed Ferrara and Bill Banks) were told to keep his current storylines going. Imagine being told such a thing. The best match on the show was the opener, which saw Mark Jindrak and Sean O'Haire beat Rey Mysterio Jr. and Billy Kidman, and Disco Inferno and Alex Wright to retain the Tag Team titles. It was all downhill from there. Mike Awesome beat Vampiro in a match that was not only horrible, but resulted in Vampiro suffering a serious head injury. Vamp, who after zero training became a main-eventer in Mexico in his very first week of wrestling, never learned how to take a real flat back bump until coming to the U.S. years later. The finish was supposed to be him taking a powerbomb off the top rope through a table. This is actually a lot less dangerous than it sounds, because when you go through a table, the table breaks your fall and it's an easier bump. Their table, however, got broken early, so Vamp had to take the powerbomb from the top rope down into the ring, a much harder landing. His head bounced super hard off the canvas and he suffered a legitimate concussion. To make matters worse, he was asked to take a second powerbomb the following night at the *Thunder* tapings. He told folks that this was the seventeenth concussion of his career, and then, years later, claimed these head injuries contributed to him developing Parkinson's disease. Main event was Goldberg beating Kronik in a bad match.

LESSON NOT LEARNED: The main event just mentioned where Goldberg had a lousy match with Kronik was not the only encounter Clark and Adams had in WCW. In fact, most of them were pretty atrocious. Amazingly, this did not stop WWE from bringing them in as a tag team and putting them against two of their biggest stars, Kane and the Undertaker. Yes, that Undertaker, the one that's been one of WWE's biggest stars for approximately twenty years. This feud led to an amazingly awful match at **Unforgiven 2001**. The match was so atrocious that despite being pushed as a top act (remember, they were battling THE UNDERTAKER!!!), they were immediately fired following the match.

The *Nitro* and *Thunder* tapings the next night in Irvine, California, were terribly sad. *Nitro*, built around Ric Flair's return to TV in the outdated commissioner role, drew—and this is absolutely true—768 paid fans. Even fans whose only joy when watching WCW was to laugh at its ineptness had to be saddened to see a company that drew 41,000 fans just two years earlier doing a number that was below what some independent shows had done that year. Backstage, virtually everyone had just completely given up, and it was quite noticeable on TV. If there was anything that could be considered even remotely good news, Flair's return helped bump the show up to a 2.52.

And hey, remember back in the last chapter where we were bemoaning the fact that the average attendance for October of 1999 was 4,200 paid? By October of 2000, that number had dropped yet again to less than 1,800. Yes, a 58 percent cut into an already horrible figure.

In early November, the WWF officially backed off on its negotiations to purchase the company. In fact, Linda McMahon's exact words to *Broadcasting and Cable Magazine* were: "We're definitely not buying it." Initially, Viacom had been upset with Vince's plan to air *Nitro* and *Thunder* on TNT and TBS respectively, since they were rival networks. At the time, this was a serious issue, because with the impending AOL–Time

Warner merger, Turner wanted to unload the money-losing company but retain the TV shows. Even though *Nitro* was doing hideous numbers in comparison to what they did at their peak, they were still above average when compared to ratings of other prime time cable TV shows. Eventually, Viacom relaxed a bit, and what prevented the deal from happening the first time had more to do with how much Turner thought WCW was worth and what the WWF, which had lost tens of millions that year with the XFL, was willing to pay.

Over the next few weeks, the lame duck television continued with almost nothing of any note happening, since the decree was still in effect to not mess up Russo's storylines. The problem with this was that none of the storylines could really advance, and it was obvious to viewers at home that nobody in the ring was giving anything even close to 100 percent. As a result, the holding pattern on TV did not result in a holding pattern for the ratings, which continued to slide. The November 20 show did a 2.27 rating, the lowest ever in the history of the show running opposed in its normal time slot.

What was sad was that the shows weren't even that horrible and were certainly better than the programs Russo had written at his most insane. (It would get even sadder in early 2001 when the shows were actually becoming mildly enjoyable just weeks before the plug was pulled entirely.) Unfortunately, by killing off all the belts, and in particular the Heavyweight title, Russo had created an atmosphere where everyone was fighting each other for really no good reason. Since the belts had been rendered worthless, there was nothing worth fighting for, and fans had no reason to get behind any of the wrestlers.

One thing of note on TV was that Kevin Nash, who in late 2000 was the reigning Smartest Man in Wrestling, suddenly started doing a bunch of jobs and buddying up with young guys like Jindrak and O'Haire. He knew that chances were very good that if he put himself over as a great team player, the WWF would show interest in him either when his contract came due, or if they bought WCW outright. It became quite humorous watching the lengths he would go to be seen as a "good guy."

A few weeks earlier, the WWF had put tickets on sale for their biggest show of the year, *WrestleMania X7*, to be held April 1, 2001 at the Houston Astrodome. On the first day they were available, 48,395 tickets were sold. In late November, tickets went on sale for WCW's biggest PPV of the year, the Grandaddy of Them All, *Starrcade*. On the first day they were available, 926 tickets were sold.

The November 22 *Thunder* was notable for being the birthplace of Booker T's new catchphrase. For historical purposes, the first time he ever uttered it, it went like this: "I've got six words for you: Don't hate the player, hate the game."

The WCW *Mayhem* PPV on November 27 from Milwaukee, Wisconsin, was similar to all the recent WCW TV; it was just a show. There were a few good matches, a few bad matches, and everything in between. The 2,871 people who paid to get in sat there and watched, reacting little to anything that happened. Several titles changed hands. Crowbar won the Hardcore title over Reno and Big Vito; General Rection beat Lance Storm to win the U.S. title; Nash and DDP beat Shawn Stasiak and Chuck Palumbo to win the Tag Team belts; and Scott Steiner beat Booker T to win the World title with his Steiner recliner finishing hold. Nobody seemed to care much at all, though they did inexplicably cheer loudly for heel Steiner when he beat babyface Booker for the belt. It was a bad night for poor Booker as not only did he get booed, but he cracked his sternum taking a full-nelson drop from Steiner in their match.

The next night, the big storyline was that Flair was going to fly in this huge superstar to face Steiner at *Starrcade*. He even went as far as to claim that this man was as big a superstar as Rock or Steve Austin. The man ended up being the self-proclaimed Master and Ruler of the World, Sid Vicious. For reference purposes, we checked with sources in

Washington, D.C., and Sid was not, in fact, the Master and Ruler of the World. The storyline was that since he had to give up his belt in April for no good reason (when Russo vacated all the belts), he deserved a chance to get it back. Yes, a rare logical storyline. Unfortunately, there was no logic in the interview, as Mr. Sid Vicious accused Steiner of having a "fictitious name." Nash was also back to his old not-caring ways as he did another interview accompanied by Dallas Page that put over Scott Hall. This was particularly bad timing since later that very day, Hall had been involved in another DUI auto accident (he claimed at the hospital that he hadn't been drinking, then immediately failed a sobriety test at three times the legal limit of 0.08). Main event was Steiner beating Booker's brother Stevie Ray in a WCW title versus career match, so Stevie had to retire forever afterwards. Earlier in the show, Stevie hyped up the match by not only calling Steiner "synthetic" (seemingly an accusation of steroid use), but also a "sad, sack-ass fruit booty" and a "sad-sack cracker jack" (seemingly accusations of, well, we have no idea). The match itself was truly atrocious as Stevie became so exhausted within a matter of moments that he was unable to perform tasks as simple as lifting his leg up in the air. It turned into one of the worst matches in *Nitro* history, a fact not lost on the tiny audience.

The following week on *Nitro*, they did an angle where Steiner attacked and destroyed Arn Anderson. When Goldberg tried to make the save, Luger waffled him with what was actually a great chairshot. This led to Flair ruling on *Thunder* that Steiner and Goldberg were both being sent home, which was hardly the brightest thing to do since they were both main-eventing *Starrcade* that weekend. He also announced that Steiner was being stripped of the belt for his actions on *Nitro*, which was unbelievably stupid given how badly the belt had been tarnished already. Thankfully, that ended up being just a storyline as Arn in a great interview talked Flair into rescinding that decision. He didn't, however, rescind the decision to send Goldberg and Steiner home, which resulted in many fans getting up and going home themselves.

On December 8, Brad Siegel met with all the WCW department heads and stated point blank that WCW was for sale. (Even though everyone knew this was the case, he'd never admitted it in previous meetings, saying only that Turner was entertaining offers from people who wanted to buy it.) This was, however, pretty much all the information he provided, so everyone left the meeting in the same state of confusion and uncertainty they were in before it started.

The December 11 *Nitro* was a disaster for reasons having nothing to do with what happened inside the ring. Months back, a David Copperfield special was scheduled to air that day, so Turner executives had bounced the idea back and forth about moving *Nitro* to Tuesday. On November 6, Craig Leathers, who was head of production for WCW, sent Terry Taylor a letter informing him that it was going to be moved. Taylor supposedly never told anyone about it. So on December 7, the Friday before *Nitro*, everyone suddenly figured out that *Nitro* wasn't going to air on Monday and they hadn't mentioned a thing about the time change on the previous *Nitro* or *Thunder* shows.

The show itself was chock-full of nothing, except for the hilarious closing angle. Sid beat up a valet and stole all his keys, then drove a bunch of cars into a circle so he could fight Steiner in the middle of it. Sadly, the footage of Sid attempting to match twenty keys to twenty different cars was never aired on the program.

The Scott Hall story of the week was that he was arrested for kicking in the door of a taxi cab after the driver told him he wouldn't accept payment via credit card. Even though he'd been fired, Kevin Nash and Dallas Page had been dropping his name regularly on TV. Following this arrest, head of WCW Legal, Diana Myers, outright banned his name from all company telecasts. This led to another legendary segment on the December 6 *Thunder*. The show featured an interview with Dallas Page and Nash conducted by the retired Stevie

Scott Hall, looking completely sober. And perhaps ready to kick in a taxi door.
[GEORGE NAPOLITANO]

Ray that, if there was a real wrestling record book of some sort, should have been listed in it. Nash and Page claimed nobody told them Hall's name was banned, so they talked about him the entire time. During this interview, there was a major lighting problem, and the overhead lamps were swinging back and forth as if they were in the middle of a windstorm. There was also a loud clanging noise, as if someone was pounding on a garbage can lid. This wasn't expected to be an issue, because the plan was to edit in footage of Hall to cover up these technical glitches. Unfortunately, when Myers heard about it she blew a gasket and refused to allow the footage or verbal references of Hall to air. Instead of pulling the segment, they aired it on TV anyway, which meant fans nationwide saw Nash and Page eyeballing this wandering overhead lamp while several dozen words were bleeped, making it totally incomprehensible. *Thunder* had become the wrestling equivalent of the Ed Wood cult flick *Plan 9 From Outer Space*.

The December 13 show was also a booking lesson in how to kill off a top contender. They actually did an interview where Sid, the supposed top babyface, was so stupid that he couldn't find the arena. He kept calling in from his cell phone saying he was lost. "Guys, can you hear me?" he asked in at least three different segments. Clearly, nobody in the company ever learned that the one thing fans will absolutely not support is an idiot babyface.

The week of December 18 saw everything go to hell again, as both participants in the *Starrcade* main event were stirring up problems behind the scene. First, Sid walked out, unhappy about being asked to lose to Steiner at *Starrcade*. He claimed he'd been promised the finish would be a double count-out, but then WCW double-crossed him and changed it to him getting pinned. He told people that he wasn't ultimately upset about the change, but rather about the fact that nobody was man enough to come up and tell him to his face, instead of just handing him a piece of paper with the new plan written on it. In the end, Sid agreed to lose, and plans to change it to a three-way so someone else could do the job were scrapped.

Then, the big fight. It started with Steiner cutting one of his now-famous unscripted promos, this time on Dallas Page. It was always funny to hear company officials get upset about things like this, because historically, it was entirely their fault. Steiner, for example, had never really been reprimanded for his behavior; if anything, he'd been rewarded, time after time after time. Earlier in the year, he buried Flair in an unscripted promo and was told by management that it was one of the best interviews of the year. Months later, he threatened Terry Taylor and was rewarded with a paid vacation over the weekend of July 4. So his antics continued, and instead of being fined or suspended, he found himself the WCW World Heavyweight champion. If management was upset with his behavior, they had nobody but themselves to blame. Even more depressing, the guys who actually worked hard, behaved themselves, and followed the rules were rewarded by being buried on television, and consequently, they gave up all hope.

Steiner's promo against Page included the following line: "Why don't you convince Diamond Dallas Page to get a sex change, so he has the balls to come out here and face me?" Page was stretching in the locker room when Steiner made his comments. Ironically, this was the same building where, earlier in the year, Steiner and Page's wife, Kimberly, had a verbal incident that resulted in her quitting the company for good. As soon as Steiner said Page had no balls, everyone in the locker room immediately turned and looked over at him, as if to see what he was going to do about it. According to one witness, "the air was totally sucked out of the room."

Page finished tying his boots and walked down the stairs near the curtain. As soon as Steiner walked backstage, Page reportedly said, "So, I don't have the balls to face you, huh?" They started swearing at each other, and a fight broke out. Steiner took Page down and started to pound on his face, with multiple witnesses saying he went straight for Page's eye. One source said that Steiner had cut his fingernails earlier in the day, and that if he hadn't, it would have been much uglier. The other wrestlers immediately jumped in to break it up, and it reportedly took them over a full minute to pry Steiner off of Page. Page was bleeding and had marks all over his face. He later told friends that Steiner wasn't just scary, he was a killer, and that he was glad he walked away from the fight alive. Page and Nash immediately grabbed their stuff and left the building, with some sources saying their last words were "We'll be back when there are new owners." Steiner then responded by cutting another promo, this time focusing on Kimberly and saying some very bad things about her.

Steiner's punishment? He continued to receive the biggest push of his professional career.

The final PPV of the year, *Starrcade*, took place on December 17 at the MCI Center in Washington, D.C., before 3,465 paying fans. It was a decent show, featuring a great opener, a few decent undercard match-es, and a shockingly good main event. Page and Nash—whose walkout lasted all of one week—beat Palumbo and Stasiak in a surprisingly good match to regain the Tag titles, thanks mostly to Page's great job working as the baby-face in peril. Goldberg versus Luger in the semi-main was surprisingly good. And when Steiner beat Sid with the recliner in the main event, the match could only be classified as a miracle.

Sadly, by this point, good show or bad, it didn't matter. *Starrcade*, tra-ditionally WCW's biggest show of the year, did a dismal 0.11.

With the year's end came the announcement of $62 million in losses. How did it happen? Hideous booking and one bad show after another caused pay-per-view buy rates and house show revenues to plummet. Advertising revenues plunged, due to *Nitro* being cut to two hours and to the elimination of *WCW Saturday Night*. Wrestlers, both on TV and in media interviews, buried the company for its incompetence, making fans feel stupid for having supported the product for so long. Countless millions were spent on stupid things: limos getting destroyed, helicopters, junkyard battle royals, contract money paid to guys who never appeared on television, booking multiple flights for individual people, commercials and newspaper ads plugging the wrong air dates for shows, and so on.

The company had become a money pit, the likes of which had never been seen before in wrestling.

And Time Warner was upset.

★ ★ ★ ★ ★ PART IV
THE DEATH

*"WCW is not a core business for Turner Broadcasting.
We've decided professional wrestling in its current incarnation just isn't
appropriate for the high-scale, upscale brand that we have built on TNT and
TBS Superstation. We're no longer interested in carrying the product."*

—Jim Weiss, Turner Spokesperson

CHAPTER
★ ★ ★ SEVEN ★ ★ ★
2001:
THE ULTIMATE SWERVE

From the beginning to the end—even as Rome burned around them—those in charge of WCW felt that if they had nothing else, at least they'd always have television.

While Vince Russo had driven both buy rates and house show attendance into the toilet, many believed the *Nitro* and *Thunder* ratings were still OK. Sure, they weren't even in the same universe as the *Raw* ratings, but many cable shows did less than a 1.0, and most *Nitro* and *Thunder* shows were in the 2.0 range. The reality, though, is that *Thunder* was dipping below the TBS ratings average, and in the last few months, the show's rating was regularly surpassed by *Ripley's Believe It or Not.*

Things were only slightly better for *Nitro*, the flagship show. Ratings were above the prime time average for the station, but they were below average in terms of ad sales. Still, while things had declined since the height of WCW's popularity back in the late '90s, there was always the possibility that the company could rebound simply by hitting upon a hot storyline or having a wrestler catch fire with the fans. While it didn't look like there was any chance of either of these things happening in the immediate future, it wasn't like they could *never* happen. After all, this was *World Championship Wrestling*. This was the organization that had reinvented the entire wrestling industry with the advent of *Nitro*. It was certainly conceivable that they could do it again at some point. WCW was, if nothing else, a company that survived. It survived times it should never have, like the lean early-'90s period when, on average, less than 1,000 fans came out to each house show. Things would turn around; they always did, and this time would be no different. All the company needed to become profitable again was to find just that right character, that right angle, and the fans would return.

WCW's ratings prior to the nWo invasion were flat, people argued, not unlike the numbers the company was doing during the collapse of 2000. Obviously, things turned out fine back then, so there was no reason to expect anything different now.

Except that there was. While the numbers in 1995 and 2000 may have appeared similar on the surface, there were major differences. The biggest was that, in 1995, the company had a $35 million to $40 million budget, compared to 2000's $185 million budget. More importantly, they'd never lost more than $6 million in any year, and all of a sudden, they'd lost $62 million in one. This sort of performance was not acceptable.

Ted Turner had been approached about shutting the company down several times in the early '90s. He'd always ixnayed the idea because he truly believed that wrestling was cyclical. Plus, because wrestling had been such an integral part of the Superstation that gave birth to his media empire, he had a soft spot for it in his heart. Pretty much everyone in the industry believed that as long as Uncle Ted was around, WCW would be safe.

But something happened in January 2000 that shattered this supposed certainty. Time Warner CEO Gerald Levin struck a $183 billion deal with America Online's Steve Case to merge the two companies into what they believed would be the ultimate media superpower. Turner ended up with 3 percent of the new company's stock and a mostly figurehead job as vice chairman. Suddenly, his days of spending millions at will on frivolities like professional wrestling were finished. In his place were boards of directors, financial analysts, and CFOs looking at the bottom line. These men were going to do something that no one ever had: make WCW fiscally responsible for its actions. And with the company losing money at an astronomical rate, it didn't take long for AOL–Time Warner to come to the conclusion that WCW was a hopeless proposition. Therefore, a shocking decision was made: they would sell the company outright.

And, for the first time ever, there wasn't a damn thing Ted Turner could do about it.

At some point, Ted Turner probably regretted having sold Turner Broadcasting to Time Warner in the mid-'90s. And although he had voted in favor of the merger, he definitely regretted having agreed to the AOL deal. His woes included a huge stock crash that cost him between $7 and $8 billion. Wrestling fans should take solace in the fact that WCW, as horribly mismanaged as it was, could not hold a candle to the incompetence of AOL–Time Warner. Sure, WCW lost $62 million one year, but did they ever lose $54 billion in one **quarter**?

"I'd rather go back and be with one of my ex-wives than go through this again," Turner once said. "It's a fascinating story of how to do everything wrong. I think part of it was that it was just too complicated. If you ever have the chance to merge with AOL, stay away."

With the company for sale, and with McMahon having pulled out in late 2000, the door was left open for one man, a person who dreamed of autonomous power and the chance to once again turn *Nitro* and *Thunder* into ratings gold: Eric Bischoff. Following his first demotion in September

1999, he spent some time hunting and fishing near his home in Colorado while still collecting large paychecks. Once Russo had thoroughly proven his incompetence, Bischoff was called about coming back.

In a 2003 interview on WWE's *Byte This* radio program, Bischoff tried to shift blame for the death of the company away from himself:

"The problem with WCW was that it really didn't fit within the Time Warner profile, meaning a lot of senior executives at the highest levels didn't want the company to be there and didn't support it. When I came back, that situation was a lot worse than when I left originally. So, I left again, and basically I was honest with Brad Siegel, who I was dealing with at the time. And I said 'Brad, the company is so screwed up, it's never going to work, I can't fix it, no one's going to fix it. Why don't you let me buy it?'"

Of course, one question remains obvious: if he claimed that nobody could fix it, including himself, why would he want to buy it? The truth is that the company didn't fit into the Time Warner profile because, thanks in good part to Bischoff, it collapsed and lost $62 million that year. If the company had still been making the kind of money it made in 1998, it would no doubt have fit the profile just fine. And his claim that his idea to buy it was a last-minute decision is false, because he'd been trying to convince Turner to sell since at least late '98. Bischoff continued:

"[Siegel] laughed at me, he thought I was nuts. And I left again, I went home again. And about two months later they called me back and said: 'If you're serious and you can raise the money, we'll talk to you.' So, I raised the money. And we had commitments for $63 million from some of the biggest blue chip investment bankers on Wall Street supporting us and some very, very smart people. And we spent about six to eight months going through a process called due diligence, where you do all the things you would need to do to buy a company, going through the books and making sure the documents are all in order and all the legal crap that goes along with it. We had a deal in place, a letter of intent had been signed, everything was going fine."

So fine, in fact, that on January 11, 2001, Bischoff and his investment group, Fusient Media Ventures, announced that they had purchased the company. When we say "announced," we mean that they told everyone: they told the press, they told everyone in the company, they told their friends, they told their families. A few noted the "coincidental" timing of the announcement, which came just hours before the AOL–Time Warner deal was finalized.

"Wrestling fans can rest assured that we will give the WCW the adrenaline shot it needs to once again become the most exciting brand of wrestling in the world," Bischoff stated in a press release.

Yet buried in all the hoopla and excitement was the tiny little part about how the sale wouldn't be finalized for forty-five days or so.

Also buried: the fact that Stuart Snyder, who was working for the WWE as their president and COO at the time, told cohorts within the company there was "zero chance" Bischoff was going to wind up with the WCW in the end. That seemed very odd, considering the press release and everything else stated publicly by both Bischoff and Turner at the time. However, Snyder had worked within Turner for years prior to his arrival in WWE in June 2000.

Interesting.

Regardless, everyone seemed to have the same question: how could Bischoff possibly turn the company around now, when he couldn't before? And more precisely, how could he do it now that he actually had to be fiscally responsible to his investors? The days of going to Turner himself were now long gone, so exactly how he planned to revert WCW back to its number-one position had everyone more than a little perplexed.

Not that it mattered to Bischoff himself. This was his chance to prove that he wasn't just a one-trick pony, that the success he'd created with the nWo was just the tip of his creative iceberg. He felt, even with a depleted roster in comparison to the glory days, that he still had the talent to get him there; he just needed time and good booking to push them over the top. He brought in John Laurinaitis as his lead booker. Laurinaitis had been lauded for his creative match scripting, and he also knew the business inside and out, having worked for virtually every wrestling promotion on the globe. If anyone knew how to properly book a promotion, it would appear to be him.

Bischoff had grandiose plans: there was going to be a brief shutdown, perhaps as long as a month, and then a huge, fresh restart. He was going to push the Cruiserweights to the moon. He was going to set up a salary system similar to the WWF's, whereby guys would be paid "downside guarantees," then bonuses based on how successful house shows and pay-per-views were. He didn't want to fall into the "trap" of guaranteed contracts again. He said he was going to phase out the older guys and push the younger guys harder. He was going to open relations with Japanese companies, including Ultimo Dragon's Toryumon group, to introduce American fans to new, hot, high-flying stars. And, perhaps best of all, he vowed there would be no more Russo.

Basically, he said all the right things. Wrestling fans, however, did not care about all the right things being said. They wanted to see action. With the major booking duties delegated to others, Bischoff began to look at the roster for anything he could trim. If he was going to own the company, that meant that he and his investors would now have to foot all the bills. No longer could he afford to pay his friends exorbitant salaries due solely to friendship. He was going to have to make the company work as a business, and realistically, the high pay rates demanded by the likes of Hulk Hogan, Kevin Nash, and Scott Hall didn't fit into his budget. So not only was the rise of such guys as Steiner and Booker T coming at the right time, but he had to make them the top stars even if they hadn't caught on yet—financially, he had little choice.

His first major plan was to do a company shutdown following the February 18 *SuperBrawl* pay-per-view. The idea was to take several weeks off to build new sets, write new storylines, and get everything set up for a brand-new beginning on March 12. Time Warner, however, said no. Ratings had dropped to such a degree that WCW had to make good to advertisers. One month with no TV whatsoever would cost them some serious cash, and with the company already losing tons of money, that was out of the question. If you're wondering why Turner cared about a company they didn't own losing money, it was because the forty-five days were not yet up, and the sale wasn't completely finalized. Everyone figured it would happen within the next week or so.

Bischoff, therefore, came up with what he thought was an ingenious storyline. He'd have Steiner, still the top heel and Heavyweight champion, take out all the remaining babyfaces one by one, leaving only Dallas Page. They'd headline the March 18 pay-per-view in Jacksonville, and then, the following night, the "new WCW owners" would be revealed and save the day by bringing all the babyfaces back at once. WCW would then scrap the April pay-per-view, so they'd have seven weeks to build up to their biggest show ever on May 6, when the entire company would be reborn.

In late February, Bischoff reconsidered his ingenious idea. The ratings were sinking fast, and he didn't think they'd be able to hold off until May before reintroducing the major stars.

Despite a few changes, programming still ranged from good to awful, depending on the week. *Thunder*, not yet canceled at this point, was by far the worst, and every program seemed to be an effort to set the record for worst in history. Sid's promos became more and more nonsensical. "See, there's only two things I care about, and I'm gonna see is the man who wins the title and the belt, and that man will be me!" he once threatened. Or stated. Or asked. Or something. The storylines were absurd. One week, a masked mystery man bedecked in what appeared to be a bumblebee costume constructed by a five-year-old, attacked Rick Steiner. The next week, he unmasked, revealing himself to be—three guesses—Rick Steiner. On another show, Heavy D sold a neck injury by stating, "The doctors told me I can never wrestle again. The slightest thing and *snap*, my head could actually fall right off my shoulders. That's sad." Announcer Scott Hudson apparently took him seriously by replying with a straight face that yes, indeed, the fact that his head might spontaneously fall off his shoulders was sad. Perhaps saddest of all was that the main event of that show was DDP versus Jeff Jarrett, and as the ring filled with brawling men following the usual DQ finish, Tony Schiavone screamed, "THEY WON'T STOP UNTIL SOMEONE DIES!" Guys retired forever on a weekly basis, including Goldberg.

Tragically, Sid's career really did end forever when, in a mishap at the **Syn** PPV in January, he jumped off the middle rope and landed on one leg, shattering his tibia and fibula in one of the most gruesome injuries anyone had ever seen.

With no major changes taking place, viewers continued to tune out. In early March, *Nitro* and *Thunder* set brand-new ratings records. Unfortunately, they were record lows, 2.05 and 1.52 respectively. The investors decided now would be a good time to really investigate the books, and they were not pleased with what they discovered. In fact, to put it gently, they totally freaked out. Time Warner then freaked out because potential brand-new owners freaking out didn't sound very promising. The deal, which still had not been finalized, nearly fell through. Fusient's lead investor, Warburg Pincus, began to realize that this was a company that was in deep, deep debt, with tons of lawsuits on its hands and a fan base departing in droves. In fact, the only real assets the company had included a name that had been horribly devalued by years of bad booking, several high-priced superstars who weren't cutting the mustard, a large tape library, and the fact that, once upon a time, it had a hot run. These were not generally considered valuable assets. Pincus, suddenly wondering why anyone in their right mind would invest in this company, hit the bricks. Once they pulled out, Fusient, which had been offering around $70 million, cut their offer almost in half. Their new plan was to offer $5.7 million down, then $2.15 million per year for twenty years. Yes, they believed they could keep WCW in business for twenty more years, or, more likely, that they could convince Time Warner that they could keep it alive for twenty more years while simultaneously looking for a new parent company to sell to.

And then it happened. A new adversary entered the fray, and it was an adversary that nobody in wrestling had ever even heard of. This man, however, would single-handedly change the entire course of pro-wrestling history. His name was Jamie Kellner, and he was the new chairman and chief executive officer of Turner Broadcasting Systems.

Kellner was not new to the television industry. He had, in fact, been the driving force behind the creation of both the FOX and the WB Networks, as well as FOX Kids. He was a strong advocate of television targeted toward the young female demographic, which led to the creation of shows such as *7th Heaven, Dawson's Creek*, and *Gilmore Girls*. He also stirred up a hornet's nest when he stated, in a 2002 interview, that personal video recorders (TiVo at the time, DVR's today), which allow viewers to skip commercials, were tantamount to stealing from the networks. If folks didn't watch the commercials that the networks aired, he reasoned, they therefore wouldn't buy any products, and if they didn't buy any products, advertisers would stop paying for future commercials. Strangely, Kellner did not go on a crusade against the remote control.

His wacky, industry-polarizing views and theories, however, were simply his way of looking at the bottom line. And that was a *huge* problem where WCW was concerned.

But that wasn't even the biggest problem. In addition to WCW's excessive financial losses, wrestling just wasn't the type of program Kellner wanted on his network. It was lowbrow, low-rent. Even when ratings were sky high, selling ad time on the programming wasn't the easiest thing to do. Car manufacturers such as Lexus and Toyota would balk at spending precious ad revenue on folks that they imagined were driving around in fifteen-year-old pickup trucks. At the end of the day, the fact was that Jamie Kellner simply didn't like pro wrestling.

And so, in his very first week on the job, Kellner simply ruled that all wrestling programming was to be canceled on TBS and TNT. No more *Nitro*, no more *Thunder*, nothing.

This no doubt led Bischoff to this articulate conclusion:

OH FUCK.

OH FUCK OH FUCK OH FUCK!!!

This was not good.

To say Bischoff was banking on those time slots would be like saying WCW lost a few bucks in 2000. How could this have happened? Wrestling had been on the Turner networks for twenty-nine years! It was a legacy, for God's sake! How could one man, some corporate suit at that, come in *on his first week* and put an end to a relationship that had lasted this long? This could not be happening.

It could NOT be happening.

None of the wrestlers believed it. After all, why would they? For six years, Bischoff and his cronies had booked storylines designed to fool not only the fans, but also the wrestlers and company employees. The company had often done this in years past, from the Ric Flair heart attack to fake fights in the back to Hogan walking out in the middle of matches. The theory behind doing this, it seemed, was that if they could fool their own employees, they'd really shock their audience.

Why, you might ask, would the company continually lie to its employees? Because in 1996, Bischoff and Brian Pillman briefly had everyone in the wrestling world talking about the fact that Pillman was out of his mind. The former "Flyin' Brian" morphed into the "Loose Cannon," a madman who could not be controlled and would say or do anything he wanted on television. He "went against the script." He had "real fights" with the bookers on live PPV. And what was the end result of this pioneering shoot angle? The wrestlers, upon discovering that they'd been lied to, stopped trusting management. Zero dollars were made by anyone other than Pillman, who got to plug his 900-phone line on **Nitro**. With everyone in a tizzy, Pillman convinced Eric to give him a real-life WCW release to make the angle "seem more legitimate." Upon receiving the very real release, Pillman immediately signed with the WWF.

So the wrestlers figured this whole "WCW sale" was just another swerve by Bischoff, an attempt to shock viewers into thinking they had lost WCW forever, only to bring it back again when it seemed things couldn't get any more bleak. The boys knew Bischoff's modus operandi, and also figured that Vince Russo, another swerve-happy booker, was likely in on it as well. It didn't help that on March 16, Brad Siegel sent everyone a memo that basically outright lied about what was going on:

> In early January, we told you about an agreement that we had reached to sell WCW and its related assets. At the time, we said that we would apprise you of any changes to the way WCW operates. Effective Tuesday, March 27, WCW programming will begin a period of hiatus. During this hiatus, WCW will review its programming plans and determine the course of future WCW-branded entertainment events. On Wednesday, March 28, please plan to attend an all-staff meeting at 10 a.m. at the Power Plant, at which time we will share with you further information regarding WCW plans. In the meantime, I hope that you will maintain the level of professionalism that distinguishes our organization, particularly as we prepare for the upcoming Panama City, Florida, event.

And so Bischoff watched his dream fall apart right before his very eyes. The company he'd made was now being pulled away from him—just when he thought he had it in the palm of his hand. It was scramble time—no way was he letting his baby get away again, not this time, not when he was this close to having it all for himself. Bischoff raced from network to network in the hope of landing a television contract for the company. Even at the end, *Nitro* had drawn strong ratings compared to your average cable fare, so there had to be a network out there that would help foot the bill for the company.

SFX? No.

USA? Barry Diller, head of the network that hosted WWF programming for eighteen years, said of the WWF's tenure, "[An] audience of twelve-to-nineteen-year-old pimply faced, mean-spirited males came, watched, and went on to whatever God-awful other pursuits."

Um, that would be a no.

That left just one last possibility: FOX. Bischoff had been negotiating on and off with the network for over a year. One of his original plans was to create a spin-off group with their own TV show on FOX to build up to an eventual interpromotional feud, something he'd been wanting to do for years prior. As a last-ditch effort, Bischoff tried to reopen negotiations in late March, but unfortunately, to no avail. So on March 20, 2001, Fusient Media Ventures announced that they were pulling out.

"Once you took the television part out of the deal," Bischoff said years later, "it really wasn't worth anything. Without television, that company wasn't worth anything to us. So we walked away from it."

And hey, remember when we mentioned Stuart Snyder earlier? Around this time, the WWF flew him in to Atlanta. Why? Why do you think? "The most surreal moment was flying into Atlanta on the WWF jet," Snyder says. "I said, 'there's no way we're going to keep this quiet, flying on a WWF jet into the home of Turner Broadcasting.'" Sure enough, their limo driver asked if he was there to buy out WCW.

He simply smirked.

Interesting.[35]

Even upon cancellation of the shows, with the end drawing ever nearer, many wrestlers refused to believe the truth. Siegel's memo didn't help. The fact that WCW never told them anything in the weeks leading up to the final program didn't help. The fact that on the final *Nitro*, instead of saying it was over, the announcers said it was simply the "season finale," didn't help. And, most of all, the fact that the company had been trying to work all of its employees since the mid-'90s didn't help. This makes little sense to those outside of wrestling, but a stunning number of performers within WCW, despite having read news stories about how their show was being canceled, thought this was just another big con, and that everything was going to turn out all right in the end.

It didn't.

And the only reason those wrestlers finally came to understand that they weren't being worked is because they stopped receiving paychecks.

"What killed us was a combination of bad management and . . . honestly, no, it wasn't a combination; it was just bad management," said a long-term high ranking WCW official under the request of anonymity. "I would say booking, but that falls under management. The frustrating part was even at the end, the revenue streams were there; people were spending money on our product, but AOL–Time Warner just wanted out. With proper management, with time, it would have worked. The revenue was there."

"The Death of WCW was a sad, very sad day for two reasons," noted J.J. Dillon. "For me personally it wasn't as bad as for many others. I had a long and successful career and life goes on. It was sad for the seventy-some wrestlers that were earning a full-time living in the business that were suddenly out of a job. I personally feel that it would have been in Vince McMahon's long-term best interest to have the company remain in business . . . they were never a serious threat to what was then the WWF, and it was a pool of talent that Vince could draw from as the better performers became available and filled a need within the WWF.

The other reason is that it was a sad day for Ted Turner. He truly loved the business and his 'rasslers,' but with all the mergers, Ted had the big title but not the clout to keep the powers in charge of day-to-day operations from pulling the plug on wrestling on their network as many had expressed a desire to do over the years. For all he had done for wrestling over the years, Ted deserved a better fate."

It seemed a shame that WCW should end in such a manner. It had, at one time, a tremendous fan base, the largest the wrestling world had ever seen. Sadly, the egos of men such as Kevin Nash and Terry "Hulk Hogan" Bollea crippled the company by forcing its spotlight to remain focused on them instead of other, younger stars. This caused many wrestlers, who could have helped WCW usher in a new era, to instead help usher in a new era in the WWF. When they left, so did much of WCW's fan base. Those wrestlers that stayed with the company until the bitter end had lost all their drawing power and were eventually nothing more than another paycheck the company had to write when it could ill afford to do so.

Eric Bischoff was also largely responsible for the company's demise. Ironically, he was the mastermind behind the unlikely rise of the promotion, which, after years of mismanagement, was perhaps even more shocking than the fact that he tanked the company in the manner he did. The way Bischoff took the reins of WCW and completely turned it around in 1996 is something that should be studied by every wrestling promoter. He was nothing short of brilliant. Sadly, those same promoters would learn even more by looking at what he did to quickly destroy the very same empire he had built. He had come up with one great idea, the nWo, which he presented over and over and over again, long past the point fans cared about it. He overspent on contracts, and when the ship began to sink, he panicked and overspent to a ridiculous degree on quick fixes like rock bands and celebrities who did nothing to help resolve WCW's primary dilemma—the fact that they were putting on horrendous TV shows, all of which were being presented with Bischoff's approval.

By the time Vince Russo came into the company, it was in pretty dire straits. Fans had been abused by WCW for years, which had presented bad show after bad show and failed to push new stars. When Russo came in, he had the opportunity to turn things around; the first week's rating showed that fans were still willing to give the company a look. Instead, he not only continued the trend of horrific television, he actually created programs that were far worse than those his predecessors had presented. This was due, in large part, to his desire to recreate an industry that had worked in more or less the same manner (two guys don't like each other, people pay to see them fight) for the past century. Despite claims that his "creative genius" was held back by Turner's standards and practices department, the fact of the matter is that he presented a product that he personally might have loved, but the fan base at large completely rejected.

In the end, the final blow to WCW was, as is often the case in television, a decision made by a TV executive in a boardroom. Jamie Kellner had never been to a pro-wrestling show in his life. He didn't see pro wrestling for what it really was: a business that could reinvent itself countless times over. He saw it as a TV program with a shelf life like any other. It was the *A-Team* or *Seinfeld* or *Married with Children*; it was a show that had done gangbuster numbers for a period but eventually ran its course. And at the end of the day, he had justification for his actions. This wasn't a company grossing hundreds of millions of dollars; it was a company that had, at one point in the last two years, lost more money in one month than any other year in its history. If it had remained wildly profitable like it had been in 1998, perhaps it would still be around today. Instead, it was a company where Hogan, Nash, Bischoff, Russo, and their band of merry misfits sealed the company's fate with nonsensical storylines, historically awful TV, ridiculous overspending, a complete inability to create new stars, and everything else that has been written about in this book. All of these things together made it very easy for Jamie Kellner in his first week on the job to look at some pieces of paper, see some numbers, and, after the highs and lows of thirteen years under Ted Turner, who due to a corporate merger no longer had the power to save it, pull the plug.

And *that* was the death of WCW.

Those in charge of the company never predicted that things would turn out this way, and, that was perhaps the biggest irony of all: for a company that took pride on fooling its fans and even its own employees, it was WCW itself that got the ultimate swerve.

1st EDITION EPILOGUE
★ ★ ★ SPITTING ON THE GRAVE ★ ★ ★

"Did I, DID I—WHOO!
Did I happen to hear Vince McMahon say he was going to
hold WCW in the palms of his hands? Is that what he said? Does that mean
that you are gonna hold Jack Brisco, Dory Funk, Harley Race, The Road War-
riors, Sting, Luger, The Steiners, Bagwell, Ric Flair, Steamboat?
Does that mean, you're going to hold us all in the palm of your hands?
To coin a phrase, I don't think so! . . . So tonight, if we're going out,
if we're going out on a high note—Stinger!
The Nature Boy wants you right here, because—That's right, that's right!
You hear it Sting? Sting, my greatest opponent, Sting, it's your last chance, your
last chance! To be—STING! STING! STING! STING! STING! STING!
STING!—To be the man, you gotta beat the man, and Sting—
I'M THE MAN! WHOO!"

—Ric Flair's promo and WCW eulogy on the final episode of *Monday Nitro*,
March 26, 2001, Panama City, Florida

With the Fusient deal dead in the water, that left just one real potential buyer: Vince McMahon. The lack of time slots meant nothing to
McMahon, who had four hours of prime time TV of his own in which
to promote the brand name. And with the price coming down from the
$500 million (yes, *five hundred million dollars*) Time Warner had rejected a
year earlier to less than $3 million, there was absolutely no reason not to
pursue it. "This is a smart business decision and a good investment for
us," cheered Linda McMahon in a press release following the purchase.
"We're grabbing it because it is simply that kind of opportunity."

To buy out your largest competitor and create a monopoly for
yourself for under $3 million? Yeah, that would be an opportunity you
wouldn't pass up.

The question, though, is this: for such a paltry sum, why would no
one else step up to offer a larger amount? It would appear that some did,
among them Jerry Jarrett and . . . "Macho Man" Randy Savage? Yes,
it's true. In a 2001 interview, Savage had this to say when questioned
about such rumors: "I was going to cut a check for that. I figured the
WCW film library alone was worth that much money. I had a production company that was going to help me do wrap arounds, introduce all
the matches, and send them overseas."[36]

Jarrett was also interested: "The day that WCW closed up they had
a $125 million annual revenue stream . . . and were losing money. My
accountant reduced these reams of documents to one or two sheets and
sent them to me. He said, 'How can you make this make money?' I
looked it all over and I said, 'You fire everybody that works there. And
I mean everybody. At the end of the meeting, you tell everyone we'll
spend the money if you want to fight it, but you're overpaid and you're
fired. But when this room clears out, I'm going to be here, and having
a wrestling company, I'm going to hire people.' And I was going to hire
everybody, but not to those contracts. There were sixteen of them that
had million dollar contracts. Konnan got paid for two years and didn't

wrestle! It was insane. We tendered a $70 million dollar offer, but we never got a response."[37]

The question remains: where *did* that $3 million price tag originate? It seems ridiculously low. Anyone in power at the time has absolutely refused to discuss it since it happened.

And while no one will go on record, we leave you with this: Remember earlier when we mentioned WWE president Stuart Snyder? Who once worked for Turner? Well, he left WWE in 2001. He later returned to . . . yes, you guessed it, Turner Broadcasting.

Again we say it:

Interesting.

When it was officially confirmed that McMahon had finally, after twenty years, completed his goal and claimed sole ownership of major-league wrestling in the United States, many questions remained. How would he integrate the WCW brand? Would McMahon give WCW its own show?

Could he bring WCW back to the prominence of its glory days?

And, perhaps most importantly to McMahon himself, how on Earth was he going to spend all the money he was about to make?

This was no ordinary wrestling storyline. This was history in the making. For years, hardcore wrestling fans had debated which company had the superior wrestlers. Who would win if Bill Goldberg wrestled Steve Austin or the Rock? What about WCW champion Scott Steiner versus WWF champion Triple H? Now, finally, McMahon would be able to promote the matchups fans had been salivating over for years and, in some cases, for over a decade. This was too good to be true.

And indeed it was.

Though most fans were delighted at the prospect of the inevitable WCW-WWF war, a few people were a bit skeptical, given Vince's track record. For example, in 1991, he'd secured the services of Ric Flair, who left WCW never having dropped the NWA World Heavyweight championship in the ring. Throughout the '80s, hardcore fans always talked about the ultimate dream match, WWF champion Hulk Hogan versus NWA champion Ric Flair. Flair's jump to the WWF opened the door for that, but instead, the WWF totally dropped the ball, not even mentioning the title by name and booking Flair as though he was some goof off the street with a fake belt calling himself the "real World Heavyweight champion." The feud was a bust at the box office compared to what it should have been. Then, in 2001, Chris Benoit jumped to WWF without having lost the WCW title in the ring. Again, the possibility existed for a dream interpromotional match, with the holder of the WCW crown facing off against the WWF champion. Instead of taking full advantage of what he'd gotten, Vince instead had WWF champion Triple H beat Benoit on his very first night in, ending all hopes of a serious money-drawing program.

Although McMahon's track record with interpromotional programs was, quite frankly, miserable, many felt that this was just too easy to screw up. WWF loyalists always had some way to justify what Vince had done previously: he *had* to beat Flair and Benoit, because even though he now had ownership of their contracts, the company they'd worked for still existed. Therefore, if they got early wins in a feud, it would show fans watching at home that the competition was in fact superior to the WWF wrestlers. This, however, was different. Vince *owned* WCW, he *owned* all the wrestlers, and WCW no longer existed except as a subsidiary of the WWF. There was therefore no logical excuse not to allow the "outsiders" to run wild on the WWF talent early to build toward big pay-per-view main events down the road.

So, believing that this was a foolproof angle, fans went crazy coming up with different fantasy booking ideas.

As any longtime wrestling fan is aware, the mainstream doesn't exactly look at followers of this sport in a positive manner. For years, books about wrestling weren't published because the belief was that wrestling fans could not read (seriously—it wasn't until Mick Foley wrote a book that hit number-one on the *New York Times* bestseller list that the golden age of wrestling books began). Angles were booked to cater to the lowest common denominator, because even those inside wrestling believed the "marks" were just one step above Neanderthals. The main characters in *Ready to Rumble,* a mainstream movie about wrestlers that supposedly catered to wrestling fans, were portrayed as the dumbest human beings walking the planet. Advertisers shied away from buying time during wrestling shows because they believed wrestling fans were poorer and dumber than the average buyer (and, sadly, television viewership studies have been done that have shown wrestling fans on average make less money and have less schooling than your average TV viewer).

Everyone who follows this sport has certainly run into a fan or two who displays a shocking lack of anything even remotely resembling intelligence. This is not just a wrestling thing, though; people like this attend other sporting events, and we see them on the street on a daily basis. But the fan so stupid that you wonder how they can even exist in society without constant aid does exist in wrestling.

Now, with all that said, the most pathetic thing about the WWF's booking of the huge and epic WCW invasion was that not even the dumbest fan could have come up with a storyline as bad as what Vince McMahon ultimately did.

One need look no further than the New Japan versus UWFi feud to see a truly successful invasion angle.

Japan's UWFi was formed in 1991 by Nobuhiko Takada. The company, which promoted "shoot-style" matches (fake wrestling bouts designed to look as real as possible), quickly took off, and at one point a few years later it was drawing over 15,000 fans to every single one of their monthly shows. By mid-1995, however, the UWFi was in horrible shape. With the company dying, New Japan, which was on a business roll and had profited from promotion versus promotion angles for decades, stepped in. Booker Riki Choshu understood that he had complete booking power over the outsiders and sought to exploit it. The company soon announced a joint show on October 9, 1995, with a main event of IWGP champion Keiji Muto versus Takada. Tickets went like crazy. The first major battle between the two companies took place on September 23 at Yokohama Arena before 16,000 fans and a $1.3 million gate. In the best match of the night, UWFi's Tatsuo Nakano and Yoji Anjoh beat New Japan's Yuji Nagata and Choshu. Yes, not only did the guy in charge of the storylines put the bad guys over, but he put them over in a match he was in. Impossible to believe, but true. Even with some major botchery (Muto won the match and largely killed the feud), the huge and well-promoted dream match still drew a packed-past-capacity house of over 57,000 fans and a $6.1 million gate. Not only that, but they also sold $2 million worth of merchandise, so the total one-day take was over $8 million. At the time, no show in history had ever done that kind of money without pay-per-view, and even among those, the only two larger were *WrestleMania III* and *WrestleMania VII*.

McMahon had plenty to learn from when it came to putting storylines together. He'd made his own dumb mistakes with Flair and Benoit in the past. He'd seen successful invasion angles booked overseas in Japan, angles that drew sellout after sellout to the 55,000-seat Tokyo Dome. And closer to home, there was the infamous UWF interpromotional battle with Jim Crockett Promotions in 1987.

Well, to call it a battle would be to give Crockett and his company way too much credit. When they bought the promotion from Bill Watts, the idea was to keep the companies separate and build toward a huge Superbowl of Wrestling card at some point down the road. Unfortunately, ego got in the way long before anything like that could even start to build. Because the two sides had been feuding for so long, Crockett wasn't able to grasp the fact that purchasing the competition meant the war was over. Instead, he was still determined to show fans that JCP was the superior organization, and to do so, he sent many of his lower-card wrestlers over to UWF TV and had them quickly win all the major titles. The UWF title was portrayed as a secondary title (say, the Intercontinental or U.S. belt) is portrayed in WWE today, and the champion would wrestle early on in the card as a "warm-up" for Crockett's big stars, who worked all the main events. Not only did this absurd booking not lead to a boom period, but things got so bad for Crockett that he ended up going out of business about a year later.

Did Vince—who surely knew this story since his head of talent relations, Jim Ross, lived through it—learn from this and book his invasion in a different manner? That is for you to decide. But first, the literal definition of the word "invasion":

NOUN: 1. The act of invading, especially the entrance of an armed force into a territory to conquer.

How about "invade"?

TRANSITIVE VERB: To enter by force in order to conquer or pillage.

Presumably, the dictionary at Titan Towers had a different definition:

TRANSITIVE VERB: To cause to be destroyed; failure to win.

The highly anticipated WCW invasion turned out to be truly preposterous. It's hard to imagine a feud booked more poorly than what should have been the simplest, biggest moneymaker in the history of pro wrestling.

Before we get into that, though, we should note that the WWF did not have all the top WCW stars at their disposal. The WWF did absorb the contracts of twenty-four mid-carders, including Lance Storm,

Chuck Palumbo, Sean O'Haire, Mark Jindrak, Mike Awesome, Elix Skipper, Shane Helms, Shannon Moore, Stacy Keibler, Chavo Guerrero Jr., Mike Sanders, Hugh Morris, Shawn Stasiak, Kaz Hayashi, Jimmy Yang, and Billy Kidman. Men like Sting, Goldberg, and Hulk Hogan, however, were under long-term deals with Time Warner, and in order to break those deals, the WWF would have had to pay to cover the difference. The same was true of the very embodiment of WCW, Ric Flair: the company claimed they *couldn't afford* to bring him in as part of the invasion.

Apparently, the WWF couldn't afford to bring in the big-name stars as it had been a very lean year for poor Vince McMahon. After all, his company was only able to gross a record-high $456 million. In fact, had it not been for his decision to start a renegade football league known as the XFL, McMahon's company would have generated a profit of $27.4 million that quarter and $84.9 million for the year. Despite the burden of the XFL, the WWF still had hundreds of millions on hand, thanks to the incredible numbers it had been producing in buy rates, ratings, merchandise, and house show attendance.

But this was not McMahon's only excuse. He also argued that if he bought out, say, Goldberg's contract for an estimated $6 million, it would upset the salary structure of the WWF and create grumblings in the locker room. What he and many of the grumbling wrestlers failed to realize was that every effort should have been made, no matter what the cost, to get the big stars and make the invasion a success. After all, if it was a success, *everyone*—from the top of the card to the bottom—was going to make a lot more money. And if the invasion was a bust because folks couldn't comprehend an "untested non-WWF performer" like Goldberg making so much money (and in reality, fans wanted Goldberg dream matches so badly at this point that he probably would have paid off his entire contract for the year with one PPV main event), well, everyone was going to end up with less spare change.

In the end, though, it didn't matter who McMahon brought in, because the WCW wrestlers weren't to be the focus of this invasion. No, the WCW invasion was about the McMahons. That became clear on the final night of the Monday Night Wars, when Vince opened up the *Nitro* broadcast himself. Just in case someone out there didn't quite get the message, the final performer in a WCW ring on the final broadcast ever of *WCW Monday Nitro* was . . . Shane McMahon.

Yes, despite having Ric Flair, Booker T, Sting, and Scott Steiner available at the show, all of whom could have fired the first shot in the WCW invasion and really put fans on the edges of their seats (and make no mistake about it, fans were prepared to open their wallets at the mere thought of interpromotional matchups), SHANE MCMAHON was the focal point. In the storyline, Shane, and not Vince, had bought WCW, so Shane would lead the invasion.

The original plan was for WCW to have its own Saturday-night TV show and to run its own house show events and PPVs; basically it was to be its own company, with Shane McMahon as the storyline president. Arenas were booked, and negotiations began with Viacom to secure a time slot for the inevitable WCW television programs. All fine in theory, but Viacom, specifically The National Network (TNN, which eventually became Spike TV, original home of UFC and TNA Impact Wrestling) on which *Raw* aired, didn't want any more wrestling programs—they had enough. And they didn't want Vince to replace his highly rated WWF show with WCW, as they'd paid top dollar for the ratings that *Raw* drew, and they didn't want those numbers to be potentially sliced in half. So there were problems on the corporate end from the get-go.

This led Vince to change his mind in late May and opt instead for a "soft-launch." His new idea was to slowly introduce the WCW performers by having them attack WWF wrestlers on *Raw* and *SmackDown*, leading to a big interpromotional pay-per-view on July 22 in Cleveland. In what would eventually become the answer to an obscure trivia question,

Lance Storm was the first guy to attack a WWF superstar on the May 28, 2001 *Raw* from his hometown of Calgary, Alberta, Canada, coming through the crowd and superkicking Perry Saturn.

"They didn't even tell me about this ahead of time," Storm said, "either to keep it secret or because it was a last minute call, I have no idea which. I was called the week before the event and told WWE was flying all of the WCW guys to Connecticut to meet with Jim Ross to discuss their future with the company. Since *Raw* and Jim Ross were going to be in Calgary the following week they thought they would save on the flight and have me meet with JR at the building Monday afternoon. I went to the event with the understanding I was just meeting with JR. Of course, I had my gear in my car, because you always bring your gear. JR was busy most of the day so I was asked if I would be heading up to Edmonton for the *SmackDown* taping, and I said I was planning to. So our meeting was bumped to Tuesday, and I was told to just hang out and enjoy the show. Later that afternoon John Laurinitis (who was the talent relations go-to guy for all WCW talent) pulled me aside and asked if I brought my gear, because I was working tonight. I laughed it off assuming he was joking, and despite him sticking to his story I ignored him and assumed he was ribbing. I was later approached by I think Dean Malenko, who mentioned me doing something tonight. At this point it was getting late, so I tracked down Johnny to confirm I was, in fact, working. He told me about the run-in, told me to get my gear, and we discussed what exactly I was doing that night. As it turned out, they wanted me in my red and white gear, not the red and black I'd been wearing the last month or two in WCW, so I had to run back to my house and get my other gear and it was quite late by the time I was ready to go. I had to put coveralls over my tights and sneak up to the concession stands so I could run in through the crowd.

"I remember being very nervous about what kind of reaction I'd get. I hadn't wrestled in Calgary since my indy days in 1995 and I wasn't getting music or a ring introduction. I had no idea if in that split second of a run-in the crowd would recognize me, register that I was a home-town boy and react. The time came. I slid out of my coveralls, ran in, superkicked Perry Saturn, got a great reaction, and then left through the crowd to meet up with Shane McMahon in his limo to ride off into the sunset, so to speak, having just fired the first shot in the WCW invasion. Everyone was quite happy, and I felt welcome and part of the team."

The next renegade to invade was the former Hugh G. Rection. Really, this was the next big invader. Keep in mind that they didn't bother to attack top stars such as the Rock or Stone Cold Steve Austin, but went after mid-carders like Bradshaw and Goldust. The one time team WCW did attack a huge WWF star, Kurt Angle, the fighting was done by—yes, you guessed it—Shane McMahon.

The first real shot in the war took place at the *King of the Ring* PPV on June 24 in East Rutherford, New Jersey, when Undertaker and the newly signed Dallas Page had an in-ring confrontation. Not a match, mind you, but a "confrontation." Page wanted to be a part of this historic angle so badly that he took a contract buyout at approximately fifty cents on the dollar. Upon entering the company, he was immediately placed in a storyline in which he portrayed a perverted stalker who had a thing for the Undertaker's wife, Sara. Of course, those who'd followed WCW for years knew that Page's wife was the white-hot Kimberly, so it made little sense that he'd be making advances toward anyone else's wife. Regardless, this led to their epic confrontation, which saw Taker beat up Page for approximately 5:39 minutes of the 5:40-minute encounter. Instead of being deadly adversaries, they were nothing but impotent goofs. This, combined with the fact that the WWF had been telling its fan base that WCW sucked for years (and, truth be told, WCW had told their own fans this for years too), led WWF fans to violently reject anything associated with WCW.

Therefore, what happened when Shane McMahon "secured" a

WCW World title match for his men at the July 2 *Raw* from Tacoma, Washington, should have come as no shock. It would be the first time ever that a WCW-sanctioned match happened on a WWF show, and it would feature two more newly signed wrestlers: WCW World and U.S. champ Booker T (who beat Steiner on the final *Nitro*) taking on Marcus "Buff" Bagwell (who, ironically, McMahon had vowed to never hire on that very same final *Nitro*). Many questioned the decision to even allow Bagwell into the company, let alone put him in such a high-profile match. He was anything but a model employee in WCW prior to the buyout, often crying like a little baby when he was asked to job. His attitude only worsened when he was informed that he was getting the title shot; he became pompous and aloof, failing to show up for required workouts. In short, his hiring did little to appease the boys in either WWF or the new WCW.

In an interesting historic twist, there was actually great debate in the WWF production meeting that afternoon about whether the match should be Booker versus Bagwell or Booker versus Lance Storm. Without question, Storm versus Booker would have been a better match, as the two had been working together at house shows frequently and getting good reviews (and, as it turns out, Booker and Bagwell had also been doing house show matches and they'd gotten terrible reviews). At the end of the day, the decision was made that Bagwell was "the more identifiable name with WCW," and so he got the match.

The match itself was a disaster of Biblical proportions. Despite announcer Arn Anderson's claim that this was "bigger than the moon landing," Bagwell and Booker tiptoed through a very mundane match and proceeded to blow spot after spot. The crowd (those who hadn't filed out, that is) entertained themselves with competing chants of "BORING!" and "THIS MATCH SUCKS!" and "GOLDBERG!" In fact, the only time the crowd truly seemed to enjoy themselves was when Steve Austin and Kurt Angle, the WWF's two lead heels, came into the ring and beat the crap out of both men. In the midst of this—the biggest event since the moon landing, remember—the cameras cut backstage to Vince McMahon making out with WCW diva Torrie Wilson. This led to *Raw*'s finale, a scene in which Vince, wearing only his boxers, was caught by his wife, Linda, with his hand in the nookie jar.

Many labeled this the worst WWF show of all time.

It also put an end to the invasion as it was originally conceived. Prior to the show, McMahon's plans had become grandiose. On the *Raw* after the *Invasion* PPV, Vince and Linda were going to do a divorce angle that would lead to the two of them splitting all their assets—assets that included the WWF itself. All of the wrestlers, WWF and WCW alike, would be drafted to one of two shows, *WWF SmackDown* on Thursday or *WCW Nitro* on Monday nights. Starting in October, the WCW crew was going to start running their own house show tours and PPV events.

Tacoma killed that idea. Vince took one look at the crowd reaction and decided there was no way WCW could survive as its own entity.

Would the proposed Tacoma alternative main event, Lance Storm versus Booker T, have changed history? Even Storm himself strongly doubts that. "The match would have been better, but it wouldn't have changed anything in the big scheme. You know, the commentary was bad, the presentation was bad, and a lot of the booking later on was bad. I wasn't changing anything. It would have been a better match but that would have been about the only difference."

With the invasion falling apart, McMahon knew something needed to be done to save the angle. And a savior of sorts appeared to have fallen into his lap. In addition to WCW, a major independent promotion based out of Philadelphia by the name of Extreme Championship Wrestling had gone under. ECW was a rogue promotion under the management of Paul Heyman, who had come up with a novel concept for wrestling in the mid-1990s: tons of sex, lots of violence, and the complete abolishment of cartoonish characters and family-friendly storylines. Ironically enough, that was the same blueprint that McMahon had borrowed (some would say "stole") for his vaunted "Attitude." ECW had a rabid fan base—even to this day, when someone gets slammed through a table in wrestling, it is not uncommon for fans to chant "ECW! ECW!"

Realistically, though, the promotion was little more than a glorified regional outfit with great booking. The company rarely drew more than 1,000 paid to their events, and their weekly television show drew less than 20 percent of what McMahon's did. Despite the brilliant storylines and groundbreaking characters, Heyman simply didn't have the funds to compete with McMahon or Bischoff on a national level. This led both of the larger companies to raid his talent and his best ideas more or less at will. By the end of 2000, ECW was in shambles, and its workers' checks were bouncing on a weekly basis. The company collapsed, and McMahon, ever the opportunist, was there to pick up the pieces. He hired Heyman and a few of his better workers on the spot, and believed, since ECW was out of business, that he could use the name and logo as he saw fit. The White Plains, New York, bankruptcy court thought otherwise. The irony of this is that WWF itself blew a gasket in 1996 when WCW did something similar with Hall and Nash, though much less blatantly. McMahon, undeterred for the time being, continued to use the name and logo while attempting to work out a settlement.

Heyman was nothing short of brilliant following the death of ECW. Ever since he'd replaced Jerry Lawler as color commentator on *Raw*, he'd been dropping ECW references constantly. Not only that, but strange emails suddenly began to arrive at all the major wrestling websites, always mentioning the same thing: Heyman was great, WCW sucked, and ECW should be resurrected with all of its former stars on WWF TV. In a "shocking coincidence," that's exactly what happened shortly thereafter. And because of it, the ruins of ECW were finally purchased by the WWF, effectively absolving Heyman of all responsibility.

Therefore, during the July 9 *Raw* in Atlanta, an ECW faction was formed when longtime ECW workers Rob Van Dam and Tommy Dreamer showed up out of the blue. All the men on the WWF roster who had ever competed for ECW joined them. Heyman himself entered the ring, giving a spirited promo about how much he hated McMahon for stealing his concepts and his talent. After teasing that the WCW and ECW factions were going to go to war with each other, they suddenly teamed up in a big swerve, with Heyman claiming that both sides were going to link up (forming the "Alliance") and kick the crap out of the WWF.

Despite running through eighteen months' worth of angles in about eighteen minutes on *Raw*, this was truly a landmark moment in wrestling. This is what the invasion should have been all along: the two promotions that Vince ran out of business teaming up to destroy McMahon and the men who had driven them into bankruptcy. All was right with the world again.

Until, of course, the final two minutes of the program, in which the viewers at home were introduced to the new owner of ECW: Stephanie McMahon.

Yes, now Vince's *daughter* was brought to the forefront of the invasion alongside her brother Shane. Again, the entire focus of the so-called "invasion" was shifted away from what fans had been dying to see for years, which was ECW or WCW versus the WWF. This alienated not only the hardcore ECW fans who might have bought into the storyline, but also many longtime WWF fans who'd already been bored to tears by the McMahon family feud angle.

Behind the scenes, things were even worse: the on-screen tension between the WWF and WCW guys was boiling over into a real-life feud. The WCW group felt the WWF crew looked upon them as second-class citizens (and unwanted ones at that). They felt they had to walk on eggshells around the WWF guys. Many within the former Turner wrestling company knew that this was realistically their last chance in the business—if this version of WCW were to fail, they had nowhere else to go now that Vince owned the U.S. wrestling industry.

It was due to the hard work of the loyal WWF wrestlers that McMahon was able to do this. At least that's how the WWF'ers felt, and that's why they thought that the WCW boys should be kissing their asses. Look at them—here were the guys who'd driven an entire company down the drain. Why should they get any special treatment? And, perhaps more to the point, why should they get opportunities that would otherwise belong to the WWF's loyal workers?

And right there in the midst of all this tension was Vince McMahon, stirring the pot as best he could. Over the years, McMahon had often pushed his wrestlers' buttons behind the scenes, hoping that fueling the real-life flames might make for better television and in-ring product. He'd done this five years earlier with Bret Hart and Shawn Michaels, resulting in the infamous Montreal double-cross that prompted Bret to leave the company.

In an effort to antagonize both sides, McMahon handed out WCW shirts for the new guys to wear, just in case someone had forgotten which side they were on. The shirts became nothing short of giant bullseye and further enraged the WWF crew, who made sure to get in a few extra stiff shots whenever the camera called for a beatdown.

And beatdowns happened often. Far too often, in fact. The biggest money-drawing feuds of all time all had one thing in common: fans believed that either side could win. That was the key to wrestling: that feeling that the men pitted against each other in the squared circle were each capable of pulling off the victory. Think back to any sporting contest you've ever seen. The most intriguing matchups are those in which both sides appear to be on equal footing. Why would anyone want to watch a wrestling match, a predetermined one at that, in which one side was portrayed as never having a chance?

But such was the plight of WCW under the rule of Vince McMahon. Perhaps it was because Vince never really wanted to acknowledge that

WCW was on equal ground with his own creation. He had, after all, refused to even acknowledge their existence on WWF television until the late 1990s, when *Nitro* was beating *Raw*'s ass in the ratings. They were the only wrestling company to successfully compete with him, and not only that, but for a while, they beat him at his own game. It was a humiliation that Vince's fragile ego seemed unable to endure. Therefore, it probably shouldn't have come as much of a shock that when he finally got the chance to pit the two companies "against" each other, he had the WWF side completely annihilate WCW.

It shouldn't have come as a shock, save for the fact that there was so damn much money to be made.

From almost the first moment that the two sides went to war on Vince's playground, WCW was made to look like a troop of pathetic losers. Page was killed dead pretty much immediately. From the moment the feud began until it ended three months later, he got in virtually no offensive moves. WWF fans hadn't seen squash matches the likes of these since the glory days of jobbers such as Mario Mancini and Barry Horowitz. Time and again, Page was humiliated in losses against the Taker, and the "feud," if you can even call it that, culminated in yet another loss—this time to Taker's wife.

"Being in WWE (formerly the WWF) sucked," noted Mike Awesome prior to his passing in 2007. "I hated it. You had to kiss everybody's ass . . . you had to be on your political toes all the time. You would not believe the backstage politics. You were getting stabbed in the back constantly. I was so happy when I was told I was gone [fired]."

Other WCW stars shared similar fates, except that the vast majority of them weren't featured anywhere near the main event. Most of the WCW crew were stuck battling men who always had been and would always be in the WWF mid-card. And the WWF guys liked it that way— God forbid these WCW slackers come in and take their spots.

Of course, if anyone from the WWF stepped back and looked at the situation objectively, they would have realized that if this invasion were a success, more people would buy tickets to the events. More PPVs would be ordered. More merchandise would be sold. And, perhaps most importantly, WCW would become reestablished, meaning that there would be even more PPVs, arena events, and merchandise. In short, there'd be more cash for everyone involved.

How much cash? This was illustrated at the *Invasion* PPV, a show so successful that it was devastatingly sad; it was a very clear demonstration of just how much revenue the company blew. The event, from the Gund Arena in Cleveland, drew a sellout 15,535 paid for an $848,060 gate. But that's peanuts compared to the buy rate: a 1.6, which translates into a whopping 760,000 buys, or about a $10 million gross.

Yes, a *$10 million* gross, for just one show.

"It [the invasion angle] was just horrible," noted Raven, who was among the ECW originals. "It was a crime against nature. But I understand why he [Vince McMahon] did it, because he wants to prove he's superior to everybody. And he's so rich he doesn't care about money, which is a shame because he could have [made so much money]. Put it this way, it was one of the highest buy rates they ever had and they did nothing to make it special. They did everything they could to hamstring it. It's so fucking sad that he's so cruel and vindictive, that he doesn't care. He has to have the biggest dick in the room."[37]

That would have more than paid off the contracts of the three biggest stars in WCW at the end, Ric Flair, Goldberg, and Scott Steiner. And God only knows how big the buy rate would have been if those men had actually been involved. You see, it was the very concept of WWF versus WCW that sold this show, but it wasn't an actual WWF versus WCW match. The main event ended up being the Dudleys and Rhyno (another creative team debate that Storm was on the wrong end of as some argued that he should replace Rhyno since there were only two WCW stars on the five-man Team WCW) and DDP and Booker T

("Team WCW") versus Steve Austin and Kurt Angle and Undertaker and Kane and Chris Jericho. In other words, of those ten men, eight were WWF guys anyway (Rhyno and the Dudleys were in the WWF long before the invasion ever began), and it wasn't like Booker T and DDP were the biggest stars WCW had at the end. It's tough to fathom the kind of numbers they might have done for this show had team WCW consisted of Flair and Goldberg and Steiner and Booker T and DDP.

It's even harder to fathom the kind of business they'd have done for at least a year afterwards had they brought all the big stars in on day one and promoted this the way it should have been promoted. The WCW stars, portrayed as equals, would have given the promotion enough dream matches to last at least a couple of years. Instead, the invasion was watered down by WWF guys pretending to be on the other team, as well as more McMahons than anyone ever wanted to see.

Ratings picked up a bit at this point, since a bunch of teenagers suddenly started to tune in, likely expecting something new and exciting. Unfortunately, this was the most interest fans would ever show for the angle, and things slowly began to drop off.

Thankfully, McMahon figured out the problem: the WCW and ECW guys didn't know how to work. Seriously, that's what he thought. Never mind the fact that WCW turned business around with Kevin Nash, who was a worse worker than all the invasion guys put together. To rectify this issue, Vince simply had two of his top stars, Steve Austin and Kurt Angle, turn heel and join the Alliance. So now, the spotlight of the Alliance was not only on Shane and Steph, but on Austin and Angle as well. The WCW and ECW guys weren't relegated to second-banana, but rather to about fifth-banana status. The plan did the exact opposite of what it was designed to do: within twelve weeks of the *Invasion* PPV, *Raw* viewership had dropped a staggering 30 percent.

Does the date September 8, 2001, ring a bell? No? That right there should indicate the kind of flop the angle had become by this point. On that day in Dallas, Steve Austin faced the Rock in the first-ever WWF champion versus WCW champion title unification match (it ended in a DQ). There was a day when this would have been one of the biggest stories in wrestling history. Within six months of purchasing WCW, however, the WWF's idiotic booking had turned it into a match virtually nobody remembers to this day.

A month and a half later, the WWF presented perhaps the most poorly booked *Raw* in history. Sure, there had been worse shows in the past, but never had a show been booked not to make money to this extent. First, Vince and Linda came out all smiling and happy, which made zero sense since, as you might recall, just prior to the invasion the storyline was that they were about to get a divorce. They were about to kiss mid-ring when Shane and Steph came out and challenged them to a winner-take-all match at *Survivor Series*. The WWF considered this to be such a huge match that they never bothered to specify what "winner-take-all" meant and quickly dropped the subject (it meant WWF versus Alliance, with the losing group having to disappear forever). Then—and this is absolutely true—to give the Alliance team, which had no credibility, that one last big push toward the PPV, they had four title matches, and in all four, *the Alliance guys lost their belts to the WWF guys.*

It was like someone from WCW had started to book *Raw.*

And that brings us to the final showdown between the Alliance and the WWF at *Survivor Series 2001*, in which the loser of the match would be forced out of wrestling forever.

The first man introduced as part of Team Alliance? Duh—Shane McMahon. Next up was Austin, who had been the embodiment of the WWF since McMahon introduced his "Attitude" concept in 1996. Then there was Angle, who had never competed anywhere but the WWF. Rounding out the team as afterthoughts were Booker T and Rob Van Dam, who were eliminated midway through the match so as not to take the focus away from anyone who, you know, hadn't worked for the WWF the majority of their career. And so, in the final match to determine the survival of WCW, the last two men in the ring were Austin and the Rock. The first person they showed after Rock pinned Austin was naturally the embodiment of ECW herself, Stephanie McMahon.

Ironically, who should appear the very next night on *Raw* but Ric Flair. Over the next year, the newly dubbed World Wrestling Entertainment, in increasingly futile attempts to reverse the downward ratings and buy rate spiral, would bring in not only Flair, but Hulk Hogan, Kevin Nash, Scott Hall, and Scott Steiner, many of the names they "couldn't afford" to bring in for the invasion.

And the two men who could potentially have meant the most, Bischoff and Goldberg? Both were eventually signed as well. Goldberg, whom fans had been dying to see in the WWF since the late '90s, was killed his first week in when he was put in a comedy sketch with Goldust that included the latter putting a shiny gold wig on the former's head. Never had a wig cost more people more money. Instead of being booked as the ultimate outsider, he was portrayed as—SURPRISE!—just another guy on the roster, and as a result, his first-ever PPV match with the Rock—which would have shattered all records years earlier—ended up doing along the lines of what every other PPV during that period did. And remember how, right after WCW folded, people said that if WWF signed Goldberg it would upset the salary structure and piss off the locker room? And how other folks said that they were going to eventually sign him no matter what, so they may as well have done it for the invasion? Well, sure enough, when he was signed, a year too late, it was for an overinflated price that upset the salary structure and pissed off the locker room.

In a 2004 interview with Alex Marvez, Goldberg reflected on his WWE tenure: "I think the way they handled my character was moronic. Any businessman who has business first and foremost on his mind wouldn't have done what they did. But as much as they tried to demean the character, they couldn't do it. The fans know the true story. And everyone knows what should have happened from a storyline and entertainment standpoint. I pretty much believe every member of WCW that came over, they had a grudge against us because we were kicking their ass when wrestling was at its pinnacle. Instead of using us to their advantage business-wise, I truly think they wanted to squash us and build us up and reinvent us as WWE entities and erase what we had done prior. When they wanted to expand the Goldberg character and make him understand people more and make people able to feel what I feel . . . people didn't want to see Goldberg have emotions or laugh. They wanted to see him rip people's heads off. That's what made me who I am. That's why I had a 176-match winning streak and Hulk Hogan and I put 40,000 asses in the seats in Atlanta. It wasn't because there was a wig on me and I was made into the laughingstock of fans. The situation was pure ignorance."

Bischoff's debut was even more absurd; instead of coming in and amassing a new horde of ex-WCW stars to try to get revenge on the company that put them out of business, his first move in his very first appearance on *Raw* was to give Vince McMahon a hug. You read that right; they HUGGED. Like the wig, never before had a hug cost so many people so much easy money. There was a time in WCW when Bischoff was known as "ATM Eric," and if ever there was a chance to do an angle in which he could live up to that reputation, this was it. Instead, he and McMahon might as well have taken millions and millions of dollars in cash and burned it all in a giant barrel on the ramp under the TitanTron, laughing maniacally at how they'd put one over on the rest of the world. The bottom line is that, no matter what anyone thought about the WWF having learned a lesson from the invasion debacle, they clearly hadn't learned a thing.

The ultimate irony is that WCW, the most incompetent wrestling organization there ever was, did an invasion right. They had three guys, Hogan, Nash, and Hall. Hogan at the time was a lame babyface who'd overstayed his welcome. Hall was a high mid-carder who'd main-event-ed a PPV or two in the WWF, but aside from his matches with Shawn Michaels, he'd never really lit the ring on fire. Nash was, without ques-tion, the worst-drawing WWF champion of all time. Yet these three men had helped to turn WCW business around because they were promoted as the biggest threats that had ever existed to the company, and they laid waste to WCW main-eventers left and right, month after month, until fans were dying to see them get what was coming to them. Of course, the fact that WCW never got their revenge was one of the reasons fans lost faith in them at the end. Still, Booker T and DDP were realisti-cally at the same level of stardom in WCW as Hall and Nash were in the WWF when they left, and if you really want to know why the nWo worked and the invasion was a disaster, go back and look at how each pair of men was promoted upon switching sides.

In short, there was a ton of money to be made, but it was all flushed away due to petty ego. A feud that should have lasted years and years, one that had been built up in fans' minds as the ultimate battle in pro wrestling, collapsed after less than six months, and the end came in front of 10,142 fans paying a little over half a million dollars.

In 1984, Vince McMahon began a long quest to become the sole ma-jor-league wrestling promoter in the United States. Through a combina-tion of cutthroat business practices, ingenious maneuvering, and flat-out good luck, he got himself to a point in the late '80s where he was making more money than many ever dreamed was possible. He had shows on net-work TV, *WrestleMania* and Hulkamania were household words, and the sky looked to be the limit. Although his company was rocked by a series of sex and drug scandals in the early '90s, he survived, and by 1995 he had only one major competitor: Ted Turner's WCW. ECW was there, and while its product was revolutionary and changed the business, financially they were always just hanging on. Bischoff created *WCW Monday Nitro* to oppose McMahon's flagship *Raw* show, and the battle was on.

The WWF lost $6 million in 1996, but by adopting many of ECW's formulas and putting everything behind the push of a WCW outcast named Steve Austin, things began to turn around. The war intensified, and by 1998, both companies were making tens of millions of dollars and broadcasting their programming to as many as 12 million viewers every Monday night. Forget Flair versus Steamboat, Funk versus Brisco, Hogan versus Andre, and even Austin versus McMahon: the biggest feud of all time was WWF versus WCW. By 2001, however, as a result of everything you've read about in this book, WCW suddenly found themselves $62 million in the hole. Still, *Nitro* was doing acceptable ratings, and between the four prime time shows the two companies aired, almost 10 million people tuned in each week. Vince, the onetime wacky announcer in the cute red bow tie, was now an evil billionaire. He'd purchased WCW and finally, after all those years, all the battles, all the raids, the last great wrestling war was about to begin, and fans everywhere anticipated perhaps the most exciting programming of their lifetimes.

Little did they know that Vince McMahon would ultimately prove himself worthy of owning the WCW name.

★ ★ ★ EPILOGUE 2014 ★ ★ ★

Here Lies World Championship Wrestling 1988–2003

Imagine for a moment that after WCW died, an idea was pitched for a new national wrestling promotion, a promotion that would serve the needs of the former WCW and NWA fans who simply didn't want to watch Vince McMahon's WWE. Imagine—if you can—that the story of this promotion involved . . .

- Hiring Vince Russo as a booker on and off for over a dozen years.
- Trying to run weekly pay-per-views with no national television with which to promote them.
- Trying to work with the National Wrestling Alliance in order to latch onto the prestigious NWA World Heavyweight title—in 2002.
- Creating a tag team called The Johnsons consisting of two men dressed as penises.

- Shooting an angle that involved a midget masturbating in a trash can.
- Shooting an angle that involved a midget pulling a gun on Jeff Jarrett.
- Shooting an angle to start the first-ever heel turn of one of the all-time greatest babyfaces in wrestling history, Ricky "The Dragon" Steamboat, which ended up never coming to fruition because Steamboat just disappeared into thin air, never to return.
- Shooting an angle to start the first-ever heel turn of WCW's lead announcer, Tony Schiavone, which ended up never coming to fruition because Schiavone just disappeared into thin air, never to return.
- Booking dozens of performers in the early years who appeared, shot angles, and were never seen again, including, but not limited to, Blue Meanie, Vader, Bart Gunn, Moondog Spot, Viscera, Mike Awesome, Roderick Strong, Jackie Gayda, Rikishi, Andrew Martin aka Test, Ayako Hamada, Sean Morley, Kim Couture and Sangriento.
- Not noticing until after a show that a wrestler had worn a shirt with a Nazi SS symbol on national pay-per-view television.
- Promoting a King of the Mountain match, which is a reverse ladder match where after pinning an opponent and sending him to a penalty box, you must climb a ladder and hang a title belt over the ring.
- Promoting a reverse battle royal, where all participants start outside the ring and have to fight to be the first to get inside, a task that involves everyone having to pretend they are clumsy and unable to crawl quickly into a ring.
- Promoting one of the worst matches in recorded history, a holiday Silent Night Bloody Night hardcore match that included a hanging barbed wire Christmas tree that grapplers took bumps into.

- Promoting a match with four boxes wherein three boxes held title shots and one box held a pink slip, which begged the question why anyone would want to open any box and risk their career when title shots were handed out regularly anyway.
- Promoting countless random pole matches.
- Promoting a lumberjack cage match, a concept too preposterous to healthily consider for any length of time.
- Promoting a Hard 10 match wherein wrestlers were encouraged to use weapons, with weapons shots garnering one point per usage and putting someone through a table garnering five points, and the only way to win was to get ten points but also be up by two points. Also, imagine that this match was so complicated and preposterous that even this company, which never learned from its mistakes, never bothered to try it again.
- Promoting something called a "Dupp Cupp" tournament wherein you received points for, among other things, goosing a woman, sticking a person's head in a toilet, and using a farm animal or a blow-up doll as a weapon, and where you could lose points for openly weeping. Also never tried again.
- Promoting an NWA title change via DQ since the original rules were that such could happen, but then eventually forgetting that rule, doing DQs in title matches, not changing the title, and never bothering to explain the change to fans.
- Promoting repeated War Games matches where the babyfaces start with the man advantage, completely destroying the most basic wrestling psychology imaginable.
- Allowing Roddy Piper to go to the ring with a live mic and ask Vince Russo on national television, "Did you kill Owen Hart?"
- Developing a faction called S.E.X., which stood for Sports Entertainment Extreme, the latter word of which does not, in fact, start with the letter X.

- Airing shots of the announcers wherein said announcers were unaware they were being filmed and thus basically read word-for-word from the script in front of a national TV audience.
- Booking various wrestling Elvises, various Nascar stars, and various country music performers solely due to being based in Nashville, Tennessee, and never successfully getting any of them over to a national television audience.
- Hiring Eric Watts, in 2003.
- Airing an angle in 2003 where Jeff Jarrett attacked Hulk Hogan at a Japanese press conference, setting the stage for Hulk Hogan's debut seven years later in 2010.
- Airing the Hulk Hogan-Jeff Jarrett angle all over television while Hogan was busy re-debuting in WWE.
- Hiring Jonny Fairplay of *Survivor* fame based solely on the fact that the president of the company was a big *Survivor* fan, paying him $150,000 for the first year, wherein he made eight appearances for a total of forty minutes of work, and then re-signing him at $150,000 for a second year, wherein he made zero appearances for a total of zero minutes of work.
- Hiring this man during a period when numerous employees made it known that they made so little money in the company that they were forced to take second jobs, and one of them, Taylor Wilde, was so embarrassed when a fan recognized her as the Women's champion while working a minimum wage job at the Sunglass Hut that she quit the wrestling company the next day.
- Hiring Dusty Rhodes to book in 2005.
- Booking an Ultimate X match where the X hanging above the ring was not secured properly so that, in the middle of the match, it fell down and they had to get a ladder to hang it back up.
- Claiming when the X fell down in an Ultimate X match that the

X had to be re-hung, and that you could not win if the X fell off the cables, and then, five minutes later, when the X fell off the cables a second time, awarding the match to the man who caught it.

- Following the death of Chris Candido due to a blood clot following surgery complications, his girlfriend, Tammy Sytch, claimed the company sent her his last paycheck in his name, which of course could not be cashed since he was deceased. When she asked the company to resend it in her name, they refused. According to Sytch, they did, however, send her a condolence gift: "A boneless fucking ham."

- Creating a drug policy that included a list of prohibited substances and drug testing, but which did not include any actual penalties. This was convenient, as when 60 wrestlers were tested in 2007 it later came out in a report to the Congressional Committee on Oversight and Government Reform that twenty-six tested positive for drugs, fifteen tested positive for steroids, and zero were punished.

- Hiring Kurt Angle immediately after WWE fired him over concern that he was a major health risk. Angle went on to be arrested four separate times (as of summer 2013) during his career, mostly for DWI offenses. He finally checked into rehab of his own volition after the fourth arrest.

- Creating a convoluted Undertaker/Kane-style storyline that involved Sinister Minister Jim Mitchell being—we think—the father of Judas Mesias and Abyss, which, based on our calculations, would have required Mitchell to have become a father at the age of nine.

- Hiring Adam Pacman Jones, who nobody outside of Tennessee had ever even heard of (he was a Tennessee Titans football player), unless, of course, they were aware of the Las Vegas strip club shooting incident that he was allegedly involved in, which left a former pro-wrestler paralyzed. He was suspended from the Titans for a year, the first time in forty-four years that a player had been suspended for anything other than substance abuse, at which point it was decided that this would be a great time to hire him for pro wrestling. Despite the fact that his football contract allowed him to appear on TV but not to get involved in any physical angles in any way, he somehow managed to win and lose the Tag Team titles.

- Expecting Pacman Jones to boost ratings and draw mainstream attention only to have his debut do 20 percent lower than the regular TV average, and the mainstream media articles on the story note that this was—swear to God—A STEP DOWN FOR PACMAN JONES.

- Booking something called a "Doomsday Chamber of Blood" match. Try to follow along: it was a cage match, and to make sure nobody could climb out, barbed wire was put around the top to shred anyone who dared to enter. The only way to win is via pinfall; however, you can pin a guy a thousand times and it doesn't count because in order to be eligible to be pinned, you must first bleed. Then the first guy to pin someone who is bleeding gets a future championship match against the winner of another match that has yet to take place. As Jim Cornette attempted to explain, "It's really quite simple." Yep, sure is.

- Having an announcer claim that an Asian female's finishing hold was called THE HAPPY ENDING, a stereotypical Asian massage parlor masturbation reference.

- Hiring one of the prettiest girls on the independent scene, cheerleader Melissa of Southern California, and giving her a Muslim gimmick that involved covering her entire body head-to-toe in a robe.

- Hiring a swimsuit model named Brooke Adams, best known for her amazing, award-winning (no joke) posterior, and sending her out every week in skirts that completely obscured said posterior.
- Pushing Sting as a top star in his fifties.
- Trying to recreate Goldberg with an unknown wrestler named Crimson, a man with neither the physical gifts of Goldberg nor anything resembling his charisma, by trying to get him over with an undefeated streak deep in the mid-card, and after 400 days when it was clearly not working, booking him to lose and then immediately taking him off TV pretty much forever.
- Booking a preposterous angle where one wrestler apparently killed another wrestler with a machete, which resulted in the latter wrestler's Wikipedia page being updated to report that he was dead as the result of being killed with a machete. The latter wrestler—Scott Steiner—was back on TV a week later with no injuries whatsoever.
- Billing a man as undefeated even though he somehow had already lost two World championships.
- Booking a match between two undefeated wrestlers where the stipulation was that neither's winning streak was on the line.
- Hiring Jenna Morasca, also, coincidentally, from *Survivor* (five years earlier), for an alleged half-million dollars, an investment that paid off in the form of quite possibly the single worst match in the entire history of professional wrestling with Booker T's wife, Sharmell, on live PPV.
- Signing Jeff Hardy and giving him the World title during a time when Jeff Hardy was facing charges of trafficking in controlled prescription pills and possession of anabolic steroids, charges to which a year later he pleaded guilty, for which he was fined $100,000 and spent ten days in jail.
- Sending Jeff Hardy to the ring during this period to work a

pay-per-view main event when it was clear he was in no condition to perform.

- Booking three Montreal-style screwjobs in a one-year period, all involving Earl Hebner, all over a decade after the Montreal Screwjob, all not meaning a single, solitary thing for business.
- Hiring Hulk Hogan as a top star in his fifties.
- Spending the last months of 2009 pushing Hogan's debut virtually the exact same way WCW pushed Hogan's debut in 1994— fifteen years earlier.
- Hiring Eric Bischoff as an executive and consultant. His first TV appearance involved him publicly TEARING UP THE SCRIPT, which backfired both creatively (fans booed Hogan a few segments later even though he was supposed to be the babyface savior), and in real life, as security had to go into the crowd and find the pieces of the script he tore up since it was the actual script for the show.
- Hiring, among others, the Nasty Boys, who could not even cut promos without getting tired, and Bubba the Love Sponge, best known for being the center of controversy when a sex tape was leaked of Hogan having sex with Bubba's wife, filmed in Bubba's home, a situation that destroyed their friendship and, according to Hogan, ruined his life.
- Booking an angle where a man in a Sting mask attacked RVD and was then unmasked, revealing, in the ultimate non-swerve, Sting.
- Firing female wrestler Awesome Kong after she beat the holy hell out of Bubba the Love Sponge backstage in what Hulk called one of the worst beatings he'd ever seen in his life. Kong was involved in Haiti earthquake relief efforts and Bubba had tweeted "Fuck Haiti"; suffice to say this enraged Kong.
- Believing the pro-wrestling landscape in 2010 was the same as

the pro-wrestling landscape in 1995 and deciding the best course of action would be to run head-to-head with *Raw* on Monday nights, a decision that led to the biggest smashing in the history of head-to-head pro-wrestling competition and resulted in a move back to their original night after losing at its lowest point 48 percent of its viewers and doing an anemic 0.6 rating.

- Booking a spot where Homicide gave Rob Terry a ridiculously hard unprotected chairshot to the head on national television exactly two days after former WCW star Chris Kanyon—who had written in the past about how he believed Chris Benoit killed himself and his family as a result of multiple concussions throughout his career, and who himself claimed to have suffered at least twelve concussions—committed suicide with a drug overdose.

- Booking a gigantic—and we mean gigantic—female training student named Rosie Lottalove into a match with 100-pound former WCW star Daffney, which resulted in Daffney being severely injured in a spot gone awry that essentially ended her wrestling career. The company refused to pay for her hospitalizations, which resulted in a very bitter lawsuit that was eventually settled out of court for an undisclosed sum.

- Having Orlando Jordan spray himself with a white, milky substance that resembled semen while looking on longingly at Rob Terry . . . this following Jordan's real-life coming out as a bisexual.

- Hiring, during a time where many wrestlers were working second jobs to make ends meet and one publicly tweeted about being on food stamps, both JWoww and Angelina of *Jersey Shore* for $15,000 per appearance, and then booking them in segments head-to-head with the real *Jersey Shore*, an unsuccessful strategy.

- During this same period spending God knows how much money to put up a "WRESTLING MATTERS" billboard in Stamford,

Connecticut, home of WWE, of which no discernible value was ever gauged.

- Naming a weapon, a barbed wire baseball bat, after the president of the company's mother.
- Booking television programs that, at their peak, saw only six minutes (360 SECONDS) of professional wrestling action in a two-hour period.
- Shooting an angle where Bischoff was held hostage in his office by a bird. He was held hostage by a bird because Sting was concerned that he would interfere in a match that just happened to be taking place inside a steel cage that was surrounded by babyface lumberjacks.
- Hyping a "revolutionary rankings system" for weeks, which upon its debut made absolutely no sense and was immediately forgotten about.
- Hiring Kazuchika Okada, one of the best young workers in all of Japanese pro wrestling, and calling him O-Kato and giving him a *Green Hornet* Bruce Lee comedy gimmick.
- Rebooking the *1996 Bash at the Beach*, where Hulk Hogan turned heel, in 2010 with Hogan once again turning heel to create a modern-day nWo consisting of Hogan, Bischoff, Abyss, and Jeff Hardy, an angle so successful that in 2014 it's likely even the most hardcore fan forgot it ever happened.
- Doing a storyline where Abyss told Hulk Hogan and Jeff Hardy that an anonymous THEY were coming; THEY proceeded to lay waste to them both in storyline on six shows over the next four months; and then THEY ended up being, among others, Abyss, Jeff Hardy, and Hulk Hogan.
- Instituting a rule where X-Division matches could only— ONLY—be contested under three-way rules, making it impossible to ever develop any sort of meaningful singles feuds or

championship programs.

- Dropping this rule less than six months later and doing a complete 180, saying that X-Division matches would ONLY be contested under one-on-one rules, apparently rendering their most popular match, the multi-man ultimate X, a thing of the past.
- Immediately dropping that rule as well.
- Falling victim to the most amazing trivia note when X-Division wrestler Brian Kendrick appeared on the new Price is Right with Drew Carey, and of the two of them, one of them was a WWE Hall of Famer—and it wasn't Brian Kendrick.
- Rotating talent in and out to cut costs, seemingly without alerting the writing crew, resulting in wrestlers winning titles on pay-per-view and then not appearing on TV for the next month.
- Historically treating their women such that when they contacted a bunch of former talents to appear on a taped womens-only PPV, nine of the women asked told them to shove it.
- Booking a PPV main event with no finish wherein the ref called for the bell after the champion was chokeslammed through the ring, it was determined that this was not a title change even though the champion could not continue, and then, to "send the crowd home happy," they had three more wrestlers take pratfalls into the hole.
- Putting the X-title, which for years had largely been built around smaller wrestlers, on The Monster Abyss, famous for being way more than 300 pounds. Shortly thereafter it was announced that the X-Division would now have a 225-pound weight limit. It was barely a year before 280-pound Samoa Joe was challenging for the belt.
- Putting one-half of the women's Tag Team titles on Eric Young. While we cannot personally confirm his sexual status, Young did ultimately admit on television that he was not, in fact, a woman.

This revelation led to him being stripped of said belt . . . 478 days after he and ODB had won them.

- Creating an online voting system where fans could choose who the next title contender would be, only to have Desmond Wolfe, who Bischoff didn't want to win, get the landslide victory two weeks in a row. Bischoff's response was to have Wolfe lose repeatedly on TV and then blame the fans for taking advantage of his own poll, which allowed multiple votes. The voting was then dropped, never to be mentioned again.

- Creating a concept called Gut Check wherein independent wrestlers fought to win a contract with the company, and after winning the contract they were sent to Kentucky, almost never heard from again, and ultimately cut.

- Signing a wrestler they didn't want to sign in Gut Check after judge Ric Flair decided he actually liked the wrestler and thought he cut a good promo, so he went off script and voted yes instead of no, resulting in the company being forced to give him a contract. The wrestler, Alex Silva, was immediately sent to Kentucky, seen once or twice thereafter, and then cut.

- Booking a Bound for Glory series months-long tournament where, in its inaugural year, perhaps in an homage to killing off Goldberg's heat in WCW, wrestlers were booked to face other wrestlers completely at random, competed in a completely random number of matches (one wrestler, for example, worked nineteen matches total and another only worked twelve, God knows why), and randomly racked up points—and then, at the end of the day, changing the finish of the finale on the day of the show.

- Booking a Bound for Glory series months-long tournament where, in its third year, in a tournament scheduled to have sixty-six total matches, they suddenly discovered that they only had three shows left to run thirty matches, and thus just threw every-thing out the window and wrapped it up the following week on television.

- Booking a championship match after Bobby Roode won the ti-tle with challenger Samoa Joe, best known for just coming off a Bound for Glory series run where he lost every single match in the tournament and racked up minus ten points.

- Booking an angle where Hulk Hogan—arguably the biggest star in the long and storied history of professional wrestling—an-nounced his retirement on television, only to draw a 1.01 rating for the show, the lowest of the entire year.

- Booking Hogan's return to wrestling one week later.

- Pushing Garett Bischoff, with no wrestling experience outside of some training with Team 3-D, and no qualifications outside of being Eric Bischoff's son, as a star member of the company's top heel group.

- Pushing Brooke Hogan, with no wrestling qualifications what-soever outside of being Hulk Hogan's daughter, as the general manager and mouthpiece of the women's division, despite her inability to cut anything resembling a successful promo on live television.

- Allowing Hulk Hogan to do a backstage promo where he says, in part, "No wonder this company was in the shape it's in. It's time to get rid of the trash, the garbage, the worthless piece of crap out here, and we started with Dixie Carter. Yeah, we're getting very real around here. We are so, real, it's unbelievable. Because, if you don't get over like I said, you're fired. If you don't draw a number, if you don't entertain, if you don't put asses in seats, if you don't put the coinage in the piggy bank, you're fired. No more games. No more, 'Kayfabe. It's a work. I've won thirty-four Tag Team belts.' Who gives a damn, how many fake belts you won? If you don't draw money, you get fired around here. If you don't put asses in seats, you're gone."

- Having to end a love triangle/affair/something-or-other storyline early because the actor they chose to play the character Claire Lynch quit the company when fans figured out who she really was (Julia Reilly, an actress who also played Olive Oyl at the Popeye ride at the same theme park where they shot television). Apparently, Reilly didn't think any of the one million plus national cable television viewers would ever be able to put two-and-two together.

- Shooting an angle during that feud where Serge Salinas, whose wrestling background consisted of him being the husband of Dixie, punched out AJ Styles, a multiple-time World champion and top star.

- Allowing Eric Bischoff to convince management that they needed to leave their long-time theme park home because everyone knows you can't run shows in the same building week-after-week, year-after-year, despite the fact that throughout history wrestling promotions have very successfully managed to run the same buildings month-after-month, year-after-year, drawing thousands and thousands of paying fans.

- Leaving their long-time theme park home to shoot television exclusively from the road despite a massive increase in costs with absolutely zero additional revenue being brought in to offset those costs and absolutely no increase in television ratings whatsoever since, at the end of the day, TV viewers do not, in fact, care where a television show is emanating from.

- Later concluding that, in fact, they could not afford the massive increase in costs with absolutely zero additional revenue being brought in to offset these costs and attempting to go back to their old longtime theme park home only to discover that their long-time theme park home had been rented out to someone else and they could no longer get in there.

• Dragging their feet on contract negotiations and having several wrestlers' contracts expire while they were in the middle of big storylines, including the Tag Team and Women's Tag Team champions on various occasions.

• Shooting an angle where for a few weeks you, the television viewer, could HEAR JEFF HARDY'S THOUGHTS. Disappointingly, he never had anything interesting to think.

• Shooting an angle where a masked wrestler named Suicide gets his costume stolen, at which point Hulk Hogan brings him out on stage, unmasked so we can see what he looks like, and alerts us that his name is TJ Perkins. Perkins proceeds to do all of his interviews backstage unmasked, but for inexplicable reasons still wrestles in the ring as a masked man named Manik. The logic behind this is never explained.

• Creating an action figure for Dixie Carter, the company president, which wrestlers backstage immediately take photos of in compromising positions with the Vince McMahon action figure.

• Firing ten employees, one of whom, Jesse Sorensen, had his neck broken on live PPV, nearly died, and was promised a job for life, and then that same week thinking it's a good idea to set up an #AskDixie Twitter question-and-answer session, which is ultimately deluged with thousands and thousands and thousands and thousands of negative comments about Dixie and the company.

• Booking a house show in Missouri where six of the wrestlers, including the current World Heavyweight champion, aren't licensed to wrestle in the state.

• Promoting big debuts, including that of Tito Ortiz, one of the biggest draws in the history of UFC, exclusively on the internet as opposed to on their national cable television show, which is seen by over a million viewers.

- Booking an angle where, in Hulk Hogan's last night ever in the company, Dixie gets on her knees and grabs his leg and begs him not to leave as he drags her up the ramp and out the door.
- Booking an angle where, in AJ Styles' last night ever in the company, he runs wild as triumphant babyface in his match with champion Magnus and it takes over a half dozen heels to finally beat him.
- Booking an angle where, in Sting's last night ever in the company, he runs wild as triumphant babyface in his title match with champion Magnus (this, by the way, happened after Sting had lost a match a year earlier where the stipulation was that he could NEVER challenge for the title again) and it takes over a half dozen heels to finally beat him—and that's after he got TWO visual pinfalls over Magnus.
- Booking a storyline where, after all of these big stars leave the company—for real—Dixie Carter is pushed as an incompetent owner who is killing the company with her stupidity.

Is it really possible that all this could happen? Can you imagine? Sadly, these bullet points are just the tip of the iceberg.

But the true story of the idiocy of TNA Impact Wrestling will be told another day . . .

★ ★ ★ ENDNOTES ★ ★ ★

1   Camel Clutch Blog. "Bill Watts Interview on Pro Wrestling Radio." Online video clip. *YouTube*. YouTube, 14 Feb. 2013. Web.

2   *Jim Crockett Promotions: The Good Old Days.* Highspots Inc., 2013. DVD.

3   Camel Clutch Blog. "Former WWE Champion Sid Eudy (Vicious) Interview on Pro Wrestling Radio." Online video clip. *YouTube*. YouTube, 16 Mar. 2013. Web.

4   Kleinfeld, N.R. "This is not real." *New York Times*. 26 Nov. 1989 late ed.: A1. Print.

5   "Wrestling Observer." *Wrestling Observer Radio.* F4WOnline.com. 16 Feb. 2001. Web.

6   "Episode 113." *Steve Austin Show.* PodcastOne.com. 6 May 2014. Web.

7   Bischoff, Eric and Jeremy Roberts. *Controversy Creates Cash*. New York: Pocket Books, 2006. Print.

8   WZVideo. "Lex Luger Reveals the Details Behind Him Showing Up on WCW Nitro." Online video clip. *YouTube.* YouTube, 12 Sept. 2013. Web.

9   Fisherman, Scott. "Monster move for Madusa." *The Miami Herald.* 11 Aug 2009. Print.

10   "Episode 210." *WrestleCrap Radio.* WrestleCrapRadio.com. 13 Jul. 2013. Web.

11   *Off the Record.* TSN. 11 Feb. 2003. Television.

12   Bischoff, Eric and Jeremy Roberts. *Controversy Creates Cash*. New York: Pocket Books, 2006. Print.

13   "Figure Four Daily." *Figure Four Daily.* F4WOnline.com. 10 Nov. 2009. Web.

14   Jericho, Chris and Pete Fornatale. *A Lion's Tale: Around the World in Spandex*. New York: Grand Central Publishing, 2007. Print.

15   "Wrestling Observer." *Wrestling Observer Radio.* F4WOnline.com. 8 Dec. 2010. Web.

16   Foley, Mick. *Foley is Good: And the Real World is Faker than Wrestling.* New York: Harper Collins, 2001. Print.

17   TitleMatchWrestling. "Bam Bam Bigelow Shoot Interview 3 Hours." Online video clip. *YouTube*. YouTube, 12 Jan. 2012. Web.

18   Jericho, Chris and Pete Fornatale. *A Lion's Tale: Around the World in Spandex*. New York: Grand Central Publishing, 2007. Print.

19   Roberts, Jeremy. *Rey Mysterio: Behind the Mask*. London: Pocket Books, 2009. Print.

20   Hart, Bret. *Hitman. My Real Life in the Cartoon World of Wrestling*. New York: Grand Central Publishing, 2007. Print

21   Jericho, Chris and Pete Fornatale. *A Lion's Tale: Around the World in Spandex*. New York: Grand Central Publishing, 2007. Print.

22   Jericho, Chris and Pete Fornatale. *A Lion's Tale: Around the World in Spandex*. New York: Grand Central Publishing, 2007. Print.

23   "Figure Four Daily." *Figure Four Daily*. F4WOnline.com. 10 Nov. 2009. Web.

24   Jarrett, Jerry. *The Story of the Development of the NWATNA*. Victoria: Trafford, 2004. Print.

25   WGD Weekly. "S2EP01 WGD Weekly w/Steve & The Scum & The Return of Jim Cornette." Online video clip. *YouTube*. YouTube, 5 Jan. 2014. Web.

26   Guerrero, Eddie and Michael Krugman. *Cheating Death, Stealing Life: The Eddie Guerrero Story*. New York: Pocket Books, 2005. Print.

27   James Walsh. "Kimberly Page on The Interactive Interview 7/05—WCW Nitro Gril Leader Tells All." Online video clip. *YouTube*. YouTube, 27 Jul. 2012. Web.

28   TitleMatchWrestling. "Bam Bam Bigelow Shoot Interview 3 Hours." Online video clip. *YouTube*. YouTube, 12 Jan. 2012. Web.

29   Guerrero, Eddie and Michael Krugman. *Cheating Death, Stealing Life: The Eddie Guerrero Story*. New York: Pocket Books, 2005. Print.

30   TitleMatchWrestling. "ECW Perry Saturn Shoot Interview 2 Hours." Online video clip. *YouTube*. YouTube, 4 Aug. 2012. Web.

31   Russo, Vince. *Rope Opera: How WCW Killed Vince Russo*. Toronto: ECW Press, 2010. Print.

32   Bischoff, Eric and Jeremy Roberts. *Controversy Creates Cash*. New York: Pocket

Books, 2006. Print.

33 "Wrestling Observer." *Wrestling Observer Radio.* F4WOnline.com. 8 Dec. 2010. Web.

34 "Wrestling Observer." *Wrestling Observer Radio.* F4WOnline.com. 20 Nov. 2005. Web.

35 Seepersaud, Steve. "Stuart Snyder Puts on a Good Show." *Binghamton University Magazine.* Binghamton University. Fall 2011. Web.

36 Between the Ropes. "Randy Savage Shoot Interview." Online video clip. *YouTube.* YouTube, 19 Dec. 2001. Web.

37 "Wrestling Observer." *Wrestling Observer Radio.* F4WOnline.com. 29 Sep. 2010. Web.

38 TitleMatchWrestling. "Scott Levy Shoot Interview." Online video clip. *YouTube.* YouTube, 19 Jun. 2012. Web.

★ ★ ★ ACKNOWLEDGMENTS ★ ★ ★

R.D. Reynolds would like to thank: Bryan Alvarez, for being a fantastic co-author in every sense of the word; every single visitor ever to WrestleCrap .com, without whom this book would not exist; the entire Wrestle-Crap crew of Blade Braxton, "Big Cheese" Paul Kraft, Justin Henry, Emerson Witner, James Chrismer, Jed Shafer, Jordan Mishkin, Sean Carless, Troy Lowe, Harry Simon, Kelly Parmele, and Greg Ogorek; my wife, Mrs. Deal, and my son, R.D. Jr., for giving me the freedom to work on this book, as well as my entire family for believing in me; Eric, Tab, Zack, and Zoe, the best friends my family and I could ever have; Casey (Trash Losagain) Stephon, "Diamond Dan" Garza, Jeff Cohen, Bill Brown, and everyone else who got me involved in this goofy busi-ness in the first place; Trae Wisecarver; Terry and Sally Corman; Matt at DinosaurDracula.com; the entire staff of F4WOnline.com, namely Dave Meltzer, Vince Verhei, Craig Proper, Granny, and Todd Martin, all of whom have brought me hours of information and entertainment; and the entire staff at ECW Press. You are wonderful.

I would also like to thank Vince Russo, who has appeared on my podcast, *The RD & Blade Show*, several times. I offered him the opportunity to give his side of the WCW story in this book, but he declined, stating, "Well appreciated, but I really don't care what people have to say anymore. After taking thirteen years of abuse over WCW, it doesn't matter what I say. Anything from me will only be misconstrued and twisted, in an all-out effort to make me out to be a liar, failure, and whatever else they wish to label me. No, at this point in my life, I'm much more interested in making sure I collect the entire line of the new, vintage 1966 Batman figures." I urge you to check out his website, pyroandballyhoo.com.

Finally, and most importantly . . . glory be to God for giving me the opportunity to write books and (hopefully) make people laugh.

Bryan Alvarez would like to thank: His beautiful wife Whitney Neugebauer and all of her family, including Bob, Linda, Quinn, Briley, and Trent; his parents Carlos and Valerie, in wrestling parlance the legit best parents of all time of all his life; his sister, Nikki, and her husband, Tony (who is not only his brother-in-law, but without whom there would be no Figure Four Online/WrestlingObserver.com); his wonderful, wild, and crazy grandmother Gladys Gibson, who remains a regular contributor to the Bryan & Vinny Show at the ripe young age of 85, also without whom there would be no Figure Four Weekly; Dave Meltzer, the most legendary wrestling writer of this or any other generation, never to be equaled; the long suffering yet ridiculously talented Vincent Verhei of Bryan & Vinny fame, possessor of the most inconvenient Twitter handle ever (@FO_Vverhei—LOL), and his lovely new bride Bridgett; Bryan's Friend Craig and the whole Proper clan; Mike Sempervive, who helps carry on the legacy of Wrestling Observer Live and the doomed Eyada.com every week on Sports Byline USA and Sirius Satellite Radio; David

Bixenspan, who helps carry on the legacy of Figure Four Weekly; all of his aunts, uncles, nephews, and maybe (?) nieces, along with their significant others, including Crazy Wayne and Rose, Lynne and Don, Carlos and Cliffy (who is now way too old to be called Cliffy, but, as my father did with my childhood nicknames, I will continue to call him such into at least his 30s), and all the rest who he sees too infrequently; everyone who he has had the pleasure to work with over the past ten years including Todd Martin, Lance Storm, Dr. Lucha Steve Sims, Mike Coughlin, Karl Stern, Doc Young, Les Thatcher, Vic Sosa, Alan Counihan, Josh Nason, Mike Sawyer, and Oliver Copp, among countless others who help keep the website going strong; R.D. Reynolds, of course, without whom, and this is absolutely, positively, unequivocally, no exaggeration, there would be no *Death of WCW*; George and Hadley and everyone at Evergreen Karate and Jiu-Jitsu who have supported his other hobby-turned-business; Master Pedro Sauer and Justin Angelos, who taught me Gracie Jiu-Jitsu; Buddy Wayne, Dave Dobashi, and Tim Flowers, who taught me pro wrestling; Art Bell, the greatest ever, who taught me radio through osmosis; Snorki, Tiggi, and The Wolf, our feral surrogate children whom we love; and little Gracie who passed too soon; and all the others, big and small, whose tales I may some day tell. And finally, a huge thank you to all of the listeners, readers, subscribers, and students, who, at the end of the day, are not actually listeners, readers, subscribers, or students, but, rather, his friends.

GET THE EBOOK FREE!

At ECW Press, we want you to enjoy this book in whatever
format you like, whenever you like. Leave your print book at
home and take the eBook to go! Purchase the print edition and
receive the eBook free. Just send an email to ebook@ecwpress.
com and include:

- the book title
- the name of the store where you purchased it
- your receipt number
- your preference of file type: PDF or ePub?

A real person will respond to your email with your eBook
attached. Thank you for supporting an independently owned
Canadian publisher with your purchase!